D1538789

ARMS CONTROL FOR THE LATE SIXTIES

Contributors

ARCHIBALD S. ALEXANDER
RICHARD J. BARNET
LINCOLN P. BLOOMFIELD
KENNETH E. BOULDING
HEDLEY BULL
GEORGE BUNN
FRANCESCO CAVALLETTI
JOSEPH S. CLARK
JOSEPH I. COFFEY
RICHARD B. FOSTER
MARC E. GENESTE
HAROLD C. HINTON
CRAIG HOSMER
HERMAN KAHN
WILLIAM R. KINTNER
KLAUS KNORR
BETTY GOETZ LALL
WILLIAM V. O'BRIEN
CHARLES C. PRICE
JAMES R. SCHLESINGER
HELMUT SCHMIDT
JOHN SILARD
JEREMY J. STONE
ROBERT STRAUSZ-HUPÉ
EDWARD TELLER
V. C. TRIVEDI
THOMAS W. WOLFE

Princeton, New Jersey   Toronto   London   Melbourne

ARMS CONTROL FOR THE LATE SIXTIES

Editors

JAMES E. DOUGHERTY

*Saint Joseph's College and
Foreign Policy Research Institute of
the University of Pennsylvania*

J. F. LEHMAN, Jr.

*Caius College
Cambridge*

D. VAN NOSTRAND COMPANY, INC.

Van Nostrand Regional Offices: *New York, Chicago, San Francisco*

D. Van Nostrand Company, Ltd., *London*

D. Van Nostrand Company (Canada), Ltd., *Toronto*

D. Van Nostrand Australia Pty. Ltd., *Melbourne*

Library of Congress Catalog Card No. 67-27982

PRINTED IN THE UNITED STATES OF AMERICA

Preface

The present volume had its origins in the Third International Arms Control Symposium, which was held in Philadelphia in April 1966 under the joint sponsorship of The University of Pennsylvania, Saint Joseph's College, and The Bendix Corporation. The Symposium brought together a number of experts on the arms problem from here and abroad, including a leader of the German Social Democratic Party, the head of the disarmament research unit in the Foreign Office of the United Kingdom, and the ambassadors of Italy and India to the Eighteen Nation Disarmament Committee in Geneva.

The present book accordingly focuses upon arms control topics which are likely to remain crucial throughout the remainder of this decade:

- Strengthening international peacekeeping institutions or finding other ways to control conflict;
- The Sino-Soviet split and changes within the Soviet system;
- The problem of preventing nuclear weapons proliferation or of adjusting to its consequences;
- The impact of East-West negotiations upon NATO;
- The question of whether or not to deploy ballistic missile defense.

These are the issues that constitute this book.

Though the vision of a disarmed world has, in the turbulent 1960's, lost some of its luster, it can still claim the allegiance of eloquent spokesmen, as Joseph S. Clark and Charles C. Price demonstrate. Kenneth E. Boulding, in a piece that is bound to provoke lively debate, calls for raising the "warmth" level of the international system in order to thaw the cold war and facilitate disarmament. But Lincoln P. Bloomfield and William V. O'Brien, both of whom are committed to reinforcing international law and peacekeeping institutions, show that they are under no illusions as to the difficulty of building machinery to control recurring conflict and of insuring peaceful change in a revolutionary age.

The student of arms control must reflect upon the policies not only of his own country but also those of key foreign states. Archibald S. Alexander, Richard J. Barnet, Herman Kahn, William R. Kintner, and other contributors reflect upon what U.S. policy has been, is, or ought to be. Harold C. Hinton and Thomas W. Wolfe present a careful assessment of Communist Chinese and Soviet policy views in their field. V. C. Trivedi illuminates the perspective of India and of other nonnuclear weapons countries which share India's outlook.

An effort has been made here to allow some of the outstanding authorities of the leading European allies of the United States to voice their opinion concerning recent arms control developments. Marc E. Geneste presents an incisive characterization of the rule which nuclear weapons can play in preventing World War III. Hedley Bull of Britain and Francesco Cavalletti of Italy give valuable insights into the current effort to discourage countries from seeking entry into the nuclear club. Helmut Schmidt traces the subtle relationship between arms control and the aspirations of the German people for national reunification. The Europeans are not alone in their concern for the future of the Atlantic Alliance. Robert Strausz-Hupé of the United States sums up years of reflection on the importance of the link between the United States and Europe for maintaining international stability, and asks what the world might be like without NATO. Betty Goetz Lall, by way of contrast, sounds a note of caution about the tendency of this country to overemphasize its relations with Europe at the expense of the developing areas.

Since the signing of the Nuclear Test Ban Treaty in 1963, concern over the dangers of fallout has been superseded by concern over the dangers inherent in the spread of nuclear weapons. Several contributors to this book, including George Bunn, Craig Hosmer, James R. Schlesinger, and John Silard, dwell upon the diplomatic, political, technical, and strategic problems of coping with the issue of proliferation, either with or without a treaty. Within these pages the reader will find discussed most of the dilemmas over proliferation now confronting the statesmen of the world.

The final major theme in this book pertains to ballistic missile defense. Richard B. Foster, Edward Teller, Joseph I. Coffey, Jeremy J. Stone, and Klaus Knorr probe questions of the technical effectiveness and cost of ballistic missile defense and its impact upon NATO and the proliferation problem. They argue that decisions concerning this form of defense will have a vital bearing upon the arms control picture in the 1970's.

The Editors would like to express their gratitude to Mr. Robert Dechert, Esq., Chairman of the Symposium, to whom belongs much of the credit for the project's success. They also wish to thank Dr. Gaylord P. Harnwell, President of The University of Pennsylvania, Very Reverend William F. Maloney, S.J., President of Saint Joseph's College, and Mr. A. P. Fontaine, Chairman of the Board of Directors of The Bendix Corporation, Detroit, Michigan, for their encouragement and active support of the Symposium.

The members of the Advisory Board, who furnished invaluable advice and guidance during a half year of planning efforts, included Professor Kenneth E.

Boulding of the University of Michigan; Dr. Joseph I. Coffey, Chief of the Office of National Security Studies of The Bendix Corporation; Mr. Amrom H. Katz, Senior Analyst of The RAND Corporation; Mr. Addison Lanier of Thomas Emery's Sons, Cincinnati; Admiral Edward N. Parker, U.S.N. (Ret.); Professor Charles C. Price and Professor Robert Strausz-Hupé, both of the University of Pennsylvania. Dr. Coffey, who directed the Second International Arms Control Symposium at Ann Arbor in early 1964, was one of the original architects of the Third in Philadelphia.

To Dr. James H. McBride, Senior Analyst in the Office of National Security Studies at Bendix, we owe a unique debt of gratitude. Working tirelessly between Ann Arbor and Philadelphia as Secretary of the Advisory Board, he contributed signally toward the coordination of the more than thirty principal participants. A special word of thanks is due to Professor William R. Kintner of the University of Pennsylvania for his informal but indispensable advice and assistance throughout the planning phase. William H. Regnery and George Watts, Symposium Coordinators, deserve full praise and credit for the excellent logistical planning and efficient administration of the project, which involved bringing some three hundred persons together for four days. In their myriad tasks they were ably assisted by David D. Dreuding and Andrew W. Green. Paul J. Friedrich, formerly of Munich University and now of the Hoover Institution at Stanford University, coordinated the arrangements for the foreign participants. Bouquets are in order for Mrs. Mary Toelke, who typed the entire manuscript of this volume during a Philadelphia summer, and for Mrs. Marge Capotrio, who meticulously proofread every page.

Worthy of particular mention for their efforts on behalf of the Symposium were the personnel of the United States Arms Control and Disarmament Agency. The Editors wish to thank Mr. Jerome H. Spingarn, Mr. George Bunn, Esq., General Counsel of the Agency, the Honorable Archibald S. Alexander, Assistant Director of the Agency, who delivered the keynote address, and Ambassador Clare H. Timberlake, former senior State Department Representative to the Eighteen Nation Disarmament Committee.

Finally, on behalf of all those who were connected with the Symposium, the Editors wish to express gratitude for the generous support provided by The William H. Donner Foundation, The Relm Foundation, The Yarway Foundation, the Foreign Policy Research Institute, the family of the late Mrs. Sarah M. Scaife, Mr. Addison Lanier, Mr. Clifford Backstrand, and Mr. Joseph Crosby. We would be remiss if we omitted a most cordial word of thanks to the expert political and strategic analysts who contributed to the intellectual success of the Symposium and to the worth of this book.

JAMES E. DOUGHERTY
J. F. LEHMAN, JR.

Introductory Remarks

By J. F. Lehman, Jr.

From the explosion at Hiroshima in 1945 until today, about a thousand books have been published in the West on the subject of arms strategy and arms control, not to mention countless official reports, study papers, monographs, pamphlets, and articles. Two dramatic developments of the postwar era—the ideological cleavage of the industrial world and a series of revolutionary breakthroughs in the technology of war—produced a body of writers whose jeremiads have filled the bookstalls and the weeklies. Back in the 1950's, the mathematical certainty of nuclear destruction and the obsolescence, indeed the immorality, of a world organized on the principle of sovereign States were oft-repeated themes. General and Complete Disarmament (GCD) was then held forth as the only saving course of action available to man. The very real danger in that period caused by the vulnerability of U.S. and Soviet forces, which placed a premium on a strategic first strike, lent considerable appeal to that movement of thought. Advocates arose to argue that "the biological division of mankind into warring states is a scientific ineptitude." They extolled the power of love in international affairs, called for unilateral initiatives to achieve a disarmed world, and constructed elaborate constitutions to administer the peace.

Not unnaturally, the philosophers of *realpolitik* objected. Irreconcilable conflicts of interest split the world, they argued, and the instruments of defense must be retained, for there were things more to be feared from a messianic ideology than war. GCD was dismissed by these critics as presupposing that the reasons why arms existed in the first place had diminished, when they had in fact multiplied. Even when the realists agreed with the idealist contention that the nature of modern weaponry made disarmament more desirable than ever, they insisted that the same factor made disarmament less practicable than ever. The debate could be described in Sorelian terms as between those who would refashion the world to suit their policy and those who would arrange their policy to suit the world.

One of the contributors to this volume, Hedley Bull, has noted elsewhere[1] that the real choice with which governments are confronted is not between opting for the present structure of the world or of opting for some other structure, but between attempting to maintain a balance of power and failing to do so. Indeed, it is arguable that the power balance of the last twenty years, marked by the severest conflict of ideas the

[1] *The Control of The Arms Race,* New York: Praeger, 1961. See especially Chapter 2, "Disarmament and the Balance of Power."

world has known since the Reformation and sustained by the most powerful States in history, owes its relative stability in no small measure to the existence of nuclear weapons. One can go further, not without justification, and espouse the hope that the world may have finally traversed the tragic cycle of total military conflict between the major industrial powers and may now be entering upon a much more complex pattern of political interrelationships.

Modern statesmen are confronted with many important opportunities in this current period of strategic stability, a period which seems likely to extend through the late sixties by the grace of invulnerable deterrents and by the existence of a plateau, albeit ephemeral, in weapons technology. Perhaps they will manage to overcome the perennial tendency of their species to apply the lessons of youth to the problems of old age. Perhaps strategic analysts will break out of the "Ptolemaic" mental framework that has characterized so much of the literature in the last twenty years. The contributors to this volume have made an excellent beginning in this direction and have begun to lay the intellectual foundations of what Amrom Katz has called a "metastable strategy."

A metastable strategy involves none of the millenarian visions of the *horribles simplificateurs,* but it has a clear set of goals that statesmen can realistically try to attain. Such a strategy provides orderly procedures for changing the international status quo. It renders nuclear weapons virtually unusable, both physically and politically. It does not prejudice regional security arrangements, like NATO, which have made their own important contribution to peace. Such a strategy is not rigid but is susceptible to organic development.

It aims, insofar as possible, at limiting proliferation and also at limiting damage in the event of conflict. Finally, the metastable strategy is resilient enough to withstand occasional breaches. Such a strategy requires that attention be directed toward the reduction of the irrational and the unpredictable in national policies. It demands a continuous search for areas of common interest, for example, in agreeing to forgo the deployment of those weapons whose development technology has made possible but whose relationship to the strategic balance is marginal. There will have to be full realization that arms control is not a separate discipline unto itself. It is not the domain only of the physical scientist, nor is it the exclusive preserve of the political scientist. To be of use, an idea must be both politically palatable and technically feasible, and it may need testing against the insights of several other disciplines, including sociology, psychology, mathematics and games theory, cybernetics, and psychometrics.

It is a truism that major wars are never the result of accidents but spring from objective conflicts, over territory or power or ideology, which give rise to the will to war. But in an era, however temporary, when offense has the advantage over defense, the implications of accident, miscalculation, or unintended escalation cannot be underestimated. Possible accidents must be decoupled from any automatic or spasmodic responses. In order to maintain such a decoupled posture without detracting from the credibility of the deterrent, there must be an invulnerable strategic capability which, through dispersion, hardening, and mobility, can undoubtedly withstand a first strike, no matter how severe. More important, the potential opponent must be left with no doubt concerning the survivable effectiveness of the retaliatory capability.

Careful attention must be given to the evolving state of the art in weapon research. It is popular now to speak of the technological plateau. However valid this description may be when applied to the past ten years, it would be imprudent to postulate its continuance for the next ten. With major weapons-systems lead times hovering near ten years, the development and deployment by only one of the superpowers of a new weapons system affecting the central bipolar balance would have profoundly unsettling effects. Not only dramatic weapons such as the laser or neutron bomb could have such effect, but also breakthroughs in material technology; in thixotropic and cryogenic fuels; in oxide dispersion metals, metalloid fibres, and polymers; or in radio, stellar, inertial, and laser guidance.

Indeed, it may be fairly put that the technological "plateau" is already coming to an end. The age old see-saw balance of sword and shield, so long down firmly on the side of the sword, is again showing signs of teetering. The technology of the advanced ballistic reentry system (ABRS) continues to progress. The art of invisible reentry, making a vehicle's optical and radar signature so small as to be undetectable, has reached the point where it is possible to make an object the size of a dining-room table appear like the end of a pencil. Passive and active countermeasures now employ real and electronic decoys and highly sophisticated methods of simulation and deception. The level of development of maneuverability offers considerable room for refinement; when the "threat-tube" is thus widened, the problems of making an effective antiballistic missile will be greatly compounded.

The whole question of the feasibility of an antiballistic missile is perhaps the most crucial challenge to the forging of a metastable strategy in the late sixties. That such a weapon can be developed now seems agreed by most experts. But is it worth the cost? Will it unsettle the bipolar balance? Will it strengthen the bipolar balance by raising the price of continued membership in the nuclear club beyond the reach of China or France?

Another imperative challenge is that of weapons proliferation. Foremost, of course, is the question of *nuclear* proliferation, with nine countries having the unquestioned capability of developing a system for delivering nuclear weapons and at least four more able to produce a bomb. Is it possible for the superpowers to prevent this spread, and if so at what price?

Less dramatic, but perhaps as crucial, is the proliferation of conventional weaponry among the countries of the developing world. The major powers have the ability to stanch the flow of the means of making war in the third world, causing such conflicts there to wither, or at least preventing them from becoming as devastating and potentially escalatory as a conflict between Egypt and Israel, for example, might otherwise be.

The keystone of a metastable strategy is a set of procedures for peaceful settlement of disputes and revision of the status quo. Customary usages may be developed from precedents tacitly set during the first twenty years of nuclear age crises. It is not, however, to the conclusion of general conventions and particular treaties that we must look for a solution to this dilemma. The mass of draft treaties and universal conventions that lie dormant for want of ratification, and the number of ratified agreements that remain unapplied, give ample testimony to the fact that codification has already far outrun the political consensus. The potentialities of international law are promising, but to confuse political agreement with international law destroys the real benefits of the latter. There is at present a particular caveat which diminishes the effectiveness of the international legal method. Soviet legal thinkers such as Pashukanis and Vyshinsky have argued that treaties based on voluntarily created reciprocity and equal reciprocal performance can in no circumstances bind the Soviet Union; and that *pacta sunt servanda* is antithetical to Marxism-Leninism. Such an ideological strait jacket is undeniably a hindrance for the Soviet Union in concluding meaningful arms control treaties, but Stalin demonstrated amazing dexterity in escaping dogmatic shackles when necessities dictated, and the present generation of Soviet leaders have also shown themselves to be highly gifted practical casuists.

While the Clausewitzian strategies of war are no longer applicable to states within the bipolar balance, it would be foolish to think that states outside the central balance, such as Israel and the Arab states, or India and Pakistan, could not perceive advantage in resorting to war in some circumstances. Realistic methods and procedures are needed for dealing with conflicts that have become violent, so that thresholds of violence are not crossed unnecessarily, so that the scope of violence at no point can exceed the scope of the real conflict of interests involved in the dispute, and in order that peaceful settlement can be achieved before the escalation of violence drags in other powers. Every war in the nuclear age, no matter how small or conventional, is a nuclear war in the sense that the fighting will take place in a nuclear environment.

These are the complex challenges that must be met by the architects of a metastable strategy. To be sure, the voices of the simplifiers are still to be heard, but the dialogue has passed beyond them. In the following pages we have endeavored to bring together analysts whose policy critiques and recommendations, while containing a vision of the ideal, do not allow the centrifugal force of ideas having only the merit of desirability, to pull their feet from the firmament of political reality. They are not Bacon's philosophers "who make imaginary laws for imaginary commonwealths, and whose discourses are as the stars which give little light because they are so high."

Contributors

ARCHIBALD S. ALEXANDER is the Assistant Director of the United States Arms Control and Disarmament Agency.

RICHARD J. BARNET is the Codirector of the Institute for Policy Studies, Washington, D.C., and a former Fellow in the Russian Research Center of Harvard University. He is the author of *Who Wants Disarmament?* (1960), coeditor of *Security and Disarmament* (1965) and coauthor of *After Twenty Years* (1965).

LINCOLN P. BLOOMFIELD is Director of the Arms Control Project, Center for International Studies, Massachusetts Institute of Technology, and Professor of Political Science at MIT. His published books include *International Military Forces* (1964); The *United Nations and U.S. Foreign Policy* (1967); and *Khrushchev and the Arms Race* (1966). He has been Consultant to the Department of State and the U.S. Arms Control and Disarmament Agency.

KENNETH E. BOULDING is Professor of Economics at the University of Michigan and Director of the University's Center for Research on Conflict Resolution. He has written widely in the fields of economic analysis, peace research and international systems. Among his recent works are *Conflict and Defense* (1962); *Disarmament and the Economy,* with Emile Benoit (1963) and *The Meaning of the Twentieth Century* (1964).

HEDLEY BULL is Director of the Arms Control and Disarmament Research Unit, in Her Majesty's Foreign Office, the United Kingdom. He has been Visiting Research Associate at the Center of International Studies at Princeton University and Reader in International Relations at the London School of Economics. His major work in this field is *The Control of the Arms Race* (1961).

GEORGE BUNN has been the General Counsel of the United States Arms Control and Disarmament Agency almost from its creation. He was formerly Special Assistant to John McCloy when the latter was Adviser to the President on Disarmament.

FRANCESCO CAVALLETTI is the Chief of the Delegation of Italy to the

Eighteen Nation Disarmament Committee at Geneva. As a career diplomat, he has served in several European and Latin American capitals and has frequently represented Italy at the Council of Europe, the European Economic Community, and the General Assembly of the United Nations.

JOSEPH S. CLARK is a United States Senator from Pennsylvania and serves as a member of the Foreign Relations Committee. During World War II he was Chief of Staff of the Eastern Air Command, China-Burma-India Theater of War. He is the author of two books, *The Senate Establishment* (1963) and *Congress: The Sapless Branch* (1964).

JOSEPH I. COFFEY is Chief of the Office of National Security Studies at the Bendix Systems Division, Ann Arbor. He was formerly with the Institute for Defense Analyses and the Special Studies Project of the Rockefeller Fund, and he has served as a consultant to the Policy Planning Council of the Department of State. A retired Army Colonel who holds his doctorate from Georgetown University, he has written several specialized works on strategic deterrence, arms control, and international stability.

RICHARD B. FOSTER is Director of the Strategic Studies Center of the Stanford Research Institute, where he has been engaged in the analysis of U.S. strategic policies, with emphasis on damage-limiting programs of air and missile defense. He was Director of the Strategic, Economic, and Cost Studies of the Department of the Army's Nike-X Threat Analysis study. His published works include articles on cost-effectiveness calculations in strategic decision-making and unilateral arms control measures.

MARC E. GENESTE is a retired Colonel of the French Army. He is a member of the Editorial Staff of *Revue de Defense Nationale,* and has written several articles on nuclear deterrence and arms control problems. He was formerly French Liaison Officer at the U.S. Army Command and General Staff College, Fort Leavenworth, Kansas.

HAROLD C. HINTON is Associate Professor of International Affairs at The George Washington University and Senior Staff Member of the Institute for Defense Analyses. He holds the doctorate in modern Chinese history from Harvard University and has taught at Georgetown, Oxford, and Columbia Universities. His published works include *Communist China in World Politics* (1966).

CRAIG HOSMER is a Member of the House of Representatives from the 32nd District of California. He is now the ranking House minority member on the Joint Committee on Atomic Energy. Congressman Hosmer has served as Adviser to the U.S. Atoms-for-Peace Delegation in Geneva.

HERMAN KAHN, a physicist and specialist in national security affairs, is Director of Hudson Institute. He was associated for twelve years with The

RAND Corporation, working on problems in applied physics and mathematics, operations research and systems analysis, weapon design and diffusion, civil defense, and strategic warfare. He is the author of three books, *On Thermonuclear War* (1960), *Thinking About the Unthinkable* (1962), and *On Escalation* (1965). He has served frequently as a consultant to governmental agencies and has lectured widely at leading U.S. universities and service colleges, as well as at defense study centers abroad.

WILLIAM R. KINTNER is Deputy Director of the Foreign Policy Research Institute at the University of Pennsylvania, where he is also Professor of Political Science in the Wharton School. As a Colonel in the U.S. Army (now retired), he served as a member of the planning staff of the National Security Council, and he was a member of the staff of Nelson A. Rockefeller when the latter was Special Assistant to President Eisenhower. He is the coauthor of several books, including *Forging a New Sword* (1958), *Protracted Conflict* (1959), *The Haphazard Years* (1960), *A Forward Strategy for America* (1961), and *Building the Atlantic World* (1963).

KLAUS KNORR is Director of the Center of International Studies, Princeton University, where he holds the William Stewart Tod Professorship of Public Affairs. He is an economist and an authority in the field of international relations, and his books include *The War Potential of Nations* (1956), *NATO and American Security* (1959), and *Limited Strategic War* (co-editor, 1962). He has been a consultant to several government agencies and is Chairman of the Editorial Board of *World Politics*.

BETTY GOETZ LALL is a Research Associate for the School of Industrial and Labor Relations, Cornell University. She has served as Staff Director of the Senate Subcommittee on Disarmament and Staff Member, Senate Foreign Relations Committee (1955-1961); Special Assistant to the President's Disarmament Adviser (1961); and Special Assistant to the Deputy Director of the United States Arms Control and Disarmament Agency (1961-1963). She is a frequent contributor to the *Bulletin of the Atomic Scientists*.

WILLIAM V. O'BRIEN is Associate Professor of Government at Georgetown University and Chairman of the Institute of World Policy at the University. He is the Washington Consultant for the Council on Religion and International Affairs and Associate Editor of *World Justice* (Louvain). At present he is President of the Catholic Association for International Peace. Books that he has coauthored or edited include *Christian Ethics and Nuclear Warfare, International Law,* and the World Policy Yearbook, Vol. III, entitled *The New Nations in International Law and Diplomacy*.

CHARLES C. PRICE is Blanchard Professor of Chemistry at the University of Pennsylvania. He has served as Chairman of the Departments of Chemistry at the Universities of Notre Dame and Pennsylvania, and he has lectured at Kyoto and Osaka Universities in Japan. His research has been principally concerned with the mechanism of various organic compounds. He was President of the American Chemical Society for 1964.

JAMES R. SCHLESINGER is a member of the staff in the Economics Department of The RAND Corporation in Santa Monica, where he has written several specialized studies on defense economics, systems analysis, and the consequences of nuclear proliferation. He was formerly a Professor of Economics at the University of Virginia. His major published work is *The Political Economy Security* (1960).

HELMUT SCHMIDT is the Chairman of the Social Democratic parliamentary caucus of the Bundestag. He has long been regarded as one of the leading defense experts of the SPD, and his book that was published in English under the title of *Defense or Retaliation?* (1960) established him as West Germany's most prominent authority on arms control questions.

JOHN SILARD is Counsel to the Council for a Livable World in Washington, D.C. Since 1955 he has been associated in the practice of law with Joseph L. Rauh, General Counsel of the United Automobile Workers, AFL-CIO. In 1963 he served as consultant to the Senate Labor Committee on Arms Industry Diversification, and he has written on arms control for the *Bulletin of the Atomic Scientists*.

JEREMY J. STONE is a Research Associate with the Harvard University Center for International Affairs. Previously he was on the Staff of the Hudson Institute. He is a frequent contributor to the *Bulletin of the Atomic Scientists* and has published several monographs on bomber reduction, antimissile missiles, and civil defense. His latest book is *Containing the Arms Race: Some Specific Proposals* (1966).

ROBERT STRAUSZ-HUPÉ is Professor of Political Science and Director of the Foreign Policy Research Institute at the University of Pennsylvania. He is also the Editor of *Orbis*. His books include *The Balance of Tomorrow* (1945), *The Zone of Indifference* (1952), *International Relations* (1954), *Protracted Conflict* (1959), and *Building the Atlantic World* (1963), as well as his autobiography, *In My Time* (1965). Within recent years he has taught in Europe as Visiting Professor at Madrid, Bruges, and Heidelberg.

EDWARD TELLER, a native of Hungary, was educated in the Technical Institute at Karlsruhe and the University of Leipzig before coming to the United States in 1935. He was Professor of Physics at George Washington University and later moved to the University of Chicago, where he was associated with the Institute for Nuclear Studies and helped to develop the atomic bomb. He became director of the United States' H-bomb project in 1950. In 1953 he became Professor of Physics at the University of California, and in 1958 he was named head of the University's Livermore Radiation Laboratory. His major book is *The Legacy of Hiroshima* (1962).

V. C. TRIVEDI is the Head of the Delegation of India to the Eighteen Nation Disarmament Committee at Geneva. Educated at Cambridge University, he has held a number of distinguished posts in the Indian Diplomatic Service, including Counsellor to the High Commissioner of India in London, 1955-1959; Deputy and Acting High Commissioner for India in Pakistan, 1959-1961; and Joint Secretary to the Government of India in the Ministry of External Affairs, 1961-1964. Besides representing his country at the ENDC, he has served as Ambassador to Switzerland since 1964.

THOMAS W. WOLFE is Senior Staff member of The RAND Corporation (Washington Office). He is a retired Colonel, U.S. Air Force, and a member of the Faculty of the Sino-Soviet Institute of The George Washington University. He was a member of the U.S. Delegation to the 10-Nation Disarmament Conference in Geneva, 1960; a member of the U.S. Delegation to the Summit Conference in Paris, 1960; and an Advisor at the McCloy-Zorin talks in Moscow, 1961. He was the coeditor and translator of V. D. Sokolovskii, *Soviet Military Strategy* (1963), and the author of *Soviet Strategy at the Crossroads* (1964).

Contents

Introduction

By James E. Dougherty

The mid-1960's witnessed a remarkable maturing process in the attitude of governments toward the arms problem. It is now widely conceded that both the Soviet Union and the United States have, since the early part of 1963, shifted their attention in international negotiations away from general and complete disarmament toward partial arms control and limitation measures. Less animated today is the discussion over such issues as inspection for total disarmament, the economics of large-scale arms reductions, and the strengthening of international peacekeeping machinery during the transition to a disarmed world. These issues, which had always sounded somewhat abstract, have been replaced by more immediate and realistic problems—the impact of arms negotiations on the Atlantic alliance and the future status of Germany, decisions to be made in respect to ballistic missile defense, the proliferation of nuclear weapons, and the applicability of arms control concepts to the conduct of limited conflict in Vietnam and elsewhere. These will undoubtedly constitute the focal points of the debate about arms control in the late 1960's.

General Disarmament

In retrospect, it is difficult to believe that any government could have looked upon the blueprints for complete disarmament tabled by the Soviet Union in 1959 and by the United States in 1961 as representing a feasible policy goal to be achieved within the foreseeable future. A few years of negotiations at Geneva and of study by Western specialists served the useful purpose of demonstrating the profound difficulties involved—difficulties of a technological, strategic, and political character. It soon became clear that the geostrategic situation of the two superpowers is quite asymmetrical, a fact that compels them to adopt divergent perspectives of their security requirements. (Ocean-based deterrent systems, for example, are more important for the United States than for the Soviet Union.) The task of reaching agreement on first-stage reductions in conformity with the McCloy-Zorin principle that neither side should be placed at an unfair disadvantage thus proved to be much more complex than had been originally thought by the advocates of total disarmament.

The longer the negotiators and the experts grappled with the subject of general and complete disarmament, the more they realized that modern military technology does not lend itself easily to regulation by the traditional diplomatic device of the written treaty. Despite the coincident interest of the superpowers in avoiding a mutually destructive nuclear cataclysm, the dispute since 1964 over the financing of United Nations peace forces and voting in the

xxi

General Assembly showed that Soviet-Western differences over the development of international organization and order are still sufficiently wide to bar progress toward a disarmed world. The Sino-Soviet split seemed to dispose Moscow toward a rapprochement with the West, at least across the intermediate terrain of Europe. But if the Soviets are genuinely apprehensive over China's long-range foreign policy objectives, then they are hardly likely to embrace plans for substantial disarmament which do not apply effectively to the Peking regime.

Probably none of the five existing nuclear weapon States wants nuclear war now or within the foreseeable future. Yet not one of them has consistently acted as if it regards total disarmament as the only way or the best way of safeguarding its security. Perhaps all five would agree that disarmament is a desirable ultimate goal. But none appears willing to move away from an international political-military environment in which the conditions of equilibrium are relatively familiar toward a radically transformed kind of international politics, except on terms so patently designed to produce unilateral advantage as to be unacceptable to the adversary side. At the present time, each nuclear power attaches a higher priority to policy objectives other than general disarmament. In the long view of history, this may or may not prove to have been a myopic attitude. No one can say for sure. But the current posture of the powers is not a mere matter of stubbornness or ill will. Rather it results from the nature of governments, the nation-state system, and international diplomacy; from the characteristics of contemporary advanced weapons technology, which makes disarmament both more desirable and more difficult to achieve; and from the intensity of the political, ideological, and other value conflicts which mark the twentieth century world.[1]

Fortunately, the fact that total disarmament is perceived as lying beyond man's present reach has not led to despair on the part of governments. The nuclear powers in varying degrees have manifested some awareness of the need for managing military power wisely and cautiously. All five powers at present seem to shun nuclear war as a means of accomplishing their foreign policy objectives. Thomas W. Wolfe, while adopting a prudently cautious interpretation of the significance and extent of the changes which have occurred in Soviet society since the time of Stalin, expresses the opinion that the two superpowers will probably continue to steer clear of a frontal collision. China, according to Harold C. Hinton, recognizes its own vulnerability to nuclear attack and pursues a course of "strategic boldness and tactical caution." In a world where such dangerous crises as the Middle East War of June 1967 can occur at any time, no one would predict that the self-restraint of the five nuclear powers—all of them—will prevail indefinitely. Strategic circumstances might be altered in the future, and this book does not ignore such an unpleasant possibility. But for the time being at least, most if not all of the nuclear powers share, in varying degrees, an interest in arms control, despite the fact that at present formal agreements among all five lie beyond the art of what is politically possible.

Arms Control

In contrast to disarmament, which entails the elimination of armaments, arms control as a theoretical concept reflects a strategic philosophy which accepts the continued existence of national military establishments. Frequently but not always the notion of arms control implies some form of collaboration between adversary States— whether it involve formal agreement, tacit cooperation, or unilateral decisions taken with the expectation of reciprocal action—in those areas of military policy that are thought to be of common or coincident interest to the parties concerned. (We say "not always" because arms control also embraces those unilateral decisions which are deemed worthwhile because they enhance controllability, stability, and security against war even if the adversary does not reciprocate or respond.) The purpose of arms control is generally at least twofold: first, to improve the safety of the international environment against the occurrence of dangerous wars by reducing certain risks inherent in the present military situation; and second, to increase the chances that if military conflicts do occur, as they are likely to from time to time, governments will pursue policies of intelligent restraint rather than engage in operations which lead to uncontrolled escalation, uninhibited violence, and unlimited damage to civilian populations. Many advocates of arms control would insist upon a third purpose—to support policies that will be conducive eventually to disarmament agreements and the growth of peacekeeping institutions in a world where all nation-states have been persuaded to set aside the rule of force in favor of the rule of law. Whether or not this third purpose is "realistic" or "utopian" remains a matter of considerable debate among students of international relations.

The term "arms control," looked at theoretically, is an extremely permissive one and may refer to such diverse measures as the following: 1) administrative, technical, or political arrangements calculated to minimize the risk of nuclear accident, unauthorized use of nuclear weapons, precipitate response to an ambiguous warning, or strategic miscalculation of the adversary's intentions; 2) a program of weapons research, development, and deployment, as well as a strategic doctrine, which stresses the nonprovocative and defensive aspects of national security postures, especially those associated with an "invulnerable second-strike capability;" 3) regional tension-reducing arrangements, such as disengagement, "thinning out" of forces, or the creation of demilitarized or nuclear-free zones; 4) decisions to hold quantitative rates of weapons production below those levels which a nation is economically and technically capable of sustaining in a genuine "arms race;" 5) tension-reducing declarations such as a "no-first-use" pledge or a "nonaggression pact;" 6) the improvement of facilities for emergency communications and prolonged arms control dialogues between adversaries; 7) efforts to separate nuclear forces and strategies from conventional forces and strategies through the utilization of various "firebreaks"—e.g., time, geography, and command; 8) the prohibition of certain activities, such as the sale of conventional arms and delivery systems to countries in "tinderbox areas," nuclear weapons testing in proscribed environments, the emplacement of weapons of mass destruction in orbit, or the establishment of spheres of influence in outer space; 9) a formal verified freeze on the production of specified items, such as fissionable materials for weapons purposes or strategic delivery vehicles; 10) efforts to prevent or retard the proliferation of nuclear weapons to nations not already in possession of them;

and 11) the prudent management of crisis diplomacy and limited conflict strategy. This may be, both from a literary and logical standpoint, an unaesthetic inventory, but it serves to illustrate the variety of measures that can be comprehended under the rubrics of "arms control" as this term has been employed in the recent literature.[2]

The foregoing list is a theoretical one; it contains many more proposals than governments have thus far been able to accept. But a little bit of progress has been registered since the Cuban missile crisis. The United States, the United Kingdom, and the Soviet Union have taken the lead in arms control by entering into a few international agreements of a limited-risk character within recent years, the Partial Test Ban Treaty of 1963 being the most notable example to date. This, along with the few modest accompanying and "follow-on" measures adopted after mid-1963, will be discussed and evaluated frequently in the articles which make up this book. Only a cursory summary need be given here, with special reference to developments that have occurred since the following papers were written.

The Hot Line

The Washington-Moscow "hot line," agreed upon before the conclusion of the Test Ban Treaty, was installed for the purpose of facilitating crisis communications under such circumstances as those which surrounded the Cuban confrontation of October 1962, when in the opinion of some observers war was brought closer by a confusion over the proper sequence of messages from Premier Khrushchev to Washington.[3] The establishment of the "hot line"[4] was an achievement for which no one has wanted to claim too much. Indeed, U.S. arms control analysts have not been

entirely oblivious of the possibility that the "hot line" itself might someday be exploited for purposes of psychological warfare in the midst of an international strategic crisis. But the potential utility of the idea prompted President de Gaulle, during his visit to the Soviet Union in June 1966, to reach agreement on the establishment of a teleprinter link between the Elysée Palace and the Kremlin. Until June 1967, the U.S.-Soviet "hot line" had been used only for the exchange of season's greetings. Then, during the confusing days of the Mideast War of 1967, several messages were exchanged between Washington and Moscow for the purpose of giving reassurances and expressing the desire to avoid direct embroilment.[5]

Nuclear Test Ban

The Treaty Banning Nuclear Weapon Tests in the Atmosphere, in Outer Space, and Under Water, announced in a communiqué of July 25, 1963, and signed on the following August 5,[6] is sufficiently well known as to require no detailed explanation. The Treaty had been a subject of considerable controversy during the five years of negotiations preceding its conclusion,[7] and the debate over the effect which it might have on U.S. security reached a crescendo during the ratification hearings in the Senate.[8] In the military sector, the concern centered chiefly on the possible implications of the treaty for the acquisition of further scientific knowledge in a few crucial areas of military technology—in respect to the penetration capability of missiles, the development of antiballistic missiles, the survival capability of missile sites and systems, and the effects of atmospheric phenomena such as communications blackout (induced by nuclear blast and radiation) upon the operation of offensive and defensive nuclear weapons.[9] Along the political front, the main problem of the treaty pertained to NATO alliance relations, particularly vis-à-vis the Federal Republic of Germany, which needed to be reassured that East Germany's diplomatic status would not be enhanced as a result of being allowed to adhere to the treaty.[10]

The Test Ban Treaty has been ratified by nearly 120 States, exclusive of France and Communist China (both of which have carried on atmospheric tests). Since signing the Treaty, both the Soviet Union and the United States have continued underground testing. Up to June 1967, the United States had carried out nearly 100 underground explosions and the Soviet Union about one-quarter of that number. Within recent years, the two superpowers have both proposed a comprehensive nuclear test ban, and the neutral States at the Eighteen Nation Disarmament Conference have often called for the same thing. Agreement has been precluded, however, by differences over the question of inspection. The Soviet Union has argued that national means of detecting and identifying seismic events are sufficient to verify compliance with a ban on underground tests and that onsite inspection is not needed. The United States and the United Kingdom, on the other hand, have contended that despite improvements in national scientific capabilities, some seismic events will remain unidentified (partly because of the problem of determining epicentral location) and that hence some on-site inspections would be necessary. The United States, as part of its multimillion dollar VELA research program for improving seismic capabilities, has constructed the first Large Aperture Seismic Array (LASA) at Billings, Montana. The Soviets have been reluctant to engage in technical studies of the detection problem; they have refused to comment on the evidence made available by the West.[11]

The eight neutral States at Geneva (Brazil, Burma, Ethiopia, India, Mexico, Nigeria, Sweden, and the United Arab Republic) have long urged the conclusion of a comprehensive test ban treaty as a nonproliferation measure.[12] The U.A.R. has called for the prohibition of all underground tests above the threshold of seismic magnitude 4.75, accompanied by a moratorium on all tests of lesser magnitude, pending the conclusion of a comprehensive treaty. This proposal had the blessing of the U.S.S.R. but was unacceptable to the West.[13] Sweden has taken the lead in advancing suggestions for the formation of an international "detection club" and a system of "verification by challenge" (or "verification by invitation," as it later came to be called).[14] According to the latter idea, which was also discussed at the Scarborough Conference in June 1966, all nuclear tests would be banned for a trial period, during which time a number of methods would be relied upon to dispel suspicion concerning the nature of doubtful seismic events. The government of the country where the event had occurred would be expected to volunteer information about it and to enter into an informal dialogue concerning the scientific evidence. Perhaps observers would be invited to visit the scene. If, finally, the evidence supplied proved unconvincing to the suspicious party, the latter would be entitled to withdraw from the agreement.[15] The United States agreed to examine the idea; the Soviet Union showed little interest in it. By June 1967, it appeared that neither of the superpowers was anxious to please the neutrals by assigning priority to the comprehensive test ban over the nonproliferation treaty, or to eliminate entirely the possibility of carrying out nuclear testing underground while two nuclear powers still reserve the right to develop their technology in the atmosphere.[16]

Ban on Weapons in Space

The first "follow-on" agreement after the partial test ban was the U.N. General Assembly resolution of October 17, 1963, which called upon all States to "refrain from placing in orbit around the earth any objects carrying nuclear weapons or any other kinds of weapons of mass destruction, installing such weapons on celestial bodies, or stationing such weapons in outer space in any other manner." [17] Prior to 1963, whenever U.S. arms control strategists had discussed the possibility of a prohibition against orbital weapons, they usually took it for granted that such a prohibition would have to be linked to a system of global launch surveillance and prelaunch inspection.[18] The U.N. resolution mentioned above did not provide for any form of inspection. Rather it reflected a widespread feeling at the time that the deployment of nuclear weapons in space, although technologically feasible, was not especially desirable on political or military grounds and might prove dangerously difficult to control. Neither the United States nor the Soviet Union appeared anxious to allocate resources to the purpose. Instead of insisting upon a form of inspection which was unobtainable from the Soviets and probably not entirely attractive to American policymakers, the United States was content to rely upon the strength of a presumed mutuality of interest, and also upon the development of an antisatellite capability, which could be used if the ban on bombs in orbit should be violated.[19]

The U.N. Resolution, which was endorsed by the two superpowers, helped to prepare the way for the Treaty Governing the Activities of States in the Exploration and Use of Space, which was announced on December 8, 1966.[20] Many observers were of the opinion that the Space Treaty was directed more toward future problems in a somewhat esoteric environment than toward present arms control problems on earth. The treaty guaranteed *inter alia* that outer space, including the moon and other celestial bodies, shall be free for exploration and use by all states equally in accordance with the principles of international law; that outer space is not subject to national appropriation by claim of sovereignty, by occupation, or by other means; that parties will not place in orbit any objects carrying nuclear weapons or other weapons of mass destruction; that no military installations shall be emplaced on celestial bodies; and that the parties assume international responsibility for activities conducted in space.

It was presumed that the treaty would not hinder the two leading space powers from carrying out any military missions which they are now able to define clearly. Indeed, the treaty specified that the "use of military personnel for scientific research or for any other peaceful purposes shall not be prohibited." At present, neither side seems anxious either to orbit nuclear weapons or to place military bases on the moon. It bears noting that the treaty does not demilitarize space; it does not prohibit the powers from using military personnel for space activities; it does not rule out reconnaissance satellites or "communications-ferreting" satellites; nor does it preclude the development of the manned orbiting laboratory (MOL). Few would deny that someday the treaty might take on considerable strategic significance, either as an effective means of limiting the armaments competition in space or as a damper on the technological programs of the side which feels more constrained by it. But at the time it was announced, the treaty appeared designed to serve primarily a psychological and political purpose as a symbol of U.S.-Soviet "détente" and cooperation amidst heightening international tensions over Vietnam. The Space Treaty was signed by 62 nations on January 27, 1967. The Senate ratified it on April 25, 1967, after a surprisingly perfunctory debate in which it was apparent that the Joint Chiefs of Staff, far from thinking that the treaty would endanger national security, expected that it would lead to an increase in U.S. military efforts in space to verify Soviet adherence to the prohibition against stationing weapons in space.[21]

Production Cutback

Another "follow-on" measure, originally announced unilaterally by the United States and subsequently made the subject of reciprocal gestures by the United States and the Soviet Union, had to do with declared cutbacks in the production of fissionable materials. Two weeks before the opening of the 1964 Geneva Conference of the Eighteen Nation Disarmament Committee (ENDC), President Johnson had announced in his State of the Union Message that the United States would reduce production of fissionable materials for weapons purposes by 25 percent, by closing four of its fourteen plutonium plants. This was followed in April 1964 by simultaneous announcements, coordinated through Geneva, that the United States would decrease its production of plutonium by 20 percent

and of enriched uranium by 40 percent, while the Soviet Union would halt the scheduled construction of two new atomic reactors for producing plutonium and would also, "during the next few years," reduce substantially the production of uranium-235 for nuclear weapons.[22] The less precise character of the Soviet undertaking stemmed no doubt from the fact that the Soviet Union, which had been producing fissionable material for a shorter time and from a smaller number of plants than the United States, was less able to cut output. The West had no way of knowing for certain whether the Soviets had indeed planned to build two new reactors, or that they were actually cutting back. Some Western observers remained skeptical, as the articles by William R. Kintner and Thomas W. Wolfe indicate. Perhaps the United States deemed itself in a position to carry out the declared reductions regardless of what the Soviets did. Few would deny, however, that the move partially undermined the U.S. proposal for a formal agreement for a verified cutoff on the manufacture of all nuclear weapons materials.[23] This illustrates one of the dilemmas confronting the United States in respect to arms control policy. If the U.S., for the sake of promoting a "détente" conducive to arms control agreements, embarks upon certain policies of unilateral restraint, this sometimes diminishes the Soviet motive to negotiate a particular type of arms-limitation pact.

Military Budget Reductions

The cutting of military budgets by 10 to 15 percent had been proposed by Soviet Delegate Semen K. Tsarapkin in January 1964.[24] He argued at the time that this would not entail any lopsided alteration in the miltary balance, since each state would be able to determine for itself which components of its defense forces would be reduced. Although it looked attractive in theory, both the United States and Britain opposed the suggestion in the absence of further technical studies and agreement on the precise methods of policing the measure. Western analysts have long been skeptical of control by fiscal inspection alone, in view of the ease with which governments can disguise appropriations or transfer funds from one account to another.[25] When the British pressed for technical studies on the verification of budgetary agreements, the Soviets retorted that back in the days of the League of Nations technical studies, instead of leading to disarmament, were merely a cloak for war preparations, and demanded that the cut should be accepted in principle prior to the inauguration of technical studies.[26]

Nevertheless, in that same period it looked as though the two superpowers, despite their inability to negotiate a formal agreement at Geneva, were interested in turning down the arms burner by at least a few degrees and carrying out, informally, modest curtailments in their military budgets. The Soviets announced a 4.3 percent cut in defense spending. Shortly thereafter, the Johnson Administration said that the U.S. arms budget would be sliced from $52 billion to $51 billion by eliminating obsolescent weapons systems, dismantling installations and bases no longer required, and tightening management efficiency in the defense establishment. It was suggested that both powers were willing to see whether they might apply to the budgetary sector what Western writers called "reciprocal unilateral measures" of a "confidence-building" nature and what the Soviets described as "mutual example." At the end of 1964, both countries once again announced defense cuts, the Soviets from 13.3 to 12.8 billion rubles and the United States from $51 to $49 billion.

During 1965, however, the expansion of the war in Vietnam necessitated extraordinary U.S. military expenditures. In December of that year, the Soviets responded by announcing a five percent increase in defense spending for 1966. In January 1966 the United States unveiled a defense budget increase from $49 billion to $57.2 billion, of which $10 billion was attributed to the prosecution of the Vietnamese conflict. Actually, this estimate proved to be quite short of the mark. By December 1966, U.S. forces in the area of Vietnam were approaching a total figure of 400,000, and the government admitted that defense costs in the current fiscal year were running as much as $10 billion higher than had been officially anticipated in the previous January. In the same December the Supreme Soviet heard that the defense program for 1967 would cost 8.2 percent more than in 1966. Then in January 1967 the Johnson Administration proposed a $73 billion defense budget, including $22 billion for the cost of the Vietnam operation. This meant that U.S. spending for strategic arms systems was approximately at the 1964 spending level. How much of the Soviet increase was going to the cost of Vietnam and how much to finance strategic arms developments in offensive and defensive missile systems could not be known exactly, but it seemed likely that only a small percentage could be attributed to military aid for Vietnam.[27] At any rate, the question of budget cuts for arms control purposes had become, at least for the time being, somewhat academic.

Proposals for Arms Control in Europe

The three years since early 1964 have witnessed the discussion (primarily at Geneva) of several other arms control proposals, most of them pertaining to Europe, which have not figured centrally in the arms control debate and can be summarized briefly. The Soviets have periodically called for the withdrawal of foreign troops from all countries, the liquidation of foreign bases, the establishment of a nuclear-free zone in Central Europe, and a pledge against the first use of nuclear weapons.[28] The Ulbricht regime in East Germany has made repeated efforts since 1964 to win a semblance of diplomatic recognition at Geneva by communicating to the Eighteen-Nation Disarmament Committee (through the Soviet Union) appeals for the joint renunciation of nuclear weapons by the "two German States" and for the removal of all foreign nuclear weapons from German territory.[29] Early in 1966 Premier Kosygin indicated that the Soviet Union was willing to include in the nonproliferation treaty a clause on "the prohibition of the use of nuclear weapons against nonnuclear States parties to the treaty which have no nuclear weapons on their territory."[30] All of these moves were related to the older and better known Polish proposals (the Rapacki and Gomulka plans) for a nuclear-free zone or at least a nuclear freeze in Germany, Poland, and Czechoslovakia. Since all of these proposals have been generally thought to involve nonsymmetrical military consequences adverse to NATO, the Western powers have refused to accept them.[31]

Surprise Attack Measures

Both sides have expressed interest from time to time in measures to minimize the fears of surprise attack, particularly through the exchange of observers. Arms control specialists have been careful not to claim too much for the utility of such a proposal, pointing out that there are ways of defeating or exploiting the observer-post system. They argue, however, that such a measure could, without disturbing the existing military balance, serve a politically and psychologically useful "confidence-building" purpose, and might also, in certain circumstances, help to avert war by miscalculation.[32] The Soviet Union, however, has linked the exchange of observers to disengagement and denuclearization in Central Europe, thus making it contingent upon the acceptance of conditions known to be objectionable to the Federal Republic. Whenever a simple proposal is tied to a more complex one, agreement is rendered more difficult to achieve—indeed, this is the purpose of the "tying" clause. The Soviets have also frequently urged the conclusion of a nonaggression pact between NATO and the Warsaw grouping. The Western powers, however, recalling the threats to Berlin in the 1958-1962 period, have made it clear that agreement on a nonaggression pact would depend upon the willingness of the Soviets to give guarantees for Berlin which they have not been ready to offer.

Unilateral Arms Control in Europe

Several of the unilateral arms control policies pursued by the United States in the early 1960's had been aimed at a reduction of the nuclear danger in Europe. The Kennedy Administration had sought to build up NATO conventional forces and to shift the emphasis in U.S. military strategy in Europe from "massive retaliation" and early nuclear response in the direction of a more flexible posture designed to provide at times of crisis a larger number of options between "holocaust and surrender." In the planning of European defense, a definite effort was made to insert a wider "firebreak" between conventional and nuclear strategies. Policymakers paid a great deal of attention to the means of preventing the accidental, unauthorized, or precipitate firing of nuclear weapons. Various efforts were made to downgrade the role of tactical nuclear weapons in NATO, to enhance control through the installation of "permissive action links" and other administrative devices, to pull back apparently "provocative" nuclear weapons systems (such as the "soft" Thor and Jupiter missiles, as well as forward battlefield nuclear rockets), and to upgrade conventional capabilities for the enforcement of a "pause" in case of Soviet conventional attack.[33]

It soon became clear, however, that there were limits to how far the United States could go in deprecating the significance of the nuclear deterrent in the defense of Western Europe. First, the Europeans simply could not be persuaded to raise their conventional contributions to NATO. Their lack of interest stemmed from a concern over economic costs, from a declining perception of the threat of Soviet attack, and from a conviction that if the nuclear deterrent were maintained at a sufficiently high level there would be no need to worry much about the requirements of local defense against attack. The Germans in particular were nervous about any policy shift that seemed likely to weaken the nuclear deterrent;

they feared that this might tempt the Soviets to gamble on a probing operation which could lead to a nuclear conflict that would have been precluded if the danger of a nearly automatic nuclear response had been posed in advance. Secondly, the policy of the de Gaulle Government in the mid-1960's, deintegrating French forces from alliance commands, made it seem, in the opinion of some experienced politicians, more necessary for the United States to keep atomic warheads stockpiled on the Continent.[34]

Within recent years, U.S. balance-of-payments difficulties, combined with the pressures of the Vietnamese War, have made the reduction of U.S. forces in Europe attractive to several American political leaders, including Senate Majority Leader Mansfield. Britain, too, has been under considerable economic pressure to reduce her commitment to Continental defense. The British have had some misgivings that a sizeable reduction of Anglo-American forces in Germany would enhance the importance of the Bundeswehr in European politics —a step which might arouse the apprehensions of West Germany's neighbors and eventually lead to a demand that the Federal Republic acquire its own nuclear weapons. Responsible Germans, too, have stressed the need for care "that in the event of a withdrawal of American and British troops from Western Europe the military strength of the Federal Republic should not appear inordinate."[35] The United States announced plans in May 1967 to withdraw up to 35,000 troops, including two Army brigades and four Air Force fighter-bomber squadrons, during 1968. Britain was also expected to withdraw one of her nine brigades from the British Army of the Rhine and one fighter-bomber squadron.[36] A number of senior military men and some diplomats discerned risks in the troop cutbacks.[37] Nevertheless, in a somewhat paradoxical move one week later, the Defense Ministers of 14 NATO countries, meeting for the first time without France, instructed the military command of the alliance to abandon the longstanding concept of "massive retaliation" and to adopt in its place as official doctrine the strategy of "flexible response."[38]

U.S. officials were counting on a capability to airlift reinforcements to Europe if they should ever be needed. But they undoubtedly hoped that moderate troop reductions, carried out in close consultation with Britain and West Germany, would further promote the Soviet Western détente in Europe and might lead eventually to reciprocal measures on the part of the Soviets. According to a German correspondent, the Soviet military forces in Western Russia and Eastern Europe were, in the beginning of 1967, more than nine times larger than Soviet forces in Eastern Russia facing China. Furthermore, he pointed out, none of the twenty Soviet divisions stationed in East Germany, nor of the two in Poland and the four in Hungary, has been shifted to the Chinese border.[39] It was conceivable that the Soviets might be interested in redeploying some divisions from west to east in the future, after China's nuclear capability attains significance. But for the present it must be apparent to the Soviet Union that Britain and the United States are bent upon unilateral troop withdrawals from Europe regardless of whether Moscow intends to reciprocate. Hence the Soviet leaders are not strongly motivated to negotiate a mutual disengagement or thinning out of forces.

Ballistic Missile Defense

Ever since the beginning of this decade, many arms control writers in the West have opposed the development and/or deployment of antimissile missiles on the grounds that such weapons would undermine the strategic nuclear balance. In the past, it was frequently argued that ballistic missile defense should be eschewed because it was technically unfeasible, economically costly, militarily useless (in view of a supposed mutual cancellation effect) and strategically destabilizing.[40] Meanwhile, both the Soviet Union and the United States showed an interest in research and development in this field. In 1963, when the Partial Test Ban Treaty was under consideration, the Soviets were reported to be deploying missile defenses around Leningrad.[41]

At the opening of the Geneva talks in 1964, President Johnson proposed a verified freeze on the nature and number of strategic nuclear offensive and defensive vehicles (both aircraft and missiles).[42] The categories of weapons affected were to be defined by range and weight. The objective of the freeze agreement would be to maintain at constant levels the quantities of strategic nuclear vehicles held by the two superpowers, while providing for a suitable number of missile systems over a period of time, and permitting the production of replacements on a one-for-one basis. The official hope was that such a freeze would put an end not only to quantitative competition but also to qualitative improvements in missiles. The proposal gave rise to many difficulties—questions of defining "strategic delivery vehicles," of inspection and control, of distinguishing between military missiles and "missiles-for-peace," and of reaching agreement on permitted replacements of missiles used up in training or confidence firings, or lost through malfunction.[43] There were even more complex obstacles arising out of the computation of the effects which such a freeze would have upon the strategic distribution of power between two titans with different numbers of different-sized missiles and different strategic needs. For three years the Soviets manifested no interest in negotiating—or even in talking about—such a proposal.

In late 1965 a committee of distinguished citizens headed by Jerome B. Wiesner proposed "a moratorium of at least three years on new deployment (but not on the unverifiable research and development) of systems for ballistic-missile defense."[44] Nevertheless, nearly a year later, Defense Secretary Robert McNamara admitted that there was "considerable evidence" that the Soviet Union was building and deploying an antiballistic missile system, and he announced that the Administration would probably recommend to Congress the production and deployment of the large submarine-launched Poseidon missile, more capable than Polaris of penetrating sophisticated defense networks.[45]

McNamara's statement set off an animated public debate—for one had long been in progress among experts below the level of front page headlines —over missile defense. Virtually the entire panoply of arguments pro and con will be found in the articles by Richard B. Foster, Edward Teller, Joseph I. Coffey, and Jeremy J. Stone. The latter two are disposed to cite the case against deployment. Coffee warns that a deployment of missile defense— whether "lightly" against the Chinese or "heavily" against the Soviet Union (and the former may in time lead to the latter)—might only serve to stimu-

late the U.S.S.R. to increased military expenditures and thus further to reduce the already slim chance of arms control agreements. Stone cautions against the assumption that all Soviet military leaders want BMD, plays down its effectiveness and scores the arguments of its advocates as "more ingenious than real." Foster and Teller, on the other hand, contend along with William R. Kintner that missile defense will be necessary for the continued effectiveness of the U.S. strategic deterrent. Foster draws a connection between the possession of BMD and the ability of the United States to supply guarantees to nonnuclear weapon countries—hence he calls BMD potentially "restabilizing." Teller points out that we know little about the real costs of missile defense; a capability to blunt a Chinese attack would not be very effective against the Soviets, but the experience of building the smaller system would enable us to judge better the cost-effectiveness of a larger system. He also suggests that a missile defense effort on an alliance-wide basis could help to recement NATO and eventually furnish an incentive for France to reintegrate her military forces.

Developments in early 1967 did not strengthen the hand of the more optimistic analysts. The U.S. intelligence community buzzed with speculation that the Soviets were constructing antimissile missile facilities all over Russia, not just around Moscow and Leningrad. Moreover, it was believed that this defense network was based on long-range, solid-fuel missiles aimed at achieving interception in space hundreds of miles from the defended areas. It was estimated that the Soviets had spent from four to five billion dollars on their antimissile defense system. (This estimate included expenditures dating back to the late 1950's, such as the cost of the earlier BMD system which was reported during 1963 but which was apparently later scrapped because it proved unfeasible.) Soviet spokesmen, in both formal pronouncements and informal conversations, made it fairly clear that they, unlike many Western analysts, did not regard BMD as "provocative" and "destabilizing" and that their country was determined to purchase all the defense it possibly could. To many military officers in the United States was attributed the opinion that the Soviets were not likely to agree to halt the deployment of their defense system. These officers were inclined to think that the Department of Defense concept of BMD restraint in recent years—based on the theory that "if we don't build it, they won't"—had been shown to be invalid by reports that the U.S.S.R. was working not only on BMD but also on multiple missile warheads, each with its own individual guidance. The Joint Chiefs of Staff, considering themselves responsible for providing maximum security for the population and territory of the U.S., unanimously recommended, over the opposition of Secretary McNamara, that the construction of a missile defense system be undertaken. What the JCS proposed was a multistaged deployment of the Nike-X system, starting with a "thin" area defense around the entire country, capable of intercepting a modest attack from China or Russia, combined with a heavier defense around Minutemen missile sites, at a total cost of $5 billion. Later the system would be expanded, first to 25 of the most populous cities at a cost of $5 billion more, and then to another 25 large cities at an additional cost of $10 billion.[46]

Secretary McNamara preferred to try persuading the Soviets to enter into an agreement freezing offensive and defensive strategic weapons. Instead of emphasizing a program of missile defense, McNamara was content to rely upon the ability of the United States to improve and increase its capability to inflict what he called "assured destruction" upon the Soviet Union as a deterrent against attack. President Johnson wrote to Soviet Premier Kosygin on January 27, 1967, suggesting measures to limit the missile competition, before the U.S. would make a "final decision" to deploy BMD. Five weeks later the President announced that Premier Kosygin had "confirmed the willingness of the Soviet Government to discuss means of limiting the arms race in offensive and defensive nuclear missiles." [47] The talks were to begin in Moscow at the "earliest possible" time, but as this volume was going to press (June 1967) no further word had been made public concerning the progress of the discussions, if any. What effect the Middle East War of June 1967 might have upon the outcome of the negotiations could only be a matter of surmise among arms control strategists. If in that crisis the Soviets concluded that they were necessarily inhibited by the existing strategic equation from giving the support which they had previously promised the Arabs, then the possibility lingered that they might protract the negotiations on curbing missile deployment until they thought that they had substantially altered the prevailing assumptions concerning U.S. strategic military superiority. Meanwhile, the debate over BMD continued unabated.[48] The announcement by the People's Republic of China on June 17, 1967 that it had exploded an H-bomb increased the likelihood that the United

States would deploy at least a "light" missile defense system.

The Nonproliferation Treaty

Some years ago a Soviet mathematician expressed the danger of nuclear weapons proliferation in the formula $R = N^2$, in which R stood for the risk of nuclear war and N for the number of nuclear powers. This formula, which implied a geometric progression in the chance of war with every increase in the number of nuclear weapon States, ignored certain political realities—including the kind of governments acquiring control over nuclear weapons and the character of their foreign policies. Hence if Sweden and Switzerland were to become nuclear weapon States, the risks of war would grow (according to this mathematical representation) just as much as if the acquiring States were North Vietnam and Castro's Cuba. In this sense, if in no other, the formula was deficient. Nevertheless, in spite of the suggestions that have been made from time to time that a world of many nuclear powers might be stabler than a world of few, and that entrance into the nuclear club might compel a militant power to act with greater responsibility and caution, most arms control analysts in recent years have taken it for granted that a world of twelve or fifteen nuclear States would be less stable than a world of three or four, because it would pose a greater statistical probability of technical accident, unauthorized use, strategic miscalculation, or uncontrolled escalation from a limited to a general conflict.

Since the conclusion of the Partial Nuclear Test Ban Treaty in 1963, a nonproliferation treaty has become the principal target of arms control diplomacy, both within the United Nations General Assembly and in the Eighteen Nation Disarmament Committee in Geneva.[49] These have been the salient questions: Can the two superpowers be expected to conclude a major arms agreement while the conflict in Southeast Asia is in progress? Is a formal treaty necessary, insofar as the five nuclear powers might already be in tacit agreement that it is not in their interest to dilute the currency of nuclear prestige by helping to create other nuclear powers? Should nonnuclear weapon States renounce their option of acquiring a nuclear military capability before they are certain that the nuclear powers will make progress toward disarmament? Can the nuclear powers give credible security guarantees to the nonnuclear weapon countries? How high a price should a superpower pay in respect to the cohesion of its alliance system in order to obtain a treaty?

For several years, the United States has sought to persuade aspirants to nuclear power that the game was not worth the candle, because small deterrents are costly, provocative and accident-prone, lack credibility, become obsolescent quickly and render young nuclear powers vulnerable to attack in their early stages. But in the early 1960's, the French Government remained unimpressed by the arguments advanced by the United States, and it is possible that other States will, in the late 1960's, discern reasons for acquiring nuclear weapons. The arguments of the nuclear advocates can be grouped under three headings. *Militarily,* nuclear weapons provide unprecedented power available in no other form; they alone can deter a nuclear-equipped opponent; they do not necessarily require expensive long-range delivery systems to deter a distant great power; a country might contemplate only their tactical use for defensive purposes against an evenly matched neighbor, to prevent the foe from massing his armies, to interdict him, and to deny him access to avenues of approach, e.g., by detonating atomic mines in mountain passes when an attack seems imminent. *Economically,* nuclear weapons programs undoubtedly siphon off scarce scientific-engineering talent from immediate development purposes, but in the long run they can contribute to the growth of the technological base. Moreover, the initial investment is no longer prohibitive especially for a country which has already developed a civilian reactor program. (It has been estimated that a minimum capability of producing five bombs a year, with a proper testing program but without a sophisticated delivery system, would cost about $450 million, spread unevenly over a ten-year period.[50]) Eventually, the acquisition of nuclear weapons might permit some savings through the reduction in the size of the conventional armed forces. *Politically,* nuclear weapons provide an ultimate guarantee of a country's independence; insofar as they furnish a State with a nuclear trigger in time of crisis, they foreclose both strong-armed tactics by more powerful States and crisis deals by the superpowers at the expense of that country; they are a source of prestige within an alliance, within the region, and within the world at large, and provide one with a ticket to summit conferences. As for the argument that entrance into the nuclear club renders a country vulnerable in the infant stages, aspirants to *N*th power status merely point to the experience of Nos. 2, 3, 4, and 5, for none of whom did mere acquisition, when combined with international strategic restraint, prove to be a *casus belli.* The strength of all the foregoing arguments for is not necessarily greater than that of the arguments against, when both are weighed by an objective logician. But in at least a few of the dozen countries that now produce weapons-grade plutonium, or of the more than twenty that will do so within a few years, the case *for* might prove more attractive than the case *against,* regardless of logic.

Everyone realizes that the proposed nonproliferation treaty would place its major burdens upon the nonnuclear rather than the nuclear powers. It is the former who would be requested to make the greater sacrifice by shutting off an option that might be vital to their security and political interests, while the three likely nuclear signatories would be doing little more than protecting their privileged position. Hence it is not surprising that Ambassador Trivedi in his paper likens the diplomatic antiproliferation campaign of recent years to an effort on the part of the armed to disarm the unarmed, or that Ambassador Cavalletti describes his Government's attempt to bring about a multilateral moratorium on the spread of nuclear weapons to other countries pending progress by the nuclear powers toward nuclear arms reduction. Several of the middle and lesser States keep insisting that there must be an "equality of obligation" in respect to nuclear abstention; they are reluctant to adhere to a treaty that seeks to prevent "horizontal proliferation" to other States while allowing "vertical proliferation" among the members of the "nuclear pentapoly." As indicated previously, some of the neutrals at Geneva have seemed at times to assign a higher priority to the conclusion of a comprehensive test ban (which would impose restraint on the Nuclear Five) than to the conclusion of a nonproliferation treaty.

India undoubtedly wonders whether the international political position of the People's Republic of China will be permanently enhanced as a result of Peking's acquisition of a nuclear missile capability. For many years past, neither neutrals nor aligned middle powers have reacted favorably to the suggestion that nuclear capabilities and the U.N. Security Council veto might someday be perfectly conjoined, but India has been particularly sensitive on this point. Quite naturally, many Indian policymakers, intellectuals, scientists, and military leaders have been worried about the long-range implications of a nonproliferation treaty. Even some of those who are most opposed to a national decision to exercise the nuclear weapons option (which has not been taken up to the time of this writing) are understandably reluctant to have their government sign a treaty while Peking still shows no interest in adhering even to the partial test ban.

Through the first half of 1967 India continued to serve as principal spokesman for those nonaligned States which suffered misgivings over the proposed treaty. Indian leaders remained apprehensive of Pakistan, guilty in their eyes of rejecting Indian offers to normalize relations in the wake of the Tashkent Agreement. But they were even more suspicious of the long-range threat of Communist China, which supplies arms and guerrilla training aid to Pakistan and seeks to apply protracted political-military pressure along India's borders. India sees trouble ahead if China should seek to demonstrate that her primacy in Asia has not been jeopardized by the internal upheaval known as the "cultural revolution."

Within recent years it has often been suggested that the nuclear States tender security guarantees to nuclear-abstaining States. After the first Chinese nuclear test at Lop Nor in October 1964, President Johnson made this pledge: "The nations that do not seek national nuclear weapons can be sure that, if they need our strong support against some threat of nuclear blackmail, then they will have it." [51] But the precise form in which a guarantee would be given to the nonnuclear powers has remained unclear—whether it would be joint or unilateral; whether it would be given to every nonnuclear State or only exposed ones; whether it would come into play only in the event of nuclear aggression or threat thereof, or might be invoked in case of uncontainable conventional attack. The more carefully circumscribed the guarantee, the less willing would nonnuclear weapon countries probably be to trust their future security to it; the more sweeping the pledge, the less prepared would the United States Senate be to ratify it. (For an insight into the attitude of lawmakers on this question, see the exchange between Robert S. McNamara and Craig Hosmer excerpted in Hosmer's article.) There were few signs in mid-1967 that the question of nuclear guarantees had been satisfactorily resolved, or would be soon. As Chinese nuclear capabilities grow, the issue of the "high posture" versus the "low posture," discussed by Bull, Schlesinger, and others, is bound to take on added significance in the minds of those Indian leaders who would like to receive guarantees against Chinese attacks or threats.

India has continued to strengthen her capabilities in the field of nuclear energy, doubling the scope of the Rajasthan Atomic Plant and building another at Tarapur. At this writing, she remains cool to the idea of placing her atoms-for-peace activities completely under the control system of the International Atomic Energy Agency (IAEA), and her agreements with Canada do not require her to do so.

Meanwhile, joint communiqués issued by India and three other Asian governments—Indonesia, Afghanistan and Iraq—have stressed the need for "an acceptable balance of obligations between nuclear weapons States and nonnuclear weapon States." [52] (This is in conformity with the position detailed by Ambassador Trivedi in his paper.) In March and again in April 1967, Mohamedali C. Chagla, the Minister for External Affairs, reiterated that national security would be the paramount consideration in determining India's policy on the signing of the treaty. He said that India would welcome a treaty that was neither discriminatory against the nonnuclear weapon powers nor obstructive of the growth of peaceful nuclear technology in the developing countries. He expressed his belief that most of the countries represented at the Geneva conference appreciated India's peculiar position with respect to the treaty because she was a nonaligned country, not a member of any military alliance or under the nuclear umbrella of any country, yet faced by the long-lasting threat of a nuclear China. [53]

Critical comments about the treaty came also from Sweden, Switzerland, Japan, Israel, and Italy, but no country has been more worried about nonproliferation diplomacy than West Germany. There was little doubt by 1965 that the project for a NATO multilateral force (MLF) was moribund, as John Silard argues in his article. Its demise gradually led to an amelioration of the strident Soviet propaganda attacks against U.S. efforts to give the Germans "access" to nuclear weapons, but it did not remove Soviet opposition to the clause in the U.S. draft treaty permitting a "European option"—i.e., the possible future creation of a joint European deterrent under circumstances which would not increase the total number of nuclear powers in the world (meaning that either the British or the French must merge their nuclear force with a European force). [54] The United States began to shift emphasis within NATO from the concept of the MLF to the so-called McNamara Committee or Nuclear Planning Committee, designed to develop continuing consultation on nuclear targeting and contingency planning, military intelligence and emergency communication. The United States was reluctant to discuss NATO nuclear sharing arrangements in the open forum at Geneva, but the Soviets continued to criticize the Ten-Member Committee because of German participation. [55]

The Johnson Administration was far from certain that the McNamara Committee would prove sufficient to satisfy Bonn. Indeed, official spokesmen of the Federal Republic said on several occasions that the Committee could not be regarded as a substitute for the MLF. Just a few weeks before the fall of his coalition government in the fall of 1966, Chancellor Erhard visited Washington. The communiqué issued at that time paid lip service to the idea of the MLF, and the Chancellor reciprocated by calling the Nuclear Committee a useful device whose full value was yet to be seen. [56] Then Foreign Minister Andrei Gromyko met with President Johnson and Secretary of State Dean Rusk early in October 1966. Both sides issued guardedly optimistic statements, and one journalist reported from Washington his description of a "feeling . . . that the President may have made some commitment about Bonn to ease Soviet fears of a rearmed Germany." [57] Once again, the West Germans came down with a case of acute political nervousness. According to one leading German newspaper, "It is plain that this has been an occurrence which could alter the whole tenor of East-West relations." It went on to say, "It won't happen today, but it will definitely happen. The time is fast approaching, but there is still time to prepare for it." [58]

The Christian Democratic-Social Democratic coalition government headed by Kiesinger and Brandt which came to power in December 1966 has shifted somewhat from the arguments which marked the debate over a nonproliferation treaty during the Erhard days—Germany has already given her West European allies a treaty pledge that she will not build atomic weapons; Germany must have a share in a NATO nuclear force; Germany should not formally renounce the NATO sharing option in a treaty with the Soviets prior to the settlement of the whole German question. The still urgent issue of strategic security has been of late partially muted. The insinuation that the Federal Republic looks upon the nuclear sharing question as a bargaining instrument for the negotiation of national reunification has been set aside. The new government has expressed misgivings about the treaty primarily on two grounds: 1) it might hinder the development of peaceful nuclear technology and lead to industrial espionage in that sector; and 2) the effort to bring Euratom under IAEA controls could have adverse repercussions upon the European unity movement.

The United States has maintained that the nonproliferation treaty would not obstruct a country's progress in the area of "atoms for peace." In mid-1966 the United States offered to make available to signatory nations nuclear explosive services for peaceful purposes on a nondiscriminatory basis and under appropriate international safeguards. [59]

President Johnson reiterated this offer when the Eighteen Nation Disarmament Committee resumed its talks in February 1967. [60] Soviet Delegate Alexei A. Roshchin agreed with the U.S. position that a nonproliferation treaty should not hinder other countries from using nuclear energy for peaceful economic development, but that a device for carrying out peaceful nuclear explosions cannot be distinguished from devices serving a military purpose. [61]

Despite U.S. reassurances, West German misgivings continued. The Federal Republic has invested heavily in fast breeder reactors, and it fears that the United States might use the nonproliferation treaty to protect the foreign markets of the American reactor industry by preventing the Germans from exporting plutonium in the future. [62] The Germans further suspect that if East European Communist inspectors from the IAEA are allowed to visit West German plants, they might carry out industrial espionage and pass along to the Soviet Union secrets concerning the construction design of German reactors. [63] Voices were also raised in the Federal Republic insisting that, if the superpowers are about to deploy ballistic missile defense, then the nonproliferation treaty must be worded in such a way as not to prevent the nonnuclear powers from later acquiring their own means of defense. [64]

Moreover, the Germans and their partners in the European Community are reluctant to see Euratom lose its self-inspection prerogatives which it won from the United States back in 1958 (much to the chagrin of the neutrals) and pass under the IAEA control system. Euratom is the nuclear agency of the Six; it would play a crucial role if the Community should someday take the decision to acquire a joint deterrent.

Thus, in a sense, to subordinate Euratom to the Vienna Agency would be tantamount to closing out the "European option." By the time the Geneva Conference opened in February 1967, the United States had already deleted from its draft treaty the unambiguous endorsement of the "European option." The Federal Republic finally brought itself to acquiesce in this when Bonn came round to the view that a United Europe is now such a remote possibility that there was no point of making an issue of it at Geneva. German legalists also contended that if a United Europe should ever come into being, it would be a new political entity, not bound by a treaty signed earlier by its individual member States.[65] Hence the Germans could live with a noncommittal treaty phraseology. But neither they nor the Italians seemed willing to give in on the Euratom issue itself, not even after the United States offered to delay inspection of the Euratom countries by the IAEA until three years after the effective date of the treaty. Both Bonn and Rome were reported to have decided to make of the three-year transition a trial period for the treaty, and to reserve the right to withdraw when they would become subject to inspection by the IAEA instead of by Euratom, if at that time they did not like all the effects of the treaty.[66] In this position they were supported by France.[67]

The West Germans have sought to avoid the appearance of being, along with India, a major obstacle to the conclusion of a nonproliferation treaty. Unlike New Delhi, Bonn has not sought to line up formal support for its position in other capitals. In early 1967 there were garbled reports concerning Premier Kosygin's opinion that the Federal Republic would have to sign the treaty whether it liked it or not, or that there

would be a treaty whether the West Germans liked it or not. The Kiesinger Government, naturally, had to make it clear that if it signed the treaty it would do so of its own free will, not under coercion. What all this diplomatic activity added up to was the inability of the Soviet Union and the United States to agree upon a joint treaty draft to be submitted to the ENDC when it reconvened after a seven-week recess in mid-May 1967. By mid-June, it looked as though no joint text could be produced at this time unless the controversial Article III, which dealt with the question of inspection, would be dropped entirely.

Conclusions

The prospects for arms control in the second half of 1967 were uncertain indeed. Within the previous year, the Soviet Union and the United States had concluded a consular treaty and an air traffic agreement, as well as a treaty for outer space. Both powers endorsed the agreement for the creation of a nuclear-free zone in Latin America.[68] Both had agreed to enter into talks over the damping of missile defense preparations, but their outcome remained in doubt. After three years of efforts to obtain a nonproliferation treaty, there were signs that both sides looked with a certain resignation upon the mounting opposition to it in other capitals and realized that it might not prove possible to obtain a treaty no matter what concessions they were willing to make to each other.

Just what effect the Mideast War, the visit to the U.S. of Premier Kosygin in June 1967, and the Glassboro meeting will have upon the détente and upon Soviet-Western arms control negotiations no prudent analyst would venture to predict. Certainly the Soviets bore a considerable share of the responsibility for the development of the political crisis which led to the Arab war. The U.S.S.R. had, for more than a decade, constituted the principal military supplier of the Egyptian and Syrian armies and had shown little or no interest in proposals to limit arms shipments into that region. The Soviet leaders helped to stimulate Nasser's nationalist adventurism by offering declaratory support to the Arab States before and after the U.A.R. decision to close the Gulf of Aqaba to Israeli shipping. Prior to the outbreak of hostilities, they deprecated the seriousness of the crisis in the U.N. Security Council. At one critical point, they ominously moved part of their fleet from the Black Sea through the Straits, and called for the withdrawal of the U.S. Sixth Fleet from the Mediterranean. Yet when the war broke out, they behaved with restraint while watching their Arab allies suffer a quick and decisive defeat. What this bizarre series of events portended for the tone of international relations and for arms control in the late 1960's can only be surmised and debated. It might mean that the Soviets will become more amenable to cooperative efforts at international stabilization; or it could mean that, as Communist strategic power grows, the pace and scope of conflict at a level below that of nuclear war will be speeded up.

Throughout early 1967 it was often suggested that the only serious obstacle to further progress toward a U.S.-Soviet détente and additional arms control agreements was the conflict in Vietnam. Terminate the war, many demanded, and then rapid strides could be taken toward international agreements. At this point a caveat must be entered against such a *simpliste* prescription. There is no single conflict which can be cited as the cause of the world's woes. Indeed, one can make a plausible case that the development of détente within the West (i.e., across Europe) in recent years has been a function of the conflict in the East—a necessary condition for keeping the military conflict under control in Asia at a time when all the major adversaries seem to realize that the limited Vietnam War involves stakes that are extremely high and risks that are enormous. The termination of that conflict, however much it is to be desired on terms that will establish a fair and stable equilibrium in Asia, will not resolve the China problem, nor the German question, nor the Arab-Israeli conflict. Nor will it assuage for long the enduring dilemmas which arise to face the statesmen of the world out of the confrontation of rival political-ideological systems which, while they all want peace rather than nuclear holocaust, cannot yet agree on the quality of the peace that is to be.

Notes

[1] In a study undertaken for the United States Arms Control and Disarmament Agency, Arnold Wolfers suggests that a world balance of power, based upon mutual deterrence, constitutes a highly rational goal for the United States, both as the minimum and maximum objective of its military effort. He points out that whereas proportionate reductions in armaments are attractive in theory, they are extremely difficult to attain in practice, and that complete disarmament can usually be expected to prove disadvantageous to the side which originally enjoyed military superiority. Finally, he questions whether an international peacekeeping force of the kind proposed in the U.S. Outline Plan for General and Complete Disarmament could really be relied upon by this country where matters of security and other important interests were concerned, or whether "American vital interests could become exposed to new threats emanating from such a force, instead of being protected by it." "Disarmament, Peacekeeping and the National Interest," in *The United States in a Disarmed World*, prepared at The Washington Center of Foreign Policy Research, Baltimore: The Johns Hopkins Press, 1966, pp. 3-32. See especially pp. 12, 25, and 32. For an exposition of the present author's views concerning the impracticability of general disarmament under the prevailing circumstances of the international system, see the Editor's Introduction to *The Prospects for Arms Control*, New York: Macfadden-Bartell, 1965; "The Status of the Arms Negotiations," *Orbis*, Vol. IX, Spring 1965; "Soviet Disarmament Policy: Illusion and Reality," Chapter 7 in *Détente: Cold War Strategies in Transition*, edited by Eleanor L. Dulles and Robert D. Crane, New York: Praeger, 1965; and *Arms Control and Disarmament: The Critical Issues*, Special Report Series, Washington: The Center for Strategic Studies, Georgetown University, 1966.

[2] See, e.g., Donald G. Brennan, ed., *Arms Control, Disarmament and National Security*, New York: George Braziller, 1961; Hedley Bull, *The Control of the Arms Race*, for the Institute for Strategic Studies, New York: Frederick A. Praeger, 1961; David H. Frisch, ed., *Arms Reduction: Program and Issues*, New York: Twentieth Century Fund, 1961; Louis Henkin, ed., *Arms Control: Issues for the Public*, Englewood Cliffs: Prentice-Hall, 1961; Ernest Lefever, ed., *Arms and Arms Control*, New York: Frederick A. Praeger, 1962; Thomas C. Shelling and Morton H. Halperin, *Strategy and Arms Control*, New York: Twentieth Century Fund, 1961; J. David Singer, ed., *Weapons Management in World Politics*, Proceedings of the International Arms Control Symposium, Ann Arbor, Michigan, December 1962 (Joint Issue of *The Journal of Conflict Resolution*, Vol. VII, September 1963, and *Journal of Arms Control*, Vol. I, October 1963); Alastair Buchan and Philip Windsor, *Arms and Stability in Europe*, for the Institute for Strategic Studies, New York: Frederick A. Praeger, 1963; and James E. Dougherty with John F. Lehman, Jr., eds., *The Prospects for Arms Control*, op. cit., 1965.

[3] Theodore C. Sorensen acknowledges this possibility but adds that he regards it as "highly doubtful." *Kennedy,* New York: Harper and Row, 1965, p. 712. Writing later, Elie Abel did not mention the view that the Khrushchev letter, tougher in tone, which was broadcast by Radio Moscow on Saturday, October 27, might have been drafted prior to the more conciliatory letter from the Premier received on Friday, October 26, through the teletype linking the Department of State with the American Embassy in Moscow. *The Missile Crisis,* Philiadelphia: Lippincott, 1966, pp. 179-186 and 189-191.

[4] The agreement which was reached on June 20, 1963, called for the establishment of two terminal points with telegraphic-teleprinter equipment in Washington and Moscow; a full-time duplex wire telegraph circuit, routed Washington-London-Copenhagen-Stockholm-Helsinki-Moscow; and a full-time duplex radio telegraph circuit, routed Washington-Tangier-Moscow. Cf. the Annex to the Memorandum of Understanding, in *Documents on Disarmament 1963,* U.S. Arms Control and Disarmament Agency Publication No. 24, Washington: G.P.O., October 1964, pp. 236-237.

[5] *New York Times,* June 9, 1967.

[6] Text in *Documents 1963, op. cit.,* pp. 291-293.

[7] See *Geneva Conference on the Discontinuance of Nuclear Weapon Tests: History and Analysis of Negotiations,* Department of State Publication 7258, October 1961; *International Negotiations on Ending Nuclear Weapon Tests September 1961-September 1962,* U.S. Arms Control and Disarmament Agency Publication 9, October 1962; and *Review of International Negotiations on the Cessation of Nuclear Weapon Tests September 1962-September 1965,* U.S. Arms Control and Disarmament Agency Publication 32, May 1966; Robert Gilpin, *American Scientists and Nuclear Weapons Policy,* Princeton: Princeton University Press, 1962, especially Chapter IX; Harold Karan Jacobson and Eric Stein, *Diplomats, Scientists and Politicians: The United States and the Nuclear Test Ban Negotiations,* Ann Arbor: University of Michigan Press, 1966; Arthur H. Dean, *Test Ban and Disarmament: The Path of Negotiation,* New York: Harper & Row, 1966; and James H. McBride, *The Nuclear Test Ban Treaty,* Chicago: Henry Regnery, 1967.

[8] See *Nuclear Test Ban Treaty,* Hearings Before the Committee on Foreign Relations, U.S. Senate, 88th Congress, 1st Session, August 12 to 27, 1963.

[9] For a summary of the arguments on these issues, see *The Nuclear Test Ban Treaty,* Report of the Committee on Foreign Relations, U.S. Senate, September 3, 1963, pp. 10-18.

[10] Secretary of State Dean Rusk informed the Committee on Foreign Relations that the United States had no intention of accepting notification by the Soviets of adherence to the Treaty by the East German authorities. *Ibid.,* pp. 6-7.

[11] These questions have been discussed frequently at Geneva during the last three years. For summaries of the state of the question at the close of the Conference negotiations in 1966, see the statements by Soviet Delegate Alexei A. Roshchin and U.S. Delegate Adrian S. Fisher in the Verbatim Proceedings of the Eighteen-Nation Disarmament Committee (hereafter referred to as ENDC/PV. 286, August 25, 1966, pp. 8-9 and 25-27. Cf. also the earlier statement on the subject by the U.K. Delegate, Lord Chalfont, ENDC/PV. 279, August 4, 1966, pp. 11-15.

[12] See the *Joint Memorandum on a Comprehensive Test Ban Treaty* submitted by the eight neutral States, ENDC/177, August 17, 1966.

[13] Statements by Mr. H. Khallaf, Delegate of the UAR, ENDC/PV. 259, April 25, 1966, pp. 25 ff. and by Mr. Alexei A. Roshchin, ENDC/PV. 286, August 25, 1966, p. 9.

[14] See the statement by Mrs. Alva Myrdal of Sweden, ENDC/PV. 279, August 4, 1966, pp. 4-11.

[15] This explanation is given by Lord Chalfont, who attended the Scarborough Conference, ENDC/PV. 279, August 4, 1966, pp. 13-15.

[16] One of the contributors to this volume, Congressman Craig Hosmer of the Joint Committee on Atomic Energy, declared that the "Sterling" Experiment of December 4, 1966, in a Mississippi salt dome "definitely demonstrated" the possibility of muffling or decoupling an atomic explosion by conducting it in a large underground cavern. The reported observation of at least a 100-fold reduction of signal strength lent added support to the "big hole" theory which had been scoffed at by Soviet experts since 1959, and was expected to reduce Congressional interest in a comprehensive test ban. *New York Times,* December 30, 1966.

[17] A/RES/1884 (XVIII), October 17, 1963.

[18] See, e.g., Donald G. Brennan, "Arms and Arms Control in Outer Space," in Lincoln P. Bloomfield, ed., *Outer Space: Prospects for Man and Society,* Englewood Cliffs: Prentice-Hall (for the American Assembly), 1962, pp. 147-148.

[19] President Johnson announced that the United States possessed this capability on September 17, 1964. *New York Times,* September 18, 1964.

[20] Text in the *New York Times,* December 9, 1966.

[21] *New York Times,* April 26, 1967. By that date, 79 countries had signed the treaty, and other signatures were expected.

[22] ENDC Document 131, April 21, 1964.

[23] Early in 1967, the Johnson Administration in a budget-minded move, announced that by mid-1967 the Atomic Energy Commission would shut down another large plutonium production reactor at Hanford, bringing to five the number of reactors closed since 1964. In contrast to the cutback of April 1964, however, the Administration made no bid to the Soviet Union to reciprocate. This latest decision would leave nine U.S. reactors in operation. *New York Times,* January 25, 1967.

[24] ENDC/PV. 160, January 28, 1964, p. 7.

[25] See Morris Bernstein, "Inspection of Economic Records as an Arms Control Technique," in J. David Singer, ed., *Weapons Management in World Politics, op. cit.* In contrast to the Western position, a Soviet participant in the Pugwash Conferences declared that, since budget cuts involve no actual disarmament, international control is unnecessary. Igor Glagolev, "The Reduction of Military Expenditures," *Disarmament and Arms Control,* Summer 1964, p. 311.

[26] ENDC/PV. 166, February 13, 1964, pp. 37-39. For U.S. Delegate William C. Foster's reply, in which he insisted upon "concrete," verified disarmament agreements—not vague, unenforceable resolutions—see ENDC/PV. 168, February 19, 1964, p. 28.

[27] When Congressman Melvin Laird released a report estimating Soviet military

aid to North Vietnam at about one billion dollars, mainly in the form of SAM missiles, some Administration officials regarded the estimate as a bit high. *New York Times,* March 31, 1967.

[28] See Eighteen-Nation Disarmament Committee, Verbatim Proceedings, ENDC/PV. 160, January 28, 1964, pp. 5-10; ENDC/PV. 220, August 3, 1965, pp. 14-18; ENDC/PV. 235, January 27, 1966, p. 19; ENDC/PV. 256, April 14, 1966, pp. 18-23.

[29] On at least three occasions the Soviet Delegate requested that a communication from the Foreign Affairs Ministry of the GDR calling for the denuclearization of Germany be circulated as an official document of the ENDC Conference. The latest East German demarche is to be found in ENDC/189, March 7, 1967. The United States has consistently taken the position that these were communications from a "non-governmental organization" which could only be circulated as attachments to Soviet documents. Cf. ENDC/PV. 238, February 8, 1966, pp. 21-25 and ENDC/PV. 291, March 7, 1967, pp. 11-13.

[30] ENDC/PV. 237, February 3, 1966, p. 15.

[31] For the original Polish proposals, see *Documents on Disarmament 1945-1959,* Department of State Publication 7008, Washington: USGPO, 1960, 2 vols., Vol. II, pp. 889-892, 944-948 and 1217-1219; and *Documents on Disarmament 1960,* Department of State Publication 7172, Washington: USGPO, 1961, pp. 259-260. Fuller discussions of various proposals for disengagement, nuclear free-zones and nuclear freezes in Central Europe can be found in Alastair Buchan and Philip Windsor, *Arms and Stability in Europe,* for the Institute for Strategic Studies, New York: Frederick A. Praeger, 1963, Chapter 5; James E. Dougherty, "Zonal Arms Limitation in Europe," *Orbis,* Vol. VII, Fall 1963; and Karol Lapter, "Nuclear Freeze in Central Europe," *Disarmament and Arms Control,* Vol. 2, Summer 1964. The "no-first-use" idea is treated in Morton H. Halperin, "A Proposal for a Ban on the First Use of Nuclear Weapons," *Journal of Arms Control,* Vol. I, April 1963.

[32] See Johan J. Holst, "Fixed Control Posts and European Stability," *Disarmament and Arms Control,* Vol. 2, Summer 1964, and Philip Windsor, "Observation Posts," in Evan Luard, ed., *First Steps to Disarmament,* New York: Basic Books, 1965.

[33] For representative treatments of the conventional-nuclear issue, consult Robert E. Osgood, *NATO: The Entangling Alliance,* Chicago: University of Chicago Press, 1962, Chapter 6; Thomas C. Schelling, "Nuclear Strategy in Europe," *World Politics,* Vol. XIV, April 1962; Buchan and Windsor, *op. cit.,* pp. 116-123; Michael Brower, "Nuclear Strategy of the Kennedy Administration," *Bulletin of the Atomic Scientists,* October 1962; Bernard Brodie, "What Price Conventional Capabilities in Europe?" *The Reporter,* May 23, 1963; Kai-Uwe von Hassel, "Détente Through Firmness," *Foreign Affairs,* Vol. 42, January 1964; and "Organizing Western Defense," *Foreign Affairs,* Vol. 43, January 1965. The West German Defense Minister in the Erhard Government cautioned against raising the atomic threshold too high, lest the potential aggressor be tempted to engage in a calculus of risks. To prevent the nuclear war which nobody wanted, he argued, NATO must be ready to employ nuclear weapons "in an early phase of a recognizable attack on Europe." *Ibid.,* p. 211.

[34] In June 1966, the Assembly of the Western European Union adopted a report which contained the following passage: "The denial of French territory to NATO

would greatly reduce the area available for the organization of Western defense. . . . In present circumstances, it is inconceivable that the Western forces would allow themselves to be driven back to the French frontier without using tactical nuclear weapons . . ." "France and NATO," Report of the Committee on Defense Questions and Armaments, Assembly of the WEU, Twelfth Ordinary Session, Document 375, extracted in *NATO Letter*, September 1966, p. 24. Earlier, Secretary McNamara had announced that by mid-1966 there would be at least 7,000 atomic warheads stockpiled in the area of NATO Europe. *New York Times*, November 28, 1965.

[35] "When British Troops Leave Germany," *Manchester Guardian Weekly*, October 20, 1966. "Allied Withdrawal Could Mean Bundeswehr Predominance," translated from *Frankfurter Allgemeine Zeitung*, February 9, 1967, in *The German Tribune*, February 18, 1967.

[36] *New York Times*, May 3, 1967.

[37] *Ibid.*

[38] *Ibid.*, May 10, 1967. Yet at the same time, many military strategists in NATO remained convinced that the British-U.S. force reductions, combined with the denial of French territory, increased the likelihood that in the event of war nuclear weapons would have to be used at an early stage. *Ibid.*, May 20, 1967.

[39] Hermann Renner in *Die Welt*, January 3, 1967.

[40] Samples of these early arguments may be found in Hedley Bull, *op. cit.*, p. 61; Schelling and Halperin, *op. cit.*, pp. 12 and 52-53; David H. Frisch and Joseph Salerno, "Comments on 'Arms Reduction in the 1960's,' " in Frisch, *op. cit.*, p. 44; John B. Phelps, "Some Reflections on Counterforce and Arms Control," *Journal of Arms Control*, Vol. I, April 1963.

[41] *Nuclear Test Ban Treaty*, Hearings of the Foreign Relations Committee, U.S. Senate, 88th Congress, 1st Session, Washington: USGPO, 1963, pp. 453, 480, and 512.

[42] ENDC/PV. 162, January 31, 1964, pp. 15-20.

[43] See the statements by Adrian Fisher, ENDC/PV. 184, April 16, 1964, pp. 13-19, and by Ambassador Clare Timberlake, ENDC/PV. 211, August 27, 1964, pp. 5-11.

[44] The White House Conference on International Cooperation, *Report of the Committee on Arms Control and Disarmament*, National Citizens' Commission, pp. 14-15.

[45] *New York Times*, November 11, 1966.

[46] See the *New York Times*, December 8, 1966, and January 29, February 5, and February 10, 1967.

[47] *New York Times*, March 3, 1967.

[48] See, e.g., Roswell Gilpatric, "Are we on the Brink of Another Arms Race?" *New York Times Magazine*, January 15, 1967; Norman Moss, "McNamara's ABM Policy: A Failure of Communications," *The Reporter*, February 23, 1967; the contributions by Oran R. Young, Laurence Martin and David Inglis to the Symposium, "The ABM Debate: Part I," in *Bulletin of the Atomic Scientists*, May 1967; and Richard J. Whelan, "The Shifting Equation of Nuclear Defense," *Fortune*, Vol. LXXV, June 1, 1967.

[49] In 1959, the U.N. General Assembly pointed out that an increase in the number of nuclear States would aggravate international tensions and compound the difficulty of reaching arms agreements. Two years later, the Irish Resolution called for a treaty by which both nuclear and nonnuclear States would pledge restraint. RES/1665 (XVI), December 5, 1961. For the text of the U.S. draft treaty, see ENDC/152, August 17, 1965; also in the *New York Times,* August 18, 1965; *Documents on Disarmament 1965,* U.S. Arms Control and Disarmament Agency Publication 34, December 1966, pp. 347-349 (where ENDC document is misnumbered); for text of Soviet draft treaty, see A/5976, September 24, 1954; *Documents on Disarmament 1965, op. cit.,* pp. 443-446.

[50] Leonard Beaton, "Capabilities of Non-Nuclear Powers," in Alastair Buchan, ed., *A World of Nuclear Powers,* for the American Assembly, Englewood Cliffs, N.J.: Prentice-Hall, 1966, p. 32.

[51] Radio-Television Address, October 18, 1964. Text in *Documents on Disarmament 1964, op. cit.,* pp. 465-469; quoted on p. 468.

[52] See *Weekly India News,* February 3, February 17, and March 24, 1967.

[53] Reports of Mr. Chagla's statement to the Lok Sabha on March 27 and his press conference upon his return from Geneva April 27 can be found in *Weekly India News,* April 7 and May 12, 1967.

[54] For an account of the Soviets' use of the Geneva Conference as a platform for carrying out political attacks against NATO, see the author's article, "The Non-Proliferation Treaty," *The Russian Review,* Vol. 25, January 1966.

[55] ENDC/PV. 263, May 10, 1966, pp. 26-27.

[56] *New York Times,* September 28, 1966.

[57] David K. Willis, in the *Christian Science Monitor,* October 13, 1966.

[58] *Die Welt,* October 12, 1966. Translation in *The German Tribune,* October 22, 1966.

[59] ENDC/PV. 280, August 9, 1966, pp. 13-16.

[60] ENDC/187, February 21, 1967.

[61] ENDC/PV. 293, March 14, 1967, pp. 23-24.

[62] See "Commercial Nuclear Development is Big Business," *Die Welt,* February 24, 1967. Translation in *The German Tribune,* March 4, 1967. Cf. also the *New York Times,* February 16 and March 2, 1967.

[63] "Two Cheers for Non-Proliferation," *Die Zeit,* March 10, 1967. Translation in *The German Tribune,* March 18, 1967. Cf. also the *New York Times,* March 24, 1967.

[64] "The Geneva Talks and the Anti-Missile Missile," *Die Zeit,* March 2, 1967. Translation in *The German Tribune,* March 11, 1967.

[65] *New York Times,* February 5 and 22, 1967.

[66] *Ibid.,* April 12 and 26, 1967. Cf. also "Nuclear Non-Proliferation Treaty Jeopardizes Euration," *Deutsche Korrespondenz,* February 21, 1967, pp. 4-6.

[67] In the Fall of 1966, Poland and Czechoslovakia offered to place their atomic power reactors under IAEA controls if West Germany would do likewise. The Federal Republic, at Washington's urging, was willing to examine the proposal. See *The Bulletin,* Press and Information Service of the FRG, November 1, 1966, p. 3. But the French Government expressed opposition to the Polish-Czech over-

ture on the grounds that it might lead to interference in Euratom affairs by an international agency whose Communist members had long taken a negative attitude toward the European Atomic Agency. *New York Times,* October 25 and 27, 1966. For Soviet attacks upon the inadequacy of Euratom safeguards in respect to Germany, see ENDC/PV. 280, August 9, 1966, p. 22. The Soviets have taken the position that no inspection for compliance with the non-proliferation treaty is really necessary, but that if the U.S. insists upon an inspection provision, then the whole control function must be performed by the IAEA. *New York Times,* February 22, 1967.

[68] Cf. the Final Act of the Fourth Session of the Preparatory Commission for the Denuclearization of Latin America, ENDC/186, February 21, 1967.

Chapter 1

THE U.S. AND ARMS CONTROL: POLICY AND POSSIBILITY

A Twenty Year Quest

By Archibald S. Alexander

So far as the history of post-war disarmament and arms control efforts is concerned, the period can be divided naturally into three parts. The first is from 1945 to 1955, the second from 1955 to 1963, and the third is not yet complete. This first part of the period began with the end of World War II. The second part was ushered in by the termination of the era of Stalinism and by the rise of Khrushchev in the Soviet Union—events which were accompanied by moves in other countries which signaled a serious international effort toward détente. The third began after the Cuban Missile Crisis.

Anyone who will think back to 1945 will remember the atmosphere of hope which accompanied the cessation of hostilities and the new effort of mankind to organize the world more rationally, by the formation of the United Nations Organization; he will also remember the rapid demobilization by the West, and particularly the United States. American military expenditures declined from $81 billion in Fiscal Year 1945 to about half that in the next year and to $11.8 billion in Fiscal Year 1948. In two years the strength of American armed forces dropped from 11,440,000 to 1,590,000. Germany and Japan were virtually without arms. Unfortunately, not all the rest of the world was in similar condition.

Although a relatively few persons in government, and a handful of nuclear scientists, at that time recognized the major factor which was moving to the center of the stage, most of us did not appreciate the importance of the atomic bomb. It was to take time for the significance of the advent of atomic weapons to impress itself upon our consciousness. This, however, was the new variable which would for the next two decades have to be considered in the balance between war and peace.

In January 1946 the General Assembly of the United Nations established a commission to deal with this problem, and in June 1946 Mr. Bernard Baruch proposed the plan which took his name, based on the Acheson-Lilienthal report and some of Senator McMahon's work. The essence of the Baruch Plan was that "managerial control of ownership of all atomic energy activities potentially dangerous to world security" would be placed in an international atomic development authority. This authority would have power "to control, inspect and license" other atomic activities. The manufacture of bombs

3

would stop, existing bombs would be disposed of as agreed and the control authority would not be subject to the veto power of any of the five countries entitled to a veto in the United Nations Security Council.

Within five days, the Soviet representative to the United Nations Atomic Energy Commission gave the reaction of his country to the Baruch proposal. His salient point, destined to reappear in connection with almost all disarmament matters thereafter and down to the present, was that he regarded the absence of a veto as an attempt "to undermine" the United Nations Charter principles, "including unanimity of the members of the Security Council." Mr. Gromyko said "such attempts must be rejected."

While the hope which mankind had felt began to subside, the Soviet Union sought to extend its influence in Iran, Greece, Turkey and Berlin. It was successful in Czechoslovakia, as it had already been in the other countries of Eastern Europe, where there could be no argument, except in nuclear terms, with overwhelming superiority in conventional weapons. The United States and other Western countries thereupon made countermoves—the Marshall Plan, the North Atlantic Treaty and some steps towards rearmament, while the American nuclear umbrella limited Soviet expansion.

With the beginning of the second period, which I place in 1955, Stalin had left the stage, Khrushchev had consolidated his leadership of the government of the Soviet Union, the Anglo-American nuclear monopoly had been broken and mankind generally had begun to be aware of the impossibility of satisfactorily settling disputes with atomic weapons. There was then a con-

siderable effort to improve the international climate. President Eisenhower and Chairman Khrushchev met in the beneficent atmosphere of Camp David. The open skies proposal, some diminution of polemics, exploration of measures to prevent surprise attack and five-power disarmament meetings all suggested possibilities of progress in arms control and disarmament. It was possible for a Presidential candidate in 1956—though the unsuccessful one, Adlai Stevenson—to propose a cessation of nuclear tests. In 1959, twelve countries, including the U.S. and the U.S.S.R., signed a treaty on Antarctica, stipulating that it be used "for peaceful purposes only" and providing for inspection. Adversary inspections have since occurred there in a cooperative atmosphere.

The Soviet Union in 1959 and then the U.S. in 1962 presented proposals for general and complete disarmament. But as this second period continued, events—like the *U-2* incident—leading to the failure of the Summit Meeting, culminated in the abrogation by the Soviets of the informal moratorium on nuclear tests in 1961, the difficult confrontation between President Kennedy and Chairman Khrushchev in Vienna and finally the crisis due to emplacement of Soviet missiles in Cuba. This second phase, like the first one, thus ended on a note of hostility and crisis, after having begun in an atmosphere of hope.

The third phase, beginning with the resolution of the Cuban crisis, again began on a new note of hope. President Kennedy's American University speech in June 1963 seems to have been the final catalyst. The earlier installation of a direct communication link between Moscow and Washington was followed by the limited test ban treaty in July of that year and by the resolution of the United Nations in October calling upon all states "to refrain from placing in orbit" weapons of mass destruction, including nuclear weapons. As to the test ban treaty, Mr. Sorensen tells us, writing of President Kennedy, that "no other single accomplishment in the White House ever gave him greater satisfaction."

One is reluctantly forced to note, however, that soon the pendulum again swung the wrong way. Since 1963, new factors have intruded into the arms control and disarmament field. The struggle between the two viewpoints in Vietnam necessitating an increase in the armed forces of the United States—by about 250,000 from their 1965 low point—and the increase in the U.S. defense budget caused by Vietnam; the problem of NATO nuclear sharing; the change in the relationship between the Soviet Union and Communist China; the end of virtual bipolarity between the Soviet Union and the United States as the relatively unchallenged leaders of the two major blocs and the acquisition of a nuclear capability by France and Communist China; the increased nuclear potential of many other countries—all these factors have combined to change the scene beyond recognition.

So much for a kind of chronology of some of the events of the last two decades which seem particularly significant for arms control and disarmament. We can now examine a few trends, some favorable, some not—perhaps the most important strands in the tangled web of international relationships during that time. First and foremost, one ought to acknowledge the importance of the tremendously increased awareness on the part of statesmen and of much of the public throughout the world in respect to the whole subject of arms control and disarmament. This manifests itself in many ways.

The most important seems to be that armed strength alone, most of us now recognize, can no longer guarantee national security. From 1066 until 1940, the United Kingdom was invulnerable to external attack. The airplane of World War II put an end to that physical invulnerability. The same kind of thing has now happened to the entire globe as the result of nuclear weapons and intercontinental carriers. At present it is technically impossible for any country to prevent one or more other countries from inflicting enormous casualties and property destruction. The consolation of being able to visit the same thing on the adversary is inadequate. President Johnson was acknowledging this fact in 1963, soon after taking office, when he said of the Director of the Arms Control and Disarmament Agency, "I look on his work as part of national security just as much as the work of Secretary McNamara and the Joint Chiefs of Staff."

Second, considerable expertise and knowledge as to arms control and disarmament have been developed throughout the world. One need but recall the recognition by President Kennedy and the United States Congress in 1961 of the desirability of an Arms Control and Disarmament Agency as an integral part of the United States Government, the patient building up of this agency by Mr. Foster, and the research and policy recommendations which have resulted. Other countries, in various ways, are also developing their mechanisms for dealing with arms control and disarmament—notably the U.K., the Soviets, the Netherlands and the Federal

Republic of Germany. This new expertise is being reflected in the positions set forth by governments—for example in the Joint Statement of Agreed Principles for disarmament negotiation which Mr. McCloy and Mr. Zorin hammered out in 1961.

The International Atomic Energy Agency, which had its beginnings in 1956, and which is now a valid and going concern with participation by East and West and non-aligned, has established an effective method of inspection to insure the peaceful use of the atomic energy produced by the plants which it inspects. The earlier, sporadic meetings of disarmament experts have long since evolved into the present Eighteen Nation Disarmament Committee. The ENDC has its full share of frustrations; but it has become established as the forum in which antagonists and neutrals talk with one another and explore the needs and the desires and the attitudes of the pluralistic world. At the ENDC it has been possible to lay the groundwork for actual and potential agreements, for more restraint than would otherwise have been shown and for greatly improved understanding by the Soviet and the Western blocs and the non-aligned nations of the respective points of view of all three groups.

An important development which is frequently overlooked is the increased continuity of the personnel representing the United States and other countries in these international negotiations. This marks a great improvement over the days when the players were sent into the game without adequate preparation. Our own national policy also owes a good deal to the Committee of Principals in the United States Government, composed of the Secretary of State as Chairman, and the Secretary of Defense, the Chairman of the Joint Chiefs of Staff, the head of the Arms Control and Disarmament Agency, the head of the Central Intelligence Agency, the Chairman of the Atomic Energy Commission and certain others. Here is the mechanism, used as often as needed, for channeling to the President for his decision the questions which arise in the field of arms control and disarmament.

A third trend which I see developing during these past twenty years is the increasing awareness that arms control and disarmament questions are inseparable from the political questions which arise between countries. It has sometimes been suggested that one should not proceed with agreements on armaments until one has solved the political differences. I do not agree with this suggestion. For one thing, there will be new subjects for disagreement when the old ones are disposed of. It is not in the nature of the human animal—and we all find this refreshing, up to a point—to see eye to eye with his fellows. For another thing, if there must be disagreements, and we cannot settle them without the use of force, then it is well worth our while to try to limit the degree of force used in whatever ways we can.

Another favorable trend has been the increase of exchanges between countries, between the northern and the southern hemispheres and between the countries of the Soviet bloc and the rest of the world. Whether the exchanges have been in the form of Pugwash conferences, international arms control symposia, formal cultural exchange programs, trade or tourists, they increase understanding and improve the atmosphere for disarmament.

A fifth trend which has appeared is the increasing awareness of the richer countries that the developing countries should and must be helped. This in turn has led to a clearer understanding that we would prefer not to devote so much of our substance to military purposes when we desperately need more resources for both domestic needs and economic assistance to the developing countries. As Secretary Rusk said not long ago at his news conference, "The burden of arms in the world is simply too great to be accepted as a part of nature."

At the same time, increasing study has been given to the economic consequences of disarmament in the countries with heavy present commitments to defense spending. In the U.S., the Committee on the Economic Impact of Defense and Disarmament, under the chairmanship of Dr. Gardner Ackley (Chairman of the Council of Economic Advisers), made its first report in mid-1965. It was concurred in by all the government departments concerned, such as Defense and the Arms Control and Disarmament Agency. President Johnson wrote of the report, "What I find most encouraging of all in the report is your conclusion that our heavy current commitment to defense is not a bar to rapid progress toward disarmament. All Americans will welcome your clear conclusion that 'there is no economic reason for the Nation to undergo a major economic decline or a slow stagnation if and when defense outlays are reduced.'"

"The American people will continue to be determined that our great industrial effort for national defense is their servant and not their master. This is the tradition of the armed forces themselves, and it is the conviction, I am sure, of those who serve in the national defense industries, too."

Thus there is every reason to get on with the business of rational control and reduction of arms. This naturally requires some mutuality between opposing camps. Thus I am brought to mention a few of the dangerous trends in the last two decades.

One, of course, is the evolution of Mainland China—whether others have contributed to it or not—towards increasing hostility to most of the rest of the world.

A second adverse trend is the accelerating pace of technological development, giving at least two powers undreamed of capabilities of destruction without compensating defenses, and making possible the acquisition by a number of other countries of the capability of building and being able to deliver weapons of mass destruction.

A third has been the inability to bridge the gap between the American view that agreements must be verifiable, and the Russian objections to intrusion and relinquishment of sovereignty.

A fourth trend has been an accelerating birth rate, in many parts of the world, unaccompanied by economic development, increasing the disparity between the more and the less fortunate, and providing a fertile breeding ground for further political disputes on top of those we have not yet resolved.

A fifth trend has been the somewhat indiscriminate competition between blocs of countries, and sometimes between members of the same bloc, in the sale or grant of increasingly sophisticated conventional weapons. The result has not always been stability, and has often been a drag on economic development in the recipient countries.

A sixth adverse tendency has been the all too frequent outbreak of what we now call conventional wars, by which we mean conflicts in which conventional arms are used—we do not mean that such wars are accepted as normal. They have brought death and suffering to the innocent and the guilty alike, and they have failed by only small margins to involve the major military powers and nuclear weapons. It is perfectly clear that a nation possessing nuclear weapons which is losing a conventional war will be subject to strong internal pressures to reverse the tide.

Not to learn the mistakes of history is to be forced to repeat them. The risks are mounting. Prudent players, as the stakes rise, are more careful. It remains to be seen whether man's rational component, his innate sense of decency and his skills in political, social and economic matters can master his impetuosities, his old hatreds and his runaway scientific and technological skill. No matter what happens, we should keep thinking and communicating. This should improve the prospect of a happy answer to the major question of our times, whether we intend to survive and have skill enough to do so.

The Current Disarmament Impasse

By Richard J. Barnet

The current disarmament impasse is the product of détente in the West and war in the East. The deceptive calm that has descended on Europe since the days of the Cuban missile crisis has removed much of the incentive for concluding large-scale arms control arrangements with the Soviets. The confrontation over Europe has always been regarded as, and is the major locale of, the U.S.-Soviet arms race. The U.S. strategic buildup in the fifties and sixties was explained and defended as a counter to a possible Soviet invasion of Europe. Those of us who have been urging the United States to make disarmament and arms control a major national security strategy have pointed to the danger of nuclear war arising over the explosive mixture of the German issue, the vulnerable position of Berlin, and the mounting nuclear arms race in and over Europe. Most of the world's statesmen have stated on one occasion or another that a serious disarmament effort must deal with these problems. Today, more than ever, the political-military confrontation over Europe constitutes the central security problem for the United States.

But the feeling has been growing since the missile crisis, when President Kennedy and his advisers during that fateful week turned their eyes anxiously to Europe and found that the Soviets did not dare to move, that a real truce has been achieved in Europe without arms control or disarmament. In the immediate wake of the crisis there was a sudden surge of interest in disarmament in the U.S. government. Some saw the extremely delicate negotiation itself in late October of 1962 as a kind of arms control agreement. There were many who believed that the post-crisis atmosphere was uniquely favorable to the conclusion of more far-reaching agreements. The world, they reasoned, had just had a taste of the nuclear reality. The subject had moved from the agenda of conferences like this one into the pit of the stomach. For the first time the President of the United States had raised directly in American living rooms the prospect that within a small, finite number of days much of his audience might be dead.

There were many who believed that the common perception of a danger barely avoided would make governments take disarmament more seriously. In a limited way, of course, this happened. The nuclear test ban was negotiated in the backwash of the crisis. But as the

9

memory of the moments of terror receded, the week of October 22 began to take on a different significance. People began reading a variety of lessons from the experience. Some said it showed the need for maintaining predominant force. Others thought that it had worked a conversion on the Soviet Union and that the control of events was now effectively in the hands of the United States. Emerging from the confrontation was a consensus that in Europe no one was going to upset the status quo by force or provoke another military crisis as Khrushchev did in 1958 and in 1961. If that was the new reality, why upset it with arms control and disarmament measures which, if they are of any significance, require political realignments? It is true that as the détente with the Soviets developed, interest within the American government increased in specific arms control measures: transfer of fissionable materials, the fissionable materials cutback, the "freeze" on further production of nuclear delivery vehicles, and a nonproliferation treaty with the crucial limitation to enable nuclear sharing in NATO. But disarmament or arms control was not adopted as a serious national security strategy. When the Soviets, regrettably but not surprisingly, rejected the freeze, no real initiative was made to get at the major manifestations of the arms race: additional strategic nuclear delivery vehicles and experimental anti-ballistic missiles. It is ironic that just as the issue of accidental war was being dramatized for the public in popular novels and films such as *Dr. Strangelove* and *Fail-Safe,* governments were increasingly discounting the danger. This was partly due to some improvements in command and control made by the Defense Depart-

ment in the Kennedy Administration. However, the real source of the growing confidence in "the stability of the military environment" was an apparently successful history of having "managed" a number of technical and political crises without precipitating the disasters of which the Cassandras had so long warned.

This growing confidence in the ability to live with the bomb was reinforced by the apparent slowing down of the arms race. The United States did not have plans for a major new nuclear weapons program after the completion of the Minuteman procurement scheduled for the mid-sixties. The Soviets under Khrushchev and his successors did not seem willing to make the effort to challenge the numerical superiority of the United States. Fears of a Soviet breakthrough in weapons development which had haunted the immediate post-sputnik years no longer loomed so large. From the moment when McNamara and Gilpatric, during the Berlin crisis of 1961, disclosed that the United States had an overwhelming numerical superiority in nuclear weapons and delivery vehicles, U.S. officials found the arms race less of a threat. An additional burden was thereby imposed on those who proposed disarmament measures, for if these were to be negotiable at all, they would have the effect of at least narrowing the U.S. missile lead. A State Department convinced that the ability to hurl more nuclear weapons on the Soviets than they could hurl at us was an important political advantage was hard to convince of the merits of disarmament.

Finally, the State Department recognized, quite correctly, that if we were going to do something serious about the arms race between the Soviet Union and the United States and the question of nuclear proliferation, we would have to alter existing policies toward Germany, NATO, and the fostering of an Atlantic Community. The rise of Gaullism, the détente with the Soviet Union, the decreasing perception of a Soviet threat, the growing interest in East-West relationships in Europe and the loosening of the Soviet grip on Eastern Europe should have been viewed as an opportunity to develop new policies in such a way as to make disarmament a possibility; instead they were regarded as difficulties in the path of old policies. The recent political ferment in Europe has made the United States cautious in proposing disarmament and arms control ideas because of the deep-seated fear that the whole structure of U.S.-continental relations is shaky and that nothing must be done to disturb it further. The decision was made to try to use the détente in Europe to maintain the status quo rather than move towards arms control.

The impact of war in Asia on the prospects for disarmament can be summarized in very few words. The official American view of the war in Viet Nam is that it is a test case for Wars of National Liberation. The prospect of such wars is now the major security concern of the United States. There is no need here to argue the correctness of this perception of the bubbling pot of decolonization, revolution, and Great Power agitation. For our purposes in explaining the current arms control impasse it is enough to say that this phenomenon is viewed by the United States as primarily a military problem. Nuclear weapons have not yet been made "relevant" to the confrontation over Viet Nam, but most parts of the military establishment have been engaged in the fight. The result is obvious: the military are increasingly reluctant to accept arms control restrictions on their freedom to procure or to deploy weapons and men, and the political climate of a shooting war makes it inevitable that their views will prevail. If, as seems likely, the U.S. troop commitment in Viet Nam will go beyond 500,000, it is quite clear that we will not accept limitations on conventional armaments. As the American response to civil strife and revolutionary activity in the underdeveloped world becomes ever more military, disarmament and arms control will look even more absurdly irrelevant.

It is more difficult to speculate about the Soviet attitude towards arms control and disarmament. There is much evidence that after the missile crisis the Soviets were interested in concluding a number of agreements including a non-proliferation treaty, a NATO-Warsaw Pact non-aggression agreement and a significant cutback in missiles. Even as early as September 1962, they had apparently begun to relax their previous demand for an immediate elimination of all missiles and to accept the idea of a "nuclear umbrella" or "minimum deterrent" along the lines of a number of unofficial U.S. arms control suggestions. They also seemed prepared to relax some of their earlier positions on inspection. The seriousness of their interest in specific arms control measures is indicated by the prominence this issue assumed in party debates, particularly in the polemical correspondence with the Chinese. Khrushchev was prepared to run some political risks to engage the West in disarmament discussions. He was willing to take these risks, probably because he wished to increase Soviet security by slowing the arms race in which the Soviet Union now stood revealed as a poor second. He wished to avoid being forced to commit scarce resources to the effort of catching up. He was concerned about proliferation. He was particularly worried about the German problem. The combination of growing West German nationalism, increasing frustration at the division of the Fatherland, and the acquisition of nuclear weapons—all viewed in the Kremlin as probabilities in the absence of a European settlement based on arms control—is still the Soviet's greatest nightmare.

But it is evident that Soviet interest in arms control and disarmament has cooled. Here again the reasons seem obvious. It is difficult for them to negotiate with the United States about anything in the midst of the Viet Nam war without giving ammunition to their Chinese adversaries. To negotiate on disarmament is to confirm the Chinese charge that the Kremlin is seeking a U.S.-Soviet alliance for world hegemony. Since the United States now shows so little interest in disarmament, there is little incentive for the Soviets to come forward with plans or to bargain over U.S. proposals. Unlike the days of Stalin when the Soviets could only gain from a propaganda standpoint by putting forward a disarmament scheme, however implausible, it is now difficult for them to devise a disarmament program which does not involve some real political conflicts—with the Soviet military, the Chinese, and the East Germans. For the Soviets, it is no longer possible to manipulate disarmament rhetoric free of risk. It is now a real and difficult political issue, just as it was in the United States during the test ban negotiations, and is today.

While it is true that the Soviet Union will have to solve some of these problems and to change some of its attitudes

in order to break the present impasse, the major initiative, if there is to be one, must come from the United States. The reasons seem clear. No other nation has such military force or military potential. What the most powerful nation in the world does (more than what it says) can exert a powerful influence on the behavior of others. The real question is whether the U.S. has the incentive to try to break the impasse.

If the President of the United States decides to make the major effort required to break the current impasse, it will be the result of a revived appreciation of the immense dangers of the unrestricted arms race. The problem most likely to dramatize these dangers is proliferation. We shall examine this issue to see whether it might provide the incentive for the major powers to break the stalemate.

The Chinese explosion of an atomic device dramatized the obvious: the "nuclear club" is no longer segregated. One need be neither western nor white to belong. Furthermore, in the next few years the entrance dues will be reduced. New techniques will make it possible to lower the present staggering cost of producing the bomb. To be sure, the pace of proliferation has been slower than many had predicted. A number of the nations with the technical and financial resources to support a weapons program have elected for the present not to start one. But the blast from Lop Nor, the silence from the Geneva Disarmament Conference and the shrill cries of nationalism around the world have created a climate in which nuclear status will be increasingly difficult to resist. India, Japan, Germany, Switzerland, Sweden, Israel, and Canada all have the resources to produce an atomic bomb within five years after a decision to make one. Homi J. Bhabha, the late head of India's nuclear reactor program, claimed that he could set off a nuclear device within eighteen months. His estimate that the Chinese are capable of building from thirty to fifty bombs a year has given a boost to the growing political sentiment in India for "going nuclear."

There are serious political advocates for national nuclear weapons programs in Japan, Germany, Israel and Sweden. Some in Sweden, for example, have argued that a country cannot be neutral in the modern world without having a nuclear deterrent since it cannot depend upon other countries to protect it. In Japan the nuclear advocates argue that without nuclear weapons Japan cannot hope to counter the total dominance of China over Asia. In Germany, Franz Josef Strauss, the former Defense Minister, and others have argued that without nuclear weapons Germany will not "have a chance to be heard" in negotiations on the future of Europe. In Israel some defense officials argue that Israel needs the bomb to survive. Even in such an unlikely candidate for nuclear status as Mexico, a recent article in *Contenido* argued that Mexico should have the bomb to back up its demands for aid from the Great Powers.

A few months before his death President Kennedy gave the reasons for American concern over the spread of nuclear weapons:

I ask you to stop and think for a moment what it would mean to have nuclear weapons in so many hands, in the hands of countries large and small, stable and unstable, responsible and irresponsible, scattered throughout the world. There would be no rest for anyone then, no stability, no real security, and no chance for effective disarmament. There would be only the increased chance for accidental war, and

an increased necessity of the Great Powers to involve themselves in what would otherwise be local conflicts.*

It takes no great imagination to see in the uncontrolled diffusion of nuclear weapons quite specific new threats to the fragile peace of the atomic age. Once nuclear armament spreads into many new disputes and into the political maneuverings of a dozen little cold wars, the world is likely to look back to the generation of the U.S.-Soviet nuclear standoff as the modern golden age. We can look forward not only to nuclear confrontations among many lesser nations, but we should also be prepared for "atomic blackmail" from dissident political groups within nations such as the OAS in Algeria or the Viet Cong and, indeed, from criminal gangs interested in money rather than politics.

A number of these horrors were predicted a long time ago. Even before the first test explosion at Alamagordo, Secretary of War Stimson warned President Truman that there were no permanent secrets to the bomb and that small nations might in a few years be able to produce them. From the first days of the nuclear age it was assumed that if this happened the security of the U.S. would suffer. The Truman Administration tried to prevent proliferation through the Baruch Plan for the international ownership of atomic facilities. Congress adopted a strict policy in the Atomic Energy Law against helping other nations to get nuclear weapons of their own. But the U.S. was virtually powerless to prevent the steady spread of nuclear technology around the world.

The key to controlling the spread of nuclear weapons, if there is one, is not

* Radio-Television Address, July 26, 1963. U.S. Arms Control and Disarmament Agency Publication 16, Washington: G.P.O., 1963.

in keeping other countries from acquiring the capability to make atomic bombs. It is clearly too late for that. Indeed, it has never been possible to halt the growth of technology. The hope is to discourage a potential nuclear power from wanting to become one. Unfortunately, much of what the U.S. has said and done has had exactly the opposite effect.

Atomic devices are not particularly useful as weapons unless they can be delivered. The U.S. in its military assistance programs has spread delivery systems to potential nuclear powers. F-104 fighter-bombers capable of carrying atomic weapons have been sold to Spain, India, Japan, and Germany. (How little control the U.S. retains over the use of military aircraft once they are transferred to allies was dramatized when the Turks used U.S. planes to bomb Cyprus.) The U.S. has supplied France with tanker aircraft for in-flight refueling without which there could be no *force de frappe*. We have encouraged and assisted several candidates for the nuclear club to operate commercial jet transport service. These transports grew out of the same technology as the B-52 bomber, still the mainstay of the U.S. Strategic Air Command, and can easily be converted into bombers. We have sold to Germany Pershing missiles that make little sense as weapons without nuclear warheads. We are also helping India, Japan, Germany and Sweden to develop rockets, which, though not intended for military purpose, could be simply converted.

The U.S. has distributed vehicles capable of delivering nuclear weapons for many reasons—to strengthen alliances, to encourage scientific cooperation, and, recently, to help solve the gold flow problem. Whatever national interests have been served by this policy, it has made it more feasible for other powers to acquire atomic striking forces, and, hence, has whetted appetites for nuclear status.

But the U.S. has most profoundly influenced the decision of other countries to produce nuclear weapons through its own attitude towards them. While it has been telling other countries for years how bad it would be for them to acquire modern weapons, it has also been telling them how important the weapons are to itself. The essential point of its deterrence policy has been to impress potential enemies that it has the bombs to destroy them and that, if provoked sufficiently, it would use them. Much of what it does do with nuclear weapons, where it puts them and what it says about them, is designed to impress this audience. But such an attitude towards the bomb cannot fail to impress other audiences as well. When the U.S. boasts about its nuclear "superiority" to impress the Soviets, it makes it quite evident to non-nuclear powers that to the most powerful country in the world, nuclear weapons are the most important basis of power. Thus a clear example is set on how to derive prestige as well as security from modern military technology. The second-generation nuclear powers are even cruder in flaunting their special status. Premier Pompidou of France recently told an African audience: "Those who do not possess nuclear arms are destined to disappear or be subjected."

From the first, the U.S. decided not to make the attempt to put nuclear weapons in a special moral or political category as was done with poison gas. President Truman has written that he regarded the atomic bomb dropped on Hiroshima and Nagasaki as "just another artillery weapon." It was hinted that the atomic bomb might be used in Korea in 1951 and in Indochina in 1954. In 1956 Admiral Radford, the Chairman of the Joint Chiefs of Staff, announced to the European allies, and of course to the rest of the world as well, that the U.S. regarded nuclear weapons as "conventional," and nuclear weapons by the tens of thousands became regular equipment throughout U.S. forces. The U.S. has announced a strategy which calls for a first use of nuclear weapons against a Soviet attack with conventional forces on Berlin. The bomb has not been exploded in anger since 1945, but scarcely a day has passed since then when it has not been used for some political purpose—to threaten an enemy, to reassure an ally, or to make the world take notice.

In the face of the continuous entry of new members into the nuclear club during the past twenty years, some have suggested that it is still possible to bar the clubhouse door. A few officials within the U.S. government have urged privately what the London *Observer* has hinted at publicly, that the U.S. should bomb the Chinese atomic installations immediately. This would prevent China from making a deliverable bomb, and would, presumably, discourage others from launching nuclear weapons programs. It is not inconceivable that there are "bomb the bomb" advocates in the Soviet government as well. This is of course preventive war, a policy of moral bankruptcy that would assure a large-scale, endless conflict with China.

But, clearly, exhortations by the great powers on the advantages of nuclear abstinence will not be enough. If the U.S. can neither talk other countries out of the nuclear weapons business nor force them out, the only alternative is to try to remove the reasons for which such countries may desire them. If the principal incentive is fear for national security, then U.S. guarantees to non-nuclear powers against atomic attack might prove effective. Just after the Chinese explosion President Johnson appeared to undertake such a commitment, although it was couched in vague terms. India has informally suggested joint guarantees by all the major nuclear powers. The problem, of course, is whether such guarantees have any real meaning. Since even major nuclear powers are vulnerable to catastrophic destruction, their commitments to acts on behalf of others which would invite atomic retaliation on themselves are not wholly credible. If Europeans, like de Gaulle, doubt the value of the American pledge to go to nuclear war for France and Germany, are Asians and Africans likely to believe that the U.S. would risk New York and Washington for Bombay or Nairobi?

There is, moreover, another problem with guarantees. The assumption that fear of attack is the primary reason for wanting nuclear weapons may well be ill-founded. It is at least as likely that several countries will want them as symbols of independence and national sovereignty. Nuclear weapons are status symbols as well as the currency of international bargaining. For these purposes someone else's nuclear umbrella is of no value at all. Indeed for a nation to accept a nuclear protectorate is to admit that it is less than fully sovereign. Because national pride rather than national security is the source of much of the pressure for atomic weapons, schemes for nuclear sharing, such as the proposed NATO Multilateral Force, also fail to meet the problem. The fiction of shared control inherent in the proposed MLF (inasmuch as the U.S. would retain a veto) will not convince advanced countries, like Germany, to abandon any nuclear pretentions they may have if traditionally weaker powers, such as India, have produced their own bombs.

The harsh reality facing the nuclear powers is that there is little prospect of preventing the spread of nuclear weapons unless they themselves take some major steps to halt production and reduce their present enormous inventories. Even an agreement not to transfer or receive nuclear weapons, as has been proposed at Geneva, would not be effective if the U.S. and the U.S.S.R. continue to turn out missiles like sausages, as Khrushchev once put it. Such agreements will collapse under the pressure of the arms race. True, there are incentives for countries to refrain from becoming nuclear powers. Countries fully capable of producing the bomb have held back because of the cost, the diversion of technical resources, the increased chance of becoming involved in a nuclear war, and even the desire to make a symbolic contribution to peace. Indeed, one of the present nuclear powers, Britain, has seriously considered resigning from the club. But these incentives can develop only in a favorable political climate. They cannot survive in an atmosphere in which the major powers are themselves spreading nuclear weapons in their own countries and around the world.

The U.S. and the U.S.S.R. could set the tone for the international community by renouncing the use of nuclear weapons for bargaining, pressure, or coercion and making this pledge credible by substantial cuts in their nuclear stockpiles They could make the weapons appear far less important by making it clear to the world that they are to be used only for retaliation against nuclear attack. A no-first-use commitment would help build a consensus that nuclear weapons are not legitimate political instruments and that the attempt to use them as such is an intolerable risk to humanity. Unless the most powerful nations are willing to make a dramatic renunciation of the atomic bomb as an instrument of policy and to take significant steps towards nuclear disarmament, they will have little hope of persuading lesser countries to do without it.

There seems to be no other way to break the disarmament log-jam than to start here, almost certainly in the context of fundamental political agreements looking toward a settlement in Europe. Whether the nations that have been helped to great power by the nuclear arms race will perceive the necessity is another matter.

The Diplomacy of Peace

By Joseph S. Clark

Few Americans would deny that the basic foreign policy objective of our country is a just and lasting peace. We contend that our national posture is not belligerent, that we seek no territorial acquisitions, that we are prepared to give up our foreign bases as part of a general peaceful international settlement and that we stand ready with economic aid to assist the underdeveloped nations of the world in solving their problems of misery and poverty.

We support the United Nations. We are prepared to move forward in the field of arms control and disarmament. Our contention is that the intransigent aggression of international communism centered in Russia and China is the only deterrent to achieving our peaceful objectives. These belligerent policies of our adversaries, we claim, require us to arm to the teeth, to devote our best brains and a huge share of our Gross National Product to preparing for and actually waging war. We deplore this necessity for the added reason that it requires drastic cutbacks in our domestic programs to build a better America.

We tend to view with suspicion suggestions looking toward a relaxation of the Cold War and the establishment of peaceful coexistence with the communist states on the ground that our enemies are utterly untrustworthy. Agreements reached with them, accordingly, would be both meaningless and damaging to our ability to create and maintain freedom and democracy around the world.

It is the purpose of this article to examine the validity of this viewpoint and to suggest policies and programs which might contribute to the achievement of our basic objective: world peace.

1.

Let us review the efforts we and others have made to create the international institutions and to negotiate the treaties which could bring peace and world order under law.

For present purposes we can begin our story with 1945.

(1) At the end of that year the victorious allies created the United Nations, an international institution whose main purpose was to establish and maintain international peace and security.

The U.N. has had its victories and its defeats. Its charter is clearly inadequate to today's needs. But there are few in-

17

telligent men who would wish to destroy it or who would contend it has not served a useful purpose.

(2) One of the preoccupations of the U.N. has been disarmament. Its members, particularly those from the medium-sized and smaller states, are gravely concerned about the danger which threatens their peoples from the angry confrontation of the great powers armed to the teeth with lethal weapons which no longer respect national boundaries.

At the Fourteenth General Assembly of the United Nations in 1959, a resolution was unanimously adopted endorsing the "goal of general and complete disarmament under effective international control," and calling upon governments "to make every effort to achieve a constructive solution of this problem."

(3) In 1960, Secretary of State Christian Herter first publicly stated that the foregoing objective of the U.N. was also the goal of the United States. President Eisenhower told the Fifteenth General Assembly of the U.N. on September 22: "Thus we see as our goal, not a super state above nations, but a world community embracing them all, rooted in law and justice and enhancing the potentialities and common purposes of all peoples."

(4) On September 20, 1961, the McCloy-Zorin 8 Point Agreement on General and Complete Disarmament was signed by the representatives of our country and the Soviet Union. Three days later, under the leadership of then Senator Hubert Humphrey and at the urging of President Kennedy, Congress created the Arms Control and Disarmament Agency.

(5) President Kennedy brought the twin concepts of general disarmament and enforceable world law together at the United Nations on September 25, 1961, when he stated that we must create "worldwide law and law enforcement as we outlaw worldwide war and weapons."

Russia had announced its support of general and complete disarmament under strict international controls some time before we had. However, in June of 1960 the United States and the Soviet Union produced preliminary proposals for a treaty of general and complete disarmament. Up to that point both sides had been content with generalities. The McCloy-Zorin Agreement significantly narrowed the differences between the two superpowers, although it still left a wide and, to date, unbridgeable gap on matters of substance.

(6) The United States Plan for a World without War was published in September 1961. It called for achieving, in three stages, general and complete disarmament under strict international control. Implementation could take perhaps twelve years. The Russian plan was similar in broad outline but contemplated only four years to complete and was quite vague in terms of the verification process. It was also faulty in that it rejected as "espionage" any inspection of armaments retained during the various stages of the disarmament process. It ignored the specifics for enforceable world law except to the extent the phrase "strict international control" could be construed as meeting the requirement.

As a result of this activity in the fall of 1961, the Eighteen Nation Disarmament Conference was convened in Geneva in the spring of 1962. Elaborate discussions, in which the draft treaties tabled by the U.S.S.R. and the United States came under scrutiny by all of the states represented at the conference, were initiated and have continued to date without much progress in narrowing the gap between the two documents. In all candor it must be admitted that both draft treaties are totally inadequate as definitive documents capable of achieving their purposes. The conference, stalled on its major objective, has increasingly turned its attention to nibbling away at arms control instead of attacking general disarmament with "barracuda bites."

(7) Nevertheless, President Kennedy, during his lifetime, continued to press forward. On June 10, 1963, in his American University address, perhaps the greatest speech he ever made, he said: "Our primary long-range interest is general and complete disarmament designed to take place by stages, permitting parallel political developments to build the new institutions of peace which would take the place of arms."

And at his last appearance before the United Nations on September 20, 1963, shortly before his death, he called for a revision of the charter of the United Nations to permit the development of that body into "a genuine world security system."

To recapitulate, the heart of the United States and Russian plans for disarmament is a staged reduction and eventual elimination of all armaments down to the level of small police weapons required to maintain internal law and order, accompanied by the simultaneous evolution of international institutions which would create, administer and enforce the international world law of disarmament.

Chief among the international institutions called for in the United States plan are:

(1) An International Disarmament Organization charged with supervising and administering the process of disarmament;

(2) International juridical institutions to decide disputes arising in the disarmament process and also to determine political disputes of every nature which, after disarmament, would no longer be resolved by force; and

(3) An International Peace Force to enforce the findings of the IDO and the decrees, judgments, arbitration awards, and the like, of the international judicial institutions.

Although the United States plan makes no mention of the subject, it is clear that substantial international financing would be required to support the activities of these institutions. It is also clear that, under present conditions, the United Nations has no capability for raising the required funds. Perhaps a small tax on international trade, possibly aided through annual payments of a part of the surplus of the World Bank for Reconstruction and Development, would provide the necessary funds to carry the plan into effect.

The United States Plan for a World without War and the outline of a draft treaty tabled at Geneva are both in effect rather pale adaptations of a much more specific and elaborate plan prepared by Mr. Grenville Clark and Professor Louis B. Sohn of the Harvard University Law School, published in 1958 by the Harvard University Press and since translated into nearly all major foreign languages. Adlai Stevenson, several years ago, presented the Russian translation to Premier Khrushchev.

The authors detailed, article by article, a revision of the charter of the United Nations required to implement the disarmament treaty. Later they drafted and sent to the State Department the disarmament treaty itself.

The deficiencies of the U.N. as a vehicle for disarmament have become increasingly apparent. Notable among them are: (1) the veto in the Security

Council; (2) the one-nation one-vote rule in the General Assembly; (3) the inadequacy of the money-raising capabilities of the U.N.; and (4) the lack of any adequate executive power.

Concerned with these problems and much influenced by the more recent thinking of Grenville Clark and Louis B. Sohn, I introduced into the United States Senate in April 1965 a revised version of a "Planning for Peace" resolution which, in one form or another, I had been proposing since 1959. Cosponsored by twenty-five of my colleagues, this resolution calls upon the President

to formulate as speedily as possible specific and detailed proposals for the implementation of the foreign policy objectives of the United States regarding the establishment of an international authority to keep the peace under conditions of general and complete disarmament effectively guaranteed by adequate inspection and controls. In formulating such proposals, the President is requested to consider whether the development of effective international machinery for the supervision of disarmament and the maintenance of peace, including (1) an International Disarmament Organization; (2) a permanent World Peace Force; (3) world tribunals for the peaceful settlement of all international disputes not settled by negotiations; (4) other international institutions necessary for the enforcement of world peace under the rule of law; and (5) appropriate and reliable financial arrangements for the support of such peacekeeping machinery, may best be achieved by revision of the Charter of the United Nations, by a new treaty, or by a combination of the two.

Sections 3 and 4 of the resolution call upon the President to make his proposals available to the Congress and to the public generally, and to transmit copies of the resolution to the heads of government of all the nations of the world, urging them to initiate studies of matters germane to the resolution and to formulate recommendations based on such studies.

Two days of hearings on this resolution were held by the Senate Committee on Foreign Relations in May 1965. It elicited strong support from all the public witnesses save two representing right-wing splinter groups. The testimony of the State Department and Arms Control and Disarmament Agency witnesses was correct but cool.

Nevertheless, the resolution has not been acted on by either the Committee or the Senate.

2.

General and complete disarmament under enforceable world law has been stalled both at Geneva and in the United Nations for the past four years, in part because of the deteriorating international situation, in part because neither France nor China has been present at Geneva (France, under the leadership of General de Gaulle, having refused to attend, and China not having been invited nor, indeed, having shown any interest in the project); but also in large part because neither the United States nor the U.S.S.R. has made any real effort to close the gap between their separate approaches on means for reaching the agreed end of disarmament. Behind this want of progress lurks, of course, the innate suspicion and mistrust that has clouded the relations of these two great giants ever since the Bolshevik Revolution of 1917. Until this mistrust between the rulers of the two countries is alleviated, there seems little chance of arriving at a just and lasting peace through the goal of disarmament under enforceable world law.

Yet, despite the eruption of the war in Vietnam, there are some hopeful signs. First among them is the successful negotiation and implementation of the limited test ban treaty. The danger of radioactive fallout has been virtually eliminated as a present worry for all mankind. The conclusion of the "hot line" agreement bringing the White House and the Kremlin into instantaneous communication with each other is another. A third is the continuation of the people-to-people cultural and technological exchange programs which have stimulated respect and friendship between the two nations. As this article is written, hope has not been abandoned for conclusion of a treaty eliminating the further proliferation of nuclear capabilities to nations not now having access to nuclear weapons.

Within Russia there are also hopeful signs. Our NATO partners are convinced that the Kremlin is no longer determined to achieve hegemony by force in Western Europe. Not long ago, on March 21, 1966, former West German Chancellor Konrad Adenauer declared the "Soviet Union has entered the ranks of the nations that desire peace." The Russian satellites, with the exception of East Germany, have reasserted a measure of independence. They are conducting increasing trade with the West. Jamming of Western broadcasts ceased several years ago. Messrs. Brezhnev and Kosygin appear to be far more cautious in their international diplomacy than their predecessors. The widening breach between China and Russia almost inevitably tends to turn the thoughts of the latter westward to render its European front safe while it deals with its communist neighbor to the east.

Finally, and perhaps most important

of all, Russia has become a "have" nation. The upgrading of education, improvement in housing, the spread of the amenities, the ever-increasing distribution of consumer goods, all tend to blunt any remaining urge for war which might exist among a less satisfied people. There may be many hawks among the Russian leaders just as there are in our own country. But it seems reasonably clear that in both the United States and the Soviet Union, the overwhelming majority of the people are opposed to chauvinism and an aggressive and belligerent foreign policy. Russia has come a long way since the Bolshevik Revolution and the days of the Stalinist terror. It is well for us to recognize and take account of this new attitude in our diplomacy.

There remain the problem of American public opinion and the attitude of our government toward Russia and world peace. First, let us deal with the former. There is still vast skepticism among the American people about the possibility of friendly relations with Russia. There is further a widespread feeling that disarmament and world peace are Utopian goals incapable of being realized in the foreseeable future. Despite the earnest efforts of President Kennedy, there is still a big job to be done in bringing public opinion in the United States to the point where meaningful disarmament treaties can be negotiated and ratified by the Senate.

And yet, truculence and belligerence in the United States are, in my judgment, more apparent than real. The military-industrial complex against which General Eisenhower warned in his last speech as President has staunch allies in the press, among the columnists and certain radio and television commentators. Nevertheless, almost every poll of public opinion taken in the recent past ends with some such conclusion as this: We want peace, we want the arms burden lifted off the backs of the taxpayers, we want an end to the threat of our children being killed in war and of bombs dropping on our homes; but history has taught us not to trust the Russians or, for that matter, the Chinese either. We are accordingly both skeptical and fearful of the possibility of arriving at agreements to achieve the goals we so ardently desire.

It is obvious that changes in public opinion must precede the achievement of meaningful international agreements to obtain peace and disarmament. No one who sat through the long debate in the Senate over ratification of the limited test ban treaty could come to any other conclusion.

Yet, in the end, the treaty was ratified by a vote of 81 to 19 over the strenuous objection of some very able Senators who took the hard line of distrust. And there is presently in this country an on-going peace offensive which is likely to turn the country away from the antics of the "gamesmen" and to support a solid effort to achieve a pragmatic and workable agreement with our adversaries.

In the last twelve months this peace offensive has shown itself in a number of ways, among them:

(1) The celebration of the twentieth anniversary of the founding of the United Nations in San Francisco in June 1965. At that meeting U Thant, Secretary General of the U.N., asked:

Is it really only the scourge of war or the lash of terror that can move us to the goal of peace and justice in the world? Can we not make the effort to advance out of our own sense of responsibility and knowledge, rather than be driven like refugees before a storm

which may be unleashed by our own inability to take hold of the future?

(2) The Washington Conference on World Peace Through Law, in September 1965, was attended by 3,000 delegates, mainly jurists, presidents of bar associations and lawyers from 115 countries. These molders of world opinion returned to their own countries prepared to secure the cooperation of their governments in advancing the concept of world peace through world law.

(3) The visit of Pope Paul to the U.N. in October 1965 had an immense impact on public opinion all over the world. His dramatic plea for a vigorous and relentless full-scale peace offensive ended with the simple but eloquent statement: "No more war, war never again."

(4) Thirty separate committees reported to the White House Conference on International Cooperation at the end of November on ways and means of increasing cooperation among the peoples of the world.

There can be measured optimism that the trend of public opinion in our country is turning away from belligerence toward support for a peace offensive in which the United States will take the initiative. We may well be closer to a breakthrough for peace than many would think.

3.

World power today is primarily in the hands of the United States and the Soviet Union. China may some day join them, but her time has not yet come. Despite the war in Vietnam, she has little offensive capability for making mischief outside her borders and has recently sustained a series of humiliating diplomatic defeats, notably in Indonesia. Indeed, the effects of the chaos of the cultural revolution may delay her emergence by many years.

The other countries of the world are, for the time being, too weak economically and militarily to have more than a peripheral influence on the behavior of the two superpowers.

NATO, having accomplished its primary purpose of restraining the western movement of Russia, has no offensive steam in it, although the potential for increased social, economic, and political integration is still great. The Warsaw Pact powers, the Scandinavians, the Arab League, the countries of Latin America and Africa, indeed, all the rest of the world, while their views must be respected and while they will unquestionably exercise a temporizing influence on the unrestrained belligerence of both Russia and the United States, are neither capable nor desirous of asserting claims to more than regional power.

The United Nations, hope of the past and perhaps also of the future, is presently incapable because of organizational defects and financial stringency of doing more than supplying help to put out international brush fires as they break out, and providing a useful forum for debate.

There are no major controversies between the United States and Russia incapable of solution by skillful diplomacy. The venom has been drained from both Russian communism and American capitalism. The differing attitudes toward individual freedom, while substantial, are not in themselves a *casus belli*. Fanaticism is out of date in both the Kremlin and the White House, although no doubt it still has its disciples at lower governmental levels in both countries.

What, then, stands in the way of a far-reaching *détente?* Vietnam and Germany.

With respect to the former, one may hope that Hanoi and the Viet Cong can be persuaded that a military victory is impossible for them, that American "hawks" can be turned into "owls," and that a settlement which is honorable without being unrealistic can be obtained at the conference table.

With respect to the latter, the breakup of NATO as a military alliance and the incipient flirtation of General de Gaulle with Moscow, coupled with the recently announced peace offensive of the West German government, may well bring the German problem within the area of a feasible solution in the reasonably near future. Here the preoccupation of our State Department with West Germany is the principal stumbling block. The best example is our stubborn refusal to abandon the proposed Multilateral Force in order to secure a workable nonproliferation treaty with Russia. The recommendations for dealing with the German problem made by the Wiesner Committee on Arms Control and Disarmament of the White House Conference on International Cooperation may well supply a way to the solution. In broad general terms, they called for a non-aggression pact between the NATO and Warsaw powers; the inspected withdrawal of Russian, American, French and British troops a suitable distance from Berlin; the stationing of observers at key points to prevent surprise attack on adversary territory; and the encouragement of the West German and East German states to increase their already substantial commercial contacts with a view to achieving a workable *modus vivendi,* perhaps in the form of a loose federation among themselves, without the intervention of either the NATO powers or the U.S.S.R.

None of this, of course, will come overnight. We cannot unfreeze the Cold War until we unfreeze our own government's thinking on the problems which separate Russia and the West and bar the path to better relations. Our foreign policy has been hampered by the persistence of fixed attitudes which were formed during the Stalinist era, but which have far less relevance now. Just as there is a "Senate establishment," about which I have commented elsewhere, I believe there is a "foreign policy establishment," both in the State Department and in the universities, which clings to old-fashioned and outmoded ideas and plans long after they have outlived their usefulness. The Multilateral Force, which I referred to earlier, is a prime example, but far from the only one.

Nevertheless, I suggest again that the problem is not beyond the capability of a skillful, forward-looking diplomacy emanating from the Kremlin and the White House; and, once the superpowers had achieved a *détente,* the road would be open for persuading—through superior force if necessary—a presently belligerent China to turn its great capabilities inward toward building a Chinese Great Society and joining in the internationalization of world peace through disarmament under world law.

In short the prospects for peace are brighter than many think. What is needed as much as anything else is an aroused public opinion, international as well as American, and leaders in government persuaded that an initiative toward a peaceful settlement of the world's problems is good politics as well as good sense. Cooperation, not conflict, must be the wave of the future.

Semantics and Asymmetries

By Craig Hosmer, H. R.

These comments might not inappropriately be entitled "The Chinese Point of View," not because they have anything to do with that subject, but because they may outrage some readers to the same extent as would those of a Red Chinese spokesman—but for different reasons.

Although complaints are sometimes voiced about the number of divergent viewpoints to be heard in the area of arms control and disarmament thinking, and although these often give rise to confusion, nevertheless one of the premises of our democratic system is that controversy is a very good thing. Discussion of a topic from different and often antagonistic viewpoints is one of the best ways of arriving at practical political wisdom and of determining both the assets and liabilities of particular proposals relative to arms control. Both scholars and politicians do well to listen attentively to points of view contrary to their own.

This observation is relevant to the progress of arms control on a worldwide basis because the divergence in viewpoint found within the covers of this book represents in miniature the much more profound asymmetries in attitude toward the subject that exist on the international plane. At least we can be thankful that most Europeans and Americans use the same semantics in discussing arms control. At the level of East-West diplomacy, there is little semantic symmetry on the subject. Therefore, in considering proposals we must not fall into the trap of "mirror imaging" and attributing to others the same thought-processes as our own. As Dr. William R. Kintner points out in his paper, it is quite possible that the communist world regards the subject of disarmament and arms control with much less sophistication than do we ourselves. Such discussion as they conduct on the subject may be quite proletarian and basic compared to ours. He who is deft at fencing, if he is not careful, may be "done in" by a clumsy fellow with a heavy iron sword.

In passing, a word should be said about the related subject of "convergence," which invariably comes up in discussions of the relations of the United States and Western Europe vis-à-vis the Soviet Union. Personal encounters with a number of Soviet scientists have induced in this writer a certain amount of caution about the idea that cultural and scientific exchanges between our two countries may ulti-

25

mately lead to a convergence of our political philosophies and outlook. The system of rewards in the Soviet Union is much different from our own. Men and women who make substantial contributions in the Soviet Union are rewarded with adequate housing, better education for their children, the use of an automobile—if contributions are particularly outstanding, a snappy Czechoslovakian automobile. These people are remarkably conservative in the sense that they do not want to jeopardize these rewards. One of the ways in which they could risk a fall from grace would be to stray from their own specialty into the realm of politics. *So* deep is their conservatism in this respect that they actually seal off that portion of their minds which might be used for political thought. Therefore, although they may converge with us in non-political areas, simply through the operation of natural economic, technological and social tendencies, it is very doubtful that we can expect much convergence in the political area. Politically, the Soviet Union is still one of the most underdeveloped of all industrialized states, and seems likely to remain so.

Soviet political leaders also share the characteristic of extreme conservatism, but this does not necessarily reduce the possibility of war between the Soviet Union and the West. It will, of course, tend to reduce estimates by Soviet political leaders of the amount of physical damage they might be willing to accept in return for carrying out their responsibility under communist dogma to "universalize" their system. But the dogmatic imperative endures: they are still compelled by the logic of their belief to proceed by force toward world conquest, whenever the risks of retaliation are tolerable. This should not be taken to imply that Soviet leaders are

reckless or irresponsible. As a matter of fact, they have shown considerable strategic caution throughout the last two decades—except perhaps in their decision to place missiles in Cuba. But they are constantly assessing potential gains versus potential risks, and constantly wondering how far they dare exert outward pressure, and when prudence demands an easing off.

Let us hypothesize the existence in the Western world of a "button" which could be pushed with the instantaneous result of a worldwide elimination of communism, with nobody being hurt on either side of the Iron Curtain. Upon pushing the button, simply and magically all communist governments would suddenly be transformed into Western democracies, totally compatible with our own. Probably few of us would hesitate to push that button under such benign circumstances. But what if the decision entailed the loss of thousands of lives on our side and thousands of lives on their side? Probably the temptation to push it would still exert its attraction despite this cost. Suppose now the price escalates another step, and another, and still another. Depending upon our varying outlooks, at some point each of us would make the judgment that the button should not be pushed because the cost had become high for achieving the objective. Communist leaders continually and inescapably are faced with this kind of decision-making process. We have got to maintain the kind of military-technological posture which will keep the Soviets continually convinced that, so far as the nuclear button is concerned, they will not deem the game worth the candle.

Senator Joseph S. Clark, a respected colleague, has for years been engaged in the business of "bottling instant peace." He seems able, without a bridge, to cross the gap that divides the real and troubled world of today from the peaceful and untroubled world we would all like to see. One might be forgiven if he derives from Senator Clark's statements the impression that except for the existence in Washington of a few anachronistic relics from a troubled prehistoric age the world would be peaceful.

Unfortunately the issue is not entirely within our control. The problem of peace lies less in Washington than it does in some other parts of the world. The path to peace also lies less in emotionally expressed hopes and aspirations than it does in an accurate calculation of the stubborn, discouraging realities of the world. We are all prone at times to overlook the hard, difficult, and immediate problems and instead made a quantum jump into fascinating discussions of more remote and esoteric problems. Mr. John Silard illustrates this in his discussion of certain ways to avoid unwanted consequences. His recommendations are: first to employ birth control; if that fails, abortion; if that fails, infanticide. However, he skipped over the most effective and immediate, but most difficult, means of avoidance —continence. It should not be forgotten that most of the states of the world which possess the economic and technological resources to become nuclear weapons powers during the next ten years would probably prefer to follow the example first set by Canada and to abstain voluntarily from acquisition, provided that they see the world moving toward conditions under which aggression does not pay.

Most of the contemporary discussion concerning the proposed anti-proliferation treaty does not come to grips with the immediate problem of accurately assessing whether such a treaty involves risks even more serious than those it is calculated to eliminate. The question arises in connection with the commitments existing nuclear states might have to make to non-nuclear states in return for a renunciation by the latter of their option to go nuclear. Hedley Bull suggests that the United States is already overcommitted, or at least would be overcommitted if it added a blanket pledge to come to the rescue of any nation in the world which, while practicing nuclear abstention, becomes the victim of aggression or nuclear blackmail. The United States has already had sufficient difficulty in recent years convincing some people concerning the credibility of our deterrent promise to Europe. The United States should think long and hard about a further extension of its deterrent guarantee on a global scale in order to achieve a non-proliferation treaty.

This subject was handled unsatisfactorily by Defense Secretary Robert McNamara before the Joint Committee on Atomic Energy during its 1966 hearings which resulted in a Congressional blessing upon the Administration's efforts to negotiate the non-proliferation treaty. The following excerpt from the Hearings illustrates the point:

Representative Hosmer. In connection with the worries of these nonnuclear powers, you state at one point that— "In order to have a successful nonproliferation treaty the general program must put potential aggressors on notice that possession of nuclear weapons will not make their aggression either easier or less dangerous." And again at a later point you refer to "appropriate arrangements" to guarantee nuclear states against nuclear attack. You said by that you meant some kind of a multilateral guarantee. Could you be more explicit?

Secretary McNamara. No. These are arrangements that need to be discussed among the nations. I would not want to prejudice such discussions by advancing definitive statements of our Government's views today.

Representative Hosmer. That kind of leaves us dangling as to what intentions of the administration are in this area, does it not?

Secretary McNamara. I don't believe so. The President has stated that we will not permit nuclear blackmail. He stated many times our desire to see some form of multilateral assurance to non-nuclear powers—protection in the event they are attacked by a nuclear power.

We have discussed the subject before the United Nations, and I think it is quite clear as to what the administration views are, but I don't believe we should endeavor to discuss today in public the details or particular form of multilateral relationships which we would find acceptable versus those that we would not.

In any case these are subjects that ought to be discussed by the Secretary of State and not by the Secretary of Defense.

Representative Hosmer. Sometimes I get a queasy feeling that we are being asked for a blank check in this endorsement of a non-proliferation treaty from an answer like that, Mr. McNamara.

Secretary McNamara. I see no basis for your feeling, Mr. Hosmer.

Representative Hosmer. Let us take this up then. In your response to Mr. Holifield, you said that the administration attitude is that we won't support an aggressor, speaking of a nuclear aggressor. But you failed to mention the victim. What do we intend to do in relation to the victim?

I ask you this in terms of the very statements you made at the beginning about the catalytic effect of nuclear war

on the part of small nations. If we get into some kind of multilateral arrangements here, in which certain treaty obligations automatically are called up, it seems to me we have a pretty major catalyst to get us in some kind of war. That does not seem to me to be a situation that leads to more stability. It seems to be one that leads to less. Would you like to comment on it?

Secretary McNamara. I cannot understand your reasoning.

This exchange was not very enlightening about the guarantees that may be expected to accompany the proposed treaty. It was disappointing, and somewhat astounding, that the Secretary had not been prepared by the Arms Control and Disarmament Agency to discuss the subject. Under the law the Agency is the advisor in these matters to the Secretary of Defense, to the Secretary of State, to the President, and others in Washington who have responsibilities in these matters. The Secretary was correct to say that this subject ought to be discussed by the Secretary of State but he was not correct to disqualify himself from the discussion of "appropriate arrangements" that might involve the United States in more far-flung commitments than those undertaken in the NATO Treaty. Apparently the Secretary had not been adequately briefed by ACDA. It has long been my contention that ACDA has not done its job thoroughly and fully with respect to analyzing clearly each arms control and disarmament proposal, both as to its advantages and to its disadvantages, and dispassionately laying out a judicious balance sheet. If there is a failure here, perhaps it is because ACDA's charter places upon its director the duty of negotiating—and in the give-and-take of public negotiations, often he must take positions for negotiating purposes only. Yet, when the head of the Agency does so, then ACDA must support those positions rather than analyzing them dispassionately.

As a matter of fact, there has been a large failure to make a dispassionate analysis of the entire proliferation problem. We simply are against it, period, and we leap at every opportunity to conclude a treaty. We have not really thought through sound philosophical, logical and political reasons for a treaty—even though they may exist. ACDA has refused on *a priori* grounds to study such advantages as might accrue from the natural spread of nuclear weapons. More than that, to make up a truly accurate balance sheet probably ACDA should make a study of any advantages and disadvantages which may lie at the opposite end of the spectrum—deliberately accelerated proliferation. ACDA has simply presumed as a matter of faith that there is nothing favorable to be said for any kind of proliferation.

For heuristic purposes, I will follow Dr. Boulding's precedent of making an outrageous hypothesis. Let us call it "total, controlled proliferation." Let us suppose that instead of opposing proliferation we simply gave every country, say, four 20-kiloton bombs. Everybody would have nuclear weapons; therefore, there would be no question of lack of national prestige from not having them. However, certain conditions must be attached. In the first place, we make sure that one of the four bombs will not work. But the countries receiving them do not know which of the four is the dud. An element of risk is introduced into the decision to use them. The recipient countries must also store these bombs in shelters providing protection against everyone else's 20-kiloton blasts. Therefore, their neighbors cannot elimi-

nate them quickly and easily. Moreover, once in storage, if the bombs are ever moved they will destroy themselves within four hours. Thus, there is no bluffing possible. They will either be used in anger or not used at all. A reasoned predecision must be made. In addition, the bombs will destroy themselves if fired by missile. That will keep things "local." Also recipient countries will be told, and fully understand that once they use their bombs they will not be replaced. The user will revert to the humiliating status of a non-nuclear state. The purpose of this model is merely to illustrate the point that in our search for peace we should not consider only the obvious. Possibly this, or some other outrageous supposition might come nearer to the mark than we think. It might be better calculated than our present policy to bring about conditions of international stability and to make all political leaders, even in the smallest countries, realize how the conditions of the nuclear age impose terrible responsibilities upon us all.

For the benefit of students and professors who can approach human problems with a sublime detachment, it may prove instructive to make some mention of how politicians go about dealing with the problems of arms control and disarmament. It is somewhat difficult for us because few of the people we represent understand much about the subject; they regard achieving it "as a very remote possibility," and they are basically suspicious of it anyway.

Not long ago, this writer took a political position by flatly predicting that the Geneva negotiations would result in a non-proliferation treaty during the year 1966. I explained that with the Viet Nam War going on, President Johnson would need something he could present as a "peace accomplishment" in the fall Congressional election campaigns. I alleged that a certain amount of informal cooperation has been going on between the United States and the Soviet Union, and that the latter's leaders might give President Johnson this political windfall in return for something they want. This, of course, was not a very statesmanlike suggestion on my part, but at least it served to give the public some feeling for the practicalities of arms control negotiations. Most Americans are sufficiently endowed with common sense to realize that politicians are seldom able to act like Plato's philosopher-kings with no regard for popular opinion.

My previous criticism of ACDA suggests another way in which politicians deal with an issue of public policy. Congress has a duty of "legislative oversight" of the agencies of the government to which it appropriates money. One of the ways of carrying on this oversight function is to make just such criticisms. Whether merited or not, the fact that criticism can be expected furnishes an incentive to agencies to do their jobs as effectively and efficiently as possible. This is a basic principle of public administration in a democratic society.

During the remainder of the 1960's, the United States will face many complex problems in the area of disarmament and arms control policy. The international setting in which we have to work out our foreign policy is fraught with opportunities for interesting, constructive experiments, and it is also fraught with pitfalls which are not always apparent to the eye until we are on the edge of them, or already falling in. It is necessary for us to recognize that by no amount of wishing can we change an intractable world and make it conform to our abstract blueprints. Other countries have their own aspirations, whether we like it or not. In renouncing nuclear technology the real loss to the nonnuclear countries will be not in weaponry but in the peaceful possibility of using "plowshare" techniques for such development projects as building canals, deepening harbors, and carrying out other geographical face-lifting operations. The realistic politician and statesman must examine proposed new policies from many angles, and avoid the gimmickry which often abounds in purely speculative discussions about the great issues of arms policy.

Arms Control and National Security: A Caveat

By William R. Kintner

Some years ago military planners were informed that they should take arms control considerations into account in developing new strategic concepts or recommending new weapons systems. By 1964, a subtle shift in United States security and arms control planning had taken place. Since then, security planning has become increasingly influenced by already established arms control policies. An integral and reciprocal relationship now exists in Washington between security and present or potential arms control policies.

The argument has gained currency that the United States "can no longer seek national security chiefly in arms and alliances alone."[1] The fear that a catastrophic nuclear war, unwanted by either side, might occur as a result of accident, human psychic failure, strategic miscalculation, communications breakdown, uncontrolled escalation of limited war, or the catalytic action of mischievous third parties has led to an increasing concern among U.S. policymakers with forms of arms control which might enhance national security as well as the safety of the world. Arms control considerations influence U.S. strategic planning with respect to the design, the deployment and use of military forces and weapons. Paradoxically, the man who has been given credit for building up and modernizing the armed forces of the United States is also, according to Arthur M. Schlesinger, Jr., the leader of the United States Arms Control effort. "Next to President Kennedy," wrote Schlesinger,

McNamara probably did more than anyone else to sustain the disarmament drive.

With his sense of the horror of nuclear conflict, his understanding of the adequacy of existing stockpiles, his fear of nuclear proliferation, his analytic command of the weapons problem and his managerial instinct to do something about an irrational situation, he forever sought new ways of controlling the arms race.[2]

Some analysts contend that U.S. policymakers have little choice but to seek an agreement for total disarmament with the Soviets. One authority advises that the United States should not hold out for high reliability in inspection systems because the perils of continued weapons competition are deemed greater than the dangers of an inefficiently-policed disarmament treaty.[3] Others argue that the risks inherent in unilateral disarmament are preferable to those posed by continuation of the arms race.[4]

Arms control can mean many different things: unilateral initiative or international agreements, formal or tacit, to reduce the possibilities of accidental war, strategic miscalculation or uncontrolled escalation of conflict; unilateral or reciprocal moves to lower tensions or build mutual confidence; agreements to hamper the spread of nuclear weapons to non-nuclear States; unilateral policies designed to improve the flexibility and defense preparedness of one side, or unilateral-reciprocal policies aiming at greater strategic stability through rendering nuclear strike forces "invulnerable"; agreements calculated to generate a climate favorable to actual disarmament agreements; a philosophy of R & D programming; or a strategy for waging controlled or limited-damage war if the deterrent fails. The concept of arms control is imprecise. Underlying the concept, however, is the assumption that there are certain military measures open to the United States (whether or not responded to by the Soviet Union) which are "considered advantageous by both major powers and which reduce the risks of nuclear war by design or accident and provide a stable military environment conducive to bargaining." [5]

The Soviets were, for a number of years, suspicious of the notion of arms control. Since 1962, however, they have begun to show a mild interest in the conclusion of partial measures which would fall under the heading of arms control. They have indicated a willingness to enter into partial agreements which, while contributing to an atmosphere of "détente" in Soviet-U.S. relations, would also improve their military position or promote political discord among the Western allies. Since January 1964, at the Conference of the Eighteen

Nation Disarmament Committee in Geneva, the Soviets have proposed a number of such measures including withdrawal of foreign troops from the territories of other countries, a non-aggression pact between NATO and the Warsaw Treaty partners, a nuclear free zone in Central Europe, elimination of bomber aircraft and prohibition of underground nuclear tests with compliance monitored by national detection capabilities rather than international inspection.

This slight shift in Soviet disarmament policy has usually been traced to such factors as an awareness of U.S. strategic superiority following the Cuban missile crisis, and of the obligation which this fact imposes upon the Soviet leaders to proceed with caution; a realization that advanced weapons programs are becoming increasingly costly and technologically complex; anxiety over the possible proliferation of nuclear weapons among countries not yet possessing nuclear forces, especially West Germany; and a desire to relax political tensions and dampen the rate of military-technological competition with the United States. All the foregoing interpretations of the motivating sources of current Soviet policy imply that the postwar "containment" policy of the United States has already succeeded to a significant degree—i.e., that Soviet Communism has already mellowed and will continue to mellow. This assumption requires careful examination.

Since the United States has been striving for twenty years to reach viable arms agreements with the Soviets, it would be irrational to take the position that all arms agreements concluded between the United States and the Soviet Union are necessarily detrimental to the security of the former. Nevertheless, arrangements for the control and limitation of armaments may have asymmetrical implications for the strategic security of the two contesting powers. It is not enough to praise arms agreements on the grounds that they contribute to the political goal of détente. Each agreement must be analyzed, therefore, with respect to the strategic posture of the United States, as well as the independence and integrity of the two-score countries which in one way or another are under the United States defense umbrella.

The United States and the Soviet Union, thus far, have agreed formally to three arms control measures: the installation of the Moscow-Washington "hot-line" for improving emergency communications, the Partial Test Ban Treaty, and the United Nations resolution prohibiting orbital bombs or weapons of mass destruction in outer space. Another measure, which falls under the heading of "arms control," was the 25% cutback in the production of fissionable material which President Johnson ordered early in 1964. This was followed in April 1964 by simultaneous announcements that the U.S. would further reduce the production of plutonium by an additional 20% between 1966 and 1968, while the Soviets would cancel the scheduled construction of two plutonium-producing reactors.

In assessing the U.S. and Soviet announcements in 1964 on reducing nuclear material production, some contend that the U.S. supply of plutonium was growing more rapidly than necessary for stockpiling nuclear weapons, and that this was the reason for President Johnson's announcement. If this is so, by arranging a simultaneous announcement with the Soviet Union, U.S. policymakers may have created an "image" of a bilateral arms control understanding which did not conform to the facts of the situation. Those who claim that the Soviets are reducing their planned production rely more on the veracity of Soviet declarations than on any satisfying empirical evidence.

In November 1965, Senator Henry M. Jackson declared that the Soviet leaders had reneged on their promise to reduce production of nuclear weapons material. The Senator concluded that:

Contrary to a widespread impression that Moscow is cutting its strategic military capability, in truth Moscow is diligently expanding both its offensive and defensive capacity—including ballistic missile and nuclear warhead development and production.[6]

Other unilateral actions which the United States has taken with respect to its own forces can also be considered as arms control measures. Some are advantageous only to the United States, while others may be of value to the Soviet Union as well. These measures include: SAC, "fail safe" procedures, prevention of an inadvertent missile launch, Presidential control over the release of nuclear weapons, doctrinal reconstitution of the U.S. command following a nuclear attack and the hardening or increasing of mobility of U.S. strategic offensive forces.

The Rationale of Arms Control

Those who hold that the relationship between the United States and the Soviet Union, as far as nuclear weapons are concerned, may be transformed into one of cooperation rather than competition, believe that the two superpowers have one overriding common interest: to avoid nuclear war. Although this contention may be true, there is a significant divergence in attitude: the Soviet Union apparently seeks the fruits of expansion while minimizing the risks of nuclear war, while the U.S. seeks to defend itself and its allies without resorting to nuclear conflict.

A common feature of the American arms control debate is the suggestion that both the United States and the Soviet Union would find it mutually advantageous to seek a "stable military balance" or "stable arms deterrence." The arms control experts do not agree on what separates military stability from military instability. Stability in the military environment cannot be equated with the absence of tensions, nor instability with their presence. Stability is not a mere matter of public moods, it is a function of many complex factors, including the relative strengths of opposing weapons systems, the flow of intelligence concerning such systems, and the assessments which are made by each side of its own interests and objectives, as well as the interests, objectives and characteristic modes of strategic behavior of the other side. A tension-ridden world might prove to be highly stable if the side which is committed to defend the existing order and the processes of peaceful change enjoys a sufficient margin of military superiority to deter a general nuclear war. Conversely, a world enveloped in an atmosphere of détente could suddenly become unstable if an aggressive state, tempted by potential technological advantage and confronted by a complacency on the other side, should decide to gamble on a novel weapons deployment.

The idea of stability, once it has been transferred to the military-strategic dimension, is complicated by political and psychological factors. Logically, the notion of stable balance implies some sort of parity of forces. Hence, it is often proposed that the United States try to reach agreement with the Soviet Union on limiting the number of strategic delivery vehicles (or the total number of strategic missiles, whether offensive or defensive) to be retained by each side.[7] But in a situation of mathematical equality with respect to physical power, one side might still prevail over the other if it is less afraid to brandish power in support of its diplomacy during times of international crisis. Conversely, a viable balance might be struck in a situation in which one side possesses a clear margin of physical superiority over the other, if the party of military preponderance happens to be in an essentially defensive posture. For a defensive power, the continued maintenance of military superiority ensures the preservation of international political-strategic stability.

Soviet interest in stability and the attendant arms control measures designed to achieve it appears to be diametrically opposite to that of many American arms control advocates. Indeed, the Soviets are engaged in an immense and continuing effort to destabilize the strategic balance at the top of the weapons spectrum in order to gain greater freedom of action for revolutionary warfare at the bottom. Yet, paradoxically, it is inconceivable to many Americans that the Soviets are seeking means to neutralize U.S. strategic superiority in order to destabilize the existing world situation.

While published Soviet documents spell out clearly the central nuclear thrust of Soviet military strategy, they leave unanswered many questions of Western readers. How Soviet military concepts would be executed is not spelled out. Important details are omitted. Others are obscured by a haze of ideology and semantics. Yet Soviet writings are amazingly forthright. According to one Soviet military professional:

In foreign bourgeois military literature there are statements which in essence come to this, that supposedly nuclear rocket weapons lead to the liquidation of military art, that waging armed combat in nuclear war does not require any military theory preparation of an officer cadre.

Soviet military science categorically rejects such groundless and over-simplified assertions about the nature and the ability to wage armed combat with the use of nuclear rocket weapons.[8]

The public Soviet debate concerning the nature of future war can only permit the most general kind of conclusions about the direction in which the Soviets are likely to move in the decade ahead. "The most important feature of Soviet military doctrine is that it is oriented not to past but to future war, taking into account its features, which pose specific demands on the art of the use of armed forces in it." [9]

The Soviets generally illustrate their arms control discussions with some of the more common terms employed in American strategic literature. Certain terms, such as "deliberate, selective response," however, are not used to describe a nuclear attack. The Soviets do stress matters of considerable importance. In view of the acknowledged destructiveness of nuclear war, they clearly recognize the one essential precondition for such warfare, namely, the first strike which they call a "pre-emptive" strike.

As a result of the mass use of strategic nuclear means, the possibility becomes real of the quick removal from the war of a series of countries of one or another coalition even without the simultaneous seizing of the territory of these countries by land forces and airborne troops.

This new feature of modern military strategy decisively influences the nature of waging war. *Using intercontinental means of combat can at once, from the very beginning of the war, achieve results of great strategic meaning.*[10]

Since the concept of the pre-emptive strike dominates the Soviets' strategic doctrine, their major weapons emphasis is still on strategic rocket forces rather than conventional forces, in spite of the possibility that they may have become more interested in recent years in the strategy of "flexible response" for Europe. The targeting doctrine which they discuss looks to a combination of counterforce, urban-industrial and population targets.[11] This targeting suggests little Soviet interest in restraint. It does point out, however, that political or other initiatives short of war can best be risked from a position of massive superiority. If war is to be waged at all, it must be waged totally and from a position of clear advantage. This is the single most persuasive theme in Soviet strategic writings today.

Since the Soviets believe that the initial plan of a nuclear war will be decisive, "to repel the nuclear blows of the enemy, especially in the beginning of the war, when he evidently will try to use the maximum of his nuclear power, is a problem of great national significance." [12] For this reason the Air Defense Command (PVO) which defends against air and missile attack is "one of the most important branches of the armed forces." [13] Soviet determination to proceed with the development and deployment of an anti-ballistic missile system is dictated by the logic of Soviet military doctrine.

It is quite possible that if the Soviets achieve the strategic superiority they seek they will never choose to employ it overtly. Then as now the Soviets may prefer the indirect approach. For if ever the military balance is tipped in the Soviet favor and the disastrous impact of this shift has registered in Western minds, few in the West will counsel opposing Communist inroads into countries which are now regarded as havens of stability. It really does not matter which overt path the Soviets pursue: A Soviet Union that has gained military-technological superiority will find it comparatively easy to find ways of exploiting its advantage against the United States and its allies.

Two Arms Control Proposals

For the most part, except for their relatively brief flirtation with the notion of general and complete disarmament in the early 1960's, U.S. policymakers have eschewed utopian arms control proposals and have confined themselves to a fairly realistic approach, demanding adequate verification for most of the limited arms control proposals which they have placed on the international conference table. Yet, in the light of the Soviet interest in destabilizing the world balance of power, we must always examine with great care whatever measures we might offer for negotiation, for virtually every measure which would serve any significant bilateral arms control purpose is fraught with implications for the U.S. security posture.

The United States, as pointed out previously, has officially proposed a verified freeze on the production of strategic delivery vehicles, which would include both offensive missiles, aircraft, and anti-ballistic missile systems. We put this plan forth at Geneva in 1964, 1965 and 1966. Up to the fall of 1966, the Soviets have shown no interest in a verified freeze, both because they are not yet ready to cut off production and because they dislike any on-site inspection of partial arms limitation agreements.

A position argued by some arms control specialists is that defense is provocative and destabilizing. How a weapons system designed to destroy incoming weapons rather than cities on the ground can be characterized as "provocative" (presumably even more provocative than ICBM's) will probably elude all but the supersophisticated; this argument certainly eludes the Soviets. As for the question of the potential destabilizing effects of ABM, if the United States should outpace the Soviet Union in the development and deployment of anti-missile missiles, the U.S. deterrent could very well remain as effective for the next fifteen or twenty years as it has been for the last fifteen years, and this would make for international "stability." Conversely, if the Soviets forge ahead of the United States in the ABM, which they now appear to be doing, the U.S. deterrent will undergo a major degradation resulting in "instability." Even while enjoying strategic superiority, the United States has had sufficient difficulty parrying the Communists' expansionist moves. In this connection, it behooves us to remember Churchill's somber Biblical warning: "If they do these things in the greenwood, what will they do in the dry?" There is no good reason why the United States should voluntarily surrender to the Soviet Union one iota of the margin of military-technological superiority which the former has enjoyed in recent years, and which it lies within its economic power to retain so long as the American people and their leaders are not bemused by specious arguments.

The proposition that ABM systems are unfeasible for technical and practical reasons has not been widely advanced since 1963. If such systems were really impracticable there would seem to be no need for an agreement to ban them. According to Freeman J. Dyson, of the Institute for Advanced Study at Princeton University, the race between offensive and defensive technology is an incessant one. "If at any time the offense stood still and committed itself to a fixed 'finite deterrence' system, the defense could find means to nullify the offense." [14] He concluded that after several years in which offensive technology reigned supreme and seemed to be permanent and automatic, defensive technology has begun to catch up. Even the more complicated problem of coping with multiple warheads appears capable of resolution.

The former Presidential advisor for science and technology, Jerome B. Wiesner, who first opposed the ABM as technically infeasible, sought, in 1965, to promote a three-year Soviet-United States moratorium on the deployment of anti-missile missile systems, on the grounds that any attempt to build a defense against missiles would trigger a United States-Soviet arms race in offensive as well as defensive missiles. He further argued that a U.S. decision to build an ABM would "destabilize" the existing strategic balance and disrupt the emerging Soviet-American détente. Apparently, the opponents of the ABM cannot see that the stability of the present situation is a function of U.S. strategic superiority and national will power, and that the acquisition of an effective ABM by the Soviets in advance of the United States could seriously jeopar-

dize that U.S. superiority to the point where it will become less rational and less responsible for a future President to protect the security of this country by taking the kind of decision which President Kennedy was able to take during the Cuba missile crisis.

Jeremy Stone, in the paper on "Risks, Costs and Alternatives" in this volume, bases his case on the best of all possible worlds. He tends to assume that the probability of nuclear war, in the minds of both the Soviets and ourselves, will remain low; that Soviet development of BMD implies no intention to deploy it; that General Talensky is but one military voice in the U.S.S.R. whom we have no good reason to take as the dominant one; and that BMD probably will not work very well anyway. He concludes that the United States should not be the first to deploy BMD because it might set off an undesirable "arms race." The type of argumentation he employs suggests paradoxically that a U.S. decision to acquire BMD might have negative results for national security, whereas a failure to acquire it would have beneficial effects. This, if true, would make BMD rather unique in the whole history of defensive weapons systems.

Actually, there is less chance that BMD will set off a disturbing arms race if the United States takes its own initiatives in this field, developing and deploying anti-ballistic missiles at a gradual pace set by its own requirements for deterrence and security. In this way, the United States will avoid falling behind the U.S.S.R., which can also be expected to make decisions essential to its own security irrespective of what the United States might do. If the American public should someday come to believe that the Soviets have deployed a significant defense capability ahead of the U.S., and if the Soviets should begin boasting of the implications of this for the world power equation, there would probably be an anxiety reaction in the United States similar to that of the post-sputnik period. The compelling desire for the United States to "catch up" as quickly as possible could then produce more dangerous tensions and temptations than a U.S. decision to deploy early rather than late.

The argument has gained currency since October 1964, when the Chinese tested their first nuclear weapon, that the United States should develop and deploy a ballistic missile defense system in order to neutralize the nuclear threat which aggressive "nth" countries might pose in the years ahead. This contention has a good deal of merit, but it is misleading insofar as it might convey the impression that China is the only threat against which the ABM should be developed. The ABM is far more needed to counter the rapidly growing arsenal of accurate, high-payload Soviet ICBM's. The Soviets are much more committed to ballistic missile defense than we are, not merely against the threat of smaller nuclear powers, but to reduce the U.S. margin of superiority. If it makes sense to them, it should make some sense to us. But while the Soviets are deploying an ABM the U.S. is still studying and pondering the problem.

A defensive missile capability is far more vital for the United States than for the Soviet Union. It can be argued that the U.S. should possess an ABM capability because it would not make a first strike on the Soviet Union, and so if war ensued, the U.S. would be the defender. Therefore, United States policy—at least in theory—is to be in a position to survive such an attack. A

freeze or reduction in strategic missiles, combined with a "go-slow" policy on the development and employment of an anti-missile weapon in the U.S. and a "go-fast" policy in the Soviet Union, might conceivably contribute temporarily to the atmosphere of détente by making Soviet strategic planners quite happy, but it will also weaken the defenses of the United States in the decade of the 1970's.

Since 1965, the United States has pressed for an agreement prohibiting the further spread of nuclear weapons. Spokesmen of the Administration have described such an agreement as the most important issue facing mankind. Influential public figures have assured the American people that unless the United States and the Soviet Union are able to agree on this issue, mankind courts disaster.

Presumably, the world will be a more dangerous place in which to live if other nations acquire nuclear weapons. Hence, we must seek to hold the present membership of the nuclear club to the United States, the Soviet Union, the United Kingdom, France and Communist China. No advocate of the anti-proliferation treaty, however, has been able to demonstrate convincingly how the signing of a non-proliferation agreement will guarantee limiting the nuclear club to its present membership. At the same time, both proponents and opponents of the treaty agree that one inescapable result of its signing would be the diplomatic embarrassment and isolation of West Germany and the weakening, if not the destruction, of the North Atlantic Treaty Organization which, until quite recently, has been regarded as the bulwark of United States security.

It is interesting to look at the anti-proliferation issue from the perspective of the National Citizens' Commission on Arms Control and Disarmament chaired by Jerome Wiesner:

The search for détente and the loosening of the ties of the Pact in the East has implications for the Western Alliance. The military element in Western relations must not be viewed as central, and accordingly should be given less emphasis. . . .

Solutions to the nuclear problem of the Alliance should be sought in arrangements that do not result in the creation of new nuclear forces. One possible method which meets this condition is the "Select Committee" that the Secretary of Defense has recently suggested. Properly developed, this would provide for more involvement of our Western European allies, especially Germany, Great Britain, France (if she so desires), Italy in a genuine dialogue on the detailed business of planning for the Alliance's strategic force. The point of such a Committee is to give practical institutional substance to the proposition that the U.S. nuclear forces *are* the Alliance Strategic Force.[15]

The Soviet Union has long sought to encourage divisive tendencies in the Atlantic Alliance. It is clear that the Soviets have seized upon two factors— the widespread desire in the West for a non-proliferation agreement and the divergence of political interests among the Western allies (which makes it impossible for the allies to reach agreement on sharing in nuclear weapons control and strategy planning at this time) to compound the crisis facing NATO.

The Soviet Union does not need a treaty to keep it from giving either nuclear information or weapons to other nations, for it has evinced no desire to do this anyway. Nor would the contemplated treaty prevent India, Israel or even Germany from acquiring nuclear weapons if they really wanted to build them. Hence, the proposed treaty would not materially effect the international security situation. On the other hand, if a treaty should be signed on the basis of the terms demanded by the Soviets for the last two years, this would make certain that Western Germany remains politically a second-class nation within the NATO Alliance. The Soviets have consistently refused to conclude a non-proliferation agreement unless their terms are met. It is not even enough that all plans for allied nuclear arrangements within NATO (such as MLF) be shelved; they must be formally renounced in the treaty, and the Federal Republic (which is the only nation in the world which has already signed an international treaty promising not to manufacture nuclear weapons),[16] must virtually be singled out by name in the non-proliferation treaty as the culprit with sinister ambitions. Using the issue for their own political ends, the patient and persistent Soviets appear to be playing an astute diplomatic game designed to compound the already severe political problems facing the Alliance. The efforts to negotiate an anti-proliferation treaty, even if they do not result in an agreement, provide Moscow with the opportunity of dividing the Atlantic Alliance and turning the political climate more than ever against the creation of a NATO nuclear force. If the treaty is signed, the Soviet Union will be able to influence the character of Western defense policies, by questioning whether NATO arrangements contravene the agreement.

The only two nuclear powers that will threaten the United States within the foreseeable future are the Soviet Union and eventually Communist China. The anti-proliferation treaty will do nothing to decrease the threat posed by these two powerful communist states. On the other hand, the U.S. deployment of an anti-ballistic missile system could provide a non-provocative means of inducing Soviet and Chinese Communist good behavior vis-à-vis the United States. But we may never deploy an ABM if a freeze on strategic defensive as well as offensive weapons systems is the next agreement pursued with Moscow. In fact, some urge the U.S. not to take decisions leading to even a token deployment of an ABM out of fear of upsetting current negotiations with the Soviet Union for a non-proliferation treaty. It is not inconceivable that in the future Japan, India and our NATO allies might want ABM defenses against Chinese Communist and Soviet missile threats. But if we signed an anti-proliferation treaty we could not help them acquire such defenses since a successful ABM system will require the use of nuclear warheads.

The avowed purpose of the non-proliferation treaty is to inhibit the increase in the number of nations armed with nuclear weapons. The pursuit of this goal, however, does not require a treaty. Nor does a treaty make the non-proliferation goal more attainable. By signing the treaty, the Soviet Union would merely agree to continue what she is already doing, namely, to keep her nuclear weapons to herself. The United States would continue with its present policy of not sharing nuclear weapons with anybody. This being the case, one is tempted to ask why the United States should sign a treaty that 1) is unnecessary; 2) is unenforceable unless the U.S. is willing to contemplate the use of coercion against nations newly acquiring nuclear weapons; 3) will increase rather than decrease the worldwide security obligations of the United

States; and 4) will provide the Soviet Union with a tool for applying leverage against a politically beleaguered NATO.

The arguments *against* a U.S. ABM defense and a NATO nuclear force and *for* the conclusion of an anti-proliferation treaty with the Soviet Union are based on essentially the same rationale: because of the Soviet Union's technological and economic growth, her interest in self-preservation now takes priority over ideological expansion. "Peaceful coexistence," initially a tactical expedient, we are told, has become the genuine aim of Soviet policy. Because some of us presume to know Soviet intentions, the rest of us are urged to ignore the Soviet military capability.

On Balance

No sweeping judgment can be made as to whether arms control contributes to or detracts from U.S. national security. Some forms of arms control may be desirable; other forms may not be. Each proposal must be scrutinized on its own merits in a strategic context. Measures which genuinely reduce the possibilities of war by accident, strategic miscalculation, or uncontrolled escalation are worth pursuing. Much can be done in this area through our own unilateral decisions based upon intelligent military planning. These objectives can be secured by imposing the proper political, administrative, and technical controls upon whatever types of weapons systems are deemed necessary to ensure the strategic superiority of the United States. The creation of highly reliable systems of command, control and communications, the development of credible decision-making arrangements among the Western allies, and the ability to communicate to the adversary our unambiguous defensive intentions will do more to keep the peace than premature offers to downgrade the quality of military technology upon which the Western deterrent depends.

Hans Bethe, referring to why scientists must be willing to work on nuclear weapons, wrote:

They must do this also because our present struggle is (fortunately) not carried on in actual warfare which has become an absurdity, but in technical development for a potential war which nobody expects to come. The scientists must preserve the precarious balance of armament which would make it disastrous for either side to start a war. Only then can we argue for and embark on more constructive ventures like disarmament and international cooperation which may eventually lead to a more definite peace.[17]

In view of the fact that the Soviets and the United States have as yet reached no agreement which leads to genuine, safeguarded and reciprocal disarmament, it would seem that Bethe's judgment is still just as valid today as it was in 1958. If anything, the balance has become more precarious as the evidence mounts that the Soviet Union is well on the way toward deploying an operational ABM system—while the United States still debates whether such a system is worth the price.

Consequently, one of the greatest dangers which arms control poses to U.S. security lies in the possibility that a series of partial measures, combined with a euphoric atmosphere of détente, will produce an adverse cumulative effect upon the national security and R & D effort long before it has been definitely established that the Soviet Union and other communist states subscribe to the same idea of arms control as do Western governments. Perhaps one cannot demonstrate to the perfect satisfaction of policymakers that any single measure, whether unilateral or bilateral, jeopardizes the national security. But a number of factors taken together—e.g., the Test Ban Treaty and a freeze on strategic offensive and defensive weapons—might well upset the delicate balance of United States strategic advantage which has thus far underwritten whatever degree of peace of the political quality it prefers the non-communist world has enjoyed in the nuclear age. U.S. policymakers would do well to ask themselves what may happen to the American security position if this country pursues "stability" for many years, while the Soviets attempt to exploit the "arms control" rationality of the West to create an international atmosphere of political détente for achieving, first, strategic parity, and subsequently, strategic preponderance.

Notes

[1] National Citizens' Commission, *Report of the Committee on Arms Control and Disarmament*, November 28 to December 1, 1965, Washington D.C., p. 14. The Chairman of this Committee, Dr. Jerome B. Wiesner, was former Special Consultant to the President for Science and Technology.

[2] *A Thousand Days* (Boston: Houghton Mifflin, 1965), p. 504.

[3] Seymour Melman declares that "the gains that could be obtained for the security of humankind by the relaxation of the arms race are so substantial as to be well worth the risks of successful evasion that may be involved in concluding disarmament agreements." *Inspection for Disarmament* (New York: Columbia University Press, 1958), p. 4.

[4] Erich Fromm, "The Case for Unilateral Disarmament," *Arms Control, Disarmament and National Security*, ed. Donald G. Brennan (New York:

George Braziller, 1961), p. 196.

[5] Richard B. Foster, "Unilateral Arms Control Measures and Disarmament Negotiations," *Orbis*, Summer 1962, p. 265.

[6] Chalmers Roberts, *The Washington Post*, 24 November 1965, p. 7. Senator Jackson is Chairman of the Joint Atomic Energy Committee's Military Applications Subcommittee and is a member of the Senate Preparedness Subcommittee of the Armed Services Committee.

[7] In his message to the opening session of the Eighteen Nation Disarmament Committee at Geneva in January 1964, President Johnson proposed the exploration of "a verified freeze of the number and characteristics of strategic nuclear offensive and defensive vehicles," *Washington Post*, 22 January 1964. It bears pointing out that the President avoided any reference to *equal* numbers of missiles.

[8] General Colonel Nikolai A. Lomov, "The Influence of Soviet Military Doctrine on the Development of Military Art," from *Communist of the Armed Forces*, November 1965, translated by Harriet Fast Scott.

[9] *Ibid.*

[10] *Ibid.* (emphasis supplied).

[11] V. D. Sokolovskii, ed., *Military Strategy*, RAND Corporation edition annotated and analyzed by Herbert H. Dinerstein, Leon Gouré and Thomas W. Wolfe (Englewood Cliffs, N.J.: Prentice Hall, Inc., 1963), pp. 59-60.

[12] Lomov, *op. cit.*

[13] Lomov, *op. cit.*

[14] "Defense Against Ballistic Missiles," *Bulletin of the Atomic Scientists,* June 1964, p. 14.

[15] Report of the Committee on Arms Control and Disarmament, *op. cit.*, p. 22.

[16] Compare Article 2, Protocol III, signed at Paris on 23 October 1954, with the Brussels Treaty, creating a Western European Union (WEU). Text in Wayland Young, *Existing Mechanisms of Arms Control* (London: Pergamon Press, 1966), p. 94.

[17] Robert Jungk's "Brighter Than a Thousand Suns," Review in *Bulletin of the Atomic Scientists,* December 1958, p. 428.

Chapter 2

ARMS CONTROL
AND THE ATLANTIC ALLIANCE

A French View

By *Marc E. Geneste*

Arms control is not an end in itself, but only a possible means of assuring peace. Peace will always remain the final objective. Hence, the question uppermost in the minds of Frenchmen is this: Would disarmament, and particularly nuclear disarmament, enhance the cause of peace today?

From most Frenchmen, the answer to this would be a resounding "no!" The French remember the dark Stalinist years when the Red Army was threatening Western Europe. Rightly or wrongly, they credit the A bomb for the peace they enjoyed, at least in this vital part of the world, since World War II. The French started building their own bomb when the strategy of massive retaliation from United States shores became less credible in the post-sputnik period, because it did not seem likely that the United States could be counted upon in all instances to expose its cities to missile attack in order to defend Europe against local aggression. Besides, no one living on the European Continent, not even General Norstad or General Lemnitzer, between the Red Army and the Atlantic, had the authority to shoot anything against the Red masses. Sentinels are not convincing without the authority to shoot. The French Bomb, in-tended to serve as the "Continental Bomb," was to a large extent a by-product of this apparent reluctance of American politicians to delegate their soldiers the power to do their job with modern weapons, even with the smallest Davy Crockett. The Atom was for the French the only answer to the Red Army threat, and an additional reason for the Soviets to resist temptation. It is still today an important factor on the Western side making for the establishment of a more stable balance of military power in Europe, because it reduces whatever doubts may have existed in the minds of Soviet strategic planners that a military thrust westward would be met by a nuclear response. Against the considerable potential of the Red Army mobilization, it remains, therefore, in French minds, the best guarantee of peace; one does not find many Frenchmen who would deny that World War III has been prevented primarily by the existence of nuclear weapons.

But this general agreement on the local dangers of defusing the Bomb and denuclearizing part of Europe is not the only reason for French skepticism over the practical value of nuclear disarmament efforts in the present international environment. There is another point which must be carefully considered. When one thinks of the military application of nuclear energy, one visualizes only "hell on earth" in the form of H bombs, fireballs, and fallout. In other words, he thinks of firepower only. But firepower is merely one part of the picture. The other part, in military strategy, is mobility. For instance, the Atom gives to modern submarines an unprecedented military advantage in respect to mobility, such an advantage as to render necessary the possible use of nuclear depth charges, i.e., nuclear firepower, for defense against those deadly fishes. Would it be thinkable then to discard nuclear firepower if nuclear mobility is not discarded at the same time? And if nuclear propulsion for the Navy were to be sacrificed on the altar of nuclear disarmament, would it be wise to give up nuclear propulsion for merchant ships as well? It would be quite incongruous to have a nuclear merchant marine protected by a conventional navy. This maritime example illustrates the fact that, whether we like it or not, we do live in the nuclear age. The clock cannot be turned back, nor can the genie be put back into the bottle from which he escaped. Instead of seeking refuge in Utopian dreams of a return to a pre-atomic condition, we would do better to face squarely the reality with which we have to live.

We know too, from bitter past experience, that people can fight without sophisticated weapons. The French experience in two "wars of liberation," in Indochina and in Algeria, has proved that shotguns, kitchen knives and homemade grenades constitute a very effective weaponry in the hands of dedicated men. The communists have absolutely mastered the techniques of using such weaponry coupled with psychological techniques in their strategy of national liberation wars. Do we seriously believe that an agreement on disarmament and arms control could possibly extend down to shotguns and kitchen knives? This would give back to sheer numbers the military advantage and nullify the quality factor on which rests the present security of Western man. In that sense, it is absolutely meaningless to try to control physical capabilities unless there is hope for real progress in the direction of controlling political intentions, and this is quite another matter!

Finally, assuming that the control of military capabilities could be established satisfactorily on the planet, there is one capability which cannot be limited: the capability of mind, science and technology. If, for one reason or another, war should break out anyway in a "denuclearized'" world, what could possibly prevent one opponent from building Atom Bombs during the protracted course of the conflict?

Just before the gunpowder age, a Franco-British war lasted one hundred years. If armament would be "controlled down" to limit the national arsenal to bows and arrows, the length of the possible conflict would leave plenty of time to "re-invent" TNT and the Atom Bomb before the end of it. The world cannot be "denuclearized." Any conflict would become nuclear even if the Bomb is discarded during peacetime. Then the question of nuclear disarmament boils down to the following: does the existence of nuclear weaponry in peacetime help or hamper the initiating of conflicts? Would the "prospective" bomb—assuming nuclear disarmament —enjoy the same power as the bomb-in-being to deter or to limit "conventional" wars? The bomb-in-being has already demonstrated—in Korea, in Vietnam, and in Suez—its value to limit brush-fires. There is reason to fear that any brushfire starting in a "denuclearized" world might get out of control much more easily, and finally bring about a nuclear conflagration. Furthermore, as far as a compulsory control system and "police force" is concerned, the Germans in World War II possessed a very effective police force and control system in Europe and decided to limit French armaments to bows and arrows; they completely failed. One half to two thirds of the French firearms were sequestered despite the effectiveness of the Gestapo. No control system can be made to work without the consent of the people to be controlled: in other words, a World Police would have to be fully accepted by everyone to be effective, and we are a long way from that.

To sum it up, nuclear disarmament, for the time being, does not appear feasible and may be not even desirable. But this situation might change as time goes by because nuclear weapons are gradually building up the psychological prerequisites for serious business in disarmament—a point to be touched upon.

Another problem presently very worrisome to the members of the Nuclear Club is nuclear proliferation, a subject on which France is in the limelight. This is an extremely serious matter which deserves both careful scrutiny and an unimpassioned approach; it seldom receives either. Here again, we are compelled to recognize the facts of life in an age of nuclear technology. *Nuclear Engineering,* written by nuclear engineers whose interest is purely technical and who are authorities in their field, in an article entitled "Swords and Plowshares," put it this way:

The raw materials of bomb architecture, uranium-235 and plutonium-239, are also the key materials of peaceful nuclear technology. Future exploitation of nuclear power depends on providing the one and producing the other. The essential difference between war and peace is a matter of "intention."

Such a technical statement is of paramount importance for an understanding of the proliferation problem.

This very clearly means that any nation desiring to build plowshares has to produce the steel with which it could make swords. That means also that any action taken to reduce the proliferation of swords can be interpreted as the desire to retain the monopoly of plowshares for a few *beati possedentes.* There is no question that, in a time of sharp economic competition, such an interpretation cannot be avoided. To mention one practical and recent example, French scientists had to retrace the same steps and to undergo the same labors as their counterparts in the United States in order to obtain the porous barriers necessary to obtain enriched uranium. The McMahon Act prevented them from procuring already available technical information for an achievement which has not only possible military applications, but economic as well. Such an absurd waste of efforts in the field of basic nuclear technology was explained by U.S. hostility to independent nuclear forces, but, at the same time, the United States was selling to the French a fleet of KC-135 refuelling tankers necessary in order to put their "Mirage IV" in a fully operational condition. Such an apparent contradiction could easily lead to the ridiculous interpretation that the United States was more anxious to delay French nuclear efforts in the field of plowshares than in the field of swords.

The fact is, of course, that the United States, while cooperating with Britain in atomic matters, has consistently practiced atomic secrecy in its dealings with France. If some day

NATO disintegrates, a large portion of the blame will have to be laid at the door of U.S. policy. If some day the mounting tidal wave of Soviet scientists and engineers surpasses the Western achievement in science and technology, the explanation will have to be sought there, and nowhere else. Then it might be too late. In other words, the only way to prevent people from building swords, if they so desire, would be to deny them by force the capability of building their own plowshares. In the field of nuclear explosives, the U.S. project "Plowshare" is the proof that these explosives, like TNT, can have peaceful applications. How could the monopoly of dynamite be justified? It seems neither feasible nor desirable to try to keep one's allies in the Stone Age, by preserving for a few the monopoly of knowledge concerning the fabrication of enriched uranium. Whether other nations will devote part of their strength to the building of swords is their own business. Some of the prospective builders of nuclear swords have already virtually given up the idea by signing the Partial Test Ban Treaty, at least for the time being, because they probably do not feel it is worth the money, or because they hope that the armament race will be stopped, or because they have more urgent tasks. But they have probably not forfeited forever their right to acquire the implements of modern defense if some threat were to develop in the future.

To be sure, the proliferation of nuclear weapons to those not already possessing them is not a pleasant prospect. It will, in all likelihood, place additional strains upon an already strained international system, and create new problems for statesmen. But, bad as this may be, is there reason to think that it is bound to trigger the general holocaust?

One must in all intellectual honesty challenge the presumption that every national addition to the Nuclear Club necessarily increases the danger. We must keep in mind not only the numbers of nations, but also the political quality and responsibility of their governments. If the Swiss or the Swedes get their own Bomb, this will not prevent the French from sleeping. And even if a Nasser or somebody enjoying a comparable reputation for occasional mischief-making gets the Bomb, he will immediately have a sign hung on him: "this man is dangerous." Actually, his freedom of action might not be increased at all. To the contrary, he might find the gadget rather cumbersome politically, for the slightest threat against one of his neighbors would immediately bring the world's attention to the Middle East, and he would be watched like a child playing with a cigarette lighter in a powder dump.

The ability of other nations to build nuclear weapons has been questioned in the past, and the McMahon Act implied quite clearly that other nations were incapable of doing it. Other nations, however, failed to appreciate the approach. With some, it was a matter of dignity and self-respect to prove to the world and to themselves that they were not intellectually backward. Today it seems at times that it is their mental sanity which is being questioned among the members of the Club, and they do not like it. The condescending attitude of the United States is hard on national pride. Psychologically, the efforts to prevent nuclear proliferation on such premises remind one of the way in which an earlier French minister, Parmentier, managed to insure the proliferation of potatoes throughout France. Potato seeds had been imported from the United States (naturally), but no one was interested in this exotic vegetable. Parmentier hit upon the idea of putting sentinels around the King's potato fields, whereupon the French peasants reasoned that this thing must be a highly prized commodity to be so heavily guarded, and so they started stealing the Government's potatoes. The comparison between potatoes and nuclear weapons should not be pushed too far, but all the compulsory measures aiming at the interdiction of the Bomb probably incite people to steal the secrets of the Atom, rather than deter them.

One of the leading French nuclear scientists, Bertrand Goldschmidt, has summarized the French philosophy on proliferation when he recently said: "Trying to prevent proliferation of nuclear weapons is just as realistic as trying to prevent sex among youngsters. All you can do is try to discourage it; at best, all you can hope for is to delay it." Given the inevitability of proliferation among those nations which are willing to divert part of their steel from plowshares to make swords, the main danger lies in the possibility of technical accidents, that is to say, a nuclear exchange started by some erratic warning signal. This is far more serious than the likelihood of someone blowing up the planet for fun, or because of strategic miscalculation. Naturally, the proliferation of hot lines and other electronic apparatus would considerably complicate the network. It would certainly be too bad if the survival of humanity should have to depend on the reliability of an electric wire! But this particular danger, although quite real, should not be exaggerated. Assuming an electronic alert, true or false, step number one might be to go to the basement shelter, launching the anti-ballistic missiles (if any are available) and get-

ting the retaliatory force ready. Step two, pushing the deadly button, might wait for the real thing: the first thermonuclear explosion. Since everyone has apparently agreed not to shoot the first counter-city blow and in so doing has pledged to suffer the first attack, it does not seem impossible to solve the problem satisfactorily, even if the technicians cannot guarantee one hundred per cent reliability in a warning system. Here is at least one area where some agreement appears feasible and highly desirable. Arms control has to begin with limited objectives of this kind, assuming a minimum of good faith among partners.

Let us not be too skeptical and pessimistic about the whole subject. Nuclear disarmament is probably not feasible today. It might become possible tomorrow, because the nuclear weapon in the arsenals of nations is creating slowly the psychological prerequisites, if not for its own demise at least perhaps for the transformation into an international guarantor of peace. Like the monster of the Stone Age, the nuclear bomb and war itself as instruments of national policy might eventually die of their overweight.

It is extremely interesting to notice in Europe, at least in France and probably in Germany, to what extent the old values are changing. It seems that the soldier, the warrior, is gradually losing the first place he had for one thousand years in the minds of young men to be replaced by the scientist, the engineer or the cosmonaut; that military achievement, which not so long ago was the only sure "path of glory," is gradually being replaced by other forms of action, by other types of conquest. It would be interesting to analyze, among the real causes of the two World Wars, the responsibility traceable to the ego of Wilhelm II and of Adolf Hitler. It might be possible that they wanted to earn, through military victories, the historic title of "Conquerors," like Alexander the Great or Napoleon. It might even be possible that many Chiefs of State, in the past, felt compelled to seek their glory in this direction even when their personal predilections were rather peaceful. This was the case with Napoleon III, living in the shadow of his famous uncle, Bonaparte. In that connection, Nikita Khrushchev found in the nuclear weapon a handy excuse to resist the "adventurism" of his extremists.

The Atom now stands as a formidable roadblock along the old path of glory. The fantastic absurdity of war appears to European children when they watch the television showing sequences of Verdun or other massacres; they are thereby prompted to question the mental sanity of their forefathers. War, some day, might appear to be a scourge of the past, like plague or cholera. No contemporary thinker would dare to present an *apologia* for war, as Nietzsche did in the 1880's. Beyond the living examples of two World Wars still vivid in Europe, the grim specter of nuclear war (this modern guise of the Black Death which took the lives of one half of Christendom) is very effective and necessary to complete the picture. Fear is the beginning of wisdom. The nuclear weapon might some day appear as the best medicine humanity had to take in order to be cured of its age-old sickness. We would be unwise to abandon the remedy when apparently it is just beginning to work. It might even work for the Chinese, and give their leaders something to think about. In spite of certain spoken threats by Communist leaders who are not averse to exploiting the West's fear of China's huge population, one is entitled to hope that 3500 years

of civilization might yet count for something.

But, naturally, the major question is: What should be the exact dose of the remedy? This is the number one problem of arms control today. In the long history of armaments, from stones to the H Bomb, one would not find the kind of firebreak we have reached today. We are confronted with a unique opportunity; such an opportunity we might never find again if we do not seize it now. The nuclear weapon has finally created a world-wide community: the community of hostages—the solidarity of hostages living naked and defenseless, under a reciprocal threat, on the Plateau of Deterrence. On this Plateau, they are condemned at least to nuclear peace, under penalty of death. This is an uneasy peace, of course, but much better than no peace at all. It does not matter very much if newcomers want to climb onto the Plateau. What does really matter is whether we shall be content to stay there, waiting for the time when nuclear and other armaments will appear so useless, and war so obsolete, that the steel of swords will be turned back to plowshares. *Or* shall we try to leave the Plateau and climb further? Shall we try to break the present stalemate, to jump over the firebreak, to close the gigantic gap between the present means of offense and defense in strategic exchanges? To be sure, the technicians have found the theoretical way of bridging the firebreak: anti-ballistic missiles, military satellites, moon bases and the like, coupled with civil defense, fallout shelters, and a life of cavemen. But the cost of achieving a military posture able to guarantee a hundred per cent hermetic stratospheric Maginot Line appears gigantic, as limitless as space itself, if we want to check all the possibilities that offense has already found or will eventually find in outer space. Military satellites, orbital bombs and other new germs of the modern "Black Death" might remain in the status of potentialities (like some of the more frightful agents of biological and chemical warfare). Should we then launch from the Plateau a new armament race in space, which might eventually give back to the armies their freedom of action, make war, once again, an instrument of policy and clear once more the old paths of glory? Or shall we stay where we are, protected by the psychological defensive line of nuclear peace that the international hostage system has given us? Is not this strange system, however weird, the best assurance we have to defuse human ambitions, to control intentions and later to limit capabilities?

Today and for a long time to come only two nations can break this state of affairs, if they so desire: the United States and the U.S.S.R. It depends on their choice to stop now the deadly race on the plateau, a race which began with the beginning of human time. Their considerable quantitative and qualitative advancement in nuclear and missile technology makes them safe vis-à-vis all others, including the Chinese, and their capability of going further is in itself a deterrent. If those in the vanguard agree to stop, then the rest will follow suit and probably stay where they are. Only then will it become realistic to contemplate the best technical ways of controlling the process of arms reduction, assuming naturally that the Chinese will be party to the agreement.

The French have proposed first to discard the ICBM rockets and other bulky hardware items of this kind, because they are easier to control and because these gadgets, unlike nuclear explosives, clearly have no peaceful vocation. But technicalities are not very important, once intentions are clearly demonstrated in good faith.

The United States and the U.S.S.R. are leading by years or decades in the armament competition. It is their responsibility to reverse the trend. Some spark of understanding has already been noticed between them, and it is theirs to kindle into the light of hope. Arms control is primarily in the hands of the two nuclear knights. Noblesse oblige! This might help to explain why the chair of France is temporarily empty in Geneva.

A German View

By Helmut Schmidt

Before examining the subject of arms control in Europe, it is advisable to make two observations. First, I presuppose that at present, and for the foreseeable future, it is imperative for the West to maintain an overall qualitative and quantitative balance of military forces, and thereby hold an overall balance of political power.

My second presupposition is that the necessities of equilibrium require not one single power balance over the globe as a whole, but a stably balanced position in each theater, such as Southeast Asia or the Near East or Europe and the Atlantic Area.

All thinking and any action on arms control policies such as non-proliferation or the test-ban weapons-cutback must be considered first for their effect upon the foregoing postulates.

We Germans foresee a growing awareness in both East and West of a lasting equilibrium in Central Europe. We fear that European publics and statesmen will become quite satisfied—indeed, too satisfied—with the existing situation of a divided Germany and a divided Europe. The German people, however, cannot feel satisfied with a mere stabilization or consolidation of the status quo if this excludes progress,

or at least the hope and expectation of progress, toward eventual national reunification.

At present, approximately two-thirds of the ordinary people of Western Germany attach the highest importance among all problems of German politics to security from Soviet Communism and to reunification. Gallup Polls have shown that over the past four or five years, the issue of reunification has become increasingly crucial in the mind of the general public, and this understandable concern, in my judgment, far from subsiding in the years immediately ahead, will continue to grow.

Among the new generation in Germany, those born after 1935, who have no personal experience of the Nazi state or the war, and who feel no responsibility for events between 1933 and 1945, the will to reunify is bound to become quite vigorous by 1970 and yet more vigorous by 1975.

At the same time, thanks to repeated frustrations west of the Rhine, the importance of uniting Western Europe—whether by the Common Market, by de Gaulle's policy, or by other concepts —is declining in the eyes of the general public.

As a consequence of this public attitude, any future government must undoubtedly try to tie together any modification of security arrangements, including arms control measures, with steps toward reunification. Accession to a non-proliferation or total test-ban treaty can be offered on a *quid pro quo* basis for substantial moves toward reunification.

A majority of reasonable politicians, diplomats and military people in Germany realize that reunification will demand sacrifice in at least four fields:

a) The Question of the German-Polish Boundary, i.e., the Oder-Neisse Line.

b) The Quantity and Quality of German Armament, even to the point of accepting international control thereof.

c) The Alliance Status of a Reunified Germany. (The Soviet Union would never allow a reunification resulting in a unified Germany free to remain in the Western Alliance. This does not necessarily mean that the solution must provide for neutrality; one can also conceive of a Central European collective security system.)

d) The Field of Economics, Finance and Foreign Trade.

Most political leaders in Germany now will oppose any concessions, in advance of a general settlement, on the question of the Oder-Neisse Line, as long as there is no *quid pro quo*. On the other hand, one can observe growing interest and sympathy toward de Gaulle's East European policy. Still more significant, perhaps, is the growing understanding that reunification of Germany will be achieved only in the context of restoring Europe as a whole to a condition of political stability and military security.

Thus when one examines arms control from the German viewpoint, one must carefully distinguish between in-

tention and effect. Regardless of the intentions of East or West, the effects of arms agreements on a world containing a Germany united would be far different from the effects of those same agreements on a world containing a Germany partitioned.

Of immediate concern to the German observer of the current arms control negotiations is that any universal treaty that may eventually issue from them would have an "effet étatique," in favor of the so-called *Deutsche Demokratische Republik*. Because the DDR will also sign the treaty, she will attempt to enter by that means as a de facto peer into relations with all other signers and acquire rights of initiative and amendment. What applies to universal treaties applies in special measure to settlements, such as the Rapacki Plan, which apply in a special way to the Central European region only.

Anticipating the not inconceivable possibility of the conclusion of an arms control agreement between the U.S.S.R. and the West, without German consent, and to German political disadvantage, the Bonn Government would then feel constrained to enter a claim for compensation in the reunification question.

For the period of the late sixties, in which no progress toward reunification is likely to be brought about, the Federal Republic—whether governed by conservatives, social democrats or a Grosse Koalition—will act with extreme reserve on any arms control schemes which might tend to give the Federal Republic a peculiar or unequal status among the other West European nations, or which make concessions with regard to the status of the Federal Republic which in our view should only be made regarding the whole of Germany or at least in the context of steps toward reunification.

The Atlantic Alliance

If meaningful arms control is to be attained in the late sixties or the seventies, much attention must be given, in my view and that of other Germans, to the disarray afflicting that organization which is eminent among the existing guarantors of international security, namely, NATO.

Without undue strain, one could conjure up an admirable scheme to solve the intra-alliance nuclear problems, and be quite confident of its common acceptance by the U.S., U.K., Germany, Holland, and several others. But one could be equally confident that France would not join this or any other new structure agreed upon by all the others. It follows, in my view, that it would not be wise then, to press for any new organizational structure which would force de Gaulle to act in contravention.

Nevertheless, I see no cause for despair. The present situation, of course, is a most unfortunate one. We are blessed, however, by a remarkably high degree of reliability and predictability among the main partners. The reliability of the U.S., as far as its military strategy is concerned, cannot be doubted. It is safe to predict, with a note of certainty, that the U.S. will adhere to the basic principles of its strategy and military philosophy well into the next decade. There may and probably will be alterations as far as the Asian theatres are concerned; but as long as political developments in Asia do not seriously affect the European situation, there will occur no major change in the U.S. strategy in Europe. The Europeans ought to understand this, that they can rely upon the fundamental American commitment.

The Europeans also ought to understand that the motivation of the American engagement in Vietnam has to prevail—physically, politically and in the American conscience. An appreciation of this situation is steadily spreading in Germany.

One could also show with little difficulty that the policies and strategic plans of Great Britain, Holland, Germany and other members of the Alliance are equally predictable, reliable and stable.

In this relatively stable situation—stable with the glaring exception of Paris—I really do not see that new proposals for major changes in the structure of the Alliance, or the creation of new institutions, could improve the situation or change the basic policies of the participating countries and governments, most especially those of the French government. One cannot bring about unison of policies by institutional changes.

One need not stress here that the Germans deplore the development of partial political disengagement in the Alliance, in particular by France. I need not stress that Germany—because of the battlefield character of her territory and because of the unsolved German problem as a whole—will continue in the future to depend heavily on the Alliance and its power to deter and to defend.

I am quite sure that several of the contributors to this book, who have written and lectured widely on structural reforms for NATO, are in complete disagreement with my position. It would not be advantageous for any one of us, however, to produce still more proposals. We have already a literature of hundreds of books and thousands of papers; there have been multitudinous conferences and there exist whole orders of battle of standing committees—all to the sole purpose of reforming NATO, and all to no avail.

Since the demise of MLF/ANF, no government has submitted a concrete proposal. The position of the French is altogether unclear. Since 1958 they have carped and criticized but have never tabled a clear-cut proposal. My advice would be to adjourn the Alliance-wide nervousness about reform until the French government does, in fact, table a proposal. In the meantime, the allied governments should make full use of the existing machinery, instead of talking endlessly about new institutions. For example, if the U.S. representative to the NATO Council would regularly debate the problems of nuclear strategy within the Council, I am sure the French representative would never leave the session. The regular common analysis of nuclear strategy would be an immense aid to the spread of understanding and education among allied governments.

Nuclear education is certainly one of the desperate needs of the allies today. All partners must be brought to understand and to accept the necessity of maintaining a common and joint defense, despite the lasting fact that some partners will continue to maintain different principles and different theories of nuclear organization and strategy. If one thing is patently clear since the breakdown of the attempt of NATO Paper MC 100/1 and in the light of the sad fate of the Stikker Exercises and Ottawa Committees at Porte Dauphine, it is that no one can expect any comprehensive strategic doctrine for the Alliance to be accepted in common by the allies during the late sixties at least. There must be, however, a minimum common strategic posture. Speaking as a German, I view the possibility of one-sided numerical retreat from Central Europe as an extreme danger. We must insist upon a common military presence in Europe, capable not only of deterring but also of defending Europe, without the help of nuclear weapons against any military attack short of total war. Berlin

will remain a crisis point exposed to many kinds of threats and showdowns, many of which will not be met without the presence of sufficient Western military power of a useable kind.

Emphasis must still be placed on adequate numbers of conventional troops on European soil, on mobility of those troops and on adequate conventional tactical airpower in Europe.

The decline of unity within the Alliance is obviously the direct result of the feeling of a diminution of the Russian threat. To be sure, if the threat was to be perceived to have again become acute the Alliance would snap together like filings to a magnet, but the warm wind of détente now blows and with it come the factional squalls of national autonomy.

The French government knows that its policy of autonomy is wholly dependent not only on the continuation of the present thaw, but also on the durability of the present balance of military power in Europe, dependent as it is upon the American nuclear capability, upon the maintenance of the relation of ground forces on both sides of the iron curtain in Europe, and upon the continuation of the American physical presence on the spot. These three factors our French friends often hesitate to acknowledge, but as long as they exist, France will follow her present policy of autonomy.

In December 1965, at the NATO Parliamentarians Conference in New York, I said that I did not see any reason not to trust the General when he declared he would not renounce the Alliance as such. Today I am less sure. One can at least predict that France will renounce her present military doctrine of nuclear retaliation and first (if not pre-emptive) strike when she approaches the third generation of nuclear weapons systems, i.e., mobile rockets.

One can also safely predict that even if she leaves NATO by 1969, she will, as far as her security vis-à-vis the East is concerned, rely upon the Atlantic Treaty and especially upon the U.S. French objectives toward EEC and NATO are much less clear. The question is whether the General is really aiming at the restoration of Europe or merely at the restoration of France as a world power.

I repeat that this must not be cause for despair or for overdramatization. All of us should strive to regain our composure and our calm. It is indeed a pity that the North Atlantic Defense Community is now in the process of transforming itself into a nineteenth century alliance instead of moving toward greater integration. But we must and we shall be glad to maintain the Atlantic Alliance as an Alliance of partners, who commit themselves to mutual military assistance in the case of attack.

Germany and Nuclear Proliferation

There exists a slight difference of political opinion in Germany toward the strategic debate taking place within NATO. Both parties agree more or less with the McNamara strategy of flexible response, but inside the governing party there are some influential people, among whom I must name the late Dr. Adenauer and Franz Josef Strauss, who have publicly questioned whether de Gaulle's criticisms of American strategy are based, at least partially, on a correct analysis of the direction which U.S. strategic thought has been taking since the early 1960's. The CDU people in general do agree to the principles of flexible response and graduated deterrence; but they are critical about this concept and they favor a very low nuclear threshold.

The Social Democrats, on the other hand, are not critical of the substance of the McNamara strategy, but they do object strongly to the way the U.S. government announces its changing views as *faits accomplis* to the whole public, and then to its allies, without even the window-dressing of discussion among its partners, let alone common deliberation with them.

The conservative government and the SPD opposition were therefore—even if reluctantly—originally in favor of the MLF because they wanted to act in unison with the U.S., a cooperation considered absolutely essential by both parties, for the security of Berlin and of the Federal Republic. There was also the advantage that the MLF would give the Federal Republic a more nearly equal status within the Alliance than she has at present. It has become sufficiently obvious, however, that the U.S. will not again embark on the idea of an MLF fleet. The whole issue is dead. Thus agreeing with Strauss, but disagreeing with some voices in Bonn, I should say that Germany ought to forget the MLF completely.

It is possible that the Christian Democrats might have continued to be very suspicious of regional and general arms control schemes and proposals, if the coalition government had not been formed. The presence of the SPD in the government is likely to produce a difference of emphasis and probably a much larger degree of flexibility in the Federal Republic's policy, but this does not mean consent to any policy affecting the balance of power in Europe such as a diminishing of the number of NATO troops on German soil. On the question of a non-proliferation treaty, one might still detect some differences of attitude between the CDU and the SPD. One hears in Bonn today that Germany, having declared in 1954 that she would not produce nuclear weapons, should go no further until the nuclear question within NATO is settled in a manner equitable to Germany, and not without obtaining Russian concessions on the reunification question.

In my view the second, if not the first, of these conditions is unrealistic. German diplomacy on the question of a non-proliferation treaty must not allow Germany to be maneuvered into a position in which she can be made to appear responsible for a failure in the non-proliferation negotiations, and put thereby into psychological isolation. Conclusion of such a pact would not be against German interests provided the Alliance remains free to decide its own best internal nuclear policy.

I should reemphasize that no fundamental change in the present nuclear strategy or in the present nuclear organization—especially no solution involving physical possession—is necessary. Let the so-called "McNamara Committee" be developed. In the long run it should certainly not be necessary for all NATO members to acquire physical possession of nuclear arms. I do hold, however, that it will be essential for all partners who are willing to engage themselves and to participate in nuclear planning to be given the opportunity to do so.

There is one further demand on which I would insist. Every government inside the Alliance should have the right of veto in the event that nuclear weapons of the Alliance are going to be launched in a strike from the national soil of that government only; or if nuclear weapons of Alliance partners are going to be used against targets only on the national soil for which that government is responsible. This is, of course, most pertinent to the German situation where most of the tactical targets and most of the tactical weapons

for most foreseeable conflict are located on German soil.

Conclusion

In sum, it can be said that the most fruitful area of arms control measures would be the area of communication and command/control.

The development of a more practical and effective system of inter-governmental cooperation in times of crisis is certainly a great need. The telecommunications apparatus of today is obsolete. A vastly improved communications system will be utterly essential if France withdraws from the Treaty. Washington, London, Bonn and Paris could hardly rely on the existing system of communication between heads of state and between various levels of executive officers of the respective governments. In future crises in such places as Berlin one cannot afford another fiasco of non-cooperation and non-coordination such as scandalized the world on 13 August 1961, when the Wall began to rise.

I should repeat that equilibrium of military forces remains an unalterable necessity, with or without arms control and with or without France. As long as there is no prospect of reunification, Germany will stick to the Alliance to make this equilibrium possible and lasting. This attitude reflects that of both major German parties and the vast majority of public opinion in Germany. It will remain the solid basis of German foreign policy throughout the late sixties and far beyond, regardless of the cyclic Russian thaws and the inter-allied rivalries and disputes, which crop up from time to time to compound the diplomatic headaches of those who—despite their squabbles—maintain a fundamental solidarity in the common defense of their national freedom and integrity.

The World Without NATO

By Robert Strausz-Hupé

NATO, like all social institutions, can be easily defined in the abstract; its workaday concreteness is not readily perceptible to the senses. The men and weapons assigned to NATO are "real;" according to reliable evidence, they exist. But their effective role as instruments of the Western Alliance can be inferred only from events which confirmed or failed to confirm a hypothesis, namely, that the Soviets meant to conquer Western Europe and that the Western Alliance could thwart Soviet intentions. Empirically, this hypothesis is unprovable. This does not mean, however, that it is not meaningful. It shares this distinction with all hypotheses about existential conditions. The functional effectiveness of NATO as a military alliance can be deduced only from a non-happening: The Soviets did not attack. But is that alliance which deters rather than fights aggression not the most effective kind of alliance? If this proposition holds, then NATO accomplished its mission. Conceived as a military alliance, it wrought political changes which its founders may not have intended and, certainly, did not foresee. On all counts, NATO has been as effective as any alliance organization has ever been.

It is idle to debate as to whether the communists, because they have not invaded Europe, have never intended to invade it, or as to whether, had NATO never existed, the communist threat could have been met by other devices, or might have waned because of restraints other than the counterpoise of the Western Alliance. The fact is that the Western peoples perceived the communist threat as real, and that NATO provided that climate of security and confidence in which Europe achieved political stability and economic prosperity. Hence, trying to envisage the world without NATO is, in the first place, an essay in conjecture about the West European peoples' perception of their security requirements and about the attitudes of the Soviets towards a Western Europe no longer bound to the United States by a treaty of mutual defense. Then, the conjectural alternatives of the West European-Soviet relationship might provide the basis for designing hypotheses about the global consequences which would flow from the demise of NATO.

Here, one assumption should be stated explicitly: the United States will seek to perpetuate NATO since it deems NATO of lasting value to its own and

58

the West's defense, or a means of maintaining its control over the policies of the West European states, or a useful bargaining tool in its dealings with the Soviets, or an outlet for its universalist emotions. In the light of the past, this seems a reasonable assumption. The assumption that NATO will just fade away is explicitly rejected. No alliance has gone out of business of its own accord. Always, one or several parties have pushed what was falling. Thus, the departure of NATO from the world scene will have been prompted and, certainly, speeded by the initiative of one or several European states.

What are the perceptions of the world and their own place in it which could induce European statesmen and their peoples to quit NATO? There is the widely held idea of the U.S./Soviet nuclear stalemate, or rather, its enduring, static nature. If this idea reflects an accurate evaluation of the military/technological environment, then the leaders of America and the Soviet Union, generally presumed to be rational, will eschew a mutually suicidal war. They will, as a matter of course, refrain from those provocative moves in Europe, where they confront one another directly, which could trigger general nuclear war. Thus, the very purpose for which NATO was created, namely, defense against Soviet aggression against Europe, no longer need be served. The security needs of the European states are met by the bilateral nuclear stalemate and, therefore, do not require their individual contributions to collective defense.

True enough, no European statesman sees matters quite so simply or avows that he does. Each may well have his reservations as to how stable is the stability of mutual deterrence. Each might envisage contingencies which, arising somewhere in the world, might upset the so-called balance of terror. Nevertheless, this idea—each of the two giants immobilized by the other—inspires the new maneuverability of European diplomacy, especially French and British and, albeit less ostentatiously, Italian. It is not far-fetched to assume that this diplomacy would gladly trade in NATO for a permanent guarantee of the nuclear stalemate—if such a guarantee could be gotten in the shape of either some version or the other of the Rapacki Plan, or universal arms reduction and control agreements.

What is past is prologue. President de Gaulle has supplied the model of the new maneuverable diplomacy of a West European state which has emancipated itself from NATO. For demonstration purposes, it does not matter that, on the whole, de Gaulle has stuck to the letter of the Alliance treaty and has continued to collect the revenue from NATO-leased real estate in France. In his diplomatic dealings he behaves as if NATO does not exist. The flamboyancy of his style diverts the attention of the American public from the fact that, on not a few occasions, other European NATO members, too, have broken ranks and behaved as if they felt no longer bound by the spirit, if not the letter, of the Alliance treaty. On not a few issues such as, for example, trade with the communist bloc, the policies of Britain have been about as ambiguous as those of France. A case study of Italian meanderings between commitments to NATO and diverse postures approximating neutralism would afford some interesting insights into both the objective conditions of NATO and the unchanging pattern of Italian policy from Salandra to Fanfani.

Of course, Germany is a special case. The *Bundesrepublik* is as sovereign a state as any NATO member. It is, however, also a NATO province. It owes its sovereignty to its simultaneous accession to the West European Union and the Atlantic Alliance. It is effectively garrisoned by American and British forces; its own military forces are unreservedly placed at the disposition of NATO, thus constituting the one and only "no strings attached" NATO force. Furthermore, the German leadership expects—or, at least, has said for a long time that it expects—NATO to do for Germany what NATO need not do for any other member, namely, restore national unity. The Alliance treaty provides no warrant whatsoever for this expectation. Nonetheless, it is a fact that Chancellor Adenauer won his people's allegiance to the alliance by linking meaningfully NATO with German unity, and that, at that time, his Western sponsors did nothing to disavow this implicit promise.

Here and now, among all the peoples of the Western Alliance, the people of West Germany are the people least able to imagine a world without NATO. The *Bundesrepublik* is a part of NATO, and NATO is a part of it. For a good many years, the Western Alliance has been represented to the German public as a stepping stone towards national reunification and the combined power of the West as a lever which, over time, would pry loose the communist grip from East Germany. The disappearance of NATO would confront the West Germans with a task of reorientation, if not reeducation, about as formidable as that accomplished, in the postwar years, under the stern gaze of the victors.

West German diplomacy, too, might accommodate itself successfully to an international environment without NATO. As a matter of fact, Germany is well placed historically and geographically to emulate the new maneuverable diplomacy which her West European neighbors now so proudly pursue. In a world without NATO, the Soviet Union has much to give to the Germans, much that she now ostensibly withholds because of the very existence of NATO. With the greatest of ease, the Soviet Union can give back to Germany her national unity, and in a NATO-less world, the Germans will be free to receive this gift under any and all conditions they choose to accept.

The case of Germany is unique. Some of the ambiguities of the German condition—embedded between East and West, constrained by extra-European power, but free enough to choose between alternatives of accommodation to the competing systems—are reflected in a state of mind which modern psychology calls cognitive dissonance.[1] For obvious reasons, it would be rash to deduce from the German case generalizations about all of Western Europe. The conflict of perceptions, however, tends to blur the outlook upon international politics of all Europeans.

There is a way of coping with this kind of conflict, though not one recommended by most experts. It is possible, at least for a while, to expunge from the conscious mind all those perceptions of reality which are disturbing. By this method, Europeans can persuade themselves to reason as follows: If the nuclear stalemate exists, it will continue to exist. Its existence forecloses the possibility of an escalating conflict in Europe—and what prospect could be more cheering? Then, does it not follow that, sooner or later, the two principal parties to the nuclear stalemate, too, will perceive the real state of affairs, adjust their conduct accordingly and institutionalize the mutuality of their interest in keeping the nuclear balance from slipping? Not so surprisingly, not a few Europeans have found that this rationalization of the situation provides the easiest, the most pleasant resolution of cognitive dissonance. Thus, Europeans can feel both secure and guiltless about doing nothing to ensure their security. To indulge with good conscience in this feeling, reasonable West Europeans and, especially, their political leaders, need theories which explain why the nuclear stalemate exists, why it cannot be broken, and why both the United States and the Soviet Union will settle down to peaceful coexistence.

Several theories, not all of them necessarily contradictory, are available. In a world without NATO, these theories would form the intellectual basis of European statecraft. They can be summed up as follows: First, the destructiveness of nuclear weapons has reached an absolute limit beyond which the acquisition of additional weaponry does not insure added military advantage— an explanation which, incidentally, is being advanced by some American scientists and advocates of American/Soviet reciprocal disarmament measures. Second, the Soviet power elite, having cooled to communist ideology, is turning to domestic works of peace and putting Russia's national interest ahead of that of the Communist World Revolution. Thirdly, the Russian people, beginning to enjoy the affluence of a status society, prefer prosperous safety at home to risking conquest abroad, and popular pressures will compel the new generation of Soviet leaders to heed the average Russian's wishes. Fourth, in the United States, too, ideological fervor has abated. The anti-communist crusade is flagging, and political leadership will be progressively more reluctant to stake the survival of the Great Society on the defense of any foreign territory, non-allied or allied, courting the risk of nuclear retaliation against America.

Any one of these theories chips away at the rational foundation of NATO. Together, they bring it down. At one time or another, de Gaulle has circumlocuted each of them. More or less forthrightly, British leaders have expressed themselves in accord with all except the last. In fact, a Europe without NATO needs to embrace all of these assumptions in order to live at ease with the rest of the world and with itself.

There is a fifth theory which explains why the present balance of nuclear forces precludes nuclear war in or over Europe, and why the United States and the Soviet Union can be kept frozen in nuclear immobility: West European states, either singly or collectively, are capable of developing a nuclear deterrent of their own. This nuclear force will dissuade the Soviets from launching a nuclear attack against Europe, for the Soviets are loath to either trade their cities for West European cities or touch off a "catalytic" war, i.e., a war into which the United States might be drawn.

On the grounds of scientific/technological development and economic resources, there is no reason why Western Europe could not develop its own credible nuclear deterrent. Politically, there is every reason to assume that it will not. According to de Gaulle's somewhat tenebrous pronouncements, annotated more explicitly by Generals Beaufre and Gallois, a national nuclear deterrent serves one purpose only, namely, to deter a nuclear attack against the nation which possesses it.

Only two West European powers possess a nuclear deterrent of sorts, namely, France and Great Britain. The economic resources of neither country suffice to maintain that scientific/technological establishment which the immensely expensive development of an independent national deterrent requires and which even the two nuclear superpowers barely manage to support. De Gaulle has hinted, again in his umbrageous way, at a Franco-British merger. Even if the British were willing, de Gaulle's obsession with undiluted national sovereignty poses formidable problems of command and control: exactly who would have the finger on the trigger and the safety catch? Would either the British or the French find these problems easier to solve among themselves than does the United States in relation to its European allies? Let us assume that France and Britain are capable of this staggering feat of national self-abnegation, will their joint nuclear deterrent then suffice to deter a Soviet attack against any West European country except France and Great Britain? Of course, it would not.

Neither France nor Great Britain find it now possible to meet their quota of conventional forces which they are supposed to make available to NATO. Certainly, they cannot be expected to substitute their own levies for the American divisions in Germany were these to be withdrawn upon the dissolution of NATO.

The dissolution of NATO's conventional force structure would preclude the graduated defense of any European country from Scandinavia to the Bosphorus. Conceivably, the inclusion of the *Bundesrepublik* in the French/British merger would supply that critical increment of scientific/technological manpower resources which would make a European deterrent credible—credible this side of any strategic option except all-out suicidal response. Yet, neither the French nor the British are prepared to go nuclear shares with the Germans.

It is not realistic to assume that the Germans will content themselves with supplying an Anglo-French nuclear force with technological gadgetry while fielding the foot soldiery of the Alliance. More likely than not, the Germans, confronted with this uninviting prospect, would bethink themselves of other strategic and political alternatives.

A Swedish observer, pondering the consequences which would flow from the dissolution of NATO, has this to say about the effectiveness of a European deterrent as regards the defense of his own country and, for that matter, any other West European country:

The Soviet leaders would certainly regard the possibility of Western interventions subsequent to an attack on Sweden as far less of a drawback than if the United States were still committed to defend Western Europe. . . . It may be asserted that the Western European states, or some of them, have greater interests than the United States in preventing a Soviet invasion of Sweden from being successful and, hence, should be more willing to take risks with this aim than the United States. In all probability, however, the available resources, both on a short and long term basis, would not allow military intervention but would rather compel a greater caution than at present. The immediate result of the United States' withdrawal from Europe would be a sizeable weakening of the West's resources for conducting a European conventional war. . . . If the United States were to withdraw from Europe, the Western European countries would probably find it necessary to allocate more resources to nuclear arms than now in order to compensate for the absence of the American guarantee.[2]

Neither France nor Great Britain singly nor a Franco-British nuclear consortium can furnish a credible guarantee of the defense of any other West European country. Conceivably, a post-Gaullist France might abandon the quaint concept of a Europe of the Fatherlands. Even then, a Western Europe, deprived of the NATO shelter, could not achieve that level of armament and military integration which could supply the basis for a Third Force in world politics.

By now, it should be clear that Western Europe's progress upon the road of economic integration has led nowhere politically. It can now be seen that the miscarriage of the European Defense Community project diverted Europe from the political high-road to integration to economic/functional byways. The latter have led Europe to unprecedented prosperity. Prosperity has not strengthened the will to political integration; it has deadened it. For example, the European Economic Community, having knuckled under to de Gaulle's demands, has quietly buried the high hopes for political integration which, once upon a time, its members pinned upon the Treaty of Rome. It has absorbed the European Coal and Steel Community and thus watered down the supranational powers of this, the boldest experiment in European functional integration.

More likely than not, a Europe without NATO will seek to persist in the enjoyment of commercial advantages accruing from cooperative trade arrangements. There is no empirical evidence whatsoever for avowing that an international trading consortium transforms itself, as a matter of course, into a political union. A Europe without NATO will be a divided and not a united Europe. It will be the divided Europe of 1939 with one difference: it will be weak militarily. Such a Balkanized Europe would invite piecemeal

aggression—the very salami tactics which the communists have advanced to such a high state of perfection. It is difficult to see how the smaller states of Europe, especially those in the vicinity of the communist bloc, could resist the temptation to insure their survival by making compromise deals, Finland-style, with the Soviets. Even under present circumstances, some of the citizens of the smaller countries do not fully credit the American guarantee of European security, enshrined in the Atlantic Pact and betokened by the American physical presence. They would have an easy time convincing their more trusting fellow citizens that a Europe without NATO and without the Americans is not the right place for standing up to the "reasonable" demands of the Soviets. What demands are not reasonable when one has no other choice but to accept them?

Throughout the last two decades, Europeans, for the first time in their history, have become aware of themselves as Europeans. Their ancient rivalries have abated, and, to their own and everybody else's surprise, the ancient and jealous nation states of Europe have engaged in great common undertakings. This miracle unfolded under the umbrella of NATO. Once that umbrella is removed, the whole of Europe will be exposed to forces from without vastly more powerful than her own. Whatever might be the European purposes of Russia—be she ideologically zestful, or be she ideologically quiescent and merely bent upon the pursuit of her national interests—she can hardly be expected to smile upon the unification of Europe—except under her own domination. If the postwar years can be said to have taught one categoric lesson, it is that economic and political development are variables that depend on one and the same factor, namely, security against direct or indirect aggression from without. The dissolution of NATO will reverse Europe's economic and political development from the 1940s to date.

By definition, the dissolution of NATO will cancel out all the gains which have been made in the direction of Atlantic cooperation, economic, political and military. This reversal will take place at a time when the resources of all the Atlantic peoples will probably be strained to the breaking point by the revolutionary transformation of the non-Western world. At present, the greatest single short-coming of NATO is the poor coordination which it provides for the policies of its members confronted by crisis situations outside the nominal region of the Alliance. Yet the NATO machinery, rickety as it is, has served as a coordinator of a kind, keeping the West from flying apart at critical moments in various hours-of-truth such as the several post-war crises in the Middle and the Far East and the Cuban Missile crisis. Certainly, the machinery needs improving. Were it dismantled, its absence would increase the already crushing burden which weighs on the United States, the most widely committed member of the Alliance.

Strategically minded critics of NATO, notably de Gaulle, have argued that bilateral security agreements should be substituted for the collective security pledge of the Atlantic Pact. Since neither France nor Britain, not to speak of Italy or the Benelux countries, is prepared to put muscle into the concept of "graduated" response to a Soviet military challenge, the *casus foederis* of such bilateral military alliances would place the United States before the choice of launching an all-out nuclear attack against the Soviet Union—or of doing nothing. Contrariwise, were the United States attacked, it would have to forego, for sufficient geopolitical and military/technological reasons, the support of its particular European ally. No member of the U.S. Senate, not even the most eccentric one, could be expected to cast his vote for so absurd an arrangement.

It is rumored that some American strategic critics of NATO deem the *Bundesrepublik* the one and only effective ally of the United States in Europe. Leaving aside the question of how effective an ally the *Bundesrepublik* is now or will be in the future, I must demur at the practicality of an American/German alliance. In a Europe without NATO, the West German citadel would be accessible to the succor of American power only by air or via a couple of North Sea ports. This seems to raise massive logistical problems. More important still, a good many Americans would view an exclusive American/German alliance as a travesty of Atlantic partnership—a cynical power-political arrangement that mocks the ideal of the open, the multi-racial and the multi-cultural community of the Western peoples. For the Germans, a Washington-Bonn axis would be a blind alley. It would set them apart from their Western neighbors. It would annul the rapprochement with France. It would convert Germany into an American *place d'armes*. It might insure West Germany's bare physical security; it would not bring Germany one step nearer to the goal of national reunification. The great majority of the Germans, especially German youth, would reject it.

In sum, a world without NATO would be a dangerous world for all the ex-members of NATO. For everybody else, it would be a world less stable than it is now. A Europe-without-NATO would be an indefensible Europe. The withdrawal of American power from Europe would create a vacuum which, we are told, nature abhors. That vacuum cannot be filled by bilateral alliances between European states and America. Hence, it would irresistibly attract the intervention of the great and proximate power which, in the past, has shown itself willing to fill it, i.e., the U.S.S.R.

For the United States, a world-without-NATO would signify the devaluation of a concept which, for a generation, has informed American policy: America's interest in Europe ranks first among all her interests abroad. The words spoken by President Kennedy, 4 July 1962, at Independence Hall, Philadelphia, need never, or rather, should never, have been spoken.

Some American non-strategic critics of NATO suggest that the United States should shift from NATO partnership with Western Europe to collaboration with the Soviet Union. This prescription is based upon the two superpowers' alleged common interest in the prevention of mutually destructive nuclear war and of international nuclear proliferation. The available evidence does not provide a basis for concluding that the Soviets see the situation quite that way. Be that as it may, in a world-without-NATO, it is difficult to see why the Soviets should collaborate with the United States in any but the most trivial undertakings. The United States would have lost its European allies; the Soviets would still keep theirs, for the states of Soviet-controlled Eastern Europe are not free to terminate, of their own accord, the Warsaw Pact or, rather, the strategic and ideological dominance of the Soviet Union. In brief, the Soviet Union would grow relatively stronger, the United States relatively weaker. For a certainty, the liquidation of NATO would reduce the United States' bargaining power vis-à-vis the Soviet Union. Not even the Soviets, eager as they are to break up NATO and adept as they are at dialectic rhetoric, have cared to argue that the dissolution of NATO will strengthen rather than weaken the United States. Wisely, they have left it to America's own critics of NATO to advance this stupendous argument.

It is possible to design all kinds of hypotheses for the state of a world-without-NATO. Among these, one seems most likely and ominous: the United States would be more isolated from the world than had been envisaged by the hardiest isolationists of the pre-World War II era. Of course, great progress has been made in image-making and the manipulation of public opinion. Those who will hail the collapse of NATO as a positive good will couch their arguments in the semantics of internationalism. There always has been a world order; it is likely that there will be one in a NATO-less future. Americans as well as Europeans would have to make considerable adjustments so that they will be able to live in it and with themselves.

Notes

1 Leon Festinger, *A Theory of Cognitive Dissonance* (Glencoe: Free Press, 1954).

2 Kjell Goldmann, "An 'Isolated' Attack Against Sweden," *Cooperation and Conflict,* II—1965, pp. 16-38.

Chapter 3

BALLISTIC MISSILE DEFENSE

BMD Options: A Critical Appraisal

Arms Control and Ballistic Missile Defenses

By Joseph I. Coffey

The Situation Today

One of the great problems in arms control is that advances in technology and their applications to military programs tend to invalidate or render meaningless even the soundest arms control proposals. Twice in the last decade this has occurred, once when the diffusion of nuclear technology and the production of large numbers of nuclear weapons rendered futile any hope of disarming completely the nuclear powers, and again when the advent of intercontinental missiles made necessary a complete rethinking of all the proposals for limiting or abolishing strategic strike forces. It may well be that we are about to witness a similar overtaking of current arms control proposals, because of the possibility of developing and deploying highly effective ballistic missile defenses.

Although work on anti-ballistic missiles has been under way for some years, the prospects for effective defense have in the past seemed relatively small.[1] As Secretary of Defense McNamara and others have testified, this was due largely to the development of sophisticated penetration aids (e.g., chaff, decoys,

and nose cones whose wakes were not easily identifiable by radar) so that incoming warheads could not be readily distinguished from decoys and tankage at the optimum altitudes for engagement by anti-ballistic missiles.[2] Under these circumstances, the cost/effectiveness of anti-ballistic missiles was relatively low in that an enemy could penetrate missile defenses with comparative ease. Alternatively, he could simply by-pass the defenses by striking at undefended targets or by detonating large-yield weapons up-wind from defended ones. To cope with this latter threat, and with the possibility of fallout—or even blast damage—from defending missiles detonated at low altitudes, ballistic missile defenses had to be complemented by civil defenses capable of protecting against fallout and resistant to low blast pressures. All in all, it is understandable that the United States decided not to deploy anti-ballistic missiles and that the Soviet Union apparently pushed ahead only on a limited basis.[3]

Recently, however, it has been determined that long-range exo-atmospheric interceptors could destroy incoming warheads before these dropped to altitudes at which current types of penetration aids would be effective in confusing the missile defense radars.[4] Moreover, the extended range of these interceptors meant that fewer anti-missile missiles could protect a larger area, thereby reducing both the number of batteries which would have to be deployed and the cost of a defensive system. Even when combined with terminal defenses around targets of particular importance, it would appear that new types of ballistic missile defenses would be more flexible and less costly than those which were under consideration a year or two ago.[5] And while a system composed of exo-atmospheric and terminal anti-ballistic missiles might not be very effective against a deliberate attack by a powerful and sophisticated opponent, it could reduce the damage from such an attack, seriously degrade second strikes or uncoordinated attacks, probably safeguard against accidental weapons launchings, and certainly be very effective against small nuclear powers.

Anyone concerned with the security of the United States must, therefore, pay close attention to the potentialities of ballistic missile defenses for limiting damage from a nuclear strike, or, in a larger sense, for helping to deter such a strike. However, it is not enough to consider the case in so narrow a context, since national security embraces concerns other than that of damage limitation and may prescribe means of achieving that security other than large and costly expenditures for defensive systems. Thus, those deciding whether, how, and when to deploy ballistic missile defenses must consider their broad effects, taking into account possible Soviet reactions, the impact on friends and allies of such a decision, and the political and sociological implications of such a move for the United States. They must also consider other means of ad-

vancing U.S. interests and achieving U.S. security, the impact on the arms race, the implications for agreement on further arms control measures, the possible effect on past agreements such as the nuclear test ban treaty, and the options open to the United States if it deems these important. It is on these concerns that this paper will focus, beginning with the possible impact on the strategic balance between the U.S. and the Soviet Union.

Ballistic Missile Defenses and Strategic Forces

As Secretary of Defense McNamara has testified, even an extended damage-limiting posture, including strengthened air defenses and some ballistic missile defenses, could not prevent the Soviets from inflicting on the United States deaths running in the tens of millions, even if they do not markedly increase the levels of forces toward which they are now building.[6] Should they respond by markedly augmenting their intercontinental ballistic forces or their submarine missile fleet, their ability to inflict casualties upon the United States could rise, even if the U.S. in its turn increased the size and the technical quality of both offensive and defensive forces.[7] Thus, viewed even in terms of damage-limitation, the utility of ballistic missile defenses depends markedly upon the restraint displayed by the U.S.S.R. in developing—and employing—its strategic strike forces.

It is, of course, impossible to predict the nature and the magnitude of any Soviet response to the deployment by the United States of ballistic missile defenses. Given their own predilections for defensive systems, their somewhat differing views of the impact of such systems on strategic stability, and the fact that linkages between U.S. actions and Soviet reactions are at best tenuous, it is possible that the Soviets may simply proceed to do what they were already doing or had planned to do, i.e., they may continue the rather steady buildup of Soviet strategic forces upon which they are now engaged. However, as Mr. McNamara has pointed out in another context,[8] the American "damage-limiting capability" cuts into the Soviet "assured destruction capability," and thus may leave them somewhat uneasy about the maintenance of effective deterrence, to say nothing of their capacity to fight successfully a strategic nuclear war. If the Soviets reacted by increasing the number of their ICBM's, the United States might, in the interest of damage-limitation, have to strengthen further its ballistic missile defenses, as well as increase those strategic strike forces earmarked for counterforce attacks on Soviet missile sites. Other Soviet options, such as augmenting the missile submarine fleet or expanding the Long Range Air Force, could induce varying American responses, ranging from the buildup of anti-submarine warfare units and air defenses to the further expansion of U.S. strategic strike forces. Thus, if the Soviets attempted to offset the effects of American anti-ballistic missiles by strengthening their strategic strike forces, they could in turn incite the United States to expand its strategic offensive forces, as well as to strengthen its air and submarine defenses.

Even if the response of the Soviets were directed largely to the acceleration of their own ballistic missile defense program, this could also have a significant impact upon U.S. strategic forces. At the very least, such a Soviet move could induce further expenditures for penetration aids and the accelerated development of those missiles, such as Poseidon, which are capable of carrying numerous decoys and/or multiple warheads. It might well lead to quantitative as well as qualitative improvements in U.S. strategic forces, particularly in intercontinental and submarine-launched ballistic missiles, which could be used either to saturate Soviet anti-missile missile batteries or to reach large numbers of smaller targets which might not be adequately protected by terminal defenses. Thus, whatever the nature of the Soviet response, it could lead to a new round of interactions between offensive and defensive forces and between Soviet and American programs for the construction of these forces.

The decision to deploy ballistic missile defenses is not one solely within the control of the United States inasmuch as the Soviets have the same option. In view of the tests which they have conducted, the boasts which they have made of the capabilities of their anti-missile missiles, and their thinking concerning the role of defenses as a stabilizing influence,[9] it is entirely possible that the Soviets will decide to deploy ballistic missile defenses regardless of what the United States may do in this area.

If the U.S. responds by deploying anti-ballistic missiles on its own, then many of the manifestations of the arms race previously described are likely to occur. It is, however, not necessary that the United States counter a Soviet defensive deployment with one of its own; it could, for example, react by improving the quality of its offensive weapons or by adding to their number.

In the first case, the U.S. might speed up the development of penetrations aids, accelerate the production of missiles like Minuteman III and Poseidon, which can carry more and better penetration aids, and perhaps ultimately, multiple warheads, and take similar measures to insure that its weapons could penetrate Soviet missile defenses. In the second case, the United States might augment its strategic strike forces, in order to saturate, bypass, or evade Soviet ballistic missile defenses. Both saturation and bypassing, i.e., striking at more lightly defended targets, would call for larger numbers of missiles and thus could appear to enhance the American counterforce capability.

Since a logical response by the Soviets would be to expand further their own strategic missile forces, and perhaps to place greater reliance on mobile missiles, an addition to the number of U.S. missiles could touch off a new round of increases. If, however, the United States chose to evade the Soviet missile defenses (i.e., to rely more heavily on weapons systems such as bombers or supersonic cruise-type missiles, which could not be degraded by Soviet ABM's), the results might be different; such weapons have little or no intrinsic first-strike counterforce capability, and would not pose a major threat to Soviet "assured destruction" forces.

All such assessments of possible actions and reactions are admittedly chancy; but in attempting to estimate future weapons programs, some chances must be taken. What can be said with some degree of certainty is that the deployment of anti-ballistic missiles, by either side, is very likely to stimulate countervailing measures by the other, with undeterminable consequences for the levels and the characteristics of strategic offensive and defensive forces. Only in the unlikely event that both sides were prepared to accept marked reductions in their strategic delivery capabilities is it probable that ballistic missile defenses could be introduced without causing disturbances in the strategic balance.

Ballistic Missile Defenses and Nth Powers

The above possibility is, of course, recognized, and indeed is made explicit, in Mr. McNamara's analysis of the implications of deploying extensive ballistic missile defenses. However, the alleged advantages of a defense against Nth powers—and particularly against Communist China—are frequently cited in support of at least the partial or "light" deployment of anti-ballistic missiles.[10] It is argued not only that ballistic missile defenses could reduce damage from a Chinese Communist attack, but also that they would render such an attack less likely, thereby enhancing the credibility of the American deterrent and giving the United States greater freedom of action in containing or opposing Chinese Communist expansionism in South and Southeast Asia. It is also maintained that the deployment of ballistic missile defenses may influence Chinese weapons procurement programs in ways favorable to the United States, i.e., that it may induce the Chinese not to build intercontinental ballistic missiles. A look at both these possibilities is in order.

Broadly speaking, the Chinese Communists have two choices: to attempt to develop a regional deterrent based on modern light or medium bombers, medium-range or intermediate-range ballistic missiles, and submarine-launched missiles; or to aim at a global deterrent, composed of long-range bombers, intercontinental ballistic missiles, and more advanced submarine-launched missiles. Whether they will, in the long run, follow one or both of these routes is less important than the fact that the current constraints on their resources almost force them into a minimal program; indeed, Secretary McNamara's postulated Chinese ICBM threat is placed at least ten years off.[11]

Considering these constraints, the possible uses of Chinese nuclear power, and the political advantages of deploying a visible deterrent as soon as possible, it may well be that the Chinese will forego for the time being the development of intercontinental ballistic missiles—whether or not the United States installs anti-ballistic missiles. However, this would not preclude the Chinese from developing a capability to launch small-scale attacks against the United States, which they could do with a variety of conventional and exotic delivery vehicles ranging from bombers to submarines which could fire nuclear-tipped torpedoes against U.S. port installations and coastal cities.[12] In fact, it is possible that the Chinese may find it advantageous to build submarine-launched missiles, rather than intercontinental ballistic missiles. In the first place, they now have submarines, they have fired short-range missiles, they may have early models of Soviet submarine-launched missiles, and they should find it fairly simple to build or to adapt rather crude forms of such missiles. In the second place, a submarine-launched missile force would give them both a regional and an intercontinental capability, at least so far as the delivery of small-scale attacks upon coastal cities is concerned. Furthermore, such a force would be less vulnerable to preemptive attack than either bomber units or the kinds of first-generation "soft" missiles that are likely to be within Chinese capabilities.

Furthermore, while fear of Chinese retaliation against the United States may inhibit U.S. freedom of action vis-à-vis Communist China, there are other inhibiting factors, ranging from the possibility of Soviet intervention to concern over the political and psychological consequences of drastic measures—factors which certainly operated prior to the time the Chinese developed nuclear weapons. To these must be added the deterrent effect of a regional Chinese capability, which could enable the Chinese to strike at American bases in the Far East or even to threaten the cities of America's Asian allies. While such a regional deterrent may not in itself have the impact of an intercontinental one—especially since it may not suffice to "trigger" a Soviet strategic strike against the United States—it will certainly strengthen the present barriers to U.S. military intervention in Asia.

Entirely aside from the question of whether ballistic missile defenses are necessary to deter Chinese nuclear strikes against the United States, it is also questionable whether they will have the effects desired. On the one hand, such defenses may simply push the Chinese into building forces capable of dominating "hostage Asia" and thereby indirectly deterring unfavorable U.S. policies and measures. Alternatively, they may induce the Chinese to emphasize weapons programs with which ballistic missile defenses (and particularly exo-atmospheric defenses) cannot readily cope, weapons such as submarine-launched cruise-type missiles.

In any case, as the technology and industrial capacity of Communist China grow, so also will the sophistication of its weapons. To counter this, the U.S. will probably find it necessary to extend, to deepen, and perhaps to improve its anti-ballistic missile system and to build up its air defenses and anti-submarine warfare forces. Thus, whatever the initial form of an ABM system designed for use against Communist China, it will ultimately become either largely ineffective or little different from that required to defend against Soviet forces. In the long run, therefore, ballistic missile defenses, such as those Mr. McNamara has indicated might be deployed against the Chinese Communists, are likely to increase markedly U.S. damage-limiting capabilities vis-à-vis the Soviet Union—a point which the Soviets are not likely to miss. Thus, even a "light" deployment of ABM's may start a series of perturbations in the Soviet-American strategic balance.

Ballistic Missile Defenses and Arms Control

From the above it would seem that the introduction of ballistic missile defenses—regardless of who introduces them and for what reasons—is likely to have a significant effect on the current negotiations for arms control. For instance, ballistic missile defenses, by introducing a new factor into strategic calculations and by triggering various responses such as those previously described, would necessitate a complete reorientation of the U.S. proposal for a freeze on strategic forces. The deployment of anti-ballistic missiles would largely rule out any possibility of agreement on general and complete disarmament, which is not likely to be adopted at a time when the nations principally concerned are engaged in strengthening their strategic forces. And, since bombers may take on new importance as a hedge against ballistic missile defenses, the deployment of ABM's would make less acceptable and less likely bomber disarmament, whether total or proportionate.

In addition, the deployment of ballistic missile defenses could stultify progress toward a non-proliferation agreement. For one thing, the Europeans might view Soviet ballistic missile defenses as further degrading the effectiveness of the U.S. deterrent, and hence increasing the likelihood of Soviet pressures against NATO Europe. While prior American deployment might strengthen belief in the credibility of the deterrent, it might also lead to greater European concern over the likelihood and the imminence of war, and thus to renewed efforts to buttress deterrence through the development of their own ballistic missile defenses or through control over nuclear strike forces. And should both sides deploy anti-ballistic missiles, the Europeans may again be concerned lest Europe become a battleground for the nuclear giants. While all possible reactions cannot be discussed in this paper, it is entirely possible that the deployment of ballistic missile defenses by one or both sides may strengthen the desire of some Europeans to develop national or regional nuclear deterrents and may increase their reluctance to sign agreements which would rule out such possibilities.

In the longer run, the impact of ballistic missile defenses on the prospects for arms control may be even greater. At the very least, the desire for greater information concerning warhead effects would make it difficult for either the U.S. or the U.S.S.R. to give up the underground testing of nuclear weapons. And at some stage in the expenditure of tens of billions of dollars, one side or the other might feel compelled to try out the operational effectiveness of its anti-missile missiles against incoming warheads. Even if these tests took place outside the atmosphere, so that there would be no fallout, they would constitute a clear breach of the present nuclear test ban, as would, of course, operational tests of nuclear-armed terminal defense missiles such as the U.S. Sprint or Hibex. Thus in time the deployment of ballistic missile defenses might lead to the abrogation or nullification of the nuclear test ban, as well as the inhibition of further progress towards arms control.

One reason for this is the probable impact on the negotiators themselves. As shown by Soviet reaction to U.S. intervention in Vietnam, it is hard to reach agreement on arms control during periods of increased tension, such as would probably follow stepped-up expenditures for defensive and offensive strategic weapons. Moreover, increases in strategic armaments would certainly alienate the smaller powers, such as India and Mexico, which are already seeking cutbacks in weapons stockpiles and strategic delivery vehicles as the price of their own adherence to any non-proliferation agreement.

At the very least, therefore, the deployment of ballistic missile defenses might lead to a hiatus in arms control negotiations, while both sides tried out their new weapons, decided on countermeasures to the others' deployment, and reestablished an effective and acceptable strategic balance. It could mean the loss of all chance for an early agreement on a comprehensive test ban and on the non-proliferation of nuclear weapons, leading to decisions by powers such as Italy or India to proceed with their own nuclear weapons programs.

Options Open to the United States

While no one can say with assurance that these are or will be the consequences of a decision to deploy ballistic missile defenses, their likelihood must be taken into account. In considering how the United States might attempt to hedge against these possibilities, while still assuring its own security and protecting its own interests, a number of possibilities come to mind.

The first of these is not to deploy ballistic missile defenses at all. It is questionable whether these are really needed against the Chinese Communists, who do not now possess, nor are likely to possess in the next decade, a strategic strike force sufficient to constitute a meaningful threat to the United States. If, as indicated by Mr. McNamara, the best that the Chinese can do, against present U.S. programs, is to inflict six to twelve million fatalities in the latter half of the next decade,[13] then the problem is neither urgent nor significant. For the Chinese to attack, or to threaten to attack, American cities in the face of the U.S. strategic strike forces would be the rashest of acts on the part of a people who have been noted for their caution and conservatism in the use of military force. Indeed, it is rather astonishing that the United States, which seems perfectly satisfied that its deterrent is effective against the Soviet Union, should be so concerned about its ineffectiveness against a power whose resources are minuscule, whose opportunities for meaningful gains through limited war are considerably less than those of the Soviet Union, and which, moreover, has shown no signs of undertaking such adventures since its circumspect use of "volunteers" in Korea.

With respect to the Soviet Union, it is clear that ballistic missile defenses, while they could significantly reduce damage from an attack by those Soviet forces now in being or presumably programmed, could not reduce fatalities below several tens of millions. Should the Soviets choose to augment or up-grade their strategic strike forces, as is entirely possible, the net result could be to re-establish something approximating the present levels of mutual destruction at a higher cost for both sides. Indeed, one consequence of the deployment of ballistic missile defenses might be to force the Soviet Union (and/or the United States) into developing other types of delivery vehicles, such as supersonic cruise-type missiles, or to increasing the yield, and perhaps the lethality, of nuclear warheads in order to assure equivalent damage from lesser numbers of penetrating vehicles.

The real basis for a U.S. decision to deploy ballistic missile defenses may lie not in the Chinese Communist threat, nor in the hope of reducing damage from Soviet strategic strike forces, but in a Soviet decision to further expand the areas defended by anti-missile missiles. As already suggested, a counter-deployment of ballistic missile defenses by the United States is only one possible response; there are others which may be equally effective in maintaining a strategic balance and less likely to stimulate another round in the arms race. It may be in the interest of the United States to choose responses which would not incite an intensified Soviet ABM deployment, nor induce the Soviets to build up their own strategic strike forces.

Should the United States, nevertheless, decide to go ahead with ballistic missile defenses, it should certainly try optional deployments which are not aimed at the Soviet Union nor likely to degrade markedly Soviet assured destruction capabilities. Despite all the talk about not triggering a Soviet response, it is obvious that the combination of nation-wide area coverage with terminal defenses around ten or more large cities suggested by some "Pentagon planners" [14] could in fact seriously degrade Soviet ICBM capabilities. Only if ABMs are restricted to the West Coast (in which case they provide only a limited and temporary defense against potential Chinese threats), are their effects likely to be insignificant in Soviet eyes.

There are, of course, other options, which may seem particularly attractive if one is concerned with Chinese submarine-launched missiles, rather than with Chinese ICBMs. The United States could strengthen its anti-submarine warfare defenses, to include surveillance of those Chinese ports at which missile-carrying submarines might be based, shadowing of Chinese submarines which leave port, the establishment on a permanent basis of advanced barriers in the Pacific, or even the activation of a Pacific defense zone off the West Coast of the United States. It could, alternatively or in conjunction with expanded anti-submarine warfare operations, develop a mobile defense against submarine-launched missiles, employing either surface ships or aircraft. Such a defense, while probably of lower effectiveness and higher cost than either terminal or area defenses, would be more clearly designed to cope with a limited threat and would pose much less of a problem for Soviet weaponeers. Or, if the Chinese threat is the one meriting consideration, the United States could deploy terminal defenses rather than area defenses, thereby reducing potential losses without necessarily creating a major obstacle to a large-scale attack such as that which the U.S.S.R. could mount.

Another option open to the United States would be to seek agreement with the Soviet Union on measures to limit the numbers or types of ballistic missile defenses or both, so that neither side would feel threatened by an open-ended deployment of such defensive weapons. Alternatively, the United States might seek to set limits on the numbers or types of offensive weapons which might be added to the arsenals of both sides in response to the deployment of ballistic missile defenses, in order to dampen the impact on the arms race of incremental increases in strategic strike forces. (In this connection, it should be noted that successful damage-limitation requires cooperation by the other side with respect to the numbers and types of weapons employed, as well as with respect to the targets against which they are directed, so that high level moves of this nature might well be justified even in the absence of ballistic missile defenses.) Indeed, the United States might find it desirable to suggest revisions to its present freeze proposal which would allow the limited introduction of anti-missile missiles, providing corresponding numbers of ICBM's or IRBM's were destroyed. To avoid interminable wrangling over technical details, and to allow for necessary adjustments in postures, such agreements might be tacit rather than formal, could be limited to a fixed number of years, or could, like the treaties of 1922 and 1936 limiting naval armaments, be denounced for cause upon notice.[15]

What is implicit in all these proposals and suggestions is that the United States not proceed with the deployment of ballistic missile defenses pending some attempt to reach agreement on measures to limit the consequences of such a deployment. This, in turn, implies a preliminary effort to obtain a moratorium on ballistic missile defenses, while following any or all of the avenues suggested previously. Thus, entirely aside from the unsuitability of initiating deployment during the war in Vietnam (which has already strained U.S.-Soviet relations), or the undesirability of funding such deployment on top of increased expenditures for that war, it is suggested that there may be value in a moratorium which aims at curbing or limiting the future deployment of anti-ballistic missiles.

Conclusions

It is obvious that judgments as to the desirability of building ballistic missile defenses will differ according to one's opinion as to the likelihood of war, one's desire to employ strategic forces as coercive instruments, one's theories on the causes of crises and on crisis behavior, and one's views as to how the Chinese Communists are likely to conduct themselves in the next decade. With regard to the latter point, it would seem unwise to deploy anti-ballistic missiles because of suppositions about the course of Chinese Communist behavior or the pattern of Chinese Communist weapons procurement ten to fifteen years in the future. While one cannot say that history repeats itself, mistaken American estimates of the nature of Soviet behavior, and the failure to take into account the likelihood and the consequences of internal changes in the Soviet Union, should stand as a warning against making similar judgments about Chinese rigidity and activism.

Moreover, the deployment of ballistic missile defenses, whether against the Chinese or against the Soviets, may well stimulate the U.S.S.R. to further expenditures for strategic defensive or offensive forces, particularly since these latter are already inferior to those of the United States and could be degraded by American anti-ballistic missiles. In consequence, the result may be not an incremental gain in that component of U.S. security called "damage-limitation" but losses both to that and to other and more significant components, such as relations with the U.S.S.R., ties among allies, and international cooperation in the interests of peace.

Chief among the losses is likely to be a further attrition of the already slim possibility of reaching agreement on further arms control measures. While the control of armaments may not be an end in itself, it is a meaningful—and possibly an essential—step toward the construction of a better and more secure world. Without denying the importance of military power in preserving that more secure world, it is still possible to question the relative allocation of resources to the increase of that power, and particularly the addition of increments which promise so little and risk so much as the construction of ballistic missile defenses. On this basis, the whole issue of constructing ballistic missile defenses might well be carefully reconsidered by both of the superpowers.

Notes

[1] Statement of Secretary of Defense Robert S. McNamara before the House Armed Services Committee on the Fiscal Year 1964-8 Defense Program and 1964 Defense Budget, 30 January 1963, Mimeograph, p. 48 and Statement of Secretary of Defense Robert S. McNamara before the House Armed Services Committee on the Fiscal Year 1965-9 Defense Program and 1965 Defense Budget, 27 January 1964, pp. 51-2.

[2] See the informative article by Jules Bergman, "If Zeus Fails, Can Sprint Save Us?", *The New York Times Magazine,* 20 March 1966, especially pp. 59, 68.

[3] Like the United States, the U.S.S.R. has apparently developed and tested anti-ballistic missiles, and has even shown television films of missile interceptions. While Soviet leaders and high Soviet officers have made numerous claims concerning the present effectiveness and future potential of anti-ballistic missiles (see Thomas W. Wolfe, *Soviet Strategy at the Crossroads,* Santa Monica, California: The RAND Corporation, RM-4805-PR, April 1964, pp. 236-246), there is little evidence that the Soviets have deployed ABM's—except possibly around Moscow or Leningrad. (*The Detroit News,* 20 March 1966, p. 15-A.)

[4] *The Wall Street Journal,* 26 July 1965, p. 10.

[5] Statement of Secretary of Defense McNamara before a joint session of the Senate Armed Services Committee and the Senate Subcommittee on Department of Defense Appropriations on the Fiscal Year 1967-71 Defense Program and 1967 Defense Budget, undated, Mimeograph, pp. 55, 57-58, 70 (hereafter cited as *McNamara Statement, 1966*).

[6] *McNamara Statement, 1966,* pp. 52-4.

[7] *Ibid.*

[8] Statement of Secretary of Defense Robert S. McNamara before the House Armed Services Committee on the Fiscal Year 1966-70 Defense Program and 1966 Defense Budget, Mimeograph, undated, pp. 47, 49-50 (hereafter cited as *McNamara Statement, 1965*). By "assured destruction capability" Mr. McNamara means the ability to destroy one-quarter to one-third of a potential aggressor's population and two-thirds of its industrial capacity (*ibid.,* p. 39).

[9] See, for example, Major General N. Talensky, "Anti-Missile Systems and Disarmament," *International Affairs* (Moscow), October 1964, pp. 15-19.

[10] *McNamara Statement, 1966,* pp. 56-58.

[11] *Ibid.*

[12] For a further discussion of alternative means of delivery open to the Chinese, see the author's paper, "The Chinese and Ballistic Missile Defense," *Bulletin of the Atomic Scientists,* December 1965, especially p. 18.

[13] *McNamara Statement, 1966,* p. 57.

[14] *The Wall Street Journal,* 26 July 1965, p. 10.

[15] Further details can be found in Study Paper No. 7, "An Over-all Freeze on Strategic Vehicles," Office of National Security Studies, the Bendix Systems Division, presented at the meeting of the Western Section, Operations Research Society of America, 29 September 1965.

The Impact of Ballistic Missile Defense On Arms Control Prospects[1]

By Richard B. Foster

1.

Dr. Joseph I. Coffey of the Bendix Corporation has presented a succinct summary of the arguments of those who believe that deployment of any type of a ballistic missile defense (BMD) system would have negative effects upon our efforts to negotiate arms control agreements with the U.S.S.R.[2] It seems to me that these arguments are invalid, for six principal reasons. First, they are based on an assumption that there is, at present, an "arms race" between the United States and the Soviet Union. Second, they fail to take fully into account publicly expressed Soviet attitudes toward BMD. Third, they ignore the fact that in the next two decades there will be an increasing Nth Country threat to both the U.S. and the U.S.S.R. which, given long lead times, the two major powers must take into account now in their strategic planning. Fourth, in maintaining that BMD would be destabilizing, they disregard some of the basic elements constituting strategic stability. Fifth, they take inadequate account of the probable impact of changing technology on the future strategic offensive and strategic defensive force structures

of both the U.S. and the U.S.S.R. Finally, they ignore the prospects of BMD for enhancing, rather than disrupting, arms control agreements. An examination, in turn, of each of these points should serve to sharpen our perspective of the relationships between BMD and arms control.

Despite frequent assertions to the contrary, there is no convincing empirical evidence which indicates that, at present, we are engaged in an exponential arms race with the U.S.S.R. Such an arms race would involve a tendency by each of the two powers to respond to any and all expansions or new additions to the opponent's forces by expanding or adding to their own. A continuing and increasing arms race would occur if the response of the second power were followed by a larger response of the first power, and so on, until one or both powers reached the limits of economic capacity. The actual situation has been somewhat different, with the U.S.S.R. emphasizing the buildup of its strategic defensive forces and its offensive capabilities against Eurasia while the U.S. has concentrated primarily on improving its strategic offensive forces against the U.S.S.R.

There has been, in the past, only a vaguely discernible correlation between changes in U.S. and Soviet defense expenditures on and allocations within the annual military budgets. This has been especially true for supposed changes in components of the Soviet defense budget in relation to changes in corresponding parts of the U.S. budget. Some new defense expenditures on specific items by one power have provoked no reaction at all from the other power. Others have provoked a quite irrelevant reaction—not a direct counter to the adversary's action but an imitation of it. For example, the U.S. bought more B-52's—not more active defense or even more protection for the B-52's it already had—after a Soviet display of heavy jets and turboprops in a May Day parade. Neither the U.S. nor the U.S.S.R. has permitted military expenditures to reach the full level that their respective economies are capable of supporting, nor is the trend in that direction. For the moment, in the U.S.S.R., those participants in the resource allocation debate who have argued for increased investment in non-military sectors seem to have prevailed over those who have argued for increased investment in military sectors at the expense of other development programs.

The U.S.S.R. has expressed serious interest in developing a BMD system, and the delays in Soviet deployment of this system seem attributable to technical difficulties rather than to a decision to defer action to await U.S. moves. If the United States should decide to deploy BMD, and if this decision were announced before the Soviets' present technical difficulties with their own BMD system have been overcome, certain specific measures in response to our BMD deployment could be expected from the other side. However,

their response might well draw military resources away from other weapons systems more inimical to us. Given the limits of the Soviet economy, a major increase in defense spending could be achieved only at the expense of productive investment and, hence, at the expense of over-all economic growth. Therefore, it seems likely that any Soviet responses to a U.S. decision to deploy BMD would be financed primarily by adjustment within the defense budget rather than by an over-all increase in defense spending. It is hard to see how this could lead to an "arms race" any more than did our expenditures on air defense in the mid-1950's.

2.

The favorable Soviet attitude towards BMD follows logically from the U.S.S.R.'s traditional institutional bias towards defense. This bias has been well expressed by Major General Talensky. Talensky stated:

It is obvious that the creation of an anti-missile defense merely serves to build up the security of the peaceable, non-aggressive states. The creation of an effective anti-missile defense system by a country which is a potential target for aggression merely serves to increase the deterrent effect and so helps to avert aggression. It is said that the international strategic situation cannot be stable where both sides simultaneously strive for deterrence through nuclear rocket power and the creation of defensive anti-missile systems. I cannot agree with this view either. From the viewpoint of strategy, powerful deterrent forces and an effective anti-missile defense system, when taken together, substantially increase the stability of mutual deterrence.[3]

Other Soviet spokesmen have echoed Talensky's views. It seems unlikely, therefore, that the U.S.S.R. will abandon its interest in acquiring BMD for itself irrespective of what the United States does. Of course, if the United States should deploy a BMD system, the U.S.S.R. might respond in a variety of ways. The latter might expand and/or accelerate its own BMD program, or what is more likely, it might add penetration aids to its offensive missile arsenal or increase the numbers and yields of offensive missiles. But this need not necessarily lead to an "arms race" any more than have the past interactions between the two powers. In fact, if both the major powers possessed BMD, this could, as Talensky suggests, be restabilizing rather than destabilizing —a point which will be discussed in greater detail below.

Some potential Soviet responses to a U.S. BMD might even further our own national arms control objectives. For example, if the U.S.S.R. financed its response to U.S. BMD at the expense of the forces confronting NATO in Europe, this would, in effect, serve as a curb on the arms levels in Europe. Although it is impossible to predict exactly what the Soviet response would be, it is by no means clear that the results would be disadvantageous to U.S. and NATO interests, or contrary to the objectives of arms control. It does seem reasonable to conclude, at any rate, that the U.S.S.R. intends to go ahead with BMD deployments, irrespective of what the United States does, just as soon as its scientists can overcome certain technical difficulties.

The favorable Soviet attitude towards BMD was manifested at the last three Pugwash Conferences. When Western spokesmen attempted to persuade the Soviet delegates that there were good reasons to refrain from deploying BMD, the U.S.S.R. representatives at first failed to understand the arguments. At the third conference, they informed the Western delegates that it was too late; the U.S.S.R. was going ahead with its BMD program. Given the traditional Soviet bias towards defensive systems and the search for another prestige "first" similar to Sputnik, the Soviet RDT&E program for BMD undoubtedly enjoys high priority. Instead of continuing the fruitless effort to persuade the U.S.S.R. that BMD is not a good thing, we in the West should be expending our energy on analyzing the consequences for our own strategies and weapons procurement programs of the expressed Soviet interest in obtaining a significant BMD system for the U.S.S.R. just as early as possible.

3.

As the Nth Country threat grows, both the United States and the U.S.S.R. will have a requirement to deploy BMD not only against each other but against such new nuclear powers as the Chinese People's Republic (CPR) and, in the Soviet case, against France. (England, too, is in Soviet eyes a potentially threatening nuclear power, but probably less so than France.) While the possession of nuclear weapons and crude delivery means will not vault either the CPR or France into great power status, it will permit them to undertake increasingly, in times of international crisis, destabilizing acts which could vitally affect the two major powers.

Secretary McNamara has estimated that the CPR would attain an initial operational capability (IOC) with MRBM's in 1967 and with ICBM's in 1975. In arriving at these estimates, as his public testimony shows, Mr. McNamara has taken into account the various other options open to the Chinese, such as emphasis on submarine-launched missiles. He seems to believe that in view of their limited experience as a naval power, as well as the long distances involved in mounting a submarine threat against the United States, the Chinese are more likely to concentrate initially on land-based systems.[4]

Chinese MRBM's could reach crucial targets in the U.S.S.R., and if the Sino-Soviet dispute continues unabated the U.S.S.R. may be threatened with the light attacks of which the CPR will be capable even before the continental United States is threatened by Chinese ICBM's. Similarly, the French *force de dissuasion* in a few years will pose an additional missile threat to the Soviet Union. If nuclear proliferation continues, other countries may, in the future, also be able to pose threats to the two major powers. Moreover, there is no guarantee that all the new nuclear powers will calculate correctly that their first use of nuclear weapons against a major power would provoke the infliction of unacceptable damage on them in retaliation. A country like Communist China may be so concerned about the potential use of tactical nuclear weapons by the United States in its region that it may threaten retaliation on the U.S. continent and thereby risk retaliation by the United States on its own territory under certain circumstances. The necessity to protect against the Nth Country threat adds an additional incentive for both the United States and the U.S.S.R. to deploy BMD.

The Nth Country threat soon will have another dimension. The United States, in particular, will be faced with a requirement to strengthen its nuclear guarantees to certain allies which may be threatened by a hostile Nth power. For example, the CPR may attempt to use nuclear threats against Japan or

India. If the United States itself is protected by BMD, it will be possible to counter the CPR with credible guarantees that an attack against one of our friends in Asia will provoke retaliation from the U.S. arsenal—and the United States will not have to fear a CPR retaliatory attack. The U.S.S.R., too, may under certain circumstances wish to extend a nuclear guarantee to another state threatened by an Nth power. BMD employed by both the major powers in their homelands would, through strengthening their respective nuclear guarantees, reduce the spectrum of destabilizing acts which hostile Nth powers would be able to commit against their neighbors. Both of the super-powers have shown themselves to be interested in projecting their influence on a world scale and, occasionally, in intervening abroad for the purpose of bringing under control local conflicts which might, if not checked, jeopardize their basic interests. In the future, if they should be obliged to deal with an unpredictable dictator armed with a crude nuclear capability, they would be in a better position to protect themselves against irrational nuclear blackmail if they are equipped with BMD.

In this sense, the possession of BMD by both the United States and the U.S.S.R. could serve as an anti-proliferation measure. Some lesser powers, if they were reasonably sure of the efficacy of the nuclear guarantees of a major power, might prefer this less expensive arrangement as a means of protecting themselves against the threats of neighboring Nth powers rather than pushing for rapid acquisition of their own nuclear weapons to counter the same threat. Since most nations bent on acquiring nuclear weapons of their own are unlikely to adhere to the terms of a non-proliferation treaty, even if one can be successfully negotiated, BMD may ultimately prove to be a better anti-proliferation measure than the treaty the United States is now seeking.

BMD in the possession of the two major powers could serve as an anti-proliferation measure in yet another way. If a burgeoning nuclear power like the CPR knew, through public announcements, that BMD was being deployed by either or both of the two major powers, this might serve to complicate considerably the planning for and the cost of an offensive force capable of attacking such powers. Missiles with penetration aids to overcome active defenses are more complicated and expensive than crude missiles capable of scoring a hit against a nation with no BMD. If such deployment announcements were accompanied by indications of strengthened nuclear guarantees to nations that were neighbors of the potential aggressive power, this would further complicate effective use of a crude missile force by the Nth power. In the face of such developments, some potential Nth powers might be discouraged from the effort to attain nuclear armed missiles, since their usefulness would be limited by the existence of great power BMD. Moreover, when the actual use of such a force is limited, the political or threat value of the force diminishes as well.

All of the elements of the Nth Country threat are affecting U.S.—and presumably Soviet—strategic planning now. Although a U.S. decision to go ahead with BMD deployments effective against so-called light attacks of the sort the CPR will be capable of mounting in the next two decades has been deferred, pressures on the decision-makers to approve such a deployment are increasing. Such a decision would, for the reasons outlined above, increase U.S. flexibility

to deal with the interrelated problems of the emergence of the CPR as a nuclear power and the more general dilemma posed by nuclear proliferation. Furthermore, given the favorable Soviet attitude toward BMD and the fact that a U.S. deployment against a light attack would not significantly lessen Soviet capabilities to mount a large-scale attack against the United States, such a deployment would be unlikely to introduce new tensions into the deterrent relationship between the United States and the U.S.S.R. By protecting against potential Soviet accidental or demonstration attacks, it might even serve to reduce tension to some extent.

4.

Strategic stability is a complex phenomenon. Here it will be possible only to mention some of the more significant elements which affect it in order to show that BMD, if deployed by either the United States or the U.S.S.R.—or both —need not necessarily be destabilizing.

The concept of strategic stability, as it has been applied until now, refers primarily to the relationship of mutual deterrence between the United States and the U.S.S.R. These are three categories of events which can increase tensions between the two major powers:

a) Events which may occur as a consequence of deliberate acts originated on the part of one of them;

b) Events which may occur as a consequence of deliberate acts originated by a nation aligned with one of the two major powers; or

c) Events which may occur as a consequence of great power involvement in developments in an unaligned nation.

The Cuban missile crisis is an example of a destabilizing event in the first category. It was caused by a deliberate Soviet attempt to install MRBM's and IRBM's in the Western Hemisphere. The Suez crisis, inasmuch as it involved deliberate decisions by Britain and France, is an example of a destabilizing event in the second category. The Congo crisis is an example of a destabilizing event in the third category, for both of the superpowers attempted to influence the outcome of that situation. As these examples suggest, destabilizing events within the various categories normally affect the "delicate balance of terror" with descending degrees of "criticality" from a) to c).

So far, in the crises that have occurred since the U.S.S.R. acquired a significant nuclear strike capability, it has been possible to restabilize the situation before deterrence failed. However, maintaining strategic stability has become an increasingly complex task as allies of the major powers have sought to attain an increasingly independent posture in the international arena and as the involvement of both the major powers in the unrest in underdeveloped areas has increased.

If nuclear proliferation continues, additional nations will seek increasingly to influence strategic stability. Even if nuclear proliferation goes no further, the CPR and France will, as their atomic capabilities grow, be able to exert a greater impact on strategic stability than they have in the past.

Strategic stability, then, is not a static phenomenon. Every day, events occur which serve to alter—temporarily or permanently—this relationship. But these events do not necessarily include the gradual modernization and buildup of certain portions of the strategic offensive and defensive forces of the United States and the U.S.S.R. Both powers have engaged in such acts, but in recent years their efforts have not been destabilizing with respect to the U.S./U.S.S.R. balance of power. Since the deployment of BMD is a logical evolution from the force structures currently in being, and since the U.S.S.R. views the buildup of defensive systems as a necessary, non-provocative act, it is difficult to see how BMD, if deployed by either the United States or the U.S.S.R. or both, could be destabilizing. It would be, instead, a part of the evolution of strategic stability to take into account the increasing ability of the lesser powers to engage in destabilizing moves. By reducing the likelihood that Nth powers would be able to threaten or to engage in adventurist moves, and by strengthening great power nuclear guarantees to non-nuclear allies, BMD could be to a considerable extent restabilizing.

BMD also could introduce a certain amount of additional stability under certain types of arms control arrangements, if these were agreed upon. Take, for example, the proposal for a freeze on strategic nuclear delivery vehicles. Assuming that both sides pursue current policies and strategies up to the time that an agreement for a freeze goes into effect, the agreement would start with the United States possessing numerical superiority in the inventory of strategic offensive forces. In all probability, the Soviet Union would insist on altering this arrangement to permit parity, if not in the initial stages then at some later stage in implementation of the agreement. This alteration of the status quo could be potentially destabilizing. Unless, meanwhile, a strategic first strike had been made more complicated, even under conditions of parity, by the addition of BMD, there would be a risk that the attainment of parity would change the dimensions of deterrence. At the very least, either the United States or the U.S.S.R. leaders might assume that these dimensions had changed, and this assumption would in itself introduce a destabilizing element. Similarly, no amount of inspection could rule out with assurance all possibility of cheating. As the levels of strategic nuclear delivery vehicles retained in the inventory were progessively reduced, in the absence of BMD it would require fewer and fewer additional missiles under a cheating arrangement to destabilize the balance. By increasing the aggressor's force requirements for threatening the victim, BMD in the possession of the potential victim would considerably increase the number of additional missiles which would have to be obtained and deployed clandestinely through cheating before an effective strike could be mounted.

Stability at the low force levels accompanying any significant arms control agreement would seem, therefore, to presuppose the existence of some active defense. This would be true not only of the proposed freeze on strategic nuclear delivery vehicles but of all other proposals envisaging the reduction, by stages, of present armaments levels. What many analysts overlook is the fact that any changes in the status quo, in the absence of a retention of active defense, could prove destabilizing at any stage before General and Complete Disarmament was achieved. A "pure" small force of offensive vehicles of the kind that figures in minimum deterrence doctrines gives rise to problems which flow precisely from its simplicity. Such an uncomplicated force may become vulnerable, if not as a result of violations of the agreement, then as the result of changes in the technological state of the art permissible under the agreement.[5] A mixture of offense and defense, just because it is more complex, is less calculable and more uncertain and pre-

sents greater risks for a potential violator. In addition, a reduction in the offensive forces of the great powers which is accompanied by a low level of defense by the great powers, or no defense at all, would offer temptations to ambitious prospective Nth Countries. The lower the force levels of the great powers, the more feasible it is for the small powers to play dangerous and destabilizing roles. The existence of defenses on the part of the great powers tends to keep the smaller powers outclassed. This point needs also to be considered in evaluating the stability of a multilateral agreement. Such an agreement is threatened not only by alterations in the status of the great powers that participate in the agreement but also by the destabilizing potential of the small powers, both those that are party to the agreement and those that are not. When strategic stability is examined from these perspectives, a good case can be made for the role of BMD as a stabilizing element.

5.

One of the most grossly misleading conceptions in recent discussions of arms control issues is the argument that the technology of armaments has arrived at a plateau. Military technology never stands still for long. New weapons systems are now in various stages of development which testify both to the continuing advances of technology and to the impact which changing technology will have on the force structures of the United States and the U.S.S.R. during the 1970's.

Insofar as offensive weapons systems are concerned, extremely low circular error of probability (CEP) and multiple warheads that permit a single offensive missile to attack several enemy launchers with satisfactory kill probabilities are already feasible. It will become increasingly possible to mount successful attacks against hard targets. As fixed targets become more vulnerable to counter-battery fire, the military planner must resort either to mobility or to hard point defense, or to some combination of the two in order to protect his retaliatory force. Technological limitations in the form of smaller payloads available for submarine launched ballistic missiles (SLBM) and mobile land-based ICBM's, when combined with the more complex command and control requirements of mobile systems, make hard point defense of fixed-site ICBM's the more desirable option.

This option is available at a time when the technology of BMD has advanced to a stage where it is very difficult to saturate such defenses and very expensive to fool them through the use of decoys and other counter-measures. The high cost of overcoming such defenses is measured not only in rubles or dollars; it also is determined by the effectiveness of the offensive systems designed to overcome them. The more complex the countermeasures for overcoming the defense that are included in the attacking offensive weapons system, the lesser will be the portion of the offensive payload available for a nuclear warhead or warheads to strike effectively at hardened targets. Hence, cost-exchange ratios are beginning to favor the defensive systems. Hard-site missile silos in the seventies may be defended at a cost which probably would be no greater than that of additional silos.

For the attacker, BMD has another advantage. As multiple warheads permit counter-battery fire and consequent degradation of the adversary's retaliatory force with fewer offensive missiles, an offensive force consisting primarily of multiple-warhead missiles combined with area and point BMD might limit the damage inflicted by the adversary in a retaliatory strike or strikes to recuperable levels.

Another alternative to reliance on an offensive retaliatory force consisting primarily of fixed-site, hardened ICBM's protected by hard point defense might be a greater reliance on manned bombers and low altitude cruise missiles. But again, for technological reasons, these weapons systems, as is the case with SLBM's and mobile land-based missiles, probably cannot carry the payload necessary to attack hardened targets effectively. Technological trends suggest, therefore, that the best option for both U.S. and U.S.S.R. military planners for the 1970's will be the addition of BMD to the strategic force structure. This option will not lose any of its desirability in the event that, meanwhile, progress is made in concluding various arms control arrangements. Technology will continue to influence choices—those concerning weapons systems which remain in the U.S. and Soviet arsenals—and the prospects for any substantial progress toward general and complete disarmament (GCD) within the next decade or so are not very bright.[6]

In considering the implications of ballistic missile defense for arms control, perhaps the most important factors to be weighed are the relative costs and effectiveness of ballistic missile defensive and offensive systems. This measure of cost-effectiveness is known as the "cost-exchange ratio" or the "exchange rate." A few years ago, Mr. William Foster, Director of the U.S. Arms Control and Disarmament Agency, stated that U.S. policy was based in part on a scientific assessment of the relative ineffectiveness and high cost of ballistic missile defenses. For example, he pointed out, for every $100 one might spend on BMD, it would take only $1 to $10 additional cost to perfect offensive missiles to overcome such a defense. This was, therefore, an unfavorable cost-exchange ratio—it ranged from 100:1 to 10:1 *against* the defense. More recent advances in the technology of the defense have radically changed this picture.

Today, for example, against a relatively unsophisticated attack such as the Red Chinese might mount in the next decade or two, it may be possible effectively to deny completely the penetration of U.S. cities. This may be done at a relatively low initial cost, based upon a defense of the entire continental U.S. by utilizing long-range Zeus missiles in an area defense mode. In another case, the possible use of BMD in the defense of missile silos, as stated above, might be accomplished at a relatively favorable cost-exchange ratio when one considers some of the other alternatives. One alternative, for example, would be to add to the numbers of our offensive missiles in order to add aiming points for the Soviet attacker. This in turn would increase the enemy's force levels. Hard site defense—as an alternative to adding silos—might in fact be an arms limitation measure, because it would not force the United States to increase the number of its strategic offensive forces in order to insure the survivability of the second-strike retaliatory forces. The cost would be probably lower—and the effectiveness higher—than would be the case for the other options.

A third example is worth mentioning. Certainly, a light attack defense of the U.S. hardened missiles would guard against inadvertent, unauthorized or "psychotic commander" attacks or accidental firings of missiles from the So-

viet Union. In this sense, such a defense would contribute to the United States' deliberate, selective controlled response policy—a policy which was conceived in 1961 as an arms control measure to minimize the risk of a general nuclear war from any cause. Additionally, such a defense might remove the capability—and hence the incentive—for Soviet "demonstration attacks" of the type that have been described in the paper by Herman Kahn. Every one of the improvements of ballistic missile defense outlined above is in itself an arms control measure that would have the effect of restabilizing mutual deterrence between the United States and the Soviet Union, thereby further reducing the risk of a general nuclear war from all causes except that of a calculated first strike.

One must consider the rate at which the cost-exchange ratios may change in the future between offensive and defensive weaponry. If they continue at the present rate, the defense planners may become indifferent to whether they buy offensive weaponry or defensive weaponry since the cost-exchange ratios may approach unity for some measures of effectiveness of both offense and defense. To put it another way, the very nature of deterrence may change from that of a threatened retaliation on cities to a more controlled and calculated retaliation on key military installations, plus a few cities. In this possible future world, the deterrent forces might be made up, in both the United States and the Soviet Union, of a balanced mix of strategic offensive and defensive systems. Such a balanced offensive and defensive force on both sides might be considered a more desirable two-sided posture from the viewpoint of arms control than the current postures of the two superpowers who now confront each other with their cities naked to attack by the adversary's missiles.

The technology of ballistic missile defense has been discussed in several articles, which have appeared since the latter part of 1965.[7] Of these, perhaps the most interesting is the one by Dr. Charles M. Herzfeld. He explains in layman's terms the advances in radar technology, in defensive missile technology, and in automatic data processing and computational technology. He points out that there are "building blocks" to the Nike-X ballistic missile defense system which can be arranged in many ways to give alternative deployments. This flexibility of the technology and its components furnishes a very considerable strategic flexibility to U.S. planners. For example, one could initially deploy a light attack defense based on the Nike-Zeus long-range missile of the type described above which would guard against attacks from the Communist Chinese and against so-called "small" attacks from the U.S.S.R. This defense could be followed by a deployment of hard-site defense components of Nike-X utilized to defend our missile fields and to guard against technological surprise in the Soviet ICBM force. Or such a protective deployment could be undertaken concurrently with the deployment of a light attack defense. One could stop here, carefully watching the response of both the CPR and the U.S.S.R. to such deployments. Or one could add a deployment of local defense of selected cities, such as the largest 10 or 20 cities in the United States, based on the short-range Sprint missile.

In determining which option is preferable, one must consider the rate of deployment. If the United States or the Soviet Union suddenly entered into a major deployment program in which one side spent perhaps five or ten bil-lion dollars per year on defenses, the other side would interpret this as a "crash program." Such an interpretation would probably trigger a violent response. For example, if the Soviet Union were to embark on such a program, coupled with a large-scale civil defense program, it might mean that the U.S.S.R. was preparing for a total war posture based on a first strike at U.S. forces. A more gradual rate of deployment would evoke less violent reactions. The relevance of this argument is illustrated by the progress of the U.S. civil defense program. Gradually, over the past several years, we have increased the number of effective fallout spaces from a capability to protect tens of millions of people to a capability to protect more than 100 million people. This increased capability has been accomplished without fanfare and without a large annual expenditure of funds. We have observed no violent response from the Soviet Union.

To treat ballistic missile defense, therefore, as if all deployments and all rates of deployment were equally undesirable is to fail to recognize the full range of real-world decision options open to U.S. planners and to the President due to the rapid advances in defense technology. A simplistic, monotonic treatment of ballistic missile defense has been and still is an easy way to avoid thinking about the real issues of deployment decisions and options. It hardly contributes to the clarification of the issues involved—or to an intelligent debate.

6.

The importance of retaining a defensive capability under arms control arrangements designed to reduce Soviet and U.S. offensive weapons systems has been discussed above. It remains for us to examine a few additional arguments favoring the role of BMD to enhance arms control arrangements.

First, let us consider an arms control agreement already in force. Would releasing BMD break the existing ban on nuclear tests in all environments except underground? Certainly, the release of the defensive missiles of a BMD system would lead to nuclear detonations in the atmosphere. If it was clear that BMD had been used to defend ourselves against a missile attack, or even against a single missile, the test ban would not have been violated. It does not prohibit the "wartime" use of nuclear weapons.[8] Our concern about violating the test ban, however, might conceivably lead to stringent rules for releasing BMD. Yet, one of the potential advantages of BMD is that it could prevent disaster from an accidental or an unauthorized missile firing, which would require that the system be automatically released in response to signals indicating a single incoming missile. If the evaluating system had made an error, we would have caused one (or more) nuclear detonations in the atmosphere that might be construed as a test ban violation. This speculation is somewhat academic; the risk seems well worth it, since an accidental or an unauthorized attack by the U.S.S.R. could, if not repulsed, be far more destabilizing than a potential violation of the test ban treaty undertaken in an effort to repulse such an attack.

The role of BMD in stabilizing any agreement for a freeze or a reduction of strategic nuclear delivery vehicles was mentioned previously. Such an agreement, if it comes, would in many ways be more complex, more momentous and more wide-ranging than the present test ban. It would involve for both sides difficult calculations of its effect on the relative strategic balance:

for our side, vital concerns about inspection, verification and sanctions; for the Soviet side, grave issues of intelligence and loosening political control—a further opening up of Soviet society. It is most improbable that these issues can be responsibly settled to the mutual satisfaction of both sides for several years, if they can be settled at all. So far, the Soviet negotiators have shown little interest in a freeze and have instead argued for a drastic *reduction* of delivery vehicles, with only a "strictly limited number," of ICBM's to be retained on the territory of the two superpowers until the process of total disarmament has been completed.

Since the Soviets may go ahead with some BMD deployment in the meantime with the idea of trying to freeze BMD at a zero-increment level on both sides, we would then be faced with the difficult task of inducing the U.S.S.R. to dismantle whatever BMD deployment it might have completed by that time. (Token BMD, it has been reported, is already being deployed around Moscow.)[9] This would complicate the negotiations on a freeze by linking them with negotiations on force reductions, where we would not be dealing simply with equal reductions (such as the percentage reduction envisaged in another of our disarmament proposals) but presumably with a trade of their BMD dismantling against some other reduction on our side. This particular negotiating problem would be less acute if the United States and the Soviet Union happened to possess relatively symmetrical missile defense capabilities at the time the freeze went into effect.

As has been suggested previously, the argument for including BMD in the freeze is that if we freeze only offensive vehicles (and prohibit also the testing of such vehicles except in some critical amount necessary to maintain an operational capability), then advances by one side in the development or sophistication of the defense might upset the balance aimed at in the agreement. In that case, the other side might increase its expenditures on defense to "restore the balance"—and so we would be back in an "arms race," but one restricted to a competition on active defense. Or the other side would be tempted to abrogate the offensive agreement by increasing its penetration capabilities through a test program for penetration aids in violation of the agreement. But from the point of view of long-term arms control objectives a freeze (and later reduction) of strategic delivery vehicles that permitted no BMD at all would be less desirable than a freeze that permitted a certain level of BMD.

Another question also should be examined. Are there advantages in leaving active defenses unrestricted while offensive forces are being reduced through any type of arms control agreement? Some of the advantages in leaving active defensive forces unrestricted have been discussed in the earlier section on strategic stability. It remains to summarize them here. Essentially, three considerations are involved.

First, as indicated previously, a combination of offense and active defense is more complex to analyze than a posture which involves only controlled and inspected offensive forces. Hence, a violator of the arms control agreement who wanted to plan an attack would be confronted with greater uncertainties if the remaining "mix" included defensive forces than if there were only offensive forces left. This uncertainty would strengthen the deterrent and make the intended violator of the agreement more cautious.

Second, active defenses, and especially BMD, can facilitate U.S.-U.S.S.R. disarmament agreements on strategic delivery vehicles by reducing the obstacle that the presence of ambitious independent nuclear powers (such as the CPR) otherwise would present. It is hard to see how the CPR could be induced to accept an agreement to freeze strategic delivery vehicles unless she had already acquired—or was permitted to acquire—a strategic capability of her own that was not insignificant in relation to either the U.S. or the Soviet capability. But given such a Communist Chinese capability, an agreement without active defenses would seem highly unstable. From the Soviet point of view, an agreement which left the U.K. or France free to upset stability might be equally risky. The problem will be compounded if nuclear proliferation continues.

Third, if one envisages a progressive reduction of strategic offensive forces, periods of instability may occur as these forces are reduced. Without active defenses, periods of acute instability may occur as the remaining offensive forces reach the lower levels. At lower levels of offensive armament active defenses might be restabilizing because they would reduce the incentives to violate the agreement.

For at least three reasons, then, retention of active defensive forces, including BMD, might enhance the stability of arms control agreements. To envisage such agreements solely in terms of controlling the offensive forces of the two sides is an oversimplification of the problem. More attention must be given to the role of active defense in the strategic postures of the two sides. As long as this role exists—and technological trends indicate that it will increase, not decrease, in the future—the defensive systems, including BMD, must be taken as fully into account in arms control proposals as are the offensive systems. In fact, BMD seems to hold promise of rendering otherwise risky and potentially destabilizing arms control arrangements far more stable and far less risky. It may be advisable, therefore, for the United States to start thinking now about modifying its proposal for a verified freeze on strategic delivery vehicles by excluding from its scope, at least for the time being, defensive missiles, or by making some other appropriate change in the terms of the proposal. It would be much better to make the necessary alteration before the Soviets show interest in the idea of a freeze than to be put into the awkward position, after the Soviets manifest a desire to discuss the proposal, of having to reserve our previous position or else proceeding to negotiate an agreement under increasingly uncomfortable strategic circumstances.

Notes

1 The author wishes to acknowledge the direct and indirect assistance of Dr. Albert Wohlstetter, currently Professor of Political Science at the University of Chicago, and Dr. Fred C. Iklé, Associate Professor of Political Science at Massachusetts Institute of Technology, for their insights into the questions of strategic stability and the possibility of negotiating arms control and disarmament agreements with the Soviet Union. He would also like to acknowledge the very considerable assistance of Mrs. Anne M. Jonas, Political Scientist, Strategic Studies Center of the Stanford Research Institute.

2 See the preceding article in this volume.

3 Major General N. Talensky, "Anti-Missile Systems and Disarmament," re-printed in *Bulletin of the Atomic Scientists,* February 1965.

4 For a conflicting viewpoint see J. I. Coffey, "China and BMD," *Bulletin of the Atomic Scientists,* December 1965.

5 A freeze on delivery vehicles does not imply a freeze on technological advances. For example, a single ICBM booster in 1966 might become the vehicle for a multiple warhead delivery system in the 1970's capable of attacking not one, but many, targets. In effect, this would vitiate a freeze on strategic delivery vehicles.

6 For an analysis of a shift of Soviet emphasis away from GCD proposals, see Thomas W. Wolfe, "The Soviet Union and Arms Control," The RAND Corporation, P 3337, April 1966, pp. 4-5.

7 Three representative examples are 1) Charles M. Herzfeld, "BMD and National Security." *Annals of the New York Academy of Sciences,* 22 November 1965; 2) Jules Bergman, "If Zeus Fails, Can Sprint Save Us?" *New York Times Magazine,* 20 March 1966; 3) George A. W. Boehm, "Countdown for Nike-X," *Fortune,* November 1965.

8 Article 1, Paragraph 1, of the Test Ban Treaty prohibits nuclear weapon test explosions, or "any other nuclear explosion" in the specified environments. According to the announced U.S. interpretation, this does not impose any limitation on the use of nuclear weapons "in war" (opinion of the State Department Legal Advisor, 14 August 1963).

9 *Washington Post,* 22 September 1965, and "Is Nike-X the Answer in Missile Defense?", *Business Week,* 4 December 1964, p. 33. More recent public pronouncements on this issue have appeared in 1) Stephen Rosenfeld, "Russia Gives Go-Ahead to Anti-Missile Systems," *Washington Post,* 21 April 1966, p. 1; 2) Michael Getler, "McNamara Says Soviets Err on ABM," *Missiles and Rockets,* 2 May 1966.

Risks, Costs and Alternatives

By Jeremy J. Stone

The first thing to understand about U.S. decisions concerning ballistic missile defenses is that they are, and ought to be, based primarily upon our perception of the risk of nuclear war. There is no valid reason for their purchase important enough to justify so large an expenditure, other than their capacity to protect us against the effects of war. Just as we decide each year whether or not the risk of nuclear war justifies additional civil defense preparations, so also must we decide each year whether or not these risks warrant the deployment of ballistic missile defenses. There is no escape from this choice simply because the assessment of such risks is a difficult one. We have no choice but to try to measure them. Indeed, we sometimes forget that we *do* measure them. When Secretary McNamara says Nike-X will not "add measurably to our safety," he does exactly this.

A second and much less important factor is the effectiveness of ballistic missile defenses. But, because these estimates are always changing, because they are more concrete than estimates of the likelihood of nuclear war, because these estimates have been the usual excuse for putting off deployment, we tend to talk a lot about them and

gradually to come to believe that an improvement in defensive efficiency would make "the difference," would justify a deployment not previously justified. This is an error. The probability of war is the important thing. And all of the computations concerning effectiveness do not change the basic fact: that there is an enormous range between optimistic and pessimistic estimates of an incompletely tested and enormously complex system designed against a changing threat, using unknown tactics, in an environment of exploding nuclear weapons. No man in this country knows, and no man in this country will ever know, how well ballistic missile defenses are likely to work.

Just as there is no way to get a realistic test of our air defense system (as General Partridge once testified); just as its effectiveness depends upon a variety of factors which are themselves unknown (as Secretary McNamara has asserted); just as most people believe the air defense system is full of holes (as Herman Kahn has written), so also will it be possible to say these things of a deployed missile defense. We can argue about the numbers, and the arguments can shift our estimates of what is more likely and what is less, but nonquantifiable uncertainties will remain, every bit as large as those we manipulate. The defense might work quite well in some circumstances and quite badly in others; no thoughtful president will ever be persuaded of very much more than this. And, this being so, we should avoid bemusing ourselves with talk of the primary importance of effectiveness.

Third, there are the arms control questions, especially the effect of deployment of BMD on the rate of arms procurement in the major powers. But just as calculations of effectiveness are given too much emphasis by an engineering outlook, so also are arms control questions often given too much emphasis by arms controllers. They tend to focus on what they know best, and gradually come to believe that the interaction between the two opposing systems is the important thing. It is true that we will have a further reason to show restraint ourselves—to avoid building Nike-X—if the Soviets are willing to show comparable restraint. We do not want to encourage them to build a system designed to defend against our own weapons—lest we be forced, immediately or eventually, to take those further steps deemed necessary to maintain our retaliatory capacity beyond even politically motivated doubt. Not being the first to deploy ballistic missile defense helps avoid these and many other problems.

But this does not mean that we would feel obliged, or should act as if we would feel obliged, to retaliate with a system of our own in response to a Soviet system. Why should they be allowed to make such a major decision for us? If their system is one that disturbs us, we should buy retaliatory weapons that negate it. If it does not, we should be mature enough to continue to follow our real interests, just as we did in making previous decisions about deployment. We should not brainwash ourselves into a quiet assumption that we would "have to do something" if the Soviets deployed a missile defense—until we see how they did it, what exactly they did, what domestic political forces are in fact aroused by it, and what would satisfy them. We ought not blithely to play "follow the leader" if we do not need to, or wish to.

Especially important, we should look with some perspective on the alarums that periodically infect our nervous community of strategic experts. We now have a long history of such fears going back to 1960. In April 1962, Senator Thurmond told a secret session of the Armed Services Committee that he had heard there was a missile defense battery being built around Leningrad, and in July 1962 Khrushchev said that he could hit a fly in the sky with an interceptor. Many rushed to say that the Soviets were moving ahead; they were not. Now many seize upon other bits of evidence supposed to show Soviet intentions to press ahead; sometimes it is even argued that progress in Soviet *development* of the system is evidence of intention to deploy. But obviously their development will continue in any case, as does ours, and it constitutes absolutely no independent evidence of their decision, one way or another, to deploy the system under development. My own guess is that they will not make a big effort, simply because they cannot afford it. They never bought a lot of bombers; they were slow to buy large numbers of missiles; their economy is in bad shape; and their perception of the risks of war—hence of the need for defense—must be waning steadily. Their statements about anti-ballistic missiles have been very restrained. Marshal Sokolovsky made a statement at a press conference recently that was almost word for word the statement he made five years ago: statements that in principle the problem of a ballistic missile defense had been solved. The ebullience of Khrushchev is absent in later statements.

Some say there is still a fourth factor to consider. But just as the risk of war was far more important than the effectiveness of the system, so also is this fourth factor still less important in turn. Indeed, this fourth argument is a mistaken one. It refers to the alleged dampening effect of this system on Indian desires to have a bomb. Some have said that we ought to try to persuade the Indians that we would defend them, by showing that we have ballistic missile defenses ready to defend against Chinese intercontinental missiles—missiles which the Chinese will not have for several years even if then. This argument seems a premature attempt to perpetuate an error made in Europe—with unfortunate consequences now being realized. Some years ago, we told ourselves that Europe could only be defended by threatening to respond with a massive attack upon the Soviet Union. Our decision to accept that logic is now bearing bitter fruit. As soon as the ability of the Soviet missile forces to reach our own cities was created, the credibility of our guarantees began to fall into question. Our own reasoning was promptly used against us. We had implicitly laid our prestige on the argument that we could defend others at no cost or very low cost to our cities, and when the costs no longer seemed to be at or near zero, our promise began to fall apart.

Those who made this strategic error are now arguing that we should try it again in Asia. They want us to make our ability to remain unscathed from Chinese attack the lynchpin of our explanation for the defense of India. But the appearance of the first Chinese intercontinental missile will evoke from Asians the same arguments that we now hear from France. Our commitment will again be impugned. "Now what?" the people will say. No one will think our defense perfect and, having acted as if we had to be protected to resist China, as if general war were the only way available to us to respond to China, we will undermine our own reputation as an ally. In short, ballistic missile defenses, as a method of discouraging Indian nuclear acquisition, will eventually *encourage* it.

In the case of Europe, we belatedly returned to what we should have said in the first place. We said we would defend Europe whatever the cost, and we noticed that we had other answers to the real threats. We need to do the same thing in Asia where the political terrain is such that threats of general nuclear war are going to be, if anything, still less effective than they were in Europe.

My own view is that we ought not to buy ballistic missile defenses now because they are not now worth the money—mainly because the chance of nuclear war is sufficiently small. *In addition,* to be the first to deploy ballistic missile defenses would be to stir up the Soviet interest in further offensive weapons, to encourage them to buy their own defensive weapons in response and, in turn, to stir our own interest in offensive weapons. Indeed, the systems will raise a whole variety of new questions over the next five, ten, and fifteen years —questions better avoided, if they possibly can be. We ought to act so as to contain the arms race, so as to constrain weapons procurement, so as to avoid raising new issues in the competition, so as to avoid encouraging recomputations of strategic security, so as to encourage reciprocated restraint. There is no compelling reason to stir up interest in strategic weapons when we are as far ahead as we are at present. It may be that we should not engage in formal agreements on the subject with the Russians because these issues are too sensitive and the agreements would be too complicated to work out. But there are other ways to encourage reciprocated restraint and we ought to cultivate them.

Something ought to be said about the influence of Soviet statements on our internal debate. It is not uncommon in discussing strategic problems with Russians to find that their position slowly evolves from outright rejection, to quiet interest, to assent. There are several reasons for this. They, like us, must have time to get used to ideas and to consider them carefully in private. Furthermore, it requires a good deal more time than one might suppose to communicate accurately what it is that we are proposing. Take, for example, the suggestion that both sides might somehow avoid the procurement of antiballistic missile systems, so long as these seem expensive and only marginally effective, in order to avoid unfortunate effects on the arms race. This is a complicated notion indeed. Our own newspapers sometimes report the suggestion in a variety of ways ranging from the outrageously distorted to the oversimplified: "Some believe that we ought to avoid a ballistic missile defense lest the other side fear an attack and attack himself;" "Some believe that we and the Russians should sign a treaty to avoid defensive weapons altogether so

that each will be able to hold hostage the largest possible number of civilians of the other;" and "Some believe that defenses are bad or immoral."

The Soviet audience, which is even less likely to catch our meaning than a newspaper reporter, may respond to any one of several quite different assertions when it responds negatively. It may be saying: "ballistic missile defenses could never be the cause of war;" "ballistic missile defenses could never be prohibited by treaty because this is political nonsense" or "ballistic missile defenses are not bad or immoral but good and defensive." None of these answers would address our question; but all might be taken as having done so— by both parties. Isolated answers to isolated questions are not really very useful and the tendency to misunderstanding is enormous.

These comments are made with one well-known example in mind; the now famous article of Major General Talensky, one of the few Soviet authors to address himself to the subject.* His views have been widely misquoted and deserve to be put in proper context. First of all, Talensky does not deny the arms race interactions which concern those in the United States who fear another round of arms competition. He says:

Some say the construction of antimissile defense systems may accelerate the arms race, and that the side lagging in such systems may build up its nuclear-rocket attack weapons. That is one of the arguments against defensive systems.

Such a development is not at all ruled out, in much the same way as the possibility that the nuclear-rocket race may

* "Anti-Ballistic Missiles and Disarmament," *International Affairs* (Moscow), No. 10, 1964, pp. 15-19.

be stepped up quantitatively and qualitatively even without any anti-missile systems.

But more important, Talensky misunderstands our argument. It is not the side "lagging in such systems" that may build up its nuclear-rocket attack weapons, but any side which fears a neutralization of its retaliatory force. Unaccustomed to our political system, with its opposition party looking for flaws in the Administration's defense policy, General Talensky may not understand how disruptive it could be for a U.S. Administration to have to admit that its capacity to destroy Russian targets had declined—even if that capacity were declining from 150 to 100 industrial or military complexes. The extent to which we and they may feel obliged, for internal political reasons, to maintain an enormous retaliatory force may be incomprehensible to him. This is suggested also by the apolitical quality of his writing: "It would be illogical to be suspicious of [a peace-loving] state when it creates an anti-missile defense system on the grounds that it wants to make it easier for itself to resort to aggression with impunity." Or "The advantage of anti-missile systems in the political and international law context is that their use is caused by an act of aggression, and they will simply not work unless an aggressor's rocket makes its appearance in flight over a given area. There will be no difficulty at all in deciding who is the aggressor and who the attacked."

The main obstacle to a correct interpretation of Talensky's article is the great, perhaps the insurmountable, difficulty in deciding what it is that he represents in the Soviet decision-making apparatus. Any one of a great number of our generals, retired and on active duty, share his opinions precisely. They would argue: "that anti-missile systems are defensive weapons in the full sense of the word"; that "sooner or later, every new means of attack leads to the emergence of a means of defense;" that distinctions between "peace-loving states" and "potential aggressors" are of overriding relevance to the decision. Thus, General Talensky's opinions are not notable for being arcane or even novel; they do not suggest that the Soviets are quite different from ourselves. We have heard his arguments from others on our side; they raise no new theoretical problems for us. The question about which we are really debating is whether or not his views will permeate the Soviet Government sufficiently to be acted upon eventually. "Eventually" should be emphasized because Talensky does not suggest any great urgency: "It is quite illogical to demand abstention from creating such weapons . . . ," and, ". . . if disarmament and its attendant measures are put off indefinitely, while the means of nuclear-rocket attack are being built up, it would hardly be in the interests of any peace-loving state to forego the creation of its own effective system of defense . . . ." It is unfortunate that we do not have access to enough Soviet opinions to enable us to resist the temptation to adopt uncritically the views of one writer as dominant. We have been especially ready to accept General Talensky's comments as authoritative because many believe that they are consistent with Soviet actions in buying enormous quantities of anti-bomber defenses— actions presumed to reflect a long-standing proclivity for defensive systems or important vested interests in the Soviet Union which will again argue for defenses. There is a much simpler explanation, however, for past Soviet actions, which is that the society as a whole was far more frightened than our own, far more persuaded that a war might be forced upon it, and hence far more inclined to try to protect itself. The implications of this explanation for future Soviet policy are quite different from the implications of those who posit a "defensive psychology" or a bureaucratic lobby, because it suggests reasons more likely to be affected by changing perceptions of the risk of war.

There are other arguments for missile defense and against it—too many of them. We have thought about the problem too long, too deeply, and too anxiously; most of us have lost our perspective. We argue about the issues that interest us most, or those which lend themselves best to conversation or controversy. We invent arguments that are rather more ingenious than real; we explore aspects of the situation which are far too minor to be of substantial interest. The debate becomes infected with the very curious points of view of those who have not put themselves into the shoes of one who must make the decision. Let me close by warning of at least five of these points of view for which one should watch out.

First, beware the apocalyptic point of view: those who still hear echoes of the missile gap, or worse, and see in missile defenses the possibility of Soviet ultimatums, of ripples of fear spreading around the world, of cries for appeasement. Missile defenses have not the political or strategic power to evoke such disasters.

Second, beware the lover of gadgets: those who would buy any new system, any new weapon, because it is new, novel, a technological advance and "progress," whatever its costs, its function, its effects. We do not need, we do not intend to buy, we ought not buy, every weapon possible. Beware the man who thinks we should.

Third, beware those who think that money is no object. Obviously if missile defenses cost nothing, we would buy them. Obviously they cost large sums of money. There are some whose advocacy of missile defenses can be traced to their view that "money is no object," which means, in effect, that missile defenses cost nothing for them. Such a perspective is unreal in the decision-making process and irrelevant to it.

Fourth, beware the war-game mentality: those who would estimate the relative effects of missile defense entirely in terms of their calculations; those who think that if we build a missile defense and tell China how good it is, that the Chinese will, like a good war-game opponent, forget about building ICBM's; those who think the system will work as expected; those who think of its strategic effects in war, but not much of its arms race effects in peace, and not at all of its political implications.

Fifth, beware the too subtle argument: we have been thinking about this problem so long that the debate has become filled with arguments and approaches that were not evident at first and will not be evident in the end.

Finally, we ought to try to deflate the problem. It involves serious costs and risks either way. It can be a hard choice to make, but it is not a world-shaking one. We must maintain our perspective, our balance, our confidence, if we are not to let the most dramatic, the most striking, the most fearsome, aspects of the choice distort our decision.

BMD in a Strategy for Peace

By Edward Teller

1. Vulnerability and Disarmament

Nuclear explosives and intercontinental missiles have deprived the United States of the protection of its ocean barriers. Today our country is open to a more sudden attack than Poland was in 1939. Our ability to retaliate has so far insured peace and the survival of the United States. The fact remains, however, that the security of America has become just as precarious as the security of the powers of Europe has been for hundreds of years.

On an emotional basis one can easily understand the attractive nature of the most straightforward solution. The present state of instability and danger is due to nuclear explosives and other modern armaments. The solution therefore should be disarmament. If we could get rid of the new dangerous instruments, we would free ourselves of the danger itself.

If the argument for disarmament is put into such a simple and straightforward form almost everyone will recognize inherent fallacies. The emotional driving force, however, remains powerful even though the counter-arguments are obvious.

Actually, disarmament will contribute to stability only if it applies to everyone, if it is controlled, and if it is rigorously enforced. The very first requirement, that of adequate knowledge of the state of armaments in the Communist countries, is not fulfilled and will not be fulfilled in the foreseeable future. All of these questions are closely related to the paramount question of national sovereignty. The right of self-defense will not be relinquished unless credible defense is established by a trusted agency. The difficulties are indeed recognized; most will agree that no one has presented as yet a complete and feasible plan for disarmament or arms limitation.

In the meantime, continued development of powerful weapons renders the international situation more unstable with every passing year. The name by which this danger is designated today is proliferation. The explosion of Chinese nuclear devices has demonstrated that modern weapons of destruction are within the reach of less developed countries. The recognition of this fact has furnished persuasive arguments, if not for disarmament, then at least for arms control.

What we really want is, however, not arms control or disarmament for its

99

own sake. What we do want is peace and stability. The purpose of the following note is to discuss to what extent disarmament or arms control will in fact contribute to stability, to what extent the proposed arms control agreements might give rise to additional dangers, and what other measures could be taken to approach a more stable situation in the present troubled state of the world.

2. The Consequences of Banning Nuclear Tests

It has been accepted by the majority of U.S. policymakers that some form of a test ban is in our interest because it slows down the further development of nuclear explosives and because it impedes proliferation. The history of test limitations must be discussed not to criticize past actions or to suggest radical changes but rather to find out what validity the claim has that a test ban is the first step toward lasting peace. The relevant arguments fill many volumes and no one can expect to draw a complete balance between advantages and disadvantages of a test ban.

The present test ban limits to some extent the development of Russian nuclear explosives. On the other hand, the study of the 1957-61 moratorium shows the limited nature of such an advantage. During that period of nearly four years the Russians made thorough preparations for a new test series and have claimed great progress as a result of that test series. Since they had ample time for the preparation, this claim is probably valid. It is likely that without a moratorium their overall progress would have been greater. On the other hand, one can hardly doubt that due to the moratorium the Rusians gained an advantage relative to us. Following the moratorium they executed two well-prepared atmospheric test series while we had only one similar series for which the preparation was of necessity less thorough.

It has been claimed that the present limited test ban discourages the development of nuclear explosives by additional nations. Secretary McNamara stated in public testimony that underground tests are too expensive and will therefore limit the spread of nuclear weapons. In a subsequent discussion Secretary McNamara said that an underground test is too expensive only in a political and psychological sense. Indeed the money expended in the actual operations of an underground test is quite negligible as compared to the money needed to develop the nuclear explosive itself. Therefore the present limited test ban impedes the spread of nuclear weapons at best in an indirect manner. If proliferation is to be avoided, much more effective measures must be employed.

A comprehensive test ban has been suggested as the remedy. However, the examples of France and China show that a test ban is not a fully sufficient answer to our problem. Further worries arise because of the fact that small tests can be carried out in secrecy and that a country may develop nuclear weapons and refrain from testing them except at a time immediately preceding intended use of the weapons.

The present limited test ban has the obvious advantage of eliminating further contamination of the atmosphere. Without repeating the numerous arguments concerning this important question one may mention three simple facts:

(1) Worldwide contamination due to nuclear tests has never exceeded ten per cent of the natural background.

(2) Agreement to limit the activity

released to the atmosphere can be satisfactorily policed and would be consistent with reducing radioactive contamination well below ten per cent of the natural radiation. Such limitation would not interfere with technological progress needed for defense.

(3) In some parts of Brazil and in the province of Kerala on the east India coast, natural radioactivity exceeds the worldwide average background by more than one thousand per cent and makes a contribution of more than a hundred times greater than fallout. There is no clear-cut indication that this high level of activity had harmful consequences on the population that has lived in these neighborhoods for many centuries, though it must be conceded that the proof of the absence of such consequences is exceedingly difficult and cannot be given in a rigorous sense.

One very important worry connected with present and projected test ban situations is the behavior of Russia. Radioactivity released in Siberia on 15 January 1965 shows that the Russians are not observing the limited test ban in as scrupulous a manner as we are. It is not clear to what extent secret violations may occur in case a comprehensive test ban is signed at a future date. The extensive preparations that the Russians must have made prior to their test series in the early fall of 1961 had remained secret, and the breaking of the test moratorium actually took us by surprise. All of this indicates in a clear fashion that a test ban puts stronger limitation on developments in the United States than on the developments in the Soviet Union.

The most important argument against the test ban is the fact that the Russians seem to have proceeded further toward the development of a missile defense than the United States. To catch up in this most important field and to introduce a system that is experimentally verified and which is therefore reasonably reliable requires testing. More specifically, it requires testing in the atmosphere. By accepting a limited test ban we have probably accepted a position inferior to the Russians in the important field of missile defense. The disadvantage might possibly be overcome by a great effort which we continue to postpone. A comprehensive test ban would make such an effort all but impossible. It should be understood that if the Russians possess a sufficiently good missile defense while we do not, then our present posture of deterrence will have been seriously weakened.

3. Arms Control and Enforcement

It is obvious that to set up rules which are made without providing a method of enforcement and without carrying out such enforcement will have harmful consequences. The best known historical example taken from a situation very different from arms control is the story of prohibition in the United States. In this instance the establishment of a law to operate within the United States and backed up by the Constitution of our country had not accomplished its purpose and led to the proliferation of organized crime. This was due to the fact that neither the citizenry nor the police were prepared to enforce prohibition in a consistent manner.

What holds for national enforcement, which in most cases is dependable, should be valid with much greater force for international law in which the very foundations of tradition, respect and stability do not exist. Introduction of international regulations which are not enforced is likely to result in a continuing lack of respect for international legality. At the present time international order based upon international law seems to be the only alternative to increasing danger and to eventual chaos. Therefore it would be particularly unfortunate if we would initiate a treaty or a structure of treaties which we have no means and perhaps no intention to enforce.

The problem becomes much more vivid if we try to connect it with a situation which exists at the present time. This is the question of our response to the Chinese nuclear explosions.

From a logical point of view there are four possible ways in which the Chinese nuclear explosions and agreement concerning non-proliferation can be related to each other. The first is to abolish the Chinese nuclear production capacity and to establish an international non-proliferation agreement. The second is to abolish the Chinese plant and not to introduce a non-proliferation agreement. The third is to allow the Chinese to continue the production of nuclear weapons and establish an international agreement; and the last is to do nothing, that is, to allow the Chinese to continue operation and not to undertake steps for the prevention of the spreading of nuclear arms. The discussion of each of these possibilities will give us some needed insight.

The first alternative has been advocated by many people of differing political views. The proposal possesses elements of realism. If the Chinese facilities for the production of nuclear weapons are wiped out by American action, this will lessen immediate dangers of Chinese aggression and will at the same time put teeth into any prospective non-proliferation agreement. Such a course of action would be a clear signal that a law of non-proliferation will not be handled in the same ineffective and disastrous manner as prohibition.

At the same time this energetic course of action seems to me dangerous, of doubtful eventual utility, and questionable from the moral point of view. It is true that the Chinese have engaged several times in aggressive action. This may serve to justify the bombing of Chinese plants. Such bombing may be preceded by an appropriate warning in order to free us of the reproach of having killed unsuspecting Chinese operators. But to my mind the basis of morality is to act according to principles which can be properly applied in all essentially similar cases. If we abolish Chinese production facilities, we shall have no effective reason to protest if the Russians do the same thing to French facilities. Indeed violent reprisal against proliferation may make a non-proliferation treaty effective, but the price that has to be paid is to apply force even before a new and beneficial law has been firmly established in the minds and the feelings of the people throughout the world.

The bombing of the Chinese plants would be a harsh measure and its ultimate utility may not be great. The Chinese could and probably would replace their facilities in utmost secrecy and we might not be able to wipe out these facilities a second time. The danger therefore would be merely delayed and the period of delay could be less than five years. Thus the establishment of nuclear power by additional nations would be firmly linked to the requirement of secrecy and would give great additional stimulus to secrecy measures not only in China but in other countries as well. Enforcement of non-proliferation would have to extend to the breaking of any secrecy and we would therefore be forced to interfere with the detailed internal operation of each country suspected of developing nuclear explosives.

Thus the first alternative, though apparently realistic, would be in the end useless unless it is the first step of comprehensive international control, perhaps even amounting to international tyranny. This type of operation could be exercised by the Russians. It could not be undertaken by the United States as long as we are to adhere to the basic principles on which our society is built.

The second alternative is to abolish the Chinese production units but not to establish treaties or controls prohibiting proliferation. This exceedingly hard line may be advocated by those who want to consider the interests of the United States without making concessions to liberal views or to world opinion. The argument adduced in favor of such action may be that in order to exercise control we must use our power where it counts and that we need not be concerned about public opinion at home or abroad. I feel that this course of action has most of the disadvantages enumerated above and at the same time can be defended less effectively on the basis of general principles. I certainly would not want to argue for this alternative.

The third possibility is most popular among the planners of arms control and disarmament: We should not interfere with present Chinese plants but at the same time press for an international agreement prohibiting further proliferation. The great weakness of this approach lies in the fact that it does not impose any plausible penalties on the breaking of the arms control agreement. In fact, by permitting the Chinese to arm, we lend strong probability to a prediction that development of nuclear explosives by any additional nation will not meet with any meaningful reprisal. Since the increase of Chinese power exposes additional nations to uncertainty and danger, it is quite probable that an anti-proliferation treaty will not carry sufficient authority.

A further danger of the anti-proliferation treaty lies in the weakening of the NATO Alliance. The Russians are apt to agree to this treaty for precisely this reason. Our unwillingness to share atomic information and atomic technology with the French has already produced serious disagreement within the Western Alliance. A rigorous interpretation of an anti-proliferation treaty may deprive other NATO members of effective or plausible support by the United States. If laxity of enforcement will lead to the development of atomic explosives by other and possibly less advanced countries, Western Germany and other NATO allies might indeed become restless.

Because of all of these circumstances I consider this alternative—not to stop Chinese development but to conclude an essentially unpoliced non-proliferation treaty—as the choice of greatest danger. Unfortunately the forces driving us toward this alternative are strong, and indeed this possibility of maximum treaty obligations combined with minimum action and enforcement may become a reality in the near future.

There remains only one alternative: This is not to interfere with Chinese development and not to conclude any treaty limiting proliferation. This appears to be the most probable course of action or more precisely, it is the likely outcome because it consists in taking no action whatsoever. If one considers only the alternatives that we have so far discussed, the situation is most unsatisfactory. However, the inaction as described by the last alternative leaves the door open for action in other respects. I believe that strong arguments can be adduced for not bombing the Chinese and for not concluding treaties that are apt to remain ineffective but to look for increased safety by other means. We shall turn now toward other methods that are apt to make peace more secure and the survival of our country more probable.

4. The Need for an Ample Retaliatory Force

The first step toward increased security has been already accomplished by the United States. It consists of the establishment of a reasonably secure retaliatory force. This force has been designed as a second strike force to be directed against the Soviet Union in case the United States should be attacked. A portion of the same force may have to be used if an attack is inflicted upon us by another power, for instance by Red China.

It has been frequently claimed that our second strike force must be considered as a danger and a liability because it might be triggered by a false alarm and in this way could give rise to war by accident. Some "scientific" arguments have even claimed that such an accident will become a certainty in the course of time for the simple reason that the probability of malfunction is cumulative. Such an assertion disregards the fact that the safeguards which are introduced against malfunction have been steadily increased and the sum of an ever-decreasing number of small probabilities can be held to a level which still is of negligible size.

Considering the necessary safeguards of security, it is unfortunately impossible to give explicit proof of this statement.

There is one method by which the probability of accidental war can be decreased to a considerable and decisive extent. This is to delay the retaliatory strike. An important advantage of such a proposal lies in the fact that it could rule out not only war by accident but also war by the provocation of a third party. If we are attacked we need not assume blindly that the attack must have come from the Soviet Union. It is possible to wait and check before we strike back.

On the other hand, a delayed second strike has disadvantages which may appear to have overwhelming importance. It has been argued with great plausibility that after a large-scale attack the devastation in our country would be so great that any further decisions would be meaningless and that delay of the counterattack might just serve to give the enemy time to complete his destructive action.

This brings us to a most important point. Retaliation, and most particularly delayed retaliation, is meaningful only if two additional conditions are satisfied. The most important one is that eventual retaliation must be certain. This requires ample and well-protected retaliatory power. The second is a considerable amount of passive defense or civil defense which could guarantee the survival of the major portion of our citizenry and also insure the rebuilding of our country and economy within a relatively short time. All of this could be carried out with particularly great effectiveness if we should establish active missile defense as well so as to blunt any attack on our country.

All this adds up to a clear picture. If we believe in a second strike force, and indeed our policy for the preservation of peace has been based on assured retaliation, then this second strike force must be ample to insure against surprising technological progress in Russia. The closed Russian state is particularly apt to bring forth such surprises without previous warning. Therefore our second strike force if it is to be reliable must be insured and reinsured.

One must always keep in mind that though deterrence is designed to prevent a nuclear attack and should indeed prevent it, our plan can work only if we continue to consider the possibility of such an attack as an ever-present danger. The insurance against technological surprise must consist mainly in excellent scientific work, but in addition it is necessary to have several alternatives for retaliation, such as land-based and submarine-launched missiles. At the same time it is necessary to insure the survival of the retaliatory force by appropriate means such as mobility or active defense. In this way we can prevent the destruction of our retaliatory force by a preemptive strike from Russia.

All this is in sharp contrast with the present trend of buying defense for a minimum amount of money. Such economy is connected with unavoidable risks, and there can be little doubt that the United States can afford to spend what is needed for safety.

It has been suggested that our retaliatory force should be limited so as not to make it appear unnecessarily provocative. It is, however, the nature of a reliable retaliatory force that it must be abundant. He who plans to deliver the first strike and possesses reasonably accurate information about his opponent may plan his attack using a moderately sized safety factor. If one assumes that Russia does plan a first strike in case the opportunity appears favorable,

the conditions for economic planning may be fulfilled *there*. For the forces planned by the *United States* strict economy is dangerous because we are building a second strike force to be effective at an unknown date and because we cannot and do not obtain detailed information about Russia, and particularly about the technological surprises that the Soviets may have in store for us.

An overwhelming second strike force is indeed not characterized by its provocative nature but rather by its safe and reliable character. If the retaliatory force is barely sufficient, the men responsible for the defense of our country may be exposed to most terrible psychological stresses. They may be tempted to retaliate prematurely so as to be able to retaliate at all. If on the other hand the force is ample, time is gained for deliberate action and thus mistakes can be avoided.

It is equally important that though our response may be delayed, it should be absolutely assured. In particular, our retaliatory system should be so organized that if all centers of higher command are put out of action by an attack, then the officer of more limited responsibility should automatically have the right and in fact the duty to release the retaliatory forces which are under his command. This system of organization should be not only known but in fact advertised so that it should not be in the interest of the attacker to destroy our centers of political decisions. The attacker should know that destruction of the centers would even more surely and speedily bring about retaliation. In the same measure in which we are determined not to strike first, we should make absolutely sure that the second strike will be launched. Otherwise deterrence will not be credible and will fail to accomplish its purpose.

5. Civil Defense

A realistic policy based on deterrence is not possible if we consider nuclear war as the end of our civilization. Such a war would indeed be more terrible than anything we can remember. Nevertheless effective measures are possible which give us a good chance to survive as a nation.

This statement will not be easily accepted. It hinges on the effectiveness of civil defense and the possibility of reconstruction after an enemy attack. We have done next to nothing in these important respects. Nevertheless it is true that civil defense can be effective particularly when combined with missile defense. That the latter measure is within the realm of possibility is made plausible by the Russian effort and can be borne out by detailed technological arguments. While it is not possible to prevent the penetration of some missiles to an altitude low enough so that great damage will be done, it has been recognized for quite a few years that one can hope to prevent almost all surface bursts in thickly populated areas. If one can force the enemy missiles to explode at a reasonable distance from the most heavily populated regions, then well-designed shelters which protect against fallout, fire and blast will save the great majority of our people. Since construction of such shelters requires a great proportion of unskilled labor and since we have at the present time an abundance of such labor, the building of the shelters can be carried out without upsetting the economy of our country.

A difficult problem in the immediate lifesaving effort connected with civil defense is due to the fact that in a surprise attack, warning time may be short. This requires a wide distribution of shelters and it also requires sufficient preparation not very different from the lifeboat drills which are always undertaken at the beginning of an ocean trip.

The reconstruction of our country after a nuclear attack is a less difficult job than most people imagine. It is relevant to remind that we can easily produce and stockpile the prime necessity for such reconstruction: extensive, well-protected, and reasonably distributed food reserves. Furthermore, it is possible in our abundant economy to mothball and safely store equipment before it is completely worn out and thus make it available for emergency purposes. It is important to remember that in the scarce economy of Russia, civil defense and proper preparation for reconstruction is much more difficult to develop than in the highly advanced economy of the United States. As long as we are forced to participate in a Cold War, there is every reason that we should emphasize those aspects of the Cold War where natural advantage is on our side and this is the case for civil defense.

There is perhaps one additional point which bears mentioning. The total goods in the United States have a value roughly equivalent to three times the annual national product. Most people do not realize that this figure is so low, though the fact is well known to economists. Thus reconstruction should not be an impossible task, however widespread the destruction, as long as the majority of the population is saved, food and sanitation are available, some emergency organization is maintained, and the necessary tools have been stockpiled.

The two problems of preventing a war and surviving it are of course intertwined. The more probable our survival, the less will be the temptation for a powerful enemy to attack us. If on the other hand we give up hope to survive a nuclear attack, the attack itself becomes more probable. Thus civil defense becomes an integral part of the policy aimed at stability and peace.

6. The Role of a Delayed Response

The planning of a delayed response needs particularly careful discussion. It is often assumed that delaying the response will lead to greatly reduced effectiveness both because of aggressive action against our second strike force by the enemy and because more time is available to the enemy for palliative measures such as evacuation of his population. The first of these points is fully valid only if we have not prepared the type of overwhelming retaliatory force which we are considering here.

The second point is most significant. I would like to argue that the enemy should be given every chance to save his people. If we are attacked by the Soviets, it should not be and it need not be our aim to kill Russians. What we must do is to annihilate the power base of the Communists, that is, we must flatten their cities, destroy their factories, interrupt their communications, and render the organized functioning of the country impossible. Under these conditions the Soviets will have lost the means by which to dominate the world and they will therefore have lost the very things for which they are fighting. This more than any other action is likely to deter Communist aggression.

The more Russians we can save under these conditions, the better it is. After the Communist power is demonstrably broken, the Russian people will regard their Communist masters in a very different light. This is particularly true if we warn the Russian population to leave the target areas, if we use clean explosives, if we demonstrate our respect for life, and if we do anything in our power to save lives by supplying food and medicine in any area where organized aggression is at an end. All this is in the best tradition of our own history, though this fact may have been obscured by the horror stories concerning the cataclysmic course of a thermonuclear war. It cannot and must not be forgotten that such a war is dreadful beyond imagination. But these dangers and terrors do not justify unnecessary killing and should not permit any negligence with respect to the saving of human lives under all realizable conditions.

The greatest limitation of our defense effort at present is not lack of money or means. I believe that our weakness lies in internal disunity which has its obvious roots in the feeling that nuclear war can never be justified. It is indeed true that nuclear war should be avoided under all possible circumstances, but it happens to be true that we can avoid war only by proper preparedness. In turn, this preparedness is much more justified and will be performed in a more effective manner if we do everything we can to maintain the effective power of our ideas and of our society without causing unnecessary suffering. This principle has guided us in the past. The dangers of the present situation increase the responsibility to adhere to the same principles in the future.

Thus a delayed response could lead to better preparedness based on more justified procedures. At the same time it may also pay off in laying the foundations of a lasting peace in case the horrible disaster of a nuclear war may actually be inflicted upon us. An object lesson of the most repulsive lucidity is furnished by the experience of the Nazi armies which were first welcomed in parts of the conquered Eastern regions, such as the Baltic countries; but soon the inhumanity of the Nazis turned the population against the invaders. This had more to do with the eventual defeat of Hitler than most people realize. While I am certain that no one in our country will plan destruction for its own sake, we may commit a serious mistake by not limiting the damage to human life in every possible way.

Thus delayed response may emerge as the safest, most practical, morally justifiable alternative that is open to us if we are ever forced to respond in a nuclear exchange.

7. Proliferation and Missile Defense

The last question to be discussed in connection with our retaliatory posture is how our plans have to be adjusted to the problem of proliferation. It is rightly stated that no defense is sufficient to rule out the possibility of a nuclear explosive being sneaked into our country. Such an explosive may indeed be set off with a terrifying effect. I hope to show, however, that such action would serve the advantage of none of our enemies. The real danger lies in a surprise attack of a sufficiently massive character, and this danger will have to be discussed separately.

The detonation of one nuclear device could be particularly dangerous in case it triggers a nuclear exchange between the major opponents. Our recommended procedure of appropriate delay would effectively eliminate this danger. A big blow against the United States which is, however, far short of having a crippling effect would in all likelihood be followed by proper retaliation against the government that has perpetrated such a crime.

Actually a single nuclear explosion will put our country into an alert state in which no effort will be spared to prevent further damage. The resulting complications and the toughening of the attitude of the United States would be a setback to our competitors, including the Soviet Union. There is no reason to believe that any one will find sufficient inducement to perpetrate mischief on such an enormous scale.

There remains the possibility of blackmail. That this is a dangerous course for any country to undertake is obvious. It is not likely to be undertaken unless the probability of success is great. And this probability need not be great if the threat is a single terrible explosion rather than a credible danger to our national survival. It is necessary and it will remain necessary for the leaders of our country to be tough-minded and not to give in to threats of nuclear attack. There is no substitute for determined leadership, and only determined leadership can face up to blackmail in the Nuclear Age. If great but limited damage is inflicted on our country, this will in the end bring disastrous results to the criminal party but not to ourselves. It remains difficult but it should be possible to remain firm and to find the right course of action in the face of nuclear threats. That such threats may come from more quarters as proliferation proceeds is a most unfortunate circumstance which, however, might prove to be unavoidable.

There is another and bigger danger which we should and indeed can avoid. One of the newcomers to the "nuclear club" may threaten an annihilating blow against the United States. For the reasons mentioned above, I believe that it is most unlikely that such a threat would be actually carried out; but a threat of a massive attack may put intolerable pressure upon our Administration. Let us assume, for instance (and this assumption is by no means implausible), that within the next five or ten years the Chinese acquire a sizeable arsenal of thermonuclear explosives together with fairly accurate medium-range rockets that can be delivered from shipboard. Let us further assume that China will want to conquer Taiwan. The Chinese may threaten to deliver a simultaneous annihilating blow against all the major cities of the United States if we should interfere with their aggressive plans. It will be an incredibly hard decision for our President to take the required risk if the stakes are as high as the continued national existence of the United States. It is necessary to find a way to counter threats of such dimensions. Fortunately appropriate defensive action is possible.

There has been extensive discussion of the question whether active missile defense can be carried out in an effective manner. Valid arguments can be adduced on both sides as long as we are faced with a massive and sophisticated attack, such as the Russians might launch against us. But there can be little doubt that we could establish within a few years an active missile defense which can blunt a Chinese attack. It is not claimed that our defense will be completely airtight and that not a single Chinese hydrogen bomb will get through. It is claimed, however, that we can destroy most of the missiles in a less massive Chinese attack so that the results, while dreadful, will not wreck our country. All of this does not mean that defense will cause the dangers of the Nuclear Age to disappear. It means only that the size of the danger will be reduced to dimensions which can be managed by men of wisdom and character.

The cost of the needed missile de-fense will run into billions of dollars. But this cost should be gladly paid for the safety of our country. Such a missile defense will fall short of an adequate insurance against a Russian attack. However, the uncertainties introduced by the existence of the missile defense may cause the rulers of the Kremlin to hesitate before launching an attack.

While we install a missile defense sufficient to stop the Chinese, we will obtain more experience and will be in a better position to judge the cost of a massive defense which can stop an attack launched by Russia; it may turn out that the cost for the defender is not much greater than the cost for the aggressor. In that case defense on a big scale would indeed be justified.

What is recommended here is obviously a difficult and expensive procedure. I am asking for a bigger, stronger, and more assured retaliatory force, and I am furthermore asking for passive and for active defense measures. All of these forces must be kept up to date. One must expect that any such proposal will be met with the statement that such defense will bankrupt our country. To this one might answer that in the course of the last fourteen years our defense expenditures have fallen from approximately 15% of the national product to 9% of the national product. In the same period the risks to our national survival have risen in a dramatic manner. We did not face bankruptcy in 1952. There is no reason to doubt that our country is strong enough and wealthy enough to do what need be done in order to survive.

8. The Effect of Missile Defense on NATO

What has been proposed is to replace disarmament or arms control by the buildup of national strength and by a policy of patience that can be coupled with such strength. But strength is not enough. The greatest immediate danger which we face today may not lie in Vietnam but in France. It is a remarkable fact that the danger of disintegration of NATO can be directly traced to questions connected with nuclear explosives. It was the nuclear shield that held NATO together during its first years. It was our unwillingness to share nuclear responsibility with our allies which threatens to break up NATO at the present time.

Greater strength in the hands of the United States will make our promise to protect NATO a more credible one. It might be remembered that the initial days of the Cuban missile crisis marked the only period of cordial relations between France and our country within the last few years. The determined posture of our Administration brought an immediate favorable reaction from President de Gaulle.

At the same time our proposals may have in part a damaging or even a disruptive effect upon the NATO Alliance. Let us assume that we introduce effective missile defense which will allow us to face up to Chinese blackmail. Let us assume at the same time that no similar defense is available to our European allies. That the psychological effects of this situation will be damaging is obvious. The effects may be sufficiently strong to lead to a dissolution of the Alliance. In the long run the unity of NATO and its development toward an even stronger cooperation is the best insurance we have had in the past and can possibly have in the future against Communist encroachment.

One of the significant consequences of an anti-proliferation treaty may be the exclusion of missile defense from the European area. Missile defense cannot be established without defensive nuclear warheads. Furthermore missile defense requires a most advanced and sophisticated application of nuclear technology. England, France, and other European countries may develop their own small retaliatory force. They cannot develop an effective missile defense without our full cooperation. The greatest danger in an anti-proliferation treaty might be the circumstance that it could prevent for the next decades a really effective defense of Western Europe.

If we look at the same situation from the opposite side we obtain the opposite picture. An offer of a joint missile defense could be the strongest move we can make to insure the functioning and strengthening of the NATO Alliance. French military theorists, in particular General Gallois, have asserted that in the Nuclear Age an alliance cannot be operational in the sense that one country will defend another at the risk of its own survival. Instead it is contended that even a small retaliatory force available to each of the cooperating Western nations will be sufficient to deter a Russian attack. This claim is fallacious.

The emerging fact of Russian missile defense will render a small retaliatory force useless. At the same time the effective and large-scale help of the United States in establishing a missile defense for Western Europe is a vital requirement for each of the allied countries.

The objection obviously arises that such missile defense will amount to rapid proliferation by placing nuclear explosives in the hands of many participating nations. It is clearly required that each of the Western nations should be given the full right to conduct its own defenses, with the help of nuclear explosives if need be, in case a major portion of its population is threatened by approaching missiles. At the same time one may fear that the defensive nuclear warheads may be used for the wrong purpose, namely, the initiation of a nuclear conflict.

Actually, ample safeguards can be erected against the misuse of the defensive explosives. Apparatus can be installed which will make the weapon promptly available for an appropriate aerial burst over the country that is to be defended. But if the attempt is made to use the nuclear bomb for any other purpose, for instance, if it is removed from its mounting to be used later in a tactical operation, then one can make sure that the warhead will completely ruin itself and at the same time furnish automatic notice at appropriate places (such as NATO headquarters and Washington) that an unplanned use has been attempted. The technical means fortunately exist by which we can make certain that defensive preparedness will be used for nothing except the proper kind of defense.

The establishment of an effective missile defense is a question of survival for ourselves and our allies. The problem is partly an economic one. To a very great extent it is, however, a difficult development in scientific technology of the most abstruse kind. Cooperation of the best brains in Europe is needed to accelerate our own effort. The work of experienced men in our country would in turn be of the greatest help to our European friends, and the American arsenal of fissionable materials together with our mass production facilities would be an absolute requirement if our allies are to enjoy the contribution to safety which missile defense can provide. It is of course not necessary and not desirable that we foot the whole bill. A very great portion of the defense consists in local construction work as well as in special efforts in which some of our allies excel. It is a clear case where the whole can be much more than the sum of its parts.

Meaningful cooperation for defense is the mainstay of NATO unity. This cooperation of course must be much broader than missile defense. In the touchy and hazardous field of nuclear cooperation the purely defensive measures should, however, be in the forefront of our present plans. They are urgent, and furthermore they are most obviously justified. In the long run we must share more responsibilities, and in the end, perhaps, complete Western unity in international politics may develop. This could serve as the fixed point from which we may move the world toward law and order.

9. The Question of Symmetry

In many arguments concerning disarmament and the hazards of war, the scientific fiction of symmetry has been introduced. It is assumed explicitly or implicitly that any measure serving the interest of peace is equally desired by the two great powers, that the actions and motivations of these two great powers are basically similar, and that the plans should be laid out in a manner equally affecting the two great countries. This point of view appears to have the advantage of true justice in that it is certainly not affected by prejudice or pride in one's own favor.

On the other hand, the assumption of symmetry flies in the face of a few obvious facts. Russia is and has been for the past centuries organized as a closed society. Our society is open. The Communist leaders have inherited a doctrine that is not only purposeful but is in fact overabundant in missionary zeal. Our own way to regard the world is more modest and more comfortable. I have tried in the last sentences to avoid words that imply value judgments. In fact, value judgments are intimately connected with the statements that have been made, but it should also be recognized that all such value judgments have a double edge.

It probably is not fully justified to interpret the Soviets' repeated statement that they will bury capitalism in a too literal and violent sense. At the same time it is quite possible that the Russian leaders will consider it their duty to "liberate" the world if, due to our overcautious and parsimonious defense policy or due to mistaken attempts at arms control, an opportunity is offered to the Russians to carry out their grand design while risking only a limited amount of damage. All too frequently the power of modern weapons is equated with the certainty that American retaliation will succeed. In a rapidly changing technological situation this may not be taken for granted. While clear aggressive designs may indeed be far from the thoughts of the Russian leaders, this statement cannot be made with any degree of certainty, and it is incumbent on us to provide for the real if not overwhelmingly great probability that such designs might be considered as possible alternatives by the Russian policymakers.

Finally, one must clearly realize that even without aggressive designs tensions are apt to develop and that these tensions do lead to acute situations in which only moderation or fear of retaliation will prevent war. Given the real differences between the United States and Russia, I believe that peace will be best preserved if we rely to some measure on the fear of retaliation in the minds of the Communists. We have every reason to be confident that moderation will apply on the part of the United States.

The best guarantee of peace is appropriate force in the hands of those who want peace. It was the purpose of the above pages to apply this simple rule to the present difficult and rapidly changing situation.

Chapter 4

ARMS CONTROL
IN SOVIET AND CHINESE STRATEGY

China's Attitude Toward Arms Control

By Harold C. Hinton

Communist China is a disadvantaged and anti-status-quo power and is likely to remain so, at least in the eyes of its leadership, for some years to come. It is near enough to being unified to be strong and yet just disunited enough to be troublesome and difficult. It tends to insist that an actual formal arms control and disarmament arrangement, as distinct from a mere initiative, must promote not only the security of China, but also its power and influence.

Chinese Views on War and Détente

The Chinese regime certainly realizes, contrary to certain statements that it has made in past years, that it is vulnerable to atomic attack and it does not desire a general nuclear war. Its debate with the Soviet Union over the question of general war, although sometimes carried on in terms of the results of such a war, has really been a debate over the likelihood of such a war occurring as the end product of a process of escalation. The Chinese apparently believe that a reasonable degree of strategic stability exists between the United States and the Soviet Union, and that to institutionalize this relative stability would be militarily unnecessary and would have serious drawbacks for Communist China in a variety of ways.

In general, the Chinese object to any form of détente between the United States and the Soviet Union for a number of reasons that can be inferred with near certainty. In the first place, such a détente tends to free the hands of the United States to deal with the Chinese in the Far East. On the other side, such a détente tends to give the Soviet Union a greater interest than before in preserving at least polite relations with the United States and, therefore, reduces still further its already very questionable willingness to make real efforts and take serious risks on behalf of the Chinese in the context of the Sino-American confrontation. This confrontation is not, of course, necessarily affected at all by a U.S.-Soviet détente. The latter does not, for example, affect the issue of Taiwan or other issues upon which the Chinese feel very deeply. Therefore, they feel, if anything, disadvantaged by it and they make their feelings very clear on every occasion when it seems necessary for them to do so.

115

China and Nuclear Weapons

No one would deny that the Chinese are working to make at least a token entry—whether it will be more than a token entry it is probably too early to say—into the superpower club. Among their reasons is a desire to deter a hostile attack, particularly of course an American attack, and possibly one with nuclear weapons; they expect to do this at first, presumably, by holding hostage American bases and forces in the Far East and possibly population centers of such friendly nations as Japan and India (just as the Soviets held European cities hostage before they could strike massively at the U.S. with ICBM's), and ultimately, to exercise deterrence by having an ability to strike the continental United States itself. Beyond that, of course, the Chinese want the kind of influence that they feel (whether rightly or wrongly) can only be acquired by having the various badges of superpower status, of which nuclear weapons are clearly one.

In the meantime, pending the achievement of such a situation, and since they regard Soviet protection as highly unreliable in any sort of likely crisis, the Chinese attempt to cover themselves through tactical caution, as expressed in the famous cliché "strategic boldness and tactical caution." Also useful is the threat (sometimes made explicitly but much more often made implicitly) to fight a conventional war in Asia (nowadays, of course, principally Indochina) outside China's frontiers if China is attacked by the United States. Only recently they have stated that they regard an air attack, as well as an invasion, as the necessary *casus belli*. The Chinese refuse, therefore, to accept more than purely unilateral and informal limitations upon their conventional forces, which they regard not only as a major source of internal security, but a major source of external security through their ability implicitly to hold hostage the non-communist countries on the continent of Asia. In view of this attitude toward the question of conventional disarmament, the Chinese object to GCD, and they phrase their objection in the proposition that GCD is unattainable and undesirable as long as imperialism exists.

In 1956 the Chinese decided to acquire the capacity to produce their own nuclear weapons, partly because of their increasing doubts (and one must admit justified doubts) of the reliability of Soviet strategic protection of Communist China, and partly because of their belief that their views and interests were not taken seriously enough in Moscow. Beginning in 1956, and increasing through 1957, they received very substantial aid from the Soviet Union toward the ultimate production of Chinese nuclear warheads and appropriate delivery systems. In exchange, they gave a commitment not to obstruct, and perhaps even to support actively, the Soviet approaches that were already getting under way for some kind of test ban agreement.

Going beyond this, the Chinese about at the end of 1957 seem to have demanded finished weapons from the Soviet Union in order to cover themselves during this interim period pending the fruition of their own nuclear program. It appears that the Russians countered with a demand for something resembling joint controls over any aspect of the Chinese military establishment capable of causing trouble outside China's frontiers, in particular, the Air Force and the Navy, and of course over any weapons that the Soviet Union might agree to turn over. Joint controls to the

Chinese spelled loss of independence, and it seems that the Russians had some kind of relationship in mind that would have meant Soviet controls over the Chinese forces. The Chinese declined.

The more limited program of Soviet technical assistance in Chinese nuclear weapons development in exchange for Chinese non-obstruction of the Soviet maneuvers toward a test ban continued in effect until mid-1960, when the Soviet Union was reported to have terminated its military nuclear assistance to Communist China, probably as a result of its general and mounting concern over the general trend of Chinese behavior and policy toward war and peace.

China and Disarmament

The Chinese thereupon began to withdraw their support for the idea of a test ban. According to their later protestations they complained vigorously to the Soviet Union when, in 1962, a test ban seemed about to materialize. Meanwhile the Chinese were developing with increasing shrillness a demand for complete and uninspected nuclear disarmament, without conventional disarmament, and alleged that this could best be achieved, and perhaps could only be achieved, if the Soviet Union proceeded to attain strategic superiority over the United States. The Chinese, it seems, were well aware that the strategy Khrushchev was employing in those days was one of strategic deception—in other words, an attempt to make gains against the United States by what was essentially bluff based upon an actually inferior strategic posture. They were convinced that it would not work, and that real progress on behalf of the entire communist bloc, China included, could only be achieved on the basis of

Soviet strategic superiority, or something approaching it:

We believe that it is possible to attain a complete ban on nuclear weapons in the following circumstances: The socialist camp has a great nuclear superiority; the people's struggles in various countries against nuclear weapons and nuclear war become broader and deeper; having further forfeited their nuclear superiority, the imperialists are compelled to realize that their policy of nuclear blackmail is no longer effective and that their launching of a nuclear war would only accelerate their own extinction.[1]

The Chinese objections to the test ban treaty, as everyone knows, were very strong indeed. In part they regarded it as simply the capstone in a détente between the United States and the Soviet Union which they have described as going beyond détente into the realm of entente. They describe it as a conspiracy to rule the world. Secondly, they regard the treaty as an anti-proliferation measure, which it certainly was and is, aimed against both West Germany and, to the extent feasible, against Communist China. The anti-proliferation aspect of the treaty the Chinese describe in their own inimitable language as an effort to preserve the nuclear monopoly of the United States and the Soviet Union.

In the aftermath of the test ban treaty, the Chinese in effect dropped their demand that the Soviet Union work toward strategic superiority over the United States. They realized that in all probability the Russians were not going to do this in any event, and they may even have felt that the Soviet strategic superiority would be undesirable in view of the general disregard that the Soviet Union was displaying at this time for Chinese interests.[2]

In any case, the Chinese began to

wage an essentially political struggle not only against American nuclear weapons (this had always been the case), but against Soviet nuclear weapons as well. They now came out in a much louder and more sweeping fashion than ever before in favor of complete nuclear disarmament, including the destruction of stockpiles and delivery systems. They demanded a complete test ban, including, of course, a ban on underground testing. They demanded a number of very sweeping atom-free zones, including one for the United States, Japan (meaning, of course, American bases and forces in the area of Japan), the Soviet Union, and China itself, as well as a number of others. They demanded the non-transfer of military nuclear technology and nuclear weapons, apparently without a formal non-proliferation agreement. Finally, they demanded a nuclear summit conference of all countries in the world.

After their own first test, which occurred a little over a year after the test ban treaty (on 16 October 1964), they made a set of similar demands, a bit briefer however, from which they omitted any reference to destruction of delivery systems. They explained this later on the ground that, after all, nuclear weapons can be delivered by all sorts of means, which is obviously true enough. They intended to safeguard their own future capability to deliver such weapons by means of fighter bombers. They may also have intended to safeguard their missile program so that it could ultimately be used to enter the space race, at least in a token fashion. They also dropped their demand for atom-free zones; nothing in particular has been heard about them since their own test. The Chinese added to their position of 1963, in the aftermath of their own first test, a no-first-use pledge. They

said they would never be the first to use nuclear weapons and presumably hoped, although without much optimism, one suspects, that they might extract a reciprocal concession from the United States. If this had worked, it would have amounted to trading one test for the neutralization more or less of the entire American strategic nuclear force.

The Chinese have said on many occasions, both before and since their own nuclear tests, that nuclear weapons should never be used either in support of or in opposition to national liberation wars or peoples' wars. They regard such weapons as in a sense irrelevant, both at the ethical plane and at the military or practical plane.

China and Nuclear Proliferation

The Chinese have taken a somewhat ambiguous stand from time to time, on the basis of principle, in favor of the proliferation of national nuclear forces, apparently including non-communist national nuclear forces. They have certainly been very loud in their condemnation of the MLF on the grounds, among others, that it was a device to foreclose nuclear independence for the component countries—France and Germany in particular. Why this rather cautious stand in favor of proliferation? The Chinese presumably realize that there probably will not be any further big nuclear powers, with the conceivable exception, over the long-term future, of West Germany. It is doubtful that the Chinese are overly worried by the possibility of a West German nuclear deterrent emerging at some time in the future. There are a good many possible reasons why they might be interested in cooperating with West Germany on a number of grounds that would go beyond the commercial agreements that are being concluded at the present time. Some kind of Sino-West German collaboration might emerge in the future, for example, in order to put joint pressures on the Soviet Union. In that case, one would be just as glad to remain on the North American continent.

Chinese non-opposition to proliferation may also be based upon the fairly obvious proposition that it would not seem reasonable to deny to others, at least so soon after the Chinese have made a token entry into the nuclear club, what the Chinese have been demanding for themselves and have, in fact, begun to acquire for themselves. The Chinese also gain a certain modest amount of spiritual merit in this way, at least in their own eyes, by contrasting their own comparatively generous stand with the stingy stand of the United States and the Soviet Union, who are allegedly attempting to close the door to the nuclear club behind them.

Finally, and most speculatively, it is just possible that the Chinese hope that the proliferation of national nuclear forces might conceivably frighten the United States and the Soviet Union into considering nuclear disarmament somewhat along the lines that the Chinese have advocated.

China and Arms Control

On the question of international peacekeeping machinery, the Chinese take over the attitude of Calvin Coolidge's preacher toward sin: they are "agin" it. They have taken a very dim view of the International Control Commissions in the Indochina countries. At the Geneva Conference on Laos in 1961-62, for example, they took a very restrictive view of the proper functions and freedom of movement of the Commission for Laos. They certainly are very much opposed to any form of United Nations intervention in international crises, whether crises in which they are directly involved or not. This stems in part from their very bitter memory of their own experience during the Korean War. At that time, because South Korea, a U.N.-created and sponsored state, was invaded by North Korea, the U.N. took a formal stand on behalf of South Korea, and when the Chinese joined the war on the other side they found themselves condemned for aggression—a condemnation that still rankles quite harshly in Peking. They therefore regard the U.N. involvement in that situation as having created many unpleasant political complications for themselves. They are most reluctant, then, to see the U.N. involve itself in the Viet Nam crisis or anything comparable.

A recent example of this occurred in the middle months of 1965. When it still seemed possible that there might be some kind of Afro-Asian conference at Algiers, the Chinese were very insistent —and, in fact, very rude—on the point that the U.N. must not be allowed to send an observer mission to the conference and, above all, not U Thant himself, about whom they had some very unkind things to say.

Finally, there is the question of possible Chinese participation in the Geneva disarmament talks or comparable disarmament negotiations, such as the World Disarmament Conference which is tentatively scheduled for 1967. Nobody, of course, can say what may happen in the future, for example after Mao dies. But at present, with Mao's men still in control and his policies essentially in effect, the Chinese have made it quite clear that they have no desire and no interest in joining in these negotiations, at least until they themselves are in the United Nations in full and exclusive possession of China's seat. They have consistently laid down at least one absolutely necessary condition for their own consent to join the United Nations, and that is that the Chinese Nationalists must be expelled lock, stock, and barrel, and that they cannot be allowed to remain under some deceptive label such as Taiwan.

Certainly, then, except on the basis of pure hope or optimism—an act of faith, if you like—it is rather difficult to foresee Chinese Communist participation in any sort of international peacekeeping arrangements and/or international formal disarmament or even arms control negotiations at the present time. China's behavior in these fields, which need not necessarily be totally negative or disruptive, will be based upon tacit and unilateral restraints that it is likely to place upon itself, rather than upon the acceptance of any sort of internationally worked out agreement.

The Chinese have, as a matter of fact, as noted above, observed a good deal of tactical caution and self-limitation in their own behavior. They have, for example, been very cautious indeed about *overtly* using their own armed forces on territory *admitted* to be foreign. In other words, the entire border fighting with India in 1962 was con-ducted upon territory claimed by the Chinese (whether rightly or wrongly is another question) with one solitary exception: an air field in territory admitted to be Indian even by the Chinese, which they shelled for purely military reasons. They were so embarrassed by this one departure from their normal procedure that they then denied the fact that they had shelled the air field. In a sense, therefore, this is the one exception that tends to prove the rule.

It would seem, then, that with reasonable vigilance on the part of the United States and, hopefully, other countries as well, the Chinese can be persuaded that it is wise to continue to observe unilateral restraint in their behavior in the military field and in the field of arms control and disarmament, even though it seems to me very unlikely that they will agree to come formally into any kind of multilateral arrangement.

Notes

[1] "The Difference Between Comrade Togliatti and Us," *People's Daily,* 31 December 1962.

[2] For a description of Chinese reaction to the test ban treaty, see Morton H. Halperin and Dwight H. Perkins, *Communist China and Arms Control* (New York: Praeger, 1965), pp. 114-116.

The Soviet Union and Arms Control

By Thomas W. Wolfe[1]

The primary purpose of this paper is to provide a frame of reference in which the subjects of arms control, limited war, and peacekeeping may be related to both current Soviet disarmament policy and to wider questions of the Soviet Union's aims and behavior on the international scene. The first portion of the paper contains a brief sketch of the main lines of recent Soviet disarmament diplomacy, and a few comments on what seems to be most significant about it. The second part of this paper consists of a reflection on certain broad trends of Soviet development that appear to me to bear in a meaningful way on the international climate in which arms control and peacekeeping arrangements may be pursued during the next five or ten years.

I. Current Aspects of Soviet Disarmament Diplomacy

Students of the subject have never agreed among themselves whether disarmament as a goal in itself carries great weight in Soviet policy. They have, however, generally agreed that the Soviets place great importance on disarmament from the standpoint of po-litical utility, strategic advantage, and propaganda opportunity. All three of these elements are in evidence in the disarmament menu currently being offered by the Soviet Union.

GCD

Let us look briefly first at GCD—General and Complete Disarmament, a staple item on the menu since 1959. While GCD is still ostensibly the principal object of the negotiations of the 17-Nations at Geneva, it has in fact tended to fade into the background, while various proposals for partial measures—as well as some disputative spillover from the Vietnam situation—have preempted the attention of the conferees. The Soviet draft treaty on GCD (Treaty on General and Complete Disarmament Under Strict International Control) presently on the agenda was tabled at the opening session of the 17-Nations' Conference in March 1962.[2] It need not be described in detail here —three stages, taking four years in all, with nuclear delivery vehicles to be eliminated in the first stage and nuclear weapons to be completely destroyed by the end of the second stage. At its conclusion, with all "national armies disbanded," small detachments of militia

121

would remain for maintenance of "internal order" and "general peace and security."

Since this proposal was submitted, the Soviet Union has offered what it terms several "important steps in meeting the West halfway" on GCD,[3] namely: to permit retention by the U.S. and U.S.S.R. of a "strictly limited" number of ICBM's (as well as AMM and SAM types of missiles) up to the end of the disarmament process, as a "protective umbrella"; to allow a higher level of conventional forces in the early stages; and to extend the total disarmament period from four to five years.[4] While offering these "concessions," the Soviet Union has at the same time insisted that the U.S. draft Outline of April 1962 [5] is "unacceptable" as a basis for agreement on various grounds. These include, according to the Soviet gravamen: failure to provide complete destruction of nuclear weapons unless foolproof verification methods are devised; calling for an international peacekeeping force which might have nuclear weapons; leaving U.S. foreign bases intact in the first stage; making "inordinate" inspection demands for intelligence purposes; and proposing various forms of international jurisdiction that would amount to "restricting the sovereignty of states." [6]

Besides seeking to present the Soviet GCD position in a favorable light compared to that of the United States, the Soviet Union during the past few years has employed its advocacy of GCD as a weapon in the polemics with Peking. In essence, the Soviets have argued that Chinese skepticism about the possibilities of achieving general and complete disarmament while "imperialism" still exists furnishes further proof that Peking is not really interested in peace. This use of the GCD issue in the Sino-Soviet polemics to demonstrate the

warlike nature of the Peking regime probably reached its peak in the 1963-64 period, and since then other issues have received more attention than GCD in the quarrel between Moscow and Peking.

As it stands today, the Soviet position on GCD is somewhat more malleable than it was previously, but most of the essential sticking points still remain unresolved. Meanwhile, the relative priority of GCD in the over-all Soviet approach seems to have shifted.[7] No longer is Soviet disarmament policy avowedly fixed on attainment of a totally disarmed world by the shortest possible route. Although Soviet spokesmen recurrently allude to the need for progress in GCD, and upon occasion assert that American activity in Vietnam has more than ever made the problem of general and complete disarmament "extraordinarily important," [8] one has the impression that the vigor of Soviet advocacy of GCD has appreciably declined. It is difficult to judge whether this connotes a tactical pause, or is traceable to more deep-seated considerations—such as Soviet reflection upon the future problems of being China's neighbor or a growth of confidence in the stability of mutual strategic deterrence.

In any event, however, a shift in the Soviet approach has become evident in the past two or three years, exemplified by the turnabout admission that the "ultimate achievement of general and complete disarmament can be facilitated" by seeking partial measures and separate steps.[9]

Partial Measures

The reemergence of Soviet interest in the partial measures approach began in the latter phase of Khrushchev's rule, and was attended by several initial accomplishments made possible perhaps by the then-prevailing political desire in both Moscow and Washington to nurture the spirit of détente in Soviet-U.S. relations. These accomplishments scarcely require recitation, for they stand out conspicuously on the rather bleak landscape of contemporary arms control endeavor. Most conspicuous, of course, is the partial nuclear test-ban treaty of August 5, 1963. Completing the list are the Washington-Moscow "hot line" link agreement of June 20, 1963 and the U.N. resolution of October 17, 1963 which banned the orbiting of mass destruction weapons in outer space, along with unilateral declarations in April 1964 of intent to cut back the production of fissionable materials for weapons purposes. It might be noted, incidentally, that the U.S. Atomic Energy Commission reported in November 1965 that there was "no evidence" that the Soviet Union had actually carried out the cutback in nuclear materials production that it had announced in 1964.[10]

Several assortments of partial disarmament measures, many of which had cropped up in one form or another in Soviet proposals prior to launching of the "GCD period" of Soviet disarmament diplomacy in 1959, have been offered by the Soviet Union in the past two years or so. Without going here into either the antecedents or the subtleties of these successive assortments of partial measures,[11] let me simply set down the list of eleven measures given in the last formal Soviet memorandum on the subject on December 7, 1964:[12]

(1) Reduction of Military Budgets.
(2) Withdrawal or Reduction of Foreign Troops on Foreign Territories.
(3) Dismantling of Foreign Bases.
(4) Prevention of Spread of Nuclear Weapons.
(5) Ban on Use of Nuclear Weapons.
(6) Nuclear-Free Zones in Central Europe and Elsewhere.
(7) Ban on Underground Nuclear Weapons Tests.
(8) Destruction of Bomber Aircraft.
(9) Non-Aggression Pact Between NATO and Warsaw Treaty States.
(10) Prevention of Surprise Attack.
(11) Reduction of Total Numerical Strength of Armed Forces.

A readjustment of this list—reflecting a shift of emphasis in Soviet thinking on partial measures—was set forth early last year in Kosygin's message to the Geneva conference a few days after its reopening on January 27, 1966.[13] Kosygin's enumeration of partial measures, which paralleled closely one given by Gromyko in a speech to the U.N. General Assembly on September 24, 1965,[14] omitted the last four items listed above, and at the same time put major emphasis on a non-proliferation treaty and related strictures against the use of nuclear weapons. Kosygin's failure to mention numerical strength reductions was an interesting oversight, which may have been related to internal Soviet controversy over the size of Soviet force levels in light of the worsened international situation.[15] The chief point of interest in his message, however, as in Gromyko's presentation at the U.N. several months earlier, was the attention given the non-proliferation question. It further underscored the importance this issue has acquired in Soviet policy, for reasons which perhaps are rooted less in Soviet objections to the principle of nuclear-sharing than in active concerns bearing directly on Soviet political and strategic interests.

Non-Proliferation
and the German Question

The first Soviet proposal for non-proliferation goes back to September 1957,[16] but it has been largely in the past two or three years that the Soviet Union has shifted its attention from the test-ban issue to non-proliferation as a means of dealing with the problem of the spread of nuclear weapons. It appears quite clear that Soviet interest in preventing the spread of nuclear weapons—apart from the general tendency of the nuclear powers to look with a jaundiced eye at the ambitions of others to enter "The Club"—has centered mainly on impeding nuclear progress by West Germany and Communist China.[17] Although any hopes Moscow may have once entertained of checking China's attainment of nuclear status are no longer relevant, the Soviet leaders evidently count on the leverage of a prospective non-proliferation agreement—whether a formal treaty is actually consummated or not—to forestall creation of an Atlantic nuclear force (MLF or other arrangements) through which Germany might gain closer access to nuclear weapons.

How valid may be the sources of Soviet anxiety that NATO nuclear-sharing arrangements would place Bonn in a position to make unacceptable demands on East Germany and the Soviet Union, and whether in fact Soviet long-term interests might not be better served by integration of West Germany into a system where other countries would continue to wield a nuclear veto —these are not matters for argument here. The fact remains, however, that a fixation over the German question seems to be embedded in the Soviet "political psyche," and will very likely continue to dominate Moscow's treatment of the non-proliferation issue. This means that the Soviet Union will probably continue to place a higher priority on blocking NATO sharing arrangements than on making adjustments for the sake of getting a treaty signed— which, of course, is precisely what the Soviet declaratory position indicates.[18] It probably also means that the Soviets will try to exacerbate differences within NATO by continuing to focus the non-proliferation dialogue on the dangers of Bonn's participation in NATO nuclear arrangements. The Soviet draft treaty on nuclear non-dissemination, which was tabled by Gromyko at the U.N. on September 24, 1965, is very specific in forbidding not only the actual transfer of nuclear weapons and control over them *within any military alliance,* but also the transfer of information which "may be utilized for manufacture or application of nuclear weapons." [19]

These provisos, which would preclude both access to and training in the use of nuclear weapons by Germany and other non-nuclear members of NATO, happen to cut both ways, of course. They would prevent the Soviet Union from carrying out the kind of joint exercises that have been held from time to time since 1961 with other Warsaw Pact forces, and in which simulated nuclear strikes and associated nuclear training activities have taken place. The Soviet Union has also furnished nuclear-delivery systems in the form of tactical missiles and advanced aircraft to her East European partners in the Warsaw Pact, although presumably nuclear warheads have been withheld. These and other trends toward closer military integration within the Pact obviously pose problems for the Soviet Union,[20] which must choose, in a sense, between greater military efficiency and a more potent counterthreat to NATO on the one hand, and her own proposals against proliferation on the other. The Soviet Union's reluctance to furnish information on present nuclear control arrangements within the Warsaw Pact leaves it uncertain whether it is trying to enjoy the best of both worlds for the time being.[21] But if it comes to a clear-cut choice, the Soviets probably would not hesitate to pay the price of permanent denial of nuclear access to their Warsaw allies in return for barring the same path to West Germany.

In connection with the current placing of the non-proliferation question high on the Soviet disarmament agenda, it should be noted that this has drawn bitter criticism from Peking. As in the case of the test ban, the Chinese have charged that Soviet interest in non-proliferation is part of a collusive Soviet-American attempt to perpetuate a superpower duopoly in the nuclear field.[22] That the Soviet Union has gone ahead despite Chinese attacks on its non-proliferation policy testifies both to the intractability of the Sino-Soviet dispute and to the evident importance which the Soviet Union attaches to employing a prospective non-proliferation treaty as a means of blocking German access to nuclear weapons.

Ban on Nuclear Weapons Use

Soviet proposals of one kind or another for banning the use of nuclear weapons go back to the initial Soviet rejection of the Baruch Plan in 1947 [23] and to the "Stockholm Peace Appeal" of the early fifties, and were for many years a central feature of a Soviet effort to inhibit the United States from deriving political advantage from its superior nuclear posture. With the advent of the GCD period of Soviet disarmament diplomacy, the issue of a nuclear ban remained on the agenda, but was given

somewhat less attention than previously. Only after China exploded its first atom bomb in October 1964 and at the same time proposed a world-wide conference to negotiate a prohibition on use of nuclear weapons[24] did the Soviet Union again revive its own advocacy of such a proposal, pointing out that this was a long-standing Soviet position.[25]

A new element was added to the Soviet position in Kosygin's February 1966 message to the Geneva Conference, linking the notion of a ban on use of nuclear weapons directly with a non-proliferation treaty and inferentially with the German question. Taking up where the previously-discussed question of guarantees to non-nuclear states had left off, Kosygin expressed the Soviet government's readiness to add to its draft treaty "an article on the prohibition of the use of nuclear weapons against non-nuclear states—parties to the treaty, which have no nuclear weapons on their territory." [26]

It is hardly necessary to point out that the last clause of this proposal has rather sweeping strategic and political implications. Besides fortifying the principal objective sought by the Soviet Union through the non-proliferation treaty itself—that is, denial of nuclear weapons to Germany—it would also have the effect of:

(1) Precluding the deployment of *U.S. weapons* in Germany, which would greatly reduce the NATO capabilities confronting the Soviet Union in Europe, especially with an uncooperative France also in the picture;

(2) Raising similar questions about the stationing of U.S. nuclear weapons on the territory of allies elsewhere in the world, including Vietnam, if this were ever to be contemplated.

In short, were enough countries to sign up on the Soviet dotted line, the

Soviet Union could hope by this partic-ular measure to go far toward achieving the neutralization of forward U.S. nu-clear power which it has sought over past years through such proposals as foreign base withdrawal, nuclear free zones, bans on nuclear use, and so on.

The case of the B-52 accident and the missing bomb at Palomares, Spain in January 1966 proved to be, from the Soviet viewpoint, a fortuitous propa-ganda opportunity to focus anew on the issue of U.S. bases and nuclear weap-ons. Soviet spokesmen at Geneva and elsewhere not only made rather hasty and tendentious charges that the Palo-mares incident was a violation of the test-ban treaty, but also dwelt on the theme that U.S. nuclear bases on for-eign territory pose grave dangers for the people of such countries. Some Soviet commentary also raised the spectre of accidental war ensuing from incidents like that at Palomares,[27] even though the incident itself seemed to demonstrate quite the opposite. The chances are, however, that the question of accidental war was not taken very seriously by the Soviets themselves. In general, the Soviet Union seems to be persuaded that vari-ous unilateral measures taken in the past few years with respect to command and control and the posture of strategic forces have served to reduce the danger of accidental war.

Soviet Arms Control Policy and the "Third World"

European-oriented problems like those of NATO nuclear arrangements and Germany, along with the general question of the over-all strategic balance between the Soviet Union and the United States, have been and apparently continue to be the central preoccupa-tions helping to shape Soviet disarma-ment policy. However, problems arising in the so-called third world also impinge upon the current Soviet arms control approach.

From the Soviet viewpoint, the for-mulation of a policy line in the third-world area is complicated both by the Sino-Soviet dispute and the rivalry be-tween Moscow and Peking as cham-pions of "national-liberation" struggles, and by the strain which the deepening Vietnam crisis of the past year has placed upon Soviet-American relations. In effect, the more the Soviet leaders tend toward a "hard" line that reduces their vulnerability to Chinese charges of letting down the revolutionary struggle in the third world and of "collusion" with the United States,[28] the more they jeopardize the chances of maintaining some semblance of détente in Soviet relations with the United States—as-suming this to be still a desideratum of Soviet policy, a subject which shall be taken up more fully later in this paper.

Ambivalence, that much-overworked word, seems best to describe the Soviet attitude toward arms control as it ap-plies to third-world problems. On the one hand, Soviet interest in supporting national-liberation movements in some of the underdeveloped countries tends to limit Soviet willingness to contem-plate arms control agreements that would embarrass such support, as for example, embargoes on arms shipments and other types of aid to particular countries or regions. Similarly, interna-tional peacekeeping arrangements that might be used to inhibit rebel activities in certain circumstances, as in the Congo case, are regarded with suspi-cion. In particular, "cooperative" peace-keeping measures which might be con-strued as entering into a quasi-military alliance with the United States seem virtually ruled out so far as the Soviet Union is concerned, in light of the sharp ideological and power competition with Peking for leadership of third-world revolutionary movements.

On the other hand, however, Soviet interests also have seemed to call under some circumstances for cultivation of a peacekeeping role in the third world, as in the case of the India-Pakistan clash. Even the development of international peacekeeping mechanisms to contain and pacify local conflicts may seem useful to the Soviets, depending on the particular situation. This may apply particularly to arrangements offering an opportunity to check Chinese influence without the appearance of direct Soviet action or of Soviet "partnership" with the United States. Furthermore, the symbolic value of arms control agreements, or merely of discussions, seems to carry some weight in Soviet eyes, either to demonstrate to critics in Peking that a "peaceful coexistence" line is possible, or to help reduce the temperature of an active crisis that may pose the danger of widening conflict.

These contradictory elements of the Soviet attitude have been reflected to some extent in the stand taken by Soviet disarmament negotiators at Geneva. In September 1965, for example, when the Geneva talks were about to be recessed, Tsarapkin expressed the view that arms control negotiations could not be separated from what he termed U.S. "aggression" in Southeast Asia, in the Congo, and in Santo Domingo,[29] implying that Soviet interest lay less in trying to advance a fruitful arms control dialogue than in trying to extract full propaganda advantage from troubled situations in the third world.

By the time the Geneva conference reconvened in early 1966, however, a somewhat different Soviet attitude was apparent. Tsarapkin then took the position that the war in Vietnam should not

be allowed to rule out the possibility of progress in arms control negotiations. The "dangerous circumstances" in Vietnam, he said, impose "special responsibilities" on the conferees "to halt the progress of the arms race." If a non-proliferation agreement could be reached, he added, this "could improve the climate for the solution of other problems as well." [30]

While Tsarapkin thus seemed to be saying that negotiations in Geneva need not bog down entirely over the Vietnam issue, this did not necessarily mean that a basic policy shift toward a new measure of cooperation with the United States had occurred. In fact, other Soviet spokesmen seemed intent on defending the long-standing Soviet line that Moscow's disarmament proposals actually serve the cause of national-liberation movements by creating "a more favorable environment" for revolutionary struggle in the third world.[31] In this connection, Soviet advocacy of non-proliferation was singled out by some commentators for the contribution it could make to weakening "imperialist" positions in the third world. Thus, as one Soviet commentator put it, "the struggle for non-proliferation of nuclear weapons is not only aimed at reducing the risk of nuclear war, but is directed also against the imperialists and colonialists, who would like to hold on to their position by means of nuclear weapons." [32]

Besides regarding Western nuclear power as an obstacle to the success of the national-liberation struggle, Soviet spokesmen have made the point that the buildup of U.S. conventional forces has become a main element of U.S. "aggressive" policy, "directed primarily against the national-liberation movement." [33] The problem of escalation of local wars also has been cited in Soviet commentary to buttress arguments for a non-proliferation agreement. Thus, one writer early in 1966 linked the possible acquisition of nuclear weapons "by a large number of states in different parts of the world" with increased danger that "even local conflicts, which in present circumstances can be smothered, might swiftly develop into a nuclear clash, threatening the whole world with a thermonuclear holocaust." [34]

The same oscillation evident in Soviet arms control discourse between presenting the Soviet Union in the image of an active supporter of national-liberation conflicts on the one hand and as a proponent of improving the international climate through patient deliberations at the negotiating table on the other, also has been apparent in other areas of Soviet conduct. Thus, for example, the Soviet Union in January 1966 hailed with notable initial enthusiasm the Tri-Continent Conference in Havana which set up an interim committee to "promote, increase and consolidate the national-liberation movement" in the Afro-Asian and Latin American countries.[35] At almost the same time, on the other hand, the Soviet Union was making known to the world, on the heels of Kosygin's mediation of the India-Pakistan dispute at Tashkent, that it had hit on "something completely new in the practice of international relations," namely—"socialist diplomacy," [36] by means of which hitherto obdurate international disputes might be resolved. Whether this new concept of the Soviet Union's peacemaking potential—with its implied acceptance of greater responsibility for peacekeeping in troubled areas of the third world—will coexist comfortably with the Soviet Union's other self-image as a dedicated champion and active supporter of national-liberation conflicts, is

a question which remains for history to answer.

II. Trends Bearing on Prospects for the Future

The Soviet Union's behavior on the international scene during the next decade or so—especially its readiness to seek arms control and peacekeeping arrangements that could contribute to international stability and adjustment of conflict situations—will depend on many considerations. Among these, at least two seem likely to be of central importance.

The first is the question whether the Soviet Union is undergoing a basic change in the direction of giving up its aspirations to usher in a worldwide Communist order. Or, to put it another way, has the operative behavior of the Soviet leaders come to mean abandonment of the Marxist-Leninist urge to remake the world, whatever ideological lip service may still be paid to such a goal? If so, at least one major source of international tension and potential conflict should diminish, though to be sure, others can be expected to arise.

The second, and by no means unrelated, consideration concerns the evolving character of the Soviet-American relationship. Although the bipolar pattern of the past twenty years is now giving way to a more diversified international system, and although the role of China as a challenger of the present international order will probably become a factor of increasing weight, it still seems reasonable to suppose that the relationship of the two superpowers will continue to be the dominant feature of the international scene for the next five or ten years. The direction in which this relationship may be tending—toward undiminished antagonism or wider recognition of shared interests—is therefore also critical to the prospects for future stability and mutual efforts to extend the scope and character of peacekeeping arrangements.

Taking up the first of these questions, one finds a considerable body of evidence that a process of change is at work within the Soviet system, although opinions differ as to the rate of change and the direction in which it may be moving. Some of the evidence relates essentially to internal Soviet developments— a presumed erosion of the Party *apparat's* commitment to ideologically-oriented action; the emergence of what might be called "creeping pluralism" as various institutional groups find a bit more elbow room within the system; recognition by the Soviet leadership of the need for major domestic economic reform and investment; tendencies toward gradual *embourgeoisement* of Soviet society; and so on. Other evidence relates essentially to external developments—the mutual interest of the nuclear superpowers in avoiding a world war; the Sino-Soviet dispute, which has not only punctured the myth of monolithic Communist unity, but also has served to point up certain parallel areas of U.S.-Soviet interest; a more pragmatic Soviet world view which may have led to quiet shelving of the notion of a universal Soviet state and tacit acceptance of the more or less traditional concept of the national state as the terminal form of the Soviet system.

The inference drawn from this reading of Soviet trends by many observers is that the Soviet Union can be expected henceforth to behave more "reasonably" or more "conventionally" on the international stage, defining its objectives increasingly in terms of Soviet national interests rather than those of world Communism, and seeking to promote international stability rather than to inflame endemic unrest and difficulties among and within non-Communist countries for the sake of Communist political advance. An important corollary of this image of Soviet change is the prospect that the Soviet Union and the United States may come more readily to recognize that their adversary relationship involves a web of overlapping as well as conflicting interests, and that it therefore behooves both to begin "collaborating" more explicitly than hitherto in areas of common concern.

A somewhat less sanguine view of the situation is taken by others, who find it premature to assume that the benign transformation of the Soviet system is already well advanced. Granted that the process of change is at work, how deeply it runs and where it may lead— according to this school of opinion—is still very much an open question. Even though the Soviet system may be gradually losing its revolutionary character, and even though the Soviet leaders may be on the way to recognizing that rival forms of sociopolitical and economic organization in the world are here to stay indefinitely, this does not necessarily nor immediately smooth the path for extensive policies of accommodation between the Soviet Union and the United States. Indeed, it is argued— and the present writer would tend to side with those who do so argue—that the Soviet Union will continue for a long time still to be dominated by a ruling elite of strongly authoritarian outlook whose values and objectives will serve more often than not to cast the Soviet Union in the role of a stubborn competitor, rather than an explicit collaborator, of the United States.

The term of art in this particular forecast is "explicit collaborator." Is there not room for a considerable range of "implicit" or "tacit" collaboration between the Soviet Union and the United States? And does not this prospect justify the optimism of those who hope that even if the two superpowers remain avowed antagonists for the foreseeable future, they may at the same time find it possible to maneuver carefully enough in the international arena to avoid an outright collision?

Perhaps the most appropriate answer is that Moscow and Washington have managed thus far in the nuclear age to do just this; hence, it should be conceded that the prospects for the future are at least as good, and that despite the high probability of recurrent tensions and crises, the two superpowers are likely to continue to avoid a frontal confrontation, and may even succeed in broadening the "cooperative" aspects of their adversary relationship.

Turning more specifically to the character of this relationship, and to the central concern upon which it pivots— that is, the mutual interest of the two superpowers in steering clear of a general nuclear war—there would seem to be two principal areas in which events and a clash of interests might trigger such a war. One of these is in the so-called third world, where not only Soviet and American policies are in partial collision, but where rival Sino-Soviet claims for leadership of the world Communist movement are being tested. The other is in Europe, where the more advanced countries of the NATO and Warsaw Pact alliances confront each other.

With regard to the third world, it can be argued that neither the United States nor the Soviet Union in the last analysis possesses really vital interests in this area, and that neither stands to gain or lose sufficiently in terms of its own national security from what happens in the underdeveloped third-world countries to warrant carrying their competition here to the point of setting off a general war. By the same token, it can also be argued that the marginal nature of conflicting Soviet-American interests in the third world makes this one of the more promising arenas in which to seek more meaningful, even if not explicitly institutionalized, cooperation between the two.

The Soviet Union, the argument runs, has already recognized the need for a differentiated set of policies toward the underdeveloped areas. Only in some parts of the third world, mainly where competition with Peking is most intense, has it chosen actively to support local revolutionary developments. In other countries, as in parts of the Middle East and Africa, the Soviet Union apparently has made its peace with local nationalist movements—be they "socialist" or "bourgeois" in cast—and has allowed indigenous Communist Parties to be submerged.[37] Given time, and further differentiation of Soviet policy in the third world, may not the Soviet Union come to recognize additional points of common interest with the United States, like that displayed in dampening the India-Pakistan crisis, or avoiding a direct confrontation with the United States in Southeast Asia? In the longer run, might not a desire to reduce the drain on Soviet resources from economic aid competition with the United States lead to identification of a mutual U.S.-Soviet interest in seeing the gap narrowed between the advanced countries and the laggard third world, between the haves and the have-nots? At the basis of this view, perhaps, lies the assumption that the Soviet conflict with China is driving the Soviet Union toward a community of interest with the West, which may manifest itself first in a willingness to reach arms control agreements, and other understandings in respect to the third world.

From another perspective, however, it would seem that each side perceives itself to have interests in the third world that are at least as conducive of conflict and abrasive relations as they are avenues for cooperative action. Such Soviet activities as being a major arms supplier to various third-world countries—Indonesia, the U.A.R., Iraq, Cuba, Somalia, among others—do not augur well for development of stability, even though a direct Soviet-U.S. clash of interests may not be involved. The Soviet military aid program alone seems to belie concern about reducing demands on Soviet resources where it appears that political ends can be served. In the case of such a temporary conjunction of U.S.-Soviet interest as the Kashmir cease-fire, one might suppose that mutuality of interest would rapidly dissolve should it appear that the new "flexibility" of Soviet diplomacy was drawing the sub-continent permanently into the Soviet sphere of influence. Over the longer term, it might also be argued that this is a dynamic age of ferment and breakup of the traditional order in most of the countries of the third world, where, despite—or possibly because of—its competition with China, the Soviet Union will find itself drawn further into the revolutionary process rather than seeking to underwrite stability and orderly change in concert with the West.

In immediate terms, perhaps the principal source of perturbation to be taken into account is the problem of Vietnam and its impact on the subtle and intricate character of the Soviet-U.S. relationship in the third world. The outcome of this situation remains quite uncertain at the present juncture. However, pressures upon the Soviet Union engendered by the crisis in Southeast Asia and by the sharpening competition with Peking could well prompt the Soviet leadership —even against its better judgment—to place a higher premium than hitherto upon material Soviet support of "national-liberation" movements in general and the Vietnam conflict in particular, creating a climate in which Soviet-U.S. relations are likely to be placed under increasing strain.

One should, however, recognize certain offsetting considerations that may work the other way so far as the Soviet Union is concerned—strengthening, rather than reducing, the reluctance of the Soviet leadership to become more deeply involved in a challenge to U.S. power locally on various distant fronts in the third world, including Vietnam. Perhaps the most trenchant consideration is that of avoiding a showdown situation in which the danger of nuclear war might become acute. Despite some doctrinal shifts over the past few years in the apparent direction of greater readiness to become involved in limited wars,[38] Soviet conduct evidently remains strongly conditioned by concern over escalation of local conflicts.

Another important consideration is the pressing need recognized by the present Soviet regime to make effective inroads upon the Soviet Union's accumulating internal problems. To the extent that a policy of deeper and more direct Soviet involvement in third-world conflicts would upset and delay programs of domestic economic improvement, a telling constraint would seem to apply against adoption of such a policy. So long as the character of Soviet involvement in situations like Vietnam can be kept on an essentially "proxy" basis,[39] control of sorts over an open-ended commitment can probably be more easily maintained.

Still another consideration weighing against a shift of Soviet policy toward a substantially more active military role, either in the Vietnam case or in other distant conflicts that may arise in the third world, turns upon the Soviet Union's traditional preoccupation with the military and political problems of Europe—not the least of which, in Soviet eyes, is the problem of keeping a resurgent Germany in check. Were the Soviet leaders to shift their sights from this central strategic front in order to pursue a strategy of waging peripheral local conflicts with globally-mobile U.S. military power, they would not only run the increased risk of local escalation to general war, but they might find that the relative power position of the Soviet Union and its ability to influence the politics of Europe had suffered as well.

Without trying to extend the list of pros and cons, one can say that there are at least as many reasons for the Soviet leadership to prefer a patient and cautious effort at political advance in the third world as there are for adoption of policies that would transform the third world into a more turbulent arena of open conflict with the United States. The crux of the matter, perhaps, is whether the rival Chinese prescription for more militant third-world struggle succeeds. The final returns are not yet in, but should the Chinese line be validated by events, say in the Vietnam "test case," then pressure upon the Soviet leadership to take up a more extreme and aggressive posture in the third world might become difficult indeed to resist.[40] This prospect would be heightened should leadership of the "anti-imperialist" dynamic in the third world seem likely to pass into Peking's hands as a result of developments in Southeast Asia.

In Europe, a somewhat different situation presents itself so far as the problem of minimizing acute strains upon the Soviet-American relationship is concerned. Here, as distinct from the third world, Soviet policy has tended increasingly to become one of power-bloc maneuvering against the advanced industrial countries of the West, rather than one of seeking to encourage and re-invigorate revolutionary activities by Western Communist parties.[41] Here also a real nexus of vital interests of both sides is to be found, and a serious attempt by either side to press for major political gains seems likely to be regarded as unacceptable trespass upon the interests of the other. For this very reason, perhaps, both sides in a sense have collaborated in a major peacekeeping operation in Europe for a number of years; it has been jeopardized from time to time by the pressures of the Cold War, but never to the point of real breakdown.

In the Soviet case, since the failure of Khrushchev's efforts from 1958 to 1962 to impose a unilateral solution with respect to Berlin and the German question, caution has governed Soviet European policy, which has shown little taste for tampering with the delicate balance in Europe. How long this relative quiescence may prevail, given the political dynamics of an evolving Europe, is one of the major imponderables upon which Soviet-American relations will turn in the period ahead.

It might be said that various pressures already seem to be at work for reactivation of more vigorous Soviet policies in Europe. Some of these arise out of adamant Soviet opposition to proposed nuclear-sharing arrangements within NATO. Should the present Soviet nonproliferation campaign fail to block such arrangements, the Soviet Union has threatened that it will take vigorous, though unspecified, countermeasures. Other pressures arise from Soviet difficulties in maintaining the cohesion of the Warsaw bloc, the members of which have displayed varying degrees of national restlessness that could threaten to erode Soviet hegemony in Eastern Europe.[42] None too subtle hints also have come from the Chinese that Moscow should create new diversions in Europe, where, according to Peking, the Soviets have been "colluding" with the United States to ease the European situation and thereby permit transfer of American troops "from Europe to expand the war in Vietnam."[43]

Thus far, the Soviet leaders have resisted this particular siren song from Peking. They may, however, for reasons of their own, come to feel that diversionary moves of some sort are in order in Europe. The stepped-up pursuit of divisive diplomacy against NATO, for example, utilizing perhaps a Moscow-Paris axis to fan discord within the Western alliance, might seem to constitute an inviting approach, calculated especially to impede renewal of the NATO agreement a few years hence. Whatever the reasons, it seems fair to say that a Soviet disposition to disrupt the present delicate equilibrium in Europe would place Soviet-U.S. relations under strains comparable to those in earlier phases of the Cold War.

At this point, assuming that neither in the third world nor in Europe will the situation get so far out of hand as to bring on the ultimate catastrophe of a nuclear war, in which case further speculation about the future might be largely irrelevant anyway, it would seem appropriate to consider the role that military power is likely to play as an instrument of Soviet policy in the decade ahead. Is there a reasonable prospect that either major changes in Soviet society or in the outlook of the Soviet leadership itself may lead to marked depreciation of military power and instrumentalities for support of Soviet policy objectives?

Any answer to this question is necessarily speculative, and subject to one's own conception of the process of sociopolitical change. To begin with, one can dismiss the chances that in the next decade—or even in the more distant future—Soviet society will arrive at the utopian Communist stage once envisaged in Marxist-Leninist scripture, where all institutions of state power, including the military, were expected to "wither away." Anchoring one's expectations in what appear to be the realities of the world as it is, the next five or ten years seem unlikely to bring truly radical changes in Soviet society and patterns of behavior.[44] Assuming this to be the case, in the view of the present writer at least, military power will probably continue to be regarded by the Soviet leaders as an essential ingredient of Soviet policy, performing much the same functions it serves today.

These functions are several. Most essential perhaps—to deter an opponent from launching an attack or to wage war if it should occur, functions sometimes described as providing a shield for the security of the Soviet Union and its allies against the "designs of imperialism." Closely related to these functions—to lend authority to Soviet foreign policy in general, and to provide the rationale upon which the feasibility of "peaceful coexistence" rests in particular. Next in importance—to ensure good conduct from Soviet partners within the Communist world itself, where emergent nationalisms may breed disrespect for Soviet interests. Besides these outward- and inward-looking functions, another of major significance may be added—that of discouraging Western military resistance to Communist political and proxy warfare endeavors, or what may be called the "counter-deterrent" role of Soviet military power as a political weapon.[45]

But let us suppose there are some surprises in store, and that during the next decade or so the Soviet Union not only sheds its revolutionary aspirations far more readily than one has assumed, but also accepts with good grace a more or less conventional great power role in world affairs. What then?

Plausibly, one might expect the "counter-deterrent" value of Soviet arms, as backup for a strategy of Communist political advance that would be no longer essentially operative, to decline in the eyes of the Soviet leadership. It seems doubtful, however, that the other functions of Soviet military power would shrink to marginal importance, in terms either of Soviet security from external attack or the assertion of Soviet interests against the national pretensions of other states, including those ruled by Communist regimes. On the latter score, the "containment" of Chinese encroachment upon Soviet interests could well become a growing problem in the next decade, counseling against the neglect of Soviet military preparations, even though the chances of an outright military collision between the two Communist powers should remain remote. In this connection, incidentally, it is a matter of some interest that the Soviet leadership apparently saw fit to castigate Peking in private recently for suggesting "to the Chinese people that it is necessary to prepare themselves for a military struggle with the U.S.S.R." [46]

Whether Soviet policy is mainly animated by a revolutionary drive to reshape the world or by an evolutionary tendency toward accommodation with it, two constants can be expected: First, it seems likely that the Soviet leadership will continue to look upon military power as a prime guarantee of Soviet security; second, it seems equally likely that the Soviet leaders will continue to pursue policies governed by the desire to reduce the risk of nuclear war.

Both of these constants will help shape the general environment for arms control and peacekeeping endeavors. In the first instance, the importance of military power in Soviet eyes is likely to keep the Soviet leadership sensitive to changes in the military balance, in technology and in other factors affecting the "correlation of forces." [47] Although Soviet efforts to translate such changes into political or strategic advantage might diminish under conditions of "evolutionary" development toward policies of accommodation, in any event the Soviet leaders will undoubtedly seek to prevent the other side from exploiting changes to its advantage. Thus, in a sense, one can expect that steps affecting the military balance will continue to have something of the character of moves in a "shadow war." In the second instance, the desire to keep this shadow war from being transformed into the real thing seems to mean that some basis for recognition of mutual Soviet-American interest is embedded in the future under a wide range of alternative paths of Soviet development.

In the field of arms control, this joint concern for avoidance of nuclear war would presumably keep alive an interest in so-called "preventive" measures to reduce the risk of war by accident or miscalculation, and it might encourage continued discussion of measures to limit deployment of new weapons systems, to prevent the spread of nuclear weapons, and to slow down the tempo of research and development. Whether the prospect for agreement on such measures will be any better than heretofore is, however, an open question. Likewise, it remains uncertain whether the Soviet Union will begin to display an interest, notably absent up to now, in arms control measures and associated strategic doctrines intended to limit the scale and destructiveness of a nuclear war and to help terminate it if it should occur.

Beyond a conjunction of interests growing out of the problem of preventing a nuclear war, the environment of the future does appear quite sensitive to shifts in Soviet outlook and behavior. For example, recognition of broader areas of common concern and cooperation than has been the case up to now seems intimately dependent on the Soviet Union's readiness to forgo a revolutionary strategy of Communist political advance in favor of a stabilizing role in the international arena. Some signs of a shift in this direction have been noted, but the question is still whether a few swallows betoken the spring.

The question here of interpreting the direction of Soviet development is exceedingly difficult, for it is a matter of distinguishing between the "normal" interplay of rivalries within the on-going system of international politics and competitive conflict that aims at scrapping the system itself. Which of these two tendencies best describes the Soviet case is perhaps the most vital question of all. In the author's opinion, the Soviet Union at best is moving only slowly and grudgingly toward acceptance of the ongoing system of "normal" competitive striving among national states. The prospects for the future will not greatly improve until the Soviet leadership is more fully persuaded that the time has come to lay down its messianic burdens and get on with the business of satisfying the needs and inner aspirations of the society over which it rules. In that event, the Soviet rulers may come increasingly to perceive that Soviet security and economic well-being can be better served by seeking broader areas of cooperation with the United States, rather than acting upon the assumption that the policies of the Soviet Union and its chief Western adversary are grounded upon an irreconcilable clash of interests.

Notes

1 Any views expressed in this paper are those of the author. They should not be interpreted as reflecting the views of The RAND Corporation or the official opinion or policy of any of its governmental or private research sponsors.

2 *The New York Times,* March 16, 1962. For a summary breakdown of various provisions of the Soviet draft treaty of March 15, 1962, see Alexander Dallin *et al., The Soviet Union, Arms Control, and Disarmament,* School of International Affairs, Columbia University, New York, 1964, p. 283.

3 V. Shestov, "Disarmament Problems Today," *International Affairs,* No. 11, November 1965, p. 57.

4 *Ibid.*

5 "Outline of Basic Provisions of a Treaty on General and Complete Disarmament in a Peaceful World," submitted on April 18, 1962. *The Department of State Bulletin,* Vol. XLVI, No. 1193, May 7, 1962.

6 Shestov, *International Affairs,* November 1965, p. 57.

7 See the present author's "Soviet Attitudes Toward Arms Control and Disarmament," *Temple Law Quarterly,* Vol. 38, No. 2, Winter 1965, pp. 124-125.

8 V. Maevskii, "The Triumph of Reason and the Escalation of Recklessness," *Pravda,* February 6, 1966.

9 Shestov, *International Affairs,* p. 57. See also Dallin, *op. cit.,* p. 126.

[10] " 'No Evidence' Found on Soviet A-Cutback," *The New York Times,* November 26, 1965.

[11] The first formal Soviet compilation of partial measures in the latter days of the Khrushchev period was given on January 28, 1964 in "Memorandum of the Soviet Government on Measures to Slow Down the Arms Race and Ease International Tensions," *Pravda,* January 29, 1964. For a list of these, see present author's article cited in note 7 above, p. 124.

[12] "Memorandum of the Soviet Government on Measures for the Further Relaxation of International Tensions and Restriction of the Arms Race," December 7, 1964. Text in Supplement to *Moscow News,* No. 50, December 12, 1964.

[13] "Message of the Chairman of the Council of Ministers of the U.S.S.R. to the Members of the 18-Nation Disarmament Committee in Geneva," *Pravda,* February 3, 1966.

[14] *The New York Times,* September 25, 1965.

[15] For a discussion of the sensitive issue of Soviet troop levels in internal Party-military circles, see present author's "Military Policy: A Soviet Dilemma," *Current History,* October 1965, pp. 205-207. Kosygin's failure to mention the other three measures in question did not necessarily indicate they had all been finally dropped from Soviet consideration. The destruction of bomber aircraft (a more sweeping measure according to the Soviet formula than the parallel U.S. proposal for a "bomber bonfire"), apparently has been set aside. Soviet rejection of a U.S. proposal to scrap "thousands" of nuclear weapons as part of a transfer of nuclear materials to peaceful purposes probably took the edge off the bomber destruction proposal. (See *The New York Times,* March 9, 1966.) On the other hand, the Soviet proposal for a NATO-

Warsaw Pact non-aggression accord, another item not mentioned by Kosygin, has continued to receive attention in Soviet commentary, and is a proposal of such long standing that it is unlikely to be shelved.

[16] See Soviet Government memorandum of September 20, 1957, in *Documents on Disarmament, 1949-1959,* Vol. II, Department of State, Washington, D.C., 1960, p. 878.

[17] See Walter C. Clemens, Jr., *Moscow and Arms Control: Evidence from the Sino-Soviet Dispute,* Center for International Studies, Massachusetts Institute of Technology, Cambridge, Mass., June 1965, pp. 31-33.

[18] F. Burlatskii, "The Atom Bomb and National Security," *Pravda,* January 10, 1966; Editorial, "Echo of Vietnam in Geneva," *International Affairs,* No. 10, October 1965, pp. 5-6. Some of the Soviet themes on non-proliferation have been concerned with defending the Soviet Union against Chinese accusations that a non-proliferation treaty represents a collusive attempt to maintain a U.S.-Soviet nuclear monopoly. The chief Soviet counter to this charge is that Soviet nuclear power protects "the entire socialist commonwealth" against "imperialist aggression." See, for example, Burlatskii, *loc. cit.* above. For background on earlier Chinese charges of U.S.-Soviet attempts to preserve a nuclear monopoly, see Dallin, *op. cit.,* pp. 237-273.

[19] See Article I of "Draft Treaty on the Non-Proliferation of Nuclear Weapons," text in *Pravda,* September 26, 1965. For elaboration of the Soviet viewpoint, see also M. Maratov, "Non-Proliferation and NATO Nuclear Plans," *International Affairs,* No. 1, January 1966, p. 23; Nikolai Fedorenko, "The U.N. and Nuclear Weapons," *Global Digest,* No. 1, January 1966, pp. 145-149. Soviet criticism of the U.S. "Draft Treaty to Prevent the Spread of

Nuclear Weapons" (text in *The New York Times,* August 18, 1965), has focused on the point that it "does not bar non-nuclear states from indirect access to nuclear weapons via military alliances with the help of measures like the MLF." Editorial, *International Affairs,* October 1965, p. 5.

[20] For discussion of these trends within the Warsaw Pact, see present author's *The Evolving Nature of the Warsaw Pact,* The RAND Corporation, RM-4835-PR, December 1965, especially pp. 11, 17-18, 23-27.

[21] What the Soviet Union has apparently preferred up to now is a certain facade of nuclear cooperation with the Warsaw Pact allies, combined with the substance of Soviet nuclear monopoly. A somewhat similar Soviet response to China's desire for nuclear aid, which proved unpalatable to the latter's sense of sovereignty, has been suggested by some of the Sino-Soviet polemical materials and may have been one of the factors leading to the rift. See discussion in the present author's work cited in note 20 above, pp. 38-39.

[22] "Statement by the Spokesman of the Chinese Government," in *Peking Review,* No. 33, August 16, 1963, p. 7. See also Chinese letter of refusal to attend the 23rd Party Congress of the CPSU, text in *The New York Times,* March 24, 1966.

[23] See *Documents on Disarmament, 1945-1949,* Vol. I, Department of State, Washington, D.C., 1960, pp. 17-19, 66-82, 176, 187, 191, 193.

[24] See "Premier Chou Cables Government Heads of the World" in *Peking Review,* No. 43, October 23, 1964, p. 6.

[25] See Morton H. Halperin and Dwight H. Perkins, *Communist China and Arms Control,* East Asian Research Center, Center for International Affairs, Harvard University, Cambridge, Mass., 1965, pp. 125-126. See also M. Lvov,

"Ban Nuclear Weapons," *International Affairs,* No. 1, January 1965, p. 14.

[26] *Pravda,* February 3, 1966.

[27] *The New York Times,* February 18, 1966; *Izvestiia,* February 24, 1966 interview with A. Kuzin, corresponding member of Academy of Sciences (broadcast February 23, 1966); M. Mikhailov, "Doesn't This Concern the UN?", *Izvestiia,* March 10, 1966; "The Day the Bombs Fell on Palomares," *Pravda,* March 2, 1966; Moscow radio broadcast, March 6, 1966, Professor V. Cherkasov; S. Zykov, "The Echo of an Explosion Over Spain," *Izvestiia,* January 28, 1966; L. Zamoiskii, "Belated Confessions," *Izvestiia,* March 4, 1966 (broadcast March 3, 1966); A. Korneichuk, "How Much Longer?", *Izvestiia,* February 6, 1966.

[28] See the present author's *The Soviet Union and the Sino-Soviet Dispute,* The RAND Corporation, P-3203, August 1965, pp. 22, 26-39. See also Dallin, *op. cit.,* pp. 259-260 ff.

[29] Iu. Gavrilov, "No Results," *Pravda,* September 23, 1965. See also Carlyle Morgan, "Tsarapkin Uses Geneva Platforms for Ideology Tirade," *Christian Science Monitor,* September 18, 1965; *The New York Times,* September 17, 1965.

[30] *Izvestiia,* January 29, 1966. See also, Anatole Shub, "Reds Drop Viet War as A-Talk Issue," *The Washington Post,* January 28, 1966.

[31] O. Grinev, "Before the Ninth Round at Geneva," *Izvestiia,* February 23, 1966. See also Shestov, *International Affairs,* November 1965, p. 54.

[32] Grinev, *Izvestiia,* February 23, 1966.

[33] B. Teplinsky, " 'Conventional' U.S. Forces in Vietnam," *International Affairs,* No. 10, October 1965, p. 29.

[34] Maratov in *International Affairs.* No. 1, January 1966, p. 19.

[35] *Pravda,* January 3, 1966; *Izvestiia,* January 4, 1966. See also "Red Talks Unify UN Latins," *The Washington Post,* February 27, 1966; *The New York Times,* February 8, 1966. It may be noted that following the protests of several Latin American governments, the Soviet Union tempered its initial acclaim for the Tri-Continent Conference, and offered the rather lame excuse that Soviet participants in it went to Havana as private citizens rather than official Soviet representatives.

[36] Editorial, "The Firm Basis of U.S.S.R. Foreign Policy," *Izvestiia,* January 18, 1966. See also C. L. Sulzberger in *The New York Times,* January 16, 1966.

[37] For an excellent discussion of the differentiation of Soviet policy toward the underdeveloped countries, see Marshall D. Shulman, *Beyond the Cold War,* Yale University Press, New Haven, Conn., 1966, especially pp. 66-72.

[38] See the present author's *Trends in Soviet Thinking on Theater Warfare, Conventional Operations, and Limited War,* The RAND Corporation, RM-4305-PR, December 1964, pp. 49-54, and *Soviet Strategy at the Crossroads,* Harvard University Press, Cambridge, Mass., 1964, pp. 118-129.

[39] As testimony to the "proxy" character of the Soviet involvement in the Vietnam war, one may note that throughout the conflict to date, despite the potentially inflammatory situation of Soviet-made surface-to-air missiles and antiaircraft artillery shooting down U.S. aircraft, both the Soviet Union and the United States apparently have found it in their interest to preserve the fiction of no direct Soviet involvement in the fighting. This, incidentally, can be considered a *de facto* form of arms control.

[40] See the present author's *The Soviet Union and the Sino-Soviet Dispute,* pp. 25-26, 39-40.

[41] See Shulman, *Beyond the Cold War,* pp. 56-57.

[42] See Richard Lowenthal, "Has the Revolution a Future?", *Encounter,* February 1965, pp. 16-21 *ff;* John M. Montais, "Communist Rule in Eastern Europe," *Foreign Affairs,* January 1965, pp. 331-348.

[43] Article by *Hung Ch'i* (Red Flag) Commentator, "Confessions Concerning the Line of Soviet-U.S. Collaboration Pursued by the New Leaders of the CPSU," in *Peking Review,* No. 8, February 18, 1966, p. 10.

[44] Obviously, the author's own conception of the process of social and political change shows through in this statement. He tends to believe, although this is a disputed question among cultural anthropologists and others (see, e.g., F. M. Keesing, *Cultural Anthropology,* Holt, Rinehart & Winston, Inc., New York, 1958, pp. 384-416), that the basic dimensions of a culture cannot ordinarily be shifted in a population in less than two or three generations. This is not to say that change and innovation do not occur on a shorter time scale also, but simply that some zones of a given culture are much more resistant to rapid change than others. There may occur, of course, critical junctures in the life of a society when a revolutionary break severs the old from the new. But such a revolutionary break does not seem, to the author at least, to be in prospect in the Soviet Union today. Indeed, in the Soviet case, even fifty years after a revolution of sweeping socio-political dimensions, the well-known *perezhitki,* or survivals of the past, persist. Just so, many of the new "Soviet" values and forms of behavior which have taken root in the Soviet period may prove equally persistent fifty years from now—even though the society is without doubt in the process of change.

[45] See Raymond L. Garthoff, *Soviet Military Policy: A Historical Analysis*

(New York: Frederick A. Praeger, Inc., 1966), pp. 110-114.

[46] The quotation is from a purported recent letter from the CPSU to other Communist Parties, published in the Hamburg newspaper *Die Welt* on March 21, 1966. See Anatole Shub, "Russians' China Blast is Revealed," *The Washington Post,* March 22, 1966. For a background discussion of Sino-Soviet military relations, see also the present author's *The Soviet Union and the Sino-Soviet Dispute,* pp. 40-49.

[47] An illuminating analysis of the concept of the "correlation of forces" and its influence upon Soviet policy calculations may be found in Garthoff, *Soviet Military Policy,* pp. 77-97.

Chapter 5

NUCLEAR PROLIFERATION

The Role of the Nuclear Powers in the Management of Nuclear Proliferation

By Hedley Bull

It is widely recognised that the process of nuclear proliferation will be greatly influenced by the military policies that are adopted by the present nuclear powers. There are, however, two conflicting doctrines as to what military policies on their part would best affect it.

According to the first doctrine, which I shall call that of Low Posture, the nuclear countries can best contribute to the management of proliferation by attempting to minimise the gap that separates them from the non-nuclear. If the United States and the Soviet Union (and perhaps the lesser nuclear powers) are able to reduce the level of their nuclear armaments, to restrict their qualitative development and to diminish reliance upon them in their foreign policies and strategies, then to that extent the world will be made safer for non-nuclear powers. Countries that are at present considering whether or not to acquire nuclear weapons will be the more easily persuaded that these weapons do not bring great advantages; while if some of them nevertheless go ahead and acquire these weapons, then at least precedents will have been established that will make a world of more nuclear powers less dangerous than it might otherwise be.

These are the sorts of policies for which India, Sweden and other representative non-nuclear countries have been calling at the Eighteen Nation Disarmament Conference, and which they declare to be at once the key to the problem of non-proliferation and the condition of their adhesion to a non-proliferation treaty. If the nuclear powers were to be swayed by this line of argument they would give urgent priority to the reaching of agreements such as those proposed for a freeze and reduction of nuclear warheads and delivery vehicles, a comprehensive test ban treaty, a moratorium on the deployment of ballistic missile defence systems, and a restriction on the use of nuclear weapons against non-nuclear powers. In the absence of such agreements, they might attempt to give partial effect to some of these proposals by unilateral actions. They might, for example, seek to equip themselves and their allies with conventional forces powerful enough to be independent of the use of nuclear weapons; they might commit themselves not to be the first to use nuclear weapons,

143

or not to use them against non-nuclear powers; they might desist from underground nuclear testing, from the deployment of ballistic missile defences and from further augmenting their strategic missile forces; and they might seek to reverse the trend towards "nuclearisation" of conventional military equipment and training, and conspicuously relegate the nuclear element in their arsenals to the role of weapons of last resort.

According to the second doctrine, which I shall call that of High Posture, the two major nuclear powers should on the contrary seek to preserve and indeed to widen the gap that divides them from the rest. By maintaining and increasing the high levels of their nuclear forces, by pressing on with their further improvement and by fully exploiting nuclear potential in their diplomacy and strategy, they will effectively preserve the bipolar structure of world power against the threat that proliferation poses to it; and potential nuclear powers can be effectively discouraged from entering the nuclear club or kept in their place if they do so.

This doctrine of High Posture has a number of advocates in the United States. It would seem to imply that any arms control agreement which bound the hands of the great nuclear powers, while leaving the aspirant nuclear states free to catch up—even more, one which actually diminished their present lead—would only encourage the forces of proliferation, or maximise the dangers that it will bring. Continued underground testing, the deployment of ballistic missile defences and penetration aids, willingness to rely on the use of nuclear weapons in diplomacy and war, are the policies to which this doctrine seems to point.

There are perhaps three arguments that support the idea of Low Posture. The first is that by adopting some of the measures that this doctrine calls for, the nuclear powers will satisfy the conditions that the spokesmen of the non-nuclear powers have laid down for their adhesion to a non-proliferation treaty, and pave the way for their agreement to it.

It is, of course, by no means clear how far the nuclear powers would have to go along the road of Low Posture in order to satisfy these conditions. Different countries have specified different sets of conditions: Swedish representatives have spoken simply of a cessation of further production of fissile material and a comprehensive test ban, while Indian spokesmen have called in addition for actual measures of disarmament. Moreover, it may be argued that the more conditions the nuclear powers are able to satisfy, the more further conditions are likely to be introduced by India and other potential nuclear powers, whose present declarations are a political manoeuvre rather than a position seriously intended.

There is no way of proving or disproving the seriousness of India's position except by putting it to the test. Although a desire to avoid entering into commitments is one element in the debate about nuclear weapons in India, there are others operating in a contrary direction. It would therefore seem reasonable that the nuclear powers should direct their policy towards influencing the course of this debate, rather than allow it to be determined in advance by some presentiment as to what the outcome of the debate will be.

India's conditions, moreover (to take the most radical that have so far been stated at Geneva) are by no means utopian. They do not specify that China is to be among the nuclear powers taking steps toward dismantling their armaments. They invoke general and complete disarmament only as a distant goal. And they do not require that the measures of nuclear disarmament to be carried out should be completed before the non-proliferation treaty is signed. It is true that India can have little actual strategic interest in reductions of nuclear delivery vehicles by the United States and the Soviet Union; and that if these reductions were very drastic, India would actually suffer from the augmentation of China's position relative to that of India's American and Soviet protectors. Nevertheless, it is clearly of great political importance to an Indian government willing to sign a non-proliferation treaty that it should be able to present to its parliament and people some tangible *quid pro quo*.

The second argument for the adoption of a Low Posture is that by reducing the military and political incentives that non-nuclear states have for going nuclear it would make a contribution in its own right to preventing, limiting or slowing down the spread of nuclear weapons, irrespective of its effect on the negotiation of a treaty.

Proliferation is stimulated by acceptance on the one hand of the assumption that nuclear weapons are a normal and necessary ingredient in the arsenal of any militarily powerful state, and on the other hand of the assumption that they are essential to the prestige and standing of a major power. Unfortunately both these assumptions are to a large extent founded upon fact; if they were illusions it would be easier to dispel them than it is. Moreover, while the nuclear powers continue to cling to their nuclear weapons, as they show every sign of doing, there are limits to the success they can have in convincing others of their inutility.

Nevertheless, within these limitations a policy of diminishing the importance of nuclear weapons may have a great deal of scope. If, during the years since 1945, nuclear weapons had been resorted to in war, or if some attempt had been made to institutionalise the equation of possession of nuclear weapons with great powerhood, the pressures now making for proliferation would be very much stronger than in fact they are. Measures have thus been taken in the past which, though they were not consciously formulated as part of an anti-proliferation strategy, have already had an element of success in advancing its purpose. There is little doubt that a more deliberate and systematic attempt on the part of the nuclear powers to relegate nuclear weapons to the background of their foreign policies, their strategic doctrines and the training and equipment of their armed forces would serve to arrest at least some of the forces making for proliferation, especially if it were undertaken in unison and enshrined in international agreements.

The third argument for the doctrine of Low Posture is that it will minimise the dangers that further proliferation will bring in its train, should it take place. The policies and agreements that are indicated by the Low Posture idea are desirable in themselves as measures of arms control among the present nuclear powers, and have for the most part been on the agenda of arms control conferences since well before the proliferation question came to assume the prominence it now has. The character of a world of many nuclear powers will be very much shaped by the military policies and arms control arrangements that are elaborated by the five existing nuclear states now; alarming though the prospect of further proliferation may be, it will be less so to the extent that the countries now wrestling with the problems of a world of five nuclear states have developed a body of arms control practice that may be transmitted to future generations.

Persuasive though these arguments are, there are elements of the proliferation problem of which they do not take account. Some potential nuclear countries are driven to contemplate acquiring nuclear weapons much less because of any assumption that they are necessary to a modern state's equipment or a great state's standing than because they have a pressing problem of security to which a nuclear force of their own provides a possible solution. Either like America's NATO allies in relation to the Soviet Union, or like India in relation to China, they feel themselves to be threatened by a nuclear power; or, like Israel in relation to the United Arab Republic or like Australia in relation to Indonesia, or South Africa in relation to her African neighbours, they feel that they are threatened, or might come to be threatened, by an enemy with so decisive a preponderance of conventional military strength that only nuclear weapons would provide an effective counter to it.

For many countries placed in this sort of situation the only alternative solution to nuclear weapons of their own is the protection, if it is available, of one of the existing nuclear powers. Such important potential nuclear powers as Canada, West Germany, Italy, Japan and Australia do in fact have firmly non-nuclear policies, the basis of which is their present confidence in the assurances provided by the American alliance system of which they are part. Other potential nuclear powers such as India and Sweden are outside this system, but nevertheless the belief that their security is underwritten by the United States is an unstated premise of their policies.

Part of the contribution that the United States and the Soviet Union (and possibly the United Kingdom) can make to the management of proliferation, then, is the extension of assurances or guarantees of support to non-nuclear states. In the first instance, this is a matter of preserving the assurances, or making certain existing assurances to non-aligned countries more explicit and categorical than they are at present. It may or may not prove desirable and feasible that the United States and the Soviet Union, and perhaps other nuclear powers, should join together in collective assurances of support to non-nuclear states, but whether such a development should come about or not, many states will continue to rely on the unilateral assurances emanating from the two major states that lie at the heart of the present political structure of the world.

The question is how far the adoption of Low Posture by the nuclear powers, and especially by the United States and the Soviet Union, is consistent with their fulfilling this role of guarantors. Some forms of the Low Posture doctrine require the nuclear powers not merely to desist from further building up their nuclear force, but actually to begin dismantling it; moreover, the suggestion appears to be that this process of dismantling, having begun, should go on, the initial measures of reduction of nuclear delivery vehicles being a token or down payment for further instalments to come.

It is clear that if the United States and the Soviet Union were to progress indefinitely down this road, a point would be reached at which their nuclear superiority, in relation both to China, Britain and France and to the leading non-nuclear states, would diminish.

This ability to protect states which felt threatened by one of the lesser nuclear states or by a non-nuclear state would then come to be called in question. Moreover, as their ability to exploit nuclear force in relation to one another became subject to restrictions and reservations, the confidence that their NATO and Warsaw Pact allies now place in them would be undermined.

The five nuclear powers do not of course constitute the close political combination or concert that their term "nuclear club" suggests; on the contrary, they are aligned on different sides of the most profound political divisions of our time. But even if the formula of a Soviet-American or a five power concert for the joint management of international affairs were solidly based in reality, it would still imply a strategic superiority on the part of states that were members of the concert over those that were not, and it would be threatened by a process of disarmament whose end product was a merging of their status with that of the rest.

Even some of the more modest steps called for by the doctrine of Low Posture might be held to call in question the efficacy of existing guarantees and to provide some of the countries that now enjoy them with a stimulus to proliferation. The adoption by the United States and the United Kingdom of a commitment not to use nuclear weapons first, for example, although it might have the beneficial effects mentioned above, would also have the effect of undermining the present strategy of NATO and of alienating West Germany and other European NATO countries from their present attachment to the alliance.

There are also uncertainties as to the extent to which the restriction envisaged would impair the ability of the United States (and possibly the United Kingdom) to preserve the guarantees which they now extend, explicitly or implicitly, to China's neighbours. At the present time the United States enjoys unquestioned strategic nuclear superiority in relation to China, and while this remains the position, as it may well do for a decade or more, such potential nuclear countries as India, Japan and Australia have no cause to doubt the credibility to China of an American threat to attack her in response to an attack on themselves. If, however, China should in the course of time develop a nuclear force that is both invulnerable to destruction and capable of attacking targets in the United States, the same sort of doubts that have been expressed about the validity of the American guarantee in NATO might come to preoccupy America's Far Eastern allies and dependents.

In this event it is very likely that the search for an acceptable alternative to national nuclear forces will tend to focus in Asia as it has in Europe upon devices for shoring up the American guarantee. This is not the place to examine the range of possible devices or to consider the applicability to the Far Eastern alliance system of the solutions to this problem that have been propounded in NATO. It is clear, however, that one of the most prominent ideas in this debate is likely to be that the United States can best maintain its position as the guarantor of China's neighbours by a deployment of ballistic missile defences that will in effect preserve its present position of strategic nuclear superiority. Such an idea, if it were accepted, would imply that a moratorium on ballistic missile deployment would have unfavourable consequences for nuclear proliferation; and that underground nuclear testing, because of its connection with ballistic missile defence, should be continued.

A policy of Low Posture, then, may weaken certain of the incentives making for proliferation but it may strengthen others. Indeed in its more radical form it is open to the objection not merely that it provides an inadequate formula for the management of proliferation but that it fails to recognise the fundamentally hierarchical basis of the present world order. In the Indian demand that "vertical proliferation" must be dealt with along with "horizontal proliferation," and that there must be an end to all talk of a "select club" of four or five states "to work out the salvation of the world" there is an implicit claim to equality among states which could be taken up by states much less significant than India and which if seriously pressed would lead to the undoing of the whole structure of power on which, unrecognised though it is in law and diplomacy, the everyday expectations of all present international life are based.

There is a certain justice in the note of grievance which is sometimes struck by countries which see themselves as the nuclear Have-Nots or proletarians. It is true that in an international order in which the many do not have nuclear weapons, the few that retain them will enjoy privileges, however effectively they are able to disguise them. But the alternative to an international order in which certain states have a larger stake than others is probably no international order at all. The problem is not to find an international order in which no one state or group of states has a special interest, but rather to ensure that those who do have special interests recognise the special responsibilities that go with them, and conduct themselves in such a way as to engage general support for the system whose custodians and guar-

antors they are. It is in this latter sense that the doctrine of Low Posture is most defensible.

If the doctrine of Low Posture does not in itself provide an adequate guide to the nuclear powers, the same is true of the contrary position. The idea that the United States and the Soviet Union should adopt a High Posture (no one appears to entertain the idea that all five nuclear powers should do so) has two supporting arguments.

The first is that by doing so the two leading states will deter or discourage potential nuclear countries from acquiring nuclear weapons. By demonstrating the superior size and sophistication of their missile forces, their ability to provide for ballistic missile defence and the prominence of the qualitative arms race, they will emphasise the great distances that divide a country which has merely tested a nuclear device from one which has a replete modern weapons system, and so discredit the idea that doing so provides an easy entrée into the ranks of the great. Moreover, by maintaining the ability to disarm the nuclear forces of lesser powers or to effectively defend their cities against them, they may in fact nullify the strategic effectiveness of lesser nuclear states: the British and French nuclear deterrents, as Soviet ballistic missile defences grow, and the Chinese one, as American defences do, may come to seem without value; and potential imitators of these lesser nuclear states may be expected to draw the lesson.

A weakness of this argument is that much of the present impetus towards proliferation is among countries which do not see the United States or the Soviet Union as their antagonist, but China or some non-nuclear state. Even where it is for confrontation with one of the two great nuclear powers that a nuclear force is being sought, the validity of the argument is uncertain. The present overwhelming superiority of Soviet and American nuclear resources has not had the effect of discouraging China and France from their nuclear programmes; and indeed there is a case to be made out for the strategic logic that sustains them. They may well calculate that the effectiveness of their deterrent forces has to be judged in relation to a whole spectrum of contingencies, and that even if over a wide range of this spectrum they cannot expect to have a meaningful deterrent, there will nevertheless be some area of it for which they can purchase one even with a force whose chance of creating inacceptable damage to a great power is only slight.

The second argument is that a High Posture will enable the United States and the Soviet Union to preserve the bipolar character of international politics against the proliferation that seems to threaten it, both that which has already taken place and that which might take place in the future; and that to this extent it provides a sound formula for the maintenance of order in a world of many nuclear states.

The "bipolarity" which is assumed in this argument is one that implies cooperation between the United States and the Soviet Union in the joint management of international politics. It may be that some element of tacit cooperation between the two leading states is now perceived by their leaders at least as a possible direction in which their foreign policies might move. But the sort of bipolarity which has actually characterised international politics in recent years is of course competitive rather than cooperative; and it is the perpetuation of this competitive bipolarity that would be the more likely result of some of the policies for which the advocates of High

Posture are calling. The continuation of underground testing and the deployment of ballistic missile defences, for example, have a vital bearing on the relations between the two great nuclear powers themselves, whatever their implications for relations between these two countries and lesser states. Indeed the negotiation of arms control arrangements would seem to be one of the most likely routes towards the replacement of a primarily competitive by a primarily cooperative bipolar order.

The doctrine of High Posture, moreover, does not allow for the need of the two predominant states to conciliate powers that are in the ascendant and to engage their support in the system. It may well be that the growth of new centres of power in Europe and Asia does not for the foreseeable future spell the end of Soviet-American predominance and that the changes in the structure of the international system which we are now witnessing imply no more than a qualification or loosening of the bipolar situation. This being so, it would be quite premature to treat China and France as if they were the equals of the United States and the Soviet Union, and to recast our thinking about arms control accordingly. Nevertheless, these countries have independent policies and nuclear forces of their own; and no arms control policy can be satisfactory which treats them as pariahs and does not seek to draw them into international negotiations and discussions.

The High Posture doctrine appears either to be opposed to arms control agreements as such, or at best to sanction only those sorts of agreements which preserve and solidify the Soviet and American preponderance. If, however, progress is to be made in making China above all, but also France, more arms control-minded, and in imparting to these and perhaps to future nuclear powers the restraints and disciplines which every nuclear power must practise if we are to survive, then arms control agreements must be negotiated in which these countries have a stake. To the extent that we are already living in a world in which the problems of arms control are multilateral, the search for purely bilateral solutions is unproductive.

It does not seem that we need accept as the soundest formula for managing the problems of a world of many nuclear powers this picture of struggle by the United States and the Soviet Union to overcome other contenders. It may well be that Soviet and American preponderance will continue for a long time to be a necessary presupposition of all strategic and political arrangements; but the dangers of proliferation also require that the two great powers maintain and develop the momentum of arms control, so as to strengthen traditions and precedents on which further nuclear powers

can draw; and also that they put forward schemes that are consistent enough with the strategic interests of new nuclear powers as to draw them into the international arms control conversation.

Neither of the two doctrines I have been discussing would appear by itself to provide an adequate guide to the nuclear powers; and there is little doubt that a concerted effort on their part to shape their military policies so as best to affect the spread of nuclear weapons would require them to strike some balance between the two. The question of nuclear proliferation is of course unlikely to be the decisive consideration in determining whether the United States and the Soviet Union adopt a High or a Low Posture. What prospect there is that the United States and the Soviet Union will concert themselves to follow a common policy of any sort in these matters, and what success they would have in managing the problem of proliferation if they did, it is beyond my present purpose to discuss.

U.S. Non-Proliferation Policy

By George Bunn

The purpose of this paper is to set forth U.S. policy on non-proliferation. It will first describe the background of the problem as the government sees it, then the reasons and purposes of U.S. policy in this area, and finally the elements of the U.S. non-proliferation program.

1.

When we were the only nuclear power in the world, we nonetheless thought that one was too many. You will recall the Acheson-Lilienthal-Baruch plan to remove nuclear energy entirely from the military field. This was not thought of as altruism. It was put forward because the Government felt that our national interests would be best served by a world without the bomb. Although it was not accepted, our ultimate objective remains the same today.

This proposal was the first of a long series of attempts to prevent widespread ability to trigger nuclear war. The 1946 Atomic Energy Act and its revisions in later years all had this as a basic purpose. One of the objectives of President Eisenhower's Atoms for Peace Plan was to guard against the diversion of the peaceful products of nuclear energy to

military use. That plan resulted in an International Atomic Energy Agency which today has available safeguard procedures and inspectors to monitor the peaceful activities of those nations which are willing to accept them. Widespread acceptance is, of course, essential to preventing further nuclear spread.

To make sure that only one man can pull the trigger to our nuclear weapons, the United States has developed intricate personnel, mechanical and electronic command and control arrangements for our arsenal. These are designed to insure against accidental or unauthorized explosion while at the same time maintaining the credibility of our deterrent. You may remember that this became an issue in the 1964 campaign. President Johnson in Seattle in September 1965 referred to the many steps the U.S. has taken to insure that neither a madman nor a malfunction could ever fire our nuclear weapons.

As another way to help keep additional fingers off nuclear triggers, President Eisenhower sought a comprehensive test ban treaty. The "driving force" behind his determination was, he said, his belief that there should be no increase in the number of nuclear powers.

The fear of proliferation was also the key to President Kennedy's efforts to secure such a treaty. In announcing the successful conclusion of the Moscow negotiations for a limited test ban, he described his hope that it would be the opening wedge in an all-out campaign to contain the nuclear threat.

The limited treaty was a beginning because it prohibits the form of testing which is simplest, quickest, least expensive and most productive for a country wishing to test a first device. But it has not stopped all testing, as Ambassador Trivedi frequently reminds us in Geneva. Nor have many near-nuclear nations accepted IAEA safeguards over their peaceful activities. Nor can any national legislation such as our Atomic Energy Act prevent other nations from uncovering the secrets of the bomb. Nor can we have any assurance that the care which major nuclear powers have usually exercised over their weapons will always be exercised either by them or by others.

2.

The peril of nuclear holocaust remains despite the steps taken so far. In describing it, I cannot improve upon President Kennedy's oft-quoted 1963 speech. He said:

I ask you to stop and think for a moment what it would mean to have nuclear weapons in so many hands, in the hands of countries large and small, stable and unstable, responsible and irresponsible, scattered throughout the world. There would be no rest for anyone then, no stability, no real security, and no chance of effective disarmament. There would only be the increased chance of accidental war and increased necessity for the great powers to involve themselves in what otherwise would be local conflicts.

These concerns are clearly shared both by those countries which have already tested nuclear weapons, and by those which really have no prospect of doing so in the foreseeable future. We believe they are also shared by those who could do so over the next ten years or so, either by themselves or with some help from others. But it is in this latter group of countries where the greatest problem now arises.

We can fairly easily conclude that our interests are best served by halting nuclear spread. But the important decisions to halt it will not be taken only in Washington, or for that matter, only in the capitals of those who have tested nuclear weapons.

The national decision of a near-nuclear country not to seek nuclear weapons is fraught with questions of national security, domestic politics and international prestige. We and the other members of the community of nations can attempt to influence it, and that is the point of the talk in Geneva about a non-proliferation treaty.

Such a treaty could make a valuable contribution to preventing national decisions to go nuclear. It would impose legal, moral, and political restraints upon the signatories. Probably, however, it could not alone prevent proliferation. What is needed is a combination of international restraints like the treaty, international cooperation, and an international atmosphere which would make it possible for near-nuclear countries to refrain without fear from entering the nuclear arms race.

On this point, let me quote the interesting testimony of Secretary McNamara before the Joint Committee on Atomic Energy:

Successful efforts to halt the spread of nuclear weapons . . . depend upon the development of a comprehensive program designed both to make it difficult for proliferation to take place and to create an international atmosphere in which potential nuclear states will realize that acquisition of nuclear weapons will decrease their security, and they therefore will *choose* not to develop them. Such a program must have three elements:

1. It must provide security and protection to the legitimate interests of non-nuclear states.

2. It must deny the utility of nuclear weapons for any state with aggressive purposes.

3. It must not permit the acquisition of nuclear weapons or a nuclear test to increase the prestige, political influence and power of a nation above and beyond the influence which it is due because of its political and economic position.

In other words a successful non-proliferation program must assure non-nuclear states that they can achieve their legitimate objectives without acquiring nuclear weapons. Such a program must put potential aggressors on notice that possession of nuclear weapons will not make their aggression either easier or less dangerous. It must make clear to great nations such as India, Japan and Germany that they need not acquire nuclear weapons to have the status of a major world power.

Secretary McNamara's statement well expresses the purposes behind the non-proliferation program which my Agency and other agencies of the Government are pursuing. Let me describe now some of the elements of that program.

3.

The *first* element in our program is a non-proliferation treaty. In August 1965 a draft treaty was submitted to the Geneva Conference by William C. Foster, U.S. representative to the Conference and the Director of the U.S. Arms Control and Disarmament Agency. This draft was based upon several years' consultation on the subject with our allies and with the Soviet Union. It was, however, rejected by the Soviet Union on the ground that it would permit access to nuclear weapons by the Federal Republic of Germany through a NATO multilateral force. Plans for such a force, the Soviets often said, were the sole obstacle to the negotiation of a treaty.

But Secretary Rusk's recent testimony before the Joint Committee on Atomic Energy makes it abundantly clear that "no one in NATO has been talking about any arrangement which would involve the proliferation of nuclear weapons." He responded to Senator Pastore's question whether any plans now under discussion in NATO contemplated the U.S. giving up its veto over U.S. weapons by saying:

We would have to insist . . . that the United States be a necessary party to a decision to use nuclear weapons. Because the vast arsenals of the United States are so heavily involved in that decision, we must be present for that decision and must ourselves agree to a decision taken.

With respect to the Soviet charges concerning NATO nuclear discussions, Secretary Rusk said:

[The Soviets] object to the very existence of NATO. They object to any arrangements which tie the United States and Western Europe more closely together for defense purposes. They object to the Federal Republic participating in the alliance on a basis of equality and partnership with other European members of the Western community. Their main propaganda drive has been directed against the Federal Republic in an effort to divide and weaken the NATO Alliance, but the West German Government is clearly on record as being opposed to acquiring a national nuclear weapons capability. The Soviet action in targeting hundreds of Soviet missiles on Western Europe is what created a nuclear problem in the Alliance in the first place.

In response to the draft treaty submitted by the United States at Geneva, the Soviet Union submitted a draft to the General Assembly in the fall of 1965. This draft was consistent with the Soviet view that any multilateral force should be prevented, for it would deny the right of allies not possessing nuclear weapons to participate in the ownership, control or use of such weapons. The breadth of its language was such, however, that it raised doubts about the Soviet view on consultation between allies in preparation for their defense against Soviet nuclear attack, and even about existing arrangements for the deployment of U.S.-owned and controlled nuclear weapons on the territory of NATO allies.

These doubts were confirmed in a late 1965 speech by Soviet Foreign Minister Gromyko and by more recent statements by Ambassador A. A. Roschin at Geneva. In the Soviet view, there now seem to be not one but three obstacles to a treaty—all of them dealing with the defense of NATO from possible Soviet nuclear attack. These three are, of course, the concept of a multilateral force, the so-called McNamara committee for allied consultations on nuclear defense planning, and existing arrangements for deployment of U.S. weapons abroad. The Soviets would ban any so-called "access" to nuclear weapons by non-nuclear allies, and they define access broadly enough to cover all these three forms of defense arrangements.

Whether the Soviets have upped the ante for bargaining, propaganda or some other purpose remains to be seen. But in an attempt to allay any legitimate concerns which might exist, we have amended our draft treaty in a number of ways. These amendments were submitted in March 1966 to the Geneva Conference by Adrian S. Fisher, present U.S. representative to the Geneva talks and Deputy Director of the Arms Control and Disarmament Agency.

These amendments adopt language from the Soviet draft treaty. The Soviet draft evidences concern that control of nuclear weapons might be transferred to non-nuclear states indirectly, through third states or groups of states or through armed forces under military alliances. After making clear (as before) that no transfer would be permitted into the national control of a non-nuclear state, the new U.S. amendments say this could not be done "directly, or indirectly through third States or associations of States, or through units of the armed forces or military personnel of any State, even if such units or personnel are under the command of a military alliance." Much of this language is from the Soviet text.

Another interesting point in the new draft was suggested by Ambassador Trivedi. Because a number of countries have demonstrated advanced nuclear capability through peaceful projects, our old concept of nuclear power or nuclear club was outmoded if we included only those who had tested nuclear weapons. To use language from Secretary McNamara which I quoted earlier, this concept served to raise the international prestige of those said to be in the club beyond the influence which was their due as the result of political and economic position. For this reason, the new draft language refers not to "nuclear states" as before, but to "nuclear-weapons states." And we do not intend to suggest that any special status goes with being a nuclear-weapon state beyond that resulting from the economic and political position of the country.

The underlying theory of the new U.S. amendments is that the danger of nuclear war will be increased by an increase in the number of fingers on nuclear triggers. The amendments would prohibit any increase—even by one—in the number of decision-making centers that have the right or ability to fire a nuclear weapon. They contain obligations on nuclear weapons countries not to transfer control of nuclear weapons or provide assistance in their manufacture, and on non-nuclear weapons countries not to manufacture them.

The Soviet response to our new amendments has so far been negative. But we remain convinced that it is the right approach and we hope ultimately that the clear mutual interest in achieving restraints on proliferation will bring them around.

So much then for the non-proliferation treaty.

A *second* and essential element in our program is the application of IAEA safeguards to peaceful nuclear programs. The most official statement of U.S. policy on this subject is President Johnson's message to the Geneva Conference which provides:

Second, through a non-proliferation treaty and through efforts outside such a treaty, we must continue to secure application of International Atomic Energy Agency or equivalent international safeguards over peaceful nuclear activities.

To this end, I urge agreement that all transfers of nuclear materials or equipment for peaceful purposes to countries which do not have nuclear weapons be under IAEA or equivalent international safeguards. At the same time, the major nuclear powers should accept in increasing measure the same international safeguards they recommend for other states.

Together with the application of safeguards, we must continue to find ways for international recognition of outstanding peaceful nuclear achievements. The large power reactor, not the mushroom cloud, must become the symbol of nuclear capability.

Third, to contribute to a climate which will permit national decisions to refrain from acquiring nuclear weapons, the nuclear-weapon states must give evidence of progress toward nuclear disarmament, and must themselves accept restraints on their nuclear-weapon ambitions. The limited test ban treaty was of course a step in this direction. Its limitations on non-nuclear weapon states have so far been wholly theoretical. But its restraints on the Soviet Union and the United States have been very practical.

Further steps have been proposed. The United States, for example, continues to support the extension of this treaty to cover underground tests.

We also are seeking agreement on the cutoff of production of fissionable materials for use in nuclear weapons. In our view, such a cutoff could be accompanied by the destruction of a great many nuclear weapons by the nuclear powers, and the dedication of the fissionable material released to peaceful purposes.

As another step to reduce the dangers and burdens of nuclear arms, we have proposed a freeze on offensive and defensive strategic bombers and missiles designed to carry nuclear weapons. If progress could be made here, we would be prepared to explore the possibility of significant reductions in these modern, high-speed carriers of nuclear destruction.

Any and all of these measures would contribute to a climate in which nuclear-capable countries could pursue their ambitions without seeking nuclear weapons.

A *fourth* element in a non-proliferation program is to provide assurance to non-nuclear states against nuclear attack. This must be done ultimately by strengthening the United Nations and other international security arrangements. "Meanwhile," President Johnson has stated, "the nations that do not seek the nuclear path can be sure that they will have our strong support against threats of nuclear blackmail."

4.

This summary of U.S. policy is based on the dual assumption that the spread of nuclear weapons threatens our national security, and that halting that spread is no simple problem. It can only be accomplished by the cooperation of nuclear and non-nuclear weapon states in a comprehensive program to secure a non-proliferation treaty and other international restraints, as well as an international climate permitting those who might otherwise seek nuclear weapons to refrain without fear from doing so.

An Italian Proposal of Nuclear Moratorium

By Francesco Cavalletti

The negotiations of the Eighteen-Nation Committee on Disarmament, which started off, as is known, in 1962 from too general and partly utopian positions, have become more realistic in content in the ensuing years. They have shifted from a somewhat theoretical and, in any case, very remote aim—general and complete disarmament—to tackling more immediate and specific objectives such as the banning of tests in three environments and the non-proliferation of nuclear weapons.

It is, of course, understood by most serious thinkers on arms control that only through realistic attitudes and gradual methods can it ever be managed, step by step, to rid the peoples of the burden of the arms race.

After the agreement on the partial prohibition of nuclear tests, the negotiators at Geneva are now focusing their efforts on non-proliferation, a very complicated but pressing and concrete problem which could be speedily solved despite obstacles. The solution of this problem has even become a kind of precondition to any other progress in the control of armaments.

It seems clear that the best, most complete and final way of putting an end to the proliferation of nuclear weapons is the conclusion of a general non-proliferation treaty. All the countries of the world should participate in such an agreement. But even if the adhesion to this agreement—as was the case with the Moscow Treaty—were incomplete, a non-proliferation treaty which was accepted by a large number of Powers including the U.S.S.R. and the United States, would be of tremendous military and political importance. As regards the political aspect, if one recalls the wave of hope and confidence which the Moscow Treaty gave rise to, one can easily contemplate the advantage of a non-proliferation treaty concluded in present-day circumstances and at a time of crisis in Southeast Asia. These efforts must be continued relentlessly while there is a chance for success, and there is still a chance of success.

It would, however, be unwise to close our eyes to the practical difficulties in the negotiations which could end in failure or drag on indefinitely without result.

The principal obstacles are known. First and foremost, the Soviet Government continues its opposition to any fair agreement. It seems that for the Soviets a non-proliferation agreement is not so much a means of preventing a sixth country being capable of using nuclear weapons but rather an expedient for trying to weaken the Atlantic Alliance, to divide the Western Allies and to prevent any European integration.

The Soviet Union is endeavoring to prevent nuclear consultations and cooperation that have nothing to do with the individual right to use nuclear weapons. That is the main difficulty in the way of agreement, and the Western representatives at Geneva are patiently striving to convince the Soviets that a limited collateral measure such as a non-proliferation treaty can neither eliminate the alliances nor block the process of European integration, which, despite recent difficulties, remains one of the principal objectives of the policy of many European countries, including mine.

Furthermore, another complicating and delaying factor has emerged during the debates both at the United Nations and at Geneva. Some non-nuclear and non-aligned countries, particularly some which are already approaching a nuclear military capability, have stated that they would not wish finally to renounce nuclear weapons without there being certain commitments on the part of the nuclear countries. They have said that non-proliferation must not remain an isolated fact but must be a stage in a process and be accompanied or followed by the cessation of the nuclear arms race and by a start in the destruction of nuclear arsenals.

These claims, which refer particularly to the cut-off and the test ban, partially correspond to the proposals which have long since been put forward by the United States Government, but the Soviet Government does not seem disposed, in the present state of affairs, to accept these proposals which would necessarily entail controls. On this issue then the difficulties stem once again from the Soviet Union, but it must be recognized that in any case, if we wish to accommodate the claims of the non-nuclear countries, lengthy negotiations will be inevitable so that, even if the best came to the best, the non-proliferation agreement, which is extremely urgent and by its nature could speedily be achieved, would be left in abeyance or very long delayed.

Indeed, the demands of the non-nuclear and non-aligned countries when kept within reasonable limits seem logical. One can understand that non-proliferation is one of the first measures, even the first, to agree on. But according to the concept of progressive or gradual disarmament, which is our concept, we should then envisage the adoption of other and more extensive measures which also concern the nuclear countries. Moreover, the non-nuclear non-aligned countries do not ask for equality of rights with the nuclear countries or the abolition of nuclear weapons everywhere, which would be clearly unrealistic. They ask that, within the framework of a non-proliferation agreement, the nuclear countries undertake to recognize specifically the obligation of progressive disarmament.

All these elements—Soviet opposition to a just non-proliferation treaty, the desire of the non-aligned countries for a more extensive treaty covering also other issues, the slowness of the negotiations and, finally, the extreme urgency of stopping the spread of nuclear weapons—have given rise to the idea of a provisional arrangement, an idea which, after having been debated in study groups, has been officially put forward for the first time by the Italian Government. It concerns a temporary and controlled nuclear moratorium to which the non-nuclear States would commit themselves for a definite period and through unilateral declarations.

The Italian Minister for Foreign Affairs outlined this proposal at Geneva on 29 July 1965.

It is quite conceivable that the non-nuclear countries might agree to renounce unilaterally equipping themselves with nuclear weapons for a specific length of time, it being understood that if their demands of broader disarmament were not complied with during that time limit, they would resume their freedom of action. In that way a respite would be given to the anxiety about nuclear dissemination and, moreover, a factor of pressure and persuasion would be created which could be brought to bear on the nuclear countries in order to spur them to conclude a general agreement, thus speeding up the process of a nuclear disarmament.

These ideas received the support of several delegations in the Eighteen-Nation Committee, including the delegations of Sweden, India, Brazil and Mexico. They were further elaborated by the Italian Government and on 14 September 1965, the Italian delegation at Geneva tabled at the Conference the draft of a nuclear moratorium declaration. The declaration which has been proposed is a unilateral one—a unilateral manifestation of will; it does not have the character of a contractual commitment. Nevertheless, according to the current opinion of the jurists, it would have full force of law, committing to a certain line of conduct the countries subscribing to it, in the conditions provided for by the declaration itself.

The declaration, for its unilateral character, might be worded in different ways, each country remaining free to choose the language best suited to it, provided that the essentials are maintained. The Italian draft contains some of the elements we consider essential, but it is only an outline or a guide and not a fixed and immutable model.

The principal points of this draft declaration are as follows:

First, the draft declaration recalls certain principles or obligations which appear to be fundamental. It is said that the governments issuing the declaration are convinced that a unilateral renunciation of nuclear weapons by the non-nuclear States may facilitate and encourage international agreements to prevent the spread of nuclear weapons, to halt the nuclear arms race, and to reduce nuclear arsenals, leading to general and complete disarmament.

The declaration then indicates the undertakings into which the governments signatory to the declaration should enter. It is stated that each government from the date of the entry into force of the declaration and for a certain number of years, 1) will not manufacture or otherwise acquire national control of nuclear weapons; 2) will not seek or receive assistance from other States in the manufacture of any such weapons; 3) will accept the application of IAEA or equivalent international safeguards on its nuclear activities.

The word "national" with regard to "control" is important. This is in line with the well-known Western stand, which aims at preventing the creation of any new independent national nuclear centre, while permitting possible forms of cooperation or nuclear integration which would not involve that danger. So if the declaration is issued by some non-nuclear countries of the Western Alliance, it would not prevent them from engaging in nuclear sharing even during the period of the moratorium.

On the other hand, the safeguards which are required are also important, because they give the necessary security to the parties concerned during the moratorium. This element of control distinguishes our concept of moratorium from some other uncontrolled moratoriums proposed by the Soviet Government and it complies with the general principle of the Western countries that every measure of disarmament must be inspected.

Further, the draft states that the undertakings, foreseen in the declaration, enter into force if similar declarations are issued by at least a certain number of States, within six months from the signature of the declaration. Three months before the expiration of the moratorium, the signatories of the declaration will consult, in order to prolong it, and consider the progress which has been made toward international agreements to prevent the spread of nuclear weapons, or to halt the nuclear arms race, and to reduce nuclear arsenals. The signatories of the declaration reserve all freedom of action if this progress is not satisfactory or if a non-nuclear state, in any way, acquires national control of nuclear weapons.

The moratorium must be fairly long in duration, otherwise it would not have the intended stabilizing effect. It must not be too long, however, or its effectiveness as a factor of pressure would be weakened. Between three and five years would then be an appropriate duration.

As for the second problem, the number of States issuing the declaration has perhaps less importance than their nuclear capability and the timing of their declaration. All the countries who are near to nuclear capability should issue the declaration, but it might happen that a country, though desiring to sign the declaration, would not do so unless it were quite sure that a certain other country would do likewise. It is also possible that the two countries in question might have difficulties in reaching agreement for a simultaneous decision or even in entering into direct contact. That is a problem which exists also with the treaty of non-dissemination and could hardly be solved by a rigid procedure laid down in a text. It would have to be approached in a flexible manner, on the practical level, and dealt with through prudent arrangements and appropriate soundings carried out by carefully chosen intermediaries.

The draft ends with an invitation to all States—nuclear and non-nuclear—to respect and observe the principles of the declaration and encourage their observance.

The commitment envisaged would not constitute a simple and platonic declaration of good intentions. The Italian draft provides a juridical, although unilateral instrument, accompanied by the necessary safeguards of application. Experience of the uncontrolled moratorium for nuclear tests is a sufficient precedent for advising against an uncontrolled moratorium. The value of the moratorium would disappear if we provided for uncontrolled commitments based solely on the good faith of the parties concerned.

We should not be tempted by the idea that the concept of the moratorium, valid as it is for non-proliferation, could be applied to other sectors of the nuclear arms race. The progressive stoppage of this race can only be achieved through contractual commitments which the moratorium is intended to foster.

Finally, we must not confuse the idea of the nuclear moratorium with denuclearization. Indeed, the moratorium would in no way affect the deployment and installation of nuclear weapons belonging to the nuclear countries wherever they are necessary to maintain the military balance. The moratorium is therefore neither the equivalent of nor a preparation for the denuclearization of certain zones—Central Europe, the Mediterranean or the Baltic, but clearly it would not impede—it would even favor—implementation of the projects now under examination for the denuclearization of certain continents.

The Soviets have already declared that they will find the unilateral declaration insufficient because, as noted above, it makes Atlantic nuclear sharing still possible. But as it involves an initiative by non-nuclear countries and concerns them alone, the Soviets would be in an embarrassing situation if they wanted to oppose it.

Could the unilateral declaration, furthermore, satisfy the aforementioned claims of the non-aligned countries and correspond to the concept of progressive disarmament? If it does not give immediate satisfaction to these demands, at least they are recognized as valid and there is the hope that they may bear concrete results. Thus the nuclear countries will have a reasonable period of time to conclude successfully, if they wish, their negotiations on nuclear disarmament, while being aware that in the event of failure the non-nuclear countries may reassume their freedom of action. The non-nuclear countries therefore retain, as Minister Fanfani observed, an element of pressure and persuasion. There are indeed reasons to believe—as moreover the discussion on this topic at the United Nations has shown—that many non-nuclear countries which would hesitate to renounce nuclear weapons forever, if no progress were evident in the disarmament of the great Powers, would be more inclined to assume temporary restrictions which would allow full freedom of action for them later. Under

our formula this freedom remains total; the moratorium however, if accepted by the principal countries approaching nuclear capability, would have prolonged stabilizing and dissuasive effects.

The moratorium which is an easier solution to non-proliferation—a shortcut, a contraceptive pill, if you permit the expression, and not sterilization—is, of course, neither the ideal nor complete solution.

The question arises of knowing at what moment the moratorium idea, which is for the time being kept in reserve, could or should be specifically relaunched. We submitted the proposal at a time when, in 1965, the Geneva negotiations for the treaty—after the Soviet rejection of the United States draft treaty—seemed to be in a state of dead-lock. The negotiations—encouraged by the United Nations deliberations—have now been resumed and, while they are not altogether promising, neither are they absolutely negative. These efforts must be continued while there is yet a ray of hope, with patience, tenacity and perseverance while keeping the alternative solution up our sleeves.

If at a particular moment, contrary to our hopes, it seems evident that the negotiations are doomed to failure or that dangerous delays are occurring, I believe that at that moment the non-nuclear countries should take the appropriate concrete initiatives within the limits of their proper responsibilities and in the awareness of the claims of peace.

The interest that the idea of the moratorium has aroused at Geneva and at the United Nations and elsewhere, an appreciative welcome which many non-nuclear countries and the major nuclear countries of the West have accorded it, gives grounds for hoping that this appeal will not be in vain.

Suggestions for Long-Term Anti-Nuclear Policies*

By Herman Kahn

A. Some Current Prospects

Nearly a decade has passed since any nation has announced an explicit decision to acquire nuclear weapons. Nuclear proliferation has been slow, at least by comparison with many of the pessimistic estimates made in the past, and some analysts expect that the pace of proliferation during the next ten years will remain as slow. Others take a very different view. They point out that nuclear warheads and carriers are becoming—from the technological and economic points of view—ever more widely available, and they argue that rapid proliferation is much more likely in the next decade than ever in the past simply because it will be technically more easy. Thus India and Pakistan, Israel and Egypt, Brazil, Argentina, Sweden, Switzerland, Japan and West Germany, might not in the future have to duplicate the efforts of France or China in order to acquire comparable nuclear capabilities. More important, it has become increasingly clear that

* This article is adapted from a Hudson Institute report prepared in collaboration with Carl Dibble.

quite rudimentary nuclear capabilities might satisfy the political, psychological and even strategic objectives of numerous potential "Nth" countries; it is not necessary to overtake the super-powers.

In short, so far as narrow military, technical and economic obstacles are concerned, proliferation in the coming decade or two might be unprecedentedly rapid. But this, alone, is too narrow a view for it ignores crucial political issues. We do not really know and we cannot reliably forecast the future pace of nuclear proliferation. Yet two decades of slow proliferation do raise the hope that future proliferation may likewise be slow—perhaps even slower.

We should note that there now exist certain widespread attitudes on nuclear issues which ten years ago were almost unheard-of, at least in public. Policies for dealing with nuclear proliferation should take some account of these. For example, ten years ago the strategic posture of the United States rested in large part on an ability and determination to initiate the use of nuclear weapons to thwart aggression. While this nuclear threat remains important in many respects, prevailing attitudes towards

162

"first use" of nuclear weapons are much changed. It is now likely that the U.S. will adopt a virtual "no first use" policy without making a deliberate decision to do so, and without even calculating all the results of doing so. Or again, while it once was believed that "escalation" would be more or less automatic and catastrophic, in the course of a mere five years it has come instead to be rather widely believed that escalation might be deliberately controlled and perhaps even stopped or reversed. The accompanying notion of a U.S.-Soviet "spasm war," in which all weapons were fired immediately for maximum destructivity, has ceased to guide military planning in the U.S. (and, it seems likely, in the Soviet Union, France, and elsewhere—despite much rhetoric to the contrary). A more or less implicit sense of proportionateness about the use of nuclear threats and attacks has developed. All of this is bound eventually to force even more extensive alterations in deterrent strategy, arms control thinking, and foreign policy generally—and all these changes will affect the incentive of various nations to acquire nuclear weapons.

Moreover, it should be clear that even very extensive proliferation does not necessarily make inevitable—or even particularly likely—the nightmare of worldwide holocaust. This is true even if twenty to thirty independent states have nuclear weapons of various kinds, with various systems of command and control. One might, for example, imagine that Che Guevara had two nuclear missiles available to him at some point. He has said that if this situation came about, he would be unable to restrain himself from launching the missiles at New York City and Washington. In fact, he would probably be considerably less likely to make such a statement, let alone carry it out, if he actually controlled two missiles. But let us imagine, hypothetically, that he had no sense of responsibility for the country within which he was operating at the time, and that nothing else within himself or in the circumstances of the case restrained him from launching the missiles. One would suppose that the United States would retaliate in some dramatic and decisive fashion, and other small countries with nuclear systems would as a result be induced to take a second look at their arrangements for controlling nuclear weapons. Although a scenario of this kind would entail immense suffering and destruction, it is clear that human life in general would go on, that the overall pattern of international relations might conceivably continue much as before, and that the United States would survive and rapidly recuperate from the damage that the two missiles had inflicted.

Even if there were widespread proliferation, the likelihood of a catastrophic U.S.-Soviet thermonuclear war might not increase very much, and might not even increase at all. In the first place, the kind of incident imagined above is not likely to happen more than once, if ever. In any case if, or as, proliferation continues, the attitudes about "first use," the risks of unsafe techniques, and disproportionate response, which now inhibit the United States and the United Kingdom, might prove to inhibit all or most of the other nuclear states as well.[1] Under these conditions all nations with large forces and most nations with small nuclear forces might acquire some capability for measured, controlled and deliberate response. Just as "our military and civilian leaders are unanimous," according to a Presidential assertion,[2] "in their conviction that our armed might is and always must be so controlled as to permit measured response in whatever crises may confront us," so the leaders of other nations would be likely to discover a similar need for controlled capabilities and flexible strategies. An international system in which there had been widespread proliferation might thus be much less accident-prone and aggression-prone than many people in the past have estimated. While we cannot, of course, offer definite or reliable forecasts of these uncertain matters, we can say that there are reasons to believe that although proliferation increases many dangers, it alleviates others. In any case, one cannot prove that it would necessarily increase the danger of very serious disaster for the U.S. or for mankind.

The argument can even be made that nuclear weapons present a "fair" solution to the problem of national defense, since one country does not have to buy security at the expense of its neighbor's security. Whereas in the past one country could hope to use even a moderate superiority to overwhelm another without suffering catastrophic losses, with a properly designed nuclear deterrent system any country can hope (so the argument goes) to be strong enough for deterrence and yet not be so strong as to be able to conduct a disarming first strike against another nuclear power. One country's strength need not mean its neighbor's weakness—deterrence, unlike superiority, can be both clear and symmetric. Thus one can conclude, with Pierre Gallois, that "the further we advance in the ballistic-nuclear age, the more possible it becomes to outlaw violence, even if the aggressor nation is stronger and more richly supplied with combat means than the nation it threatens." [3]

Yet despite all these arguments, one cannot be confident either that the future pace of proliferation will be slow or that its consequences would not be very serious. [4] In fact, there is a surprising consensus among analysts, scholars, policy makers, and men in the street that it is crucially important not only to decrease the likelihood of nuclear use by those who possess nuclear weapons, but also the likelihood of the spread of those weapons to other countries. While all of these people may be wrong, and there is no way to ascertain who is right, the author shares their judgment at least in its less apocalyptic form. I assume in this paper that the reader shares my concern about the threat of future proliferation and wants to improve even the current situation—perhaps at least by trying to exploit some of the seemingly "desirable" characteristics of the nuclear trends mentioned above, i.e. there may be much wisdom embodied in some of the developments that have occurred or are now occurring.

While there is a wide consensus on the need to inhibit further nuclear spread or use, there are surprisingly few long-term policy ideas on how to do this. A reasonably complete list might go as follows:

1.   Attempt, at least temporarily, to prolong the current situation, meanwhile hoping for marginal or far-reaching changes that might be desirable.

2.   If the *status quo* must change, attempt to make it evolve so slowly that much time will be bought and then hope that this time will allow other developments to occur (these other developments are rarely specified).

3.   De-emphasize or ignore all long-range problems and deal with each issue as it comes up in a pragmatic and *ad hoc* fashion.

4.   Accept the fact that proliferation

will occur and try to live with this "inevitable" large-scale diffusion of nuclear weapons—again in an *ad hoc* or pragmatic fashion.

5. Work for universal and comprehensive arms control systems or world government.

It may well be that this list covers the total range of practical policies and that one need not look for anything else; but this seems most doubtful. This writer has occasionally made the point[5] that serious changes in the international system seem most likely to be made as a result of an intense crisis or a small or large nuclear war, and that it should be a major objective of negotiations to lay the groundwork for the constructive exploitation of such crises, or of small or large wars. It seems most unlikely that the world will be sufficiently motivated to work out a safer international system as a result of peaceful negotiations around a conference table. But national plans and international negotiations may lay a basis for action in the conditions of changed power relationships and nuclear attitudes which might be the immediate aftermath of some violent world experience or dramatic crisis.

While I still believe in the value of such preparations, this paper is written in a somewhat different spirit, and focuses upon some *ad hoc* and pragmatic but important *peaceful* changes that could be made in the *current* institutional and international environment. It might be hoped that these changes could prove large enough to make important differences and yet remain small enough to be achievable. Hence I wish to present a reasonably specific set of policy proposals (as well as some more general ideas and issues), not because they necessarily have spectacular merit, but because they are alternatives to the approaches listed above, and because discussing relatively specific proposals will serve to bring out issues interesting even to those who are uninterested in the specific suggestions. Moreover, these proposals represent an attempt to start looking at relatively "messy" international arrangements which nevertheless are relatively feasible and relatively significant by comparison to most current proposals.

I will begin by proposing a set of criteria that any long-range "anti-nuclear" policy should try to meet. The description and discussion of such desiderata, are, themselves, an important part of the proposed investigation. Indeed, a debate on these criteria could prove to be more important than a debate on the specific proposals. It could, for example, clear the air for proposals quite different from the ones suggested but which are—again—either more practical or more far-reaching than many which are currently discussed.

B. Fifteen Criteria for a Long-Range Anti-Nuclear Policy[6]

The fifteen desiderata listed below are, of course, by no means sacrosanct, nor are they the only ones that could be listed. One could reasonably include others, or omit some which are included here. Moreover, few would agree to give each of these criteria the kind and degree of emphasis given here. But stimulation of the creation of alternative lists and degrees of emphasis could be one of the most useful products of this exercise. The fifteen desiderata of the policy are as follows:

1. It should be likely to prevent nuclear intimidation.
2. It should limit proliferation.

3. It should make nuclear weapons be and seem almost unusable—either politically or physically—and decrease the prestige associated with them.

4. It should be damage-limiting, if nuclear weapons should ever be used.

5. It should not be aimed at perpetuating U.S. status, power, and obligations.

6. It should not require Italy, Japan, India, West Germany, or France to accept an invidiously inferior status or unnecessarily precarious security position.

7. It should be competent to withstand crises, small and even large conventional wars, and some breaches and violations.

8. It should be responsive to national interests, sentiments, and doctrines, and be negotiable.

9. It should improve current international standards, but not require thorough-going reformation.

10. It should be conservative in using U.S. prestige, morale, and influence.

11. It should be presented as apolitical ("above the melee" of normal diplomatic in-fighting and posturing).

12. It should not have been foreclosed or embarrassed by any prior commitment of the United States.

13. It should be thoroughly planned so as to be able to become an object of "sudden diplomacy."

14. It should be potentially permanent (not necessarily a transitional arrangement) and yet flexible enough to hedge against events and opportunities in both negotiation and operation.

15. While not designed as a transitional arrangement, it should allow for major or basic developments and changes.

The most telling objection to this list may be not that it is idiosyncratic but that it is too stringent and therefore impractical. It may be that no policy can meet all of these criteria satisfactorily, but I believe it is important to go as far as one can toward meeting them, and the policy I am about to propose does attempt to meet them. And whether these desiderata are idiosyncratic or impractical, the list is intended to be rounded, nonpartisan, provocative, and of help to skeptics as well as to believers.

One Basic Proposal

Can nuclear weapons be made so limited in their usefulness that by and large, they will have relatively little effect on the conduct of international affairs, even in relatively intense crises; and, moreover, can this be done in a manner that improves U.S. security and the stability of the international order? Clearly, an affirmative answer to this question would be a good beginning for an anti-nuclear policy. The issue therefore is not necessarily whether nuclear weapons shall exist, or in what numbers. Rather we focus on the actual and perceived potential usefulness of these weapons, the prestige attached to their possession, their attributes of legitimacy, danger or terror, the felt necessity of various nations in the world to acquire them, and the special role they play in both normal and crisis situations.

As a first approach to devising a program to limit their usefulness, let us imagine a world system in which each nation agrees and expects that nuclear weapons cannot be used except, possibly, for strict retaliation. In such a system each nation would have adopted a no-first-use policy and a policy of responding in commensurate kind and equal degree if nuclear weapons were used against it. Non-nuclear nations could have made arrangements to have such proportionate retaliation carried out by others. If these expectations could be made to be, and to seem to be, reliable and certain, then it is unlikely that any nations could credibly threaten to use nuclear weapons.

Another conceivable objective, which could either be supplementary and complementary to such a system or independent of it, would be a restriction on legitimate possession (or further acquisition) of nuclear weapons by any other than international organizations—nuclear defense alliances in Western Europe, East Europe, Asia, Latin America, North America, the North Atlantic, or even nuclear defense organizations which had a basis in larger than regional interests.

A third objective might be to establish nuclear free zones, particularly in those areas of the world which do not currently seem likely to be the scene of direct nuclear confrontations, e.g., Latin America, Africa, the Middle East, parts of Asia, and possibly the rim of Europe outside the Western European Union.

All of these objectives are combined in the following long-term "anti-nuclear" policy:

1. A return to the idea of (nuclear) *lex talionis,* which we would define as not only *at least* an eye for an eye but also—at least between equals—*at most*

an eye for an eye; or to put it in the current jargon, no escalation including *no-first-use.*[7] (In other words, what we regard as ethically unacceptable in the relations between private persons appears to be an imperative of practical political wisdom in the relations between nuclear states.)

2. A European nuclear retaliatory force whose sole purpose is to enforce the *lex talionis* in Europe. (This might take the form of a European Strategic Defense Community based upon Western European Union or it might take some other form. It might not be a Community, or it might be a Community which did not include the United Kingdom, or France, or West Germany.)

3. An Asian Nuclear Defense Organization which would enforce the *lex talionis* in Asia. (Probably this could not or should not, at least initially, take the form of an independent Strategic Defense Community. Whatever form it did take, the nuclear defense organization might initially be based upon the United States, Japan, Australia, New Zealand, the Philippines, India, Pakistan, and perhaps Great Britain. It could also exclude some of these states, at least initially, and it would probably be —to some great degree—under the effective and perhaps legal control of the United States or perhaps Japan, India, and/or Australia.)

4. Nuclear-free zones in Latin America, Africa, Eastern Europe, the Middle East, and elsewhere, developed (with modification) from current proposals.

5. A more or less explicit (and perhaps interim) U.S. (and Soviet?) "talionic" guarantee to various non-nuclear areas, which could vary for different areas, and which could be established in terms of likely, minimum or maximum U.S. responses to nuclear provocations

as appropriate to each area. (The nature of the guarantee might explicitly include provision for modifications over time.)

6. For the denuclearized zones a long-term program might simultaneously be developed of a non-aligned multilateral nuclear defense organization to play the same role for denuclearized zones as the European and Asian nuclear forces play for their own areas, thus possibly eventually replacing U.S. (and Soviet?) talionic guarantees.

7. Finally the concept of a universal agency could be developed to replace, supplement, complement or absorb the various regional and national forces.

These arrangements probably sound Utopian, and might prove to be, in the sense of being desirable but unfeasible. If completely successful, these proposals would limit nuclear weapons to the U.S., the Soviet Union, one international European organization, one international Asian organization, China, and possibly certain other international organizations. The credibility of the talionic response to a nuclear provocation should be high, in order to provide the deterrence of provocation. Not only should nuclear intimidation be difficult but with time even the mere thought of it might be eliminated from crises as well as day-to-day international relations. Yet, if deterrence failed and weapons were used, Armageddon would not follow but simply whatever destruction was entailed in a tit-for-tat response. Then, conceivably, there would be a return to some previous or *ad hoc* status quo. The system could conceivably withstand several failures of deterrence and many other intense crises. Yet, except for participation in the Asian nuclear force, this system would immediately reduce

U.S. obligations, and eventually would reduce them very sharply. While these proposals tend to relegate the U.S. to a status of first among equals, it seems likely that in the long run this would be beneficial.

The idea of *lex talionis* amounts to a return to the nineteenth-century law of reprisal or the practice of primitive communities—particularly ones in which there are no reliable means for maintaining order. It is therefore not, by itself, an obviously Utopian notion. It would also seem to provide a clear improvement over a situation in which "spasm" or other all-out war could occur after the nuclear threshold is crossed. Its damage-limiting potentialities might be exceedingly valuable, especially if alternative means to limit damage prove to be unavailable or unreliable.

In such a tit-for-tat situation (as in most current peacekeeping situations), one does not usually ask who is right. The objective is to bring the violence to a conclusion—"to stop the fighting as soon as possible"—and to create precedents that prevent later repetitions. It should be transparently clear that it would be very difficult to bring violence between equals to a conclusion as long as there is clearly an open-ended account in which one side has done much more damage than the other side. Therefore it would seem almost a necessity that there be some sort of equitable, proportionate retaliation before peace can be restored. This is of course exactly the technique adopted by primitive tribes and for much the same reason—they wish to restrain violence and they have no police and judicial system with which to do it. It is, of course, true that "tit-for-tat" occasionally results in long-continued blood feuds—in other words, it may generate further violence. But more often than not it brings equilibrium. As a system it is more likely to work than not. As such it may be far superior to anything else that is actually available in the international field today.

In this regard it is worth noting that most intelligent laymen in the U.S. now readily understand such points as the following:[8] (1) if a small number of nuclear weapons are exploded in a country like the U.S., the President is more likely to ask questions than to press every button; (2) after his questions are answered and he understands the situation, he is still unlikely to lose all control of himself and launch a suicidal spasm response; rather he is likely to ask what is in the national interest of the U.S., even if—and perhaps especially because—the situation is agonizing and emotion-filled; (3) the national interest may require a deliberate, measured, controlled and selective response; (4) such a response could occur as a tit-for-tat or other reciprocal retaliation; (5) as a result, millions of people could be killed and yet the war could come to a close with most of the weapons on every side remaining unfired.

Many analysts have argued that the relatively rigid tit-for-tat procedure is a retrogression in terms of modern strategic thinking; it goes against the current trend of emphasizing complete flexibility, control, *ad hoc* calculation and a certain amount of deliberate uncertainty as to what the response will be. This proposal does tend toward fixed response, to make it almost deterministic, but in a fashion which is quite different from the old massive retaliation doctrine. Rather than prescribing a simple spasm response we argue for a response which is never larger than the situation requires.

Thus, surprisingly enough, *lex talionis* arrangements would be basically consistent with current U.S. policy and with emerging political-strategic doctrine. They would extend, make explicit, and seek to institutionalize generally the profound disposition toward proportionate response now widely held among American officials. Furthermore, this disposition, which certainly exists in other countries as well, is quite likely to affect the contingency policy of other nuclear powers whether they realize it ahead of time or not. In other words, these proposals are not "Utopian" in the sense of being based on a far-fetched principle; their Utopian character, if any, lies in requiring an unlikely degree of success in implementing already well-known, sound, and comparatively desirable principles.

It is possible and even likely that a disposition towards proportionate response will increase among nuclear powers roughly in accordance with their experience of—and deliberation about—the use of their weapons. This tendency is not as apt to affect decisions to acquire the weapons as it is the eventual strategy for utilizing them. Nuclear powers might deprive themselves for a long time of the capability of responding in corresponding degree and kind, meanwhile anticipating the choice of surrender or nightmarish calamity, but eventually, and at "the moment of truth," even small nuclear powers are likely to search desperately for alternatives to surrender or holocaust.

None of the above is certain, of course. But once concrete situations are envisaged, and sequences of events and calculation are spelled out, it is far from probable that a spasm response to nuclear attack will seem preferable. Rather the kind of layman's common sense noted here might suggest basic principles and evidently reasonable assumptions for long-range policy. The nuclear control arrangements envisaged do not presuppose that all nuclear powers will necessarily act calculatingly, and in a measured and controlled manner. But deliberate, measured and controlled behavior can be made more certain by cultivating world wide (not only in the U.S.) the disposition to act that way, and institutionalizing the principles that seem to be implied in that disposition.

Any proposal that tries to do this will, of course, have to meet many particular objections or difficulties. Let us consider here only some of the more salient ones.

C. Some Basic Assumptions and Concepts

There are certain objections which could reasonably be made on the level of principle, or basic assumption, before going into any discussion of detailed feasibility. For example, the idea of "an eye for an eye" might be manifestly unjust when it actually means a city for a city, and when a city attacked in retaliation is inhabited by persons with no particular responsibility for the initial nuclear attack. The objection is a serious one. One must examine the ethical and political questions, which in turn depend in part upon empirical and technical questions, such as what constitutes a proportionate response or whether a talionic doctrine would be more unjust or unstable than alternative doctrines. One must ponder the possible wrongness of an inflexible tit-for-tat system as compared with the possible infeasibility, risk, or even immorality of counterforce, massive city attacks, and other more or less flexible, ambiguous, or unpredictable doctrines as well as the possible consequences of not retaliating at all or not retaliating in a manner that deters further attack. At this point I can say only that all these questions are

both serious and complex, and that some allowance should be made for responsible authorities to avoid at least the most rigid kind of "city-for-city" retaliation. All these issues will be discussed in more detail in our forthcoming Hudson Institute report, although it is hardly likely that any preliminary discussion of such issues will be "adequate."

I should also mention that we are proposing a European nuclear retaliatory force that would differ in important ways from the multilateral force that was proposed by the U.S. and the Atlantic nuclear force that was proposed by the British. We envisage a truly independent nuclear deterrent for Europe, which while having a credible tit-for-tat response would not permit any membernation to launch a spasm retaliatory response. We will argue that a European nuclear defense organization designed in this way would probably represent an increase, rather than a decrease, in the kinds of independence that European nations most desire, and that distinguishing between talionic and escalatory responses makes solvable the dilemma of the "trigger" (who can authorize launching nuclear weapons?) and the "safety catch" (who can forbid launching nuclear weapons?). To take an oversimplified but illustrative possibility: everyone could have his finger on the trigger for talionic responses and his finger on the safety catch for escalation responses, i.e., any nation could authorize a proper tit-for-tat retaliation or forbid excessive escalation. More complex and practical arrangements are discussed in our forthcoming report.

One assumption underlying this proposal is that Western Europe is, to some degree, a "pluralistic security community," as described by Karl Deutsch. This implies that in Western Europe an international subsystem exists in which war is literally unthinkable among the nations concerned (as is also true, for example, in the case of the United States and Canada). In this international subsystem the threat of physical coercion plays almost no role in relations among the nations within the community, though other kinds of threats are occasionally made. Thus no provisions are necessary for the protection of Western European nations from each other. (In fact, the force could be adapted to such a purpose, if necessary; but this is not envisioned as an important purpose of the force.) It is also assumed that Western Europe needs independent power mainly because it does not want to continue to be a protectorate of the United States, and not because it seeks to advance any aggressive designs against the Soviet Union, East Germany, China, or any other nations which may acquire nuclear weapons.

The Asian countries do not constitute a pluralistic security community and, at least without the United States, there is not the same primarily bipolar (though also polycentric) international alignment as exists between Western and Eastern (including Soviet) Europe. Therefore an Asian nuclear defense organization would have to be different, perhaps more tentative and flexible, and probably involve greater U.S. involvement, perhaps along with Japan and India.

As time passes, an Asian force would have to develop according to the separate requirements of the Asian area. It might ultimately become a true collective security force which attempted to furnish security against aggression by its own members as well as by nations external to the force. If so, the force would have to be operated and designed in a different fashion. But it is premature at the present time to try to specify details, though examples could be explicated for the purposes of discussion and illustration. But at least two of the Asian nations, Japan and India, are not unlikely in the future to desire to fulfill national nuclear aspirations within the framework of a regional force, and this expectation is one of the bases (though not an essential one) on which the proposal is built.

Summary and Recapitulation

The proposals and concepts in this paper are being put forth for the purpose of discussion. It may well turn out that as far as the underlying problem is concerned—the proliferation and potential use of nuclear weapons—the current situation will be judged to be stable or at least reasonably acceptable. Or it may turn out that one or the other basic paths listed above on page 167 should be pursued by the United States. But I have tried to suggest that there is a whole class of relatively *ad hoc* proposals for different areas of the world or for different issues which are much more basic and far-reaching than most of the meliorative policies that have been suggested, but also much more practical, feasible and even desirable than some of the comprehensive reforms now being considered. There are of course many unanswered questions about the specific proposals presented. Indeed if adopted they could turn out to be contraproductive, resulting in a rather more rapid diffusion of weapons-system technology than would otherwise have occurred, or arousing ambitions for nuclear weapons in nations which are currently more or less satisfied with the *status quo*. (In particular it may increase West German and Japanese nuclear ambitions.) In any case, if the proposals were accepted many nations would be brought closer to nuclear weapons than they are today. Even the mere act of considering these proposals could create problems.

Thus even today the so-called "MLF clause" (i.e., the U.S. insistence that any anti-proliferation treaty allow for the creation of a multi-national force which absorbs one of the current nuclear forces), seems to be a major block in the negotiation of the current non-proliferation treaty. The possibility of an Asian nuclear force might create similar or greater difficulties. (But the analogy is not completely relevant. The major objection to the MLF clause comes from the Soviet Union, which is clearly worried about West Germany. Furthermore West Germany's nuclear ambitions, if any exist, do not have the approval or support of any of its allies on the Continent. In this respect Japan seems to be in a much different position both with regard to the Soviet Union and to its allies.)

Several important issues remain to be considered. For example, what would happen if the various multilateral or other nuclear forces were dissolved? These forces can be subjected to strains and survive them—but what if they do not survive? Another possibility to be considered is that at least the European nuclear organization might entail giving too much authority to its decision makers who, in the nature of the situation, are likely to feel substantially more independent of the "political authorities" than would be true of representatives of a nation-state. There are many conceivable Soviet reactions to the proposals and we have not considered any of the pressures or problems that these might or might not create, if this proposal is seriously advanced. It is possible that nations in non-nuclear regions will object to their status once they begin to perceive the political and stra-

tegic feasibility of regional (or even national) deterrents. They in turn may wish to have a regional deterrent of their own eventually, or to find security through some broader international organization. Very likely pressures toward such "solutions" would be increased by the creation of a European Strategic Defense Community. Further, the mere proposal to organize such a community might arouse latent suspicions in various European nations—and it might increase desire for national acquisition of nuclear status in Italy and West Germany, so that they will be assured of a place at the "top table" within the region. All of the foregoing points and objections must be conceded and many more as well. Nevertheless it seems clear that there is insufficient thought in the government and scholarly communities about the possibilities of implications of:

1.   The use of *lex talionis* as a guiding principle.

2.   The distinction between interior and exterior escalation or between talionic responses and escalation. (Neither of these distinctions seems to have been considered in relation to the MLF, yet they might make all the difference as to its role or to the trigger and safety-catch problem.)

3.   The need for modifying U.S. guarantees if (or as) the Soviet Union acquires a reliable and large second-strike capability.

4.   Coming to grips with a situation of increasing multipolarity in which the United States and the Soviet Union will no longer dominate international relations nearly as much as they still do, and in which guarantees which have any hint of "protectorate" about them will be more unacceptable.

5.   The need for separating current nuclear arrangements from being basi-

cally a legacy of World War II—that is, the victors must recognize that they cannot indefinitely perpetuate the "nuclear club" exclusively as a victors' club.

6. The possibility of various *ad hoc* regional or other special institutions and practices that lie between the usual melioration and comprehensive proposals, particularly suggestions that may exploit or deal with the concepts suggested above.

7. The fifteen general criteria for a long-range anti-nuclear policy, listed above on pages 165 and 166.

Finally, it should be pointed out that while the proposal set forth in this paper has many bizarre-seeming aspects, most of the bizarre quality derives from coping with an unprecedented situation in which there has not been as much thought about long-range policies and prospects as there might have been. Thus the discussion in this paper will have achieved one important objective if it simply takes the edge off the bizarreness; i.e., if it makes it easier to discuss the problem and to weigh various alternative policies on their merits.

Notes

[1] A fairly wide range of nuclear use and the possible aftereffects of the situations is considered by Edmund O. Stillman, *Predicting the International Consequences of the Introduction of Nuclear Weapons*, HI-621-RR (Harmon-on-Hudson, N.Y.: Hudson Institute, January 26, 1966). These scenarios indicate that of almost all the situations in which nuclear weapons might be used in the future, more or less plausibly, a very large U.S.-Soviet nuclear war seems relatively unlikely.

[2] *The New York Times*, January 11, 1965, p. 16.

[3] Pierre Gallois, *The Balance of Terror: Strategy for the Nuclear Age* (Boston: Houghton Mifflin Co., 1961) p. 113.

[4] See the author's *On Escalation: Metaphors and Scenarios* (New York: Frederick A. Praeger, 1965, Chapter VI, particularly pp. 97-101, for a discussion of the pros of nuclear proliferation.

[5] See, for example, *Thinking About the Unthinkable* (New York: Horizon Press, 1962), pp. 153-158.

[6] The term "anti-nuclear" is used deliberately, in recognition that some readers would find it a suitable description of the ideas advanced. The term does make a crude sort of point. And there seems to be no other acceptable term: something like "nuclear defunctionalization" might be a little more precise, but it seems to be objectionable on stylistic grounds.

[7] As discussed in the forthcoming Hudson Institute report, one might modify this rule to distinguish between interior escalation (first use of nuclear weapons on one's own sovereign territory) which does not justify any nuclear reprisal, and exterior escalation (first use of nuclear weapons on the opposite territory) which does justify reprisal against the homeland. While there are grave objections to trying to make interior escalation legitimate (it would make nuclear weapons more useable), it may be necessary to accept some such compromise to satisfy some European opinion.

[8] See Herman Kahn, *On Escalation: Metaphors and Scenarios* (New York: Frederick A. Praeger, 1965), pp. 185-186, including footnote. It is interesting to note that much current fiction as well as scholarly analysis has used proportionate response as being the only plausible response in situations in which the only other alternatives are holocaust or surrender.

The Strategic Consequences
of Nuclear Proliferation

By James R. Schlesinger[1]

The responsibility assigned to me is to examine the strategic consequences of nuclear proliferation. If we limit ourselves strictly to the strategic area—to the possible employment of additional nuclear capabilities against military or urban targets—one cannot avoid the conclusion that considerable exaggeration has crept into public discussion of proliferation's consequences. This observation rests, in part, upon a distinction between strategic and socio-political consequences, which some will regard as arbitrary and which in any event cannot be made precise. If we isolate the strategic from the socio-political consequences, it is plain that the latter could be quite serious. The very countermeasures through which harmful strategic consequences can be avoided are likely to be viewed as undesirable on social or political grounds. At the very least, the spread of nuclear weapons generates fear. When publics or governments become fearful, they can act in ways which seriously reduce the amenities of living in society. For example, one possible result of the spread would be for societies partially to close their borders and to police incoming goods and peo-

ple more carefully than at present. This might easily be associated with the decline in the tolerance of dissent within the society. In the specific case of the United States, it is sometimes felt that the idealistic flavor characterizing much of its foreign policy would tend to disappear—to the disadvantage particularly of those who live in the underdeveloped world. These are consequences which few would view without some trepidation. But these are *political* consequences. They do not imply a major alteration of the military balance or for that matter the physical security of most of the world's population.

For these reasons, most public discussion of proliferation's *strategic* consequences must be judged to be seriously defective. However, nothing said here regarding the exaggerations of these strategic consequences should be construed as a criticism of the basic objectives of U.S. policy or of the desirability of preventing further nuclear spread. It is dubious, however, whether any such policies can be completely successful. There is a danger in expecting too much as well as in being too fearful. Moreover, since the writer believes that

174

the effects of proliferation would be less severe than currently anticipated, he would be inclined to set a lower price on what the United States should be willing to pay to prevent proliferation than would some other analysts who have contributed to this book, and would be particularly reluctant to pay a very high price in terms of offending friendly nations merely to get paper acquiescence to a non-proliferation treaty.

Nevertheless, despite the exaggerations of public discussion, it is plain that we should bend our efforts to avoid or to limit the spread of weapons. Proliferation adds to the problem of managing the world. It increases the number of uncertainties and the number of variables that must be watched. One can put the menace of proliferation in another way, as has William C. Foster, the Director of the United States Arms Control and Disarmament Agency: further nuclear spread would lead to a reduction of the relative influence of the United States on the world scene. This appears like a self-serving plea, and for this reason, the argument may have less initial appeal to outsiders than to Americans. Nonetheless, the argument contains a surprisingly large element of altruism. A decline in the relative influence of the United States on the world scene may be more closely associated with increased difficulty in keeping the world relatively stable and peaceful than many non-Americans might be willing to concede at first blush. In a world in which nuclear weapons were more widely held and in which the United States sought to avoid "entanglements," the gravest misfortunes would be reserved for the populations in the unstable portions of the world rather than for the favorably-situated publics of the nuclear superpowers.

1. Some Expressions of Concern

If, then, we acknowledge that there are weighty reasons for opposing the spread, how much despair should we be prepared to feel, if our efforts at control turn out to be unsuccessful? It is on this point that prophecies of disaster appear to dominate public discussions and that public statements diverge most sharply from a sober assessment of the risks. The view that nuclear spread poses a single, overwhelming threat to the continued existence of mankind strikes many responsible analysts as a distortion of reality which, if taken seriously, could lead to a misallocation of our national efforts. The noticeable discrepancy between the paramountcy nominally attributed to the problem and the policies we stand ready to adopt indicates that the more extreme expressions of alarm are not, in fact, taken too seriously. Among leading public figures Senator Robert F. Kennedy has most vividly dramatized the disastrous consequences to be expected from proliferation. In a recent statement he asserted that alongside proliferation control "nothing else means anything." This is a bit of political hyperbole, the force of which would appear to be weakened by the Senator's allocation of his own energies. He himself devotes intense effort to numerous other issues, but aside from public statements has given relatively little attention to the problems of proliferation.

To move from the survival of mankind to the survival of the United States, we have heard on even higher authority that the survival of the United States is at stake—if we fail to prevent the spread of nuclear weapons. Once again, for reasons that will be extensively developed below, this statement is simply misleading. The risks to the American society—and in this respect we must distinguish sharply between the American society and societies in the third world—are very much exaggerated. The United States is in a position to reduce the risks to itself to very low levels. The United States can both adjust its policies and adopt countermeasures which reduce the damage that limited nuclear capabilities could inflict. Such countermeasures would maintain or increase the already enormous gap between U.S. military capabilities and those possessed by non-superpowers. A package of such countermeasures could sharply reduce the risks of proliferation in several respects: 1) the ability to inflict damage on the United States would be kept low, 2) the United States, if it so desired, would remain in a position to deter attack by lesser nuclear powers against third countries, and 3) the incentives to acquire capabilities would consequently be altered—and possibly reduced toward the vanishing point. Countermeasures taken by the Soviet Union would, of course, reinforce the process.

One can make a cogent argument that the ability to implement such countermeasures—to make crystal clear to all nuclear aspirants that acquisition of nuclear weapons cannot significantly alter the strategic balance—provides the best hope over time of controlling proliferation and its consequences. Hedley Bull has characterized this position as one of "high posture." He has—on this occasion as on prior ones—expressed misgivings regarding its suitability. There is no need at this point to argue whether the psychological repercussions of augmenting the gap between the superpowers and other states will be of

the sort that Mr. Bull foresees. My purpose at this juncture is merely to indicate a) that such countermeasures are well within the capacity of the United States, and b) that the survival of the United States is scarcely brought into question by the further spread of limited nuclear capabilities. This last specter is one we had best put to rest.

It is scarcely imaginable that any American president will fail to accept at least some of these countermeasures. However, let us place such issues to one side. Whatever their resolution, it is plain that, if proliferation to additional countries takes place, we shall go right on living with it. We may continue to complain about it, but we shall live with it—while continuing to enjoy the benefits—if that is the appropriate term—of a rising standard of living. The very leaders who now assert that non-proliferation is indispensable to our security will then find other subjects to dramatize.

The attempt to allay some of the anxieties regarding proliferation would seem to be necessary not simply because we should recognize that existence will continue to be quite tolerable, even if proliferation takes place. What is perhaps more important, an attitude of desperation regarding the spread of nuclear weapons is not merely inaccurate, but may also be counterproductive in our efforts to achieve control. By understating the difficulties of acquiring a serious nuclear capability and by exaggerating what a nuclear aspirant power may obtain through acquisition of a capability, we may actually strengthen the incentives for acquisition. The danger inherent in exaggerated chatter regarding the damage that additional capabilities can foster is that it revivifies the false notion of nuclear weapons as "the greater equalizer" in international conflict. Hopefully, most nations will penetrate the smokescreen and perceive the difficulties. However, some may be lured into believing that nuclear weapons do provide an answer to their security problems. Others may be encouraged in the notion that acquisition will provide an instrument of threat, or blackmail which can be directed toward the rest of the world.[2]

To illustrate the way in which such illusions can be fostered, Senator Kennedy has misappropriated some words of his brother, the late President, to the effect that "every man, woman, and child, lives under a nuclear sword of Damocles hanging by the slenderest of threads, capable of being cut at any moment by accident or miscalculation or by madness."[3] The Senator's point is that each additional nuclear capability, no matter how limited, automatically creates an additional Damoclean sword. But this suggestion is simply not true. In relation to the indicated levels of destruction, the damage potential of small nuclear forces is too limited. In assessing the damage that might result from nuclear spread, it is essential to recognize that the acquisition of a significant nuclear weapons and delivery capability, although it depends heavily on the quality of a nation's technology, has become even more a quantitative problem than a qualitative one; the superpowers number their nuclear weapons in the thousands or tens of thousands. The quantitative aspects are subject to calculation, but in the public excitement over the threat of proliferation these calculations are normally ignored. Such oversight seems indispensable in generating both needless anxiety and the nuclear-weapons-as-equalizers illusion.

2. Dimensions and Measurement

Any serious attempt to assess the dimensions of the proliferation threat should begin with some calculations regarding the spectrum of strategic capabilities given varying levels of investment. Further development of the point that proliferation in certain essential respects is a quantitative problem is basic to our understanding. Proliferation is really quite unlike pregnancy, though in the intuition of many something akin to pregnancy is used as a rough analogue. It is frequently observed—usually by way of admonition—that there is no such thing as being a little bit pregnant. But this is because the results and the time involved in the process are pretty well defined. In size and weight full-term babies tend towards a normal distribution; the variance is not a matter of great moment. But suppose that in pregnancy there were no tendency toward a unimodal distribution of the results and that the time involved in gestation were subject to enormous variation. Suppose again that the ultimate progeny could be Lilliputians or Brobdingnagians—or, for that matter, a varied assortment of misshapen dwarfs, possibly lacking essential organs, limbs, or faculties—and that the specific result depended upon not only the intake of the mother but her intelligence. This is really a more revealing analogy. It explains why being a *little bit proliferated* may be a meaningful concept, while being a little bit pregnant is not. In this area controlling the ultimate dimensions may be even more important than preventing conception or birth.

The range of possible nuclear capabilities is simply enormous. One must be aware of the importance of the distinctions to be drawn among capabilities —and how these distinctions relate to size and vulnerability. Consider the existing array of nuclear capabilities. The United States, which has invested most heavily, possesses a capability which is not only a solid deterrent, but which is not incredible in terms of a carefully controlled, countermilitary initial strike. The Soviet Union, which has invested less, has an impressive second-strike force, which is an effective deterrent. Britain possesses a much more limited capability, presently dependent for delivery on obsolescent aircraft; both the influence and the credibility of the British "independent contribution to the deterrent" are steadily on the wane. The French capability is even more limited in respect to its potential for inflicting damage upon the Soviet Union, though it promises to exploit more advanced delivery systems indigenously-produced. Finally, the Chinese capability—presently drawing the lion's share of attention—is barely past the embryonic stage. There is some question whether it should even be referred to as a *capability*.

The degree to which a nuclear capability is strategically exploitable—and this is substantially dependent on the credibility of the threat to employ—is determined by its size and sophistication and by the vulnerability of the society it is designed to protect. Strategic posture ultimately depends upon the ability to inflict and to limit damage. All these are roughly correlated with the volume of resources the society has invested or is able to invest in its capability. Happily for the wealthy and powerful, this ability is subject to considerable variance. As someone has astutely observed, there is no cheap substitute for money. It is doubtful whether

the inexorable requirement for money is anywhere more decisive than in relation to the development of a nuclear capability. Sophisticated nuclear weapons and sophisticated delivery systems are terribly expensive. The cost of developing a capability which could seriously disturb the superpowers (as opposed to one's unarmed neighbor) is staggering.[4]

Let me indicate roughly what kind of sums are involved. In order to develop a convincing second-strike capability against one of the superpowers, a nation must be prepared to spend billions of dollars annually—and these expenditures would continue for a decade and longer. Estimates differ; five billion dollars a year may be too high and three billion dollars a year might be adequate. These sums, however, run well beyond what most nations have been prepared to spend—including some that are present members of the nuclear club. Resources will be required not only for delivery systems and compatible weapons, but also for certain supplementary capabilities whose costs are rarely reckoned. How often do we remember to include such indispensable items as reconnaissance and intelligence in the list of required outlays? But any nation contemplating a confrontation with a superpower had better learn something about the location of targets and about the location and capabilities of its opponent's air defense and missile defense systems. The upshot is that only through very heavy outlays can a nation develop more than a very minimal threat against a superpower.

To illustrate the problem, let us consider some historic cost figures. Take the matter of weapons development and stockpiling. Down to early 1966, the United States had invested on the order of eight billion dollars in the development of nuclear weapons. For AEC operations generally, it has now appropriated close to $40 billion. These are substantial amounts. How many nations are in a position to spend even 20 percent or 25 percent of these amounts? Yet, for the creation of a serious capability, requiring deliverable weapons in the megaton range, heavy investment in weapons development is unavoidable.

Though the spread of *missile* capabilities is now a matter of increasing concern, the problem of compatibility implies that development of advanced weapons is preliminary to deployment of an effective missile force. To develop a warhead for an early-generation missile with limited thrust and size (the goal of a development program or the initial goal of a program for an aspiring nuclear power), there must be heavy investment in weapons testing in order to get yield-to-weight ratios to a point where a weapon adequate for target destruction can successfully be delivered in the vehicle. Moreover, there will have to be major investment in guidance technology simply to insure that missiles will be accurate enough to place weapons near the point targeted —whether military bases or cities. In this respect, it is vital to recognize the tradeoff between weapon size and weapon accuracy. With very large yields, considerable inaccuracy may be tolerated. However, with the very low-yield weapons of the sort that can be developed with small amounts of money, yet which must be delivered with limited-payload vehicles, the accuracy requirements become very severe. But missile accuracy is neither cheap nor easy to obtain.

The implication is that no nation is going to be in a position to develop a strategic capability that is both sophisticated and cheap. In the absence of major investments or extraordinary outside assistance the only option open to most nuclear aspirants is the aerial delivery of rather crude nuclear weapons. Though such capabilities can, of course, dramatically transform a regional balance of power (provided that the superpowers remain aloof), the superpowers themselves will remain more or less immune to nuclear threats emanating from countries other than the principal opponent. For the foreseeable future, only the Soviet Union will be able to deliver the requisite megatonnage to threaten major devastation in the United States. Threats from other quarters may be faced down.

The superpowers therefore will remain in a position in which they can dominate any nuclear confrontation. Only a superpower—and in this connection the term applies particularly to the United States—will be able to intervene in such confrontations in third areas. If it desires to pay the costs and is willing to run the risks, other nations, including the present three minor members of the nuclear club, will continually be deterred. Not only will they be precluded from implementing nuclear thrusts, but in the relevant cases, their capabilities will remain vulnerable to a disarming first strike unless they are given protection by an associated superpower. In any showdown with a superpower, a minor nuclear power relying on its own resources will simultaneously be deterred and be subject to disarming.

This asymmetrical relationship between major and lesser nuclear powers brings us back to a point raised earlier: why it may be counter-productive to talk in a panicky way about proliferation's threat to mankind-as-a-whole. If we are to dissuade others from aspiring to nuclear capabilities, what we should stress is that, if weapons spread, they are not likely to be employed against the superpowers. The penalties for proliferation would be paid, not by the United States, or the Soviet Union, but by third countries.

The likelihood that the first nuclear war, if it comes, will originate in and be confined to the underdeveloped world should play a prominent role in any assessment of proliferation's consequences. The tenor of the existing discussion of proliferation has led some people in the underdeveloped countries to conclude that the major powers would be the chief beneficiaries of curtailing the spread. If nuclear spread is to be effectively opposed, it should be made crystal clear just whose security is placed at risk and whose is not.

3. Countermeasures

The problem of nuclear spread is not exhausted by the attempt at prevention. The effort to dissuade additional states from acquiring nuclear capabilities, while good in itself, is not likely to be wholly successful. Control includes much more than simply preventing nuclear dispersion. Influencing the character and consequences of whatever nuclear spread does take place should not be neglected out of disappointment with the "failure" to prevent proliferation entirely.

We should recognize that the long-run problem is how to live with the spread at minimum risk. This implies a form of control which will require continuing effort over time; it is not an all-or-none problem to be settled in some particular time period. If we adopt the position that the issue is simply one of *counting* those nations claiming nuclear weapons status and setting this number as a ceiling on the assumption that *if this number increases* we are undone,

then we will fail to examine the second-stage opportunities for control. Given our policy of trying to minimize the number of nuclear powers, there should be additional strings to the non-proliferation bow, to be employed as the number of nuclear weapons states increases. What are these additional strings? First, if new weapons programs are launched, we may hope to keep the resulting capabilities as limited as possible. (This would reduce the damage potential of any nuclear wars taking place in third areas.) Second, we can take steps to reduce the likelihood that these capabilities, whatever their size, will or could actually be employed by rational political leaders, especially against the United States. Moreover, any actions which sharply reduce the size or the likelihood of employment of additional capabilities may also serve to weaken the motives for acquisition.

Under the heading of limiting the size of additional capabilities, the methods at our disposal are indirect ones. Recognizing the ordinary tradeoff between cost and quantity, our actions should be designed to keep the cost of strategic capabilities at a high level, thereby weakening the temptation to acquire larger capabilities. This implies a policy of withholding direct assistance from the strategic nuclear programs of other nations, save in rare and unusual circumstances. Through rigorous strategic trade controls we may also hope to limit indirect assistance. Above all, we should make every effort to see that international assistance intended for the support of peaceful nuclear programs is not diverted to support of military programs. These are not easily achievable goals, and we ought not pitch our definition of success at too high a level. The instruments for control are imperfect. Moreover, costs of themselves cannot exclude other nations from seeking nuclear capabilities. Given the existing system of national sovereignties, the ability to influence the decisions of other states is quite limited. Nonetheless, something can be achieved. To whatever extent we can prevent the deflation of costs, we can limit the size and the potential destructiveness of budding nuclear capabilities.

The second heading—reducing the likelihood that new capabilities will be actually employed or, if employed, limiting the potential damage—represents that aspect of living-with-proliferation-at-minimum-risk over which we ourselves have most control. There are certain hardware possibilities and other physical arrangements that can limit the potential for damage. One obvious possibility may be to buttress the air defense capabilities of threatened states. A more controversial possibility is the deployment of new systems that will sharply reduce the damage that Nth countries could inflict on the major nuclear powers. The most dramatic current illustration of this type of possibility—the development of an ABM system—is discussed in Chapter 3 of this book. My remarks should not be taken as an endorsement of the ABM system, for that decision involves complex arms control, strategic, and cost-effectiveness calculations, which are beyond the scope of this paper. But one factor that is relevant to the final decision deserves stressing here: deployment of an ABM system or other systems that substantially reduce the damage that can be inflicted on the United States may serve to curtail the harmful consequences which might otherwise flow from proliferation. Through such damage-limiting measures, the willingness and ability of the United States to intervene in third areas when the use of nuclear weapons is threatened is enhanced. Consequently the U.S. ability to prevent the misuse of nuclear capabilities will be strengthened. The strongest deterrent to a lesser power's employing its capability is the possibility that a major nuclear power will enter the lists against it.

Given the existing preponderance of U.S. power, the deployment of major new systems may not be essential to achieve this result. Certain types of developments do appear desirable, however, in order to exploit the discrepancy between major and lesser nuclear powers for the purpose of driving home to lesser powers how ill-advised they would be to initiate the use of nuclear weapons. For example, in a world of many nuclear powers in which anonymity is at least a hypothetical possibility, we should invest considerable effort in developing methods for "fingerprinting" nuclear weapons and parallel systems through which we may in a crisis quickly ascribe responsibility for any detonation that occurs. Then, if we wish to offer protection to threatened nations, we could see to it that punishment for any irresponsible nuclear act would be swift and condign.

An approach of this sort, which relies on superpower preponderance to withstand the potentially baleful effects of proliferation, is not one that is universally and automatically appealing. Hedley Bull has characterized this approach as "high posture" and has contrasted it with one that he prefers: the "low posture" in which the differences between the greater and lesser powers are muted. Let me therefore say a few words in defense of the so-called "high posture."

First, phrases like "high posture" and "low posture" have a certain allure, but the question must be raised whether they accurately describe the underlying realities or the true alternatives. The gap in military nuclear power between the superpowers and other nations is enormous and will continue to be so. In fact, it is more likely to increase than diminish.[5] If we accept that the strategic gap will continue to be enormous, what seems desirable is that the character and width of the gap be sufficient to permit the superpowers to exert a stabilizing influence on the restless third areas of the world. Moreover, this stabilizing function needs to be perceived by those who may come to possess a minor nuclear capability. This potential stabilizing function should not lightly be discarded in the quest for a somewhat mythical "low posture."

Second, the spread of nuclear capabilities into third areas will very much intensify the existing elements of instability and magnify the danger of instability beyond what it is today. The new nuclear capabilities will be unsophisticated and vulnerable. Given the existence of vulnerabilities and the temptation to exploit a temporary strategic edge, the likelihood of nuclear initiation through a hair-trigger response seems obvious. Most persons who seek a more peaceful world would find beneficial the ability of the superpowers to forestall the initial use of such capabilities. In seeking arms control arrangements, we must keep in mind the bilateral U.S.-Soviet relationship, but we should also remember that increases in our capabilities, when matched by the Soviet Union, may serve to diminish the risks of dangerous outbreaks in third areas of the world.

Third, most nations, even when they strongly disapprove of specific aspects of U.S. policy, desire that the United States stand ready to counter nuclear threats against nations lacking in the means of self-protection. The United

States, in particular, is being called upon to perform functions that other nations are not called upon to perform. If the United States is expected to play the role of a nuclear Galahad, risking nuclear retaliation and loss of population in behalf of others, it does not seem unreasonable for the United States to possess protective measures of a type not universally available. Nor does it seem wholly consistent for those who rely on U.S. protection simultaneously to urge the United States to accept a low posture *and* to stand ready to intervene in the defense of nuclear "abstainers." If a nation is expected to accept losses in behalf of others, it seems reasonable that plans should be laid to hold the potential losses to a minimum. That those on whom the role of nuclear Galahad is thrust should desire thicker armor seems quite understandable.

4. Conclusion

There has been a tendency to exaggerate the strategic importance of proliferation because the problem has been viewed qualitatively in respect to enumerating those nations that might acquire a small capability rather than quantitatively in respect to the destructive potential of the capability that might be achieved. As far as we can see into the future, the strategic environment will continue to be dominated by the preponderant military power of the United States and the Soviet Union. It is possible that the spread of weapons will increasingly inhibit the use of power by the United States or the Soviet Union in regions of less than vital concern. The degree of inhibition will depend upon the risks that we (or the Soviets) are willing to run. However, if we desire to accept the risks, we could, because of our preponderant power, continue to intervene in unsettled areas to diminish the risk of small-scale nuclear war.

With the spread of weapons there would be a greater likelihood of use or misuse, but the risk of use or misuse will be concentrated primarily in the third areas of the world. Given the current and prospective stable military balance between the United States and the Soviet Union, it is difficult to envisage conflicts in third areas escalating into exchanges between the homelands of the two major powers. This implies, of course, that proliferation would impose enlarged risks primarily on other nations. The superpowers will continue to be relatively immune to strikes from the parvenus; the threat to them will continue to come primarily from each other. In all analyses of proliferation this asymmetrical distribution of the risks should be stressed because of its possible impact on the incentives of aspiring nuclear powers.

A substantial diminution of the strategic gap between the superpowers and others is simply not in the offing. The only way in which reduction of the gap could be influential is if it undermines the credibility of intervention by a superpower to stabilize conditions in third areas being subjected to nuclear threat. This is not necessarily beneficial, and it is doubtful whether those in threatened areas would desire such an outcome, if they were to think seriously about the problem. What may be desirable is to make crystal clear that despite nuclear spread the major powers will retain the ability to intervene to deter nuclear threats or to punish nuclear irresponsibility without risking substantial damage to themselves. This does not necessarily mean that the major powers will be forced to deploy all those systems, like ABM, which hold some promise in this regard; it does mean that they shall be

forced to work diligently so as continually to upgrade their ability to detect, deter, disarm, or punish the national source of nuclear irresponsibility.

While nuclear spread is basically destabilizing, its strategic consequences need not be too severe. Simple nuclear capabilities cannot play the role of "equalizers" in international conflict. The strategic position that the United States and the Soviet Union currently enjoy is so unassailable that even continuing action by third parties is unlikely to upset the central strategic balance for the next twenty years. Properly exploited, this central strategic balance could continue to provide some stability in regional conflicts—even in the face of nuclear proliferation.

Notes

[1] Any views expressed in this paper are those of the author. They should not be interpreted as reflecting the views of The RAND Corporation or the official opinion or policy of any of its governmental or private research sponsors.

[2] Fortunately, a number of those nations to which such a motive might reasonably be attributed appear to have such weak technical and industrial bases that it is doubtful whether they could develop a capability, even if so moved.

[3] The nuclear sword of Damocles in President Kennedy's United Nations address quite obviously referred to American and Soviet capabilities. While some poetic license seems understandable in relation to such vast destructive power, it does not seem particularly relevant in relation to the extremely modest forces that other powers would develop.

[4] The potential of small nuclear capabilities for precipitating regional confrontations or regional destruction would remain as a major source of trouble. Its attenuation—in the case of

continued great power involvement—will be treated below.

[5] Pious comments regarding diminution of the strategic-military gap separating the superpowers from other nations, nuclear and non-nuclear alike, is reminiscent of some high-flown discussions regarding the "income gap" which were particularly popular in the 50s. It was frequently stated at that time that it was essential to diminish the gap between the affluence of the developed nations and the poverty of the under-developed nations. In the intervening period per capita GNP in the United States has risen by more than $1,000, while there remains some question whether per capita income in the under-developed countries has risen at all. Diminution of the income gap was simply not a feasible objective. Similarly, in the strategic area we are not going to have any diminution of the gap between the superpowers and the rest for the foreseeable future. It is never sensible to base one's policies on hopes for the unobtainable. Therefore, let us avoid repetition of this particular class of past errors. Whatever else our policy is based on, it should not be on an expected diminution of the strategic gap.

The Coming International Nuclear Security Treaty

By John Silard

The art of long-range weather prediction—as exemplified by the success of the Farmer's Almanac—rests on projection of past patterns into the future. In the more erratic human realm of political and social events, prediction becomes inherently more difficult, particularly when there is no historical precedent available for application to a radically altered situation. Nowhere is this better demonstrated than in the area of nuclear arms. Weapons of national annihilation having no precedent in human history, it is difficult to foresee the course of the international adjustment to this critical new factor in the relations between nation states.

But we do now have some twenty years of experience with nuclear weapons themselves. From the discernible impact they have had on international affairs, and from the progress of incipient nuclear control efforts of recent years, there begins to emerge a pattern and direction. Indications are that before the close of the century, the adjustment to the invention of nuclear arms will have run through four successive phases:

1. The first phase—*anarchic nuclear race*—was exemplified in the first decade following Hiroshima by the race for destructive capacity between the United States and the Soviets. During this era there was little real emphasis on limitation or control of nuclear development and deployment. Indeed—having actually used nuclear bombs in 1945 the United States continued occasionally to imply the possibility of use to contain "aggression" in Asia and in periodic Berlin crises.

2. From the uncontrolled nuclear race stage there unfolded the second phase—*nuclear arms limitation*—upon which the U.S. and the Soviets embarked six or seven years ago. We are now presently well within this second phase, striving to inhibit qualitatively, quantitatively, and geographically, the further spread of nuclear weapons and to "freeze" the nuclear race at its present levels.

3. There are signs that we may now also be on the threshold of a third nuclear phase—*control of existing nuclear weapons*. The focus of this nuclear control stage, as distinguished from current

185

efforts to put a "ceiling" upon nuclear spread and development, will be the establishment of international controls and guarantees—particularly among the nuclear powers—to reduce the possibility that nuclear weapons will actually be used or threatened in local conflict situations.

4. A final stage in the international adjustment to the weapons of mass annihilation will inevitably be *nuclear disarmament*. While that may now appear a remote prospect, there are signs that a modest beginning may soon be made on reductions of certain kinds and quantities of nuclear weapons deployed by the nuclear powers.

Today we are somewhere between the second and third stages of the four-step nuclear cycle—arms race, proliferation limitation, nuclear arms control, and nuclear disarmament. Following on the test ban, the international non-proliferation agreement soon to be achieved will bring stage two substantially to a close. And it now appears that as a concomitant of that treaty there will also be a beginning of nuclear arms control by the nuclear powers, necessary to guarantee the security of nations which renounce the nuclear path.

This discussion focuses upon the approaching culmination of nuclear spread limitation and likely first steps in nuclear arms control. The first portion of the analysis takes a look backward to suggest some lessons learned during the recent demise of the MLF. The second section examines the changing nuclear debate, particularly the growing political concern over the security implications of nuclear proliferation—exemplified by recent testimony of the Secretary of Defense before the Joint Committee on Atomic Energy. The third section examines the principal ingredients of the

coming nuclear compact, suggesting that it will be in substance an "International Nuclear Security Treaty" assuring international freedom from the threat of nuclear war and halting the further spread of nuclear arms which would increase the threat of nuclear war. The last section of the discussion examines some prospects for commencing nuclear disarmament and the impact of that area upon achievement of an effective end to nuclear proliferation.

1. A Look Backward: The Meaning of the MLF Demise

A seaborne multilateral nuclear force in NATO was originally suggested at the end of the Eisenhower era as a modest increment in the manifestation of NATO's unity in matters of nuclear defense. It remained a largely dormant and uninteresting proposal until General de Gaulle insisted on an independent nuclear role for France and in other ways challenged the viability of NATO's military subservience to U.S. control. The French offensive stimulated the State Department's interest in dramatizing the continuing adherence of the other allies to our NATO conceptions. Accordingly, under President Johnson and particularly in the months preceding the 1964 Presidential election, the Department of State exercised its greatest energies toward reaching a formalized agreement with some of our NATO allies to create an MLF force.

The showdown between MLF proponents in the State Department and the forces in opposition came in the fall of 1964. The opposition included France, Great Britain, other NATO nations fearing German dominance, American arms control proponents, and a great majority of the informed members of

Congress. The MLF proponents lost, and in January of 1965 President Johnson manifested the defeat of the MLF in a public statement that actually all the United States had ever proposed was our interest in the MLF, if our NATO allies actively desired it. Thereafter, the frantic MLF drive practically vanished with the disbanding of the MLF force in the State Department. Today the MLF is a dead beast which cannot return to life, but the postponement of its public funeral continues to preclude Soviet acquiescence at Geneva in the non-proliferation treaty now very much desired by agencies concerned with arms control, including the Department of Defense.

Why did the MLF die? If there was a principal cause for its defeat, it probably lies in the momentum of nuclear arms limitation achieved during the same years that the MLF drive reached its peak. In this connection it is important to recollect that the MLF was a State Department rather than a Defense Department product. Its significance lay not in any increased nuclear capability in NATO, but in the desire to face down de Gaulle by a manifestation of continuing American dominance in NATO. And while adding no significant increment to the nuclear security of the West, the MLF did threaten the prospects for international nuclear limitation.

This was less because of its multilateralized control of nuclear weapons, than because it involved the creation of a new nuclear force, armed with weapons having strategic capability against the Soviet mainland. By 1964 such a major escalation in nuclear arms deployment ran counter to an existing nuclear limitation trend. That trend was manifested not only in the 1963 test ban treaty; it was symbolized by the tacit understandings between the United States and the Soviets that neither would disseminate nuclear weapons information or capacity to others and that outer space was to be free of nuclear weapons. It was perhaps most sharply manifested by the showdown in the Cuban crisis over Soviet efforts to introduce nuclear weapons in a new area on the boundaries of the United States. The MLF was wholly inconsistent with this progression of nuclear limitation measures and understandings. Accordingly, it is hardly surprising that so significant a political force as the Department of Defense— seeing no security increment in the MLF and aware of its adverse impact on nuclear limitation—withheld the support indispensable for a State Department victory on so controversial an issue.

The MLF "peaked" too late. By 1963-64 the French challenge to NATO's preemptive military power had progressed beyond the point where what was only a symbol of solidarity could heal the rift. And the effort to halt the nuclear race had progressed during the same years to the point where a new sea-borne nuclear force targeted on the Soviet mainland was manifestly contrary to the arms limitations course upon which the two nuclear giants had embarked. But beyond this political insight, the MLF demise and the debates preceding it served to awaken awareness of the salient considerations promoting nationalistic desires for nuclear power: desire for security from nuclear force (avoidance of nuclear attack or nuclear blackmail) and desire for enhanced national prestige derived from independent nuclear capability (or from "equal partnership" status with the United States, as in a jointly-owned MLF nuclear force). The MLF debate has thus contributed to improved appreciation of the obstacles to achievement of universal agreement to and observance of a non-proliferation agreement. Before turning to examination of that subject, however, it is appropriate to note the changing debate over and emphasis upon nuclear arms limitation since the demise of the MLF.

2. 1965-1966: The Changing Political Context

With the demise of the MLF, prospects for progress in nuclear arms limitation brightened, and efforts in that direction commenced anew in 1965. The subject had meanwhile gained increased urgency from the detonation of a first nuclear device by Red China in 1964. Moreover, the Soviet representative in Geneva had stated in 1964 the immediate readiness of the Russians to subscribe to a non-proliferation treaty once the MLF hurdle was cleared away. While Premier Khrushchev was replaced soon after this public offer, it became clear after an intervening period of uncertainty that the interest in nuclear limitation manifested under Khrushchev was to be perpetuated under the new Soviet leadership.

In the United States the desire to move ahead with nuclear limitation was demonstrated in two outstanding analyses in the Congress given in 1965 by Senator Robert Kennedy. The major theme of the Kennedy speeches was the emergent importance of nuclear arms control to international peace, to European interests, and to the security of the United States. That theme was even more clearly manifested as the consensus of the American political majority by the Congressional Resolution introduced on January 19, 1966 on behalf of 55 senators by Senator Pastore of Rhode Island, ranking Senate member of the Joint Committee on Atomic Energy. In

that Resolution, the Senate commends "the President's serious and urgent efforts to negotiate international agreements limiting the spread of nuclear weapons," and supports "additional efforts by the President which are appropriate and necessary in the interest of peace for the solution of nuclear proliferation problems." Upon the introduction of the Resolution in the Senate, Chairman Pastore in colloquy with Senator Robert Kennedy revealed the staunch opposition of the Joint Committee to the MLF and emphasized the need for including China in the international discussions striving for nuclear arms limitation.

Perhaps most revealing of the increasing United States commitment to achieve nuclear arms limitation was the testimony given in March of 1965 on the Pastore resolution by Defense Secretary McNamara. Before the Joint Committee he repeatedly underlined that acquisition of nuclear weapons capability by more nations *imperils the security interests of the United States.* The Secretary indicated that the very survival of the United States would be risked in an unrestricted nuclear exchange with the Soviet Union or, within one or two decades, with China, and he made clear the reasons why increase in the number of nuclear nations would seriously increase the risk of such a nuclear exchange:

First, he outlined the difference between a conventional arms conflict not immediately involving the nuclear powers, which permits the international machinery of peace-keeping and conflict-adjustment to operate, and a situation where a smaller nation has developed a nuclear capacity which becomes employed in a local conflict. In the latter situation, as the Secretary demonstrated, because of the nature of a nuclear confrontation there might be immediate recourse to a nuclear response, involving the large nuclear powers in what might become an uncontrolled annihilative exchange. As a second increased hazard to security, the Secretary pointed out the dangers of accidental detonation of a nuclear device possessed by a smaller nation. He noted that the United States has spent billions of dollars for controls and safeguards against accidental detonation, which nations now contemplating nuclear development clearly could not afford to expand. On this basis the Secretary ventured the view that at some time an accidental detonation by one of these powers would be almost a certainty, and indicated that because of the difficulty of diagnosing such a detonation it could well trigger an international nuclear war. Finally, McNamara pointed out that with each new nation that acquires a nuclear capacity a larger and additional number of nations are prompted to follow suit. He insisted that this is true irrespective of what nation might become the sixth nuclear power; whether it might be Sweden, Switzerland, Czechoslovakia, or Indonesia, the catalytic effect would tend further to increase nuclear proliferation with each new nation that joins the nuclear "club."

It is a fair assessment from these various indicators of changing American perceptions that nuclear arms limitation is rapidly becoming a priority United States objective, and a similar sentiment prevails in Great Britain as well as in the Soviet Union. True, there are no comparable indications yet from China or France. But the logic of nuclear power indicates that these nations, too, may soon look with concern at the prospect of uncontrolled nuclear proliferation. Thus, Secretary of State Rusk recently indicated that while it may have

served the interests of France to develop its nuclear force, she will see that it disserves her interests of security, power, and prestige, for others to follow her example. Nor could it be lost upon Red China that whatever interest is served by her nuclear arms program is hardly enhanced if India, Indonesia, or Japan develop comparable nuclear power.

As encouraging as are the signs among the nuclear powers, it is often said that since to halt proliferation is but to preserve an international double standard it is hardly likely to appeal to such nations as India, Israel, or West Germany. These have the technological capacity in short time periods to achieve an initial nuclear detonation and begin national nuclear arms development. But there are other real inhibitors to national nuclear forces; and there may also be more of a case for restricting the nuclear club to its present members than mere great power self-interest. For it is a fact (substituting Red China which controls the mainland for Nationalist China which holds the United Nations seat), that today's five nuclear powers are the *same* nations which were given permanent places on the United Nations Security Council, in recognition of their superpower status. The postwar division between these nations and the nullifying effect of the veto has robbed the Security Council of its intended peace-keeping role. But the underlying premise that the great military powers of the world have an obligation to preserve the international security continues to have meaning. On that premise the non-proliferation emphasis by the nuclear powers can have a dimension beyond mere selfish interest: the five nuclear powers can guarantee the freedom of countries renouncing the nuclear course from nuclear conflict or threat of such conflict on their territory.

This, indeed, is emerging in current discussions as the principal new ingredient of the coming nuclear limitation agreement. There are now prospects for conclusion not merely of a non-proliferation pact, but for an International Nuclear Security Treaty to forestall both the threatened use of existing weapons and their spread beyond today's five nuclear powers.

3. The Coming Treaty: Culmination of Proliferation Limitation and a Beginning of Nuclear Arms Control

It is generally anticipated that the next international nuclear agreement will have as a principal ingredient a pledge against proliferation of nuclear weapons. Therein, the nuclear nations will pledge not to disseminate weapons or know-how to non-nuclear nations, which in turn will promise to refrain from developing their own nuclear weapons. The substance of these complementary pledges, as proposed in alternative texts in Geneva by the Soviet Union and the United States, has remained relatively unchanged in recent years. The only significant difference between the two versions—one which presents a threshold obstacle to the conclusion of a treaty—concerns the MLF, which the United States continues to treat as consistent with and not precluded by our proposed treaty.

Possibilities of overcoming the MLF hurdle are much more favorable than they were as recently as a year ago. This is because of significant changes affecting each of the three major grounds of alleged German desire for the MLF: 1) The MLF was thought desired by the Germans because it might ultimately lead to their "full partnership" in Eu-

ropean nuclear defense through attenuation of the American veto on the use of our nuclear weapons. However, in March of 1966 any such German anticipation was firmly renounced when the West German Defense Minister stated the understanding that there will be no deterioration of the U.S. nuclear veto in any new NATO arrangements. 2) During the MLF debates there was also expressed concern about the inadequate joint planning of nuclear matters within NATO. On this score, McNamara's Select Committee is now functioning, and promises quite soon to provide an increased level of regularized joint nuclear planning, which should go far toward satisfying this element of the German interest in the MLF. 3) There was formerly the anticipation that the MLF would provide a "hardware" solution in the sense that the Germans would achieve joint ownership of a nuclear force and thus a larger say in NATO nuclear matters. While there continue to be manifestations of interest in a hardware solution, even German politicians now recognize the irreparable demise of the MLF.

Accordingly, it appears that President Johnson is now in a position to declare that after due consideration and deliberation the MLF no longer seems desirable to or for our European friends. On that basis he could conclude a non-proliferation agreement which both the Soviets and the Germans could be induced to sign.

Yet as time has tended to dissolve the MLF roadblock there has simultaneously arisen a new and serious worry about achieving an effective non-proliferation pact. Not so long ago it was a fair expectation that a non-proliferation treaty could command acceptance by almost every nation in the "free world," as well as the countries in the

Soviet orbit. Today, however, there is serious doubt whether certain "Nth" countries such as India, Japan, Israel, Egypt, or even some European nations, will sign a non-proliferation treaty if much more time passes before the moment for decision is at hand. And even now there is doubt whether there would be widespread agreement and adherence to a nuclear renunciation pledge without some significant security guarantees from the nuclear powers to the renouncing nations. The principal concern of non-nuclear powers about the possibility of a nuclear exchange on their territory must be met, for these nations appreciate General de Gaulle's *force-de-frappe* argument that even against the nuclear superpowers there is a deterrent effect from capacity to inflict a painful even though not annihilative nuclear response.

The form of the guarantee to the non-nuclear powers against a nuclear exchange on their territory is not yet clear, but its substance is predictable. From the point of view of India, for instance, what is desirable is a guarantee by Red China that it will not unleash or threaten to unleash a nuclear weapon on Indian territory, and a guarantee from the United States, and hopefully the Soviet Union, that it would assuredly come to the defense of India with nuclear power to forestall any such nuclear attack or threat by China. It is noteworthy, taking India again as an example, that the respective guarantees by China, by the United States, and by the Soviets, have differing but complementary value. From the Chinese, who are regarded as the only likely nuclear aggressor in India, a promise against initiating a nuclear attack adds little assurance in the short run. But over one or two decades the guarantee could take on significance if, consistent

with it, the Chinese refrained from deploying any serious nuclear capability near to or targeted upon Indian territory.

The guarantee from the United States has far greater significance. Of course, India hardly needs assurance today of United States defense in the event of a conventional or nuclear attack by China. But there is always latent concern in non-nuclear nations that in the long run even their staunchest allies would hesitate to come to their defense in a situation in which they might consequently suffer annihilative retaliation from the initial nuclear aggressor. For this reason it is advisable for the United States to manifest to India in the strongest terms in connection with the non-proliferation treaty and on other appropriate future occasions, its continuing determination —even at the risk of its own survival— to preclude a nuclear attack on India.

Finally, perhaps the most significant pledge for India is that from the Soviet Union. A guarantee from the Soviets to deter Chinese nuclear aggression in India would afford increased assurance that by forgoing her own nuclear forces India would not be left at the mercy of Chinese nuclear power in Asia.

The foregoing example demonstrates the significance of the "no nuclear attack" guarantee from the nuclear powers to nations promising abstention from nuclear arms. In the "no-nuclear attack" pledge there is a real measure of inducement to the non-nuclear powers to subscribe to the non-proliferation treaty, as Secretary McNamara's 1966 testimony clearly recognized in its emphasis that such a pledge should accompany the non-proliferation pact.

Indeed, it may be appropriate to give emphasis to the "no nuclear attack" pledge even beyond that given the non-proliferation element of the coming treaty. After all, that pledge by the nuclear powers is in a sense the "offer" and inducement for the non-nuclears' "acceptance" of the compact to refrain from nuclear arms. Moreover, the no attack pledge would be the first international *nuclear arms control* measure as distinct from mere *nuclear development limitation,* and in the long run is likely to have much greater significance. Accordingly, the appropriate emphasis of the coming treaty may be upon the larger conception of an "International Nuclear Security Agreement" to secure world-wide freedom from nuclear war *and* to preclude the spread of nuclear armaments which further endangers that freedom.

In addition to nuclear security and non-proliferation pledges, the coming treaty will in all probability include safeguards against secret violation of the non-proliferation commitment. Without some safeguards there would be legitimate concern whether over a period of years a signatory nation might not secretly develop a nuclear capacity in violation of its treaty commitment. The safeguards required will likely involve both periodic inspection in non-nuclear nations and controls upon their use and disposition of nuclear materials acquired from other nations—preferably by way of the International Atomic Energy Agency. However, the present lack of experience with periodic general inspection may indicate the desirability of limiting the "safeguards" consent of the non-nuclear powers to a generalization to be implemented by future agreements governing the details of material controls and periodic general inspection. Doubtless, the nuclear powers will have to pay an appropriate price in exchange for the safeguards against secret development of nuclear weapons by renouncing nations. But that is a price well worth paying, for the longer the non-

proliferation pact is postponed the longer will be the cost of acquiescence by the non-nuclear nations in permanent nuclear renunciation.

4. Beyond Tomorrow: Nuclear Reductions

Ever since the United States ended the Second World War with nuclear weapons, the possession of nuclear bombs has been looked upon in the United States as a national asset. Not only did the bomb end the war, but its threatened or implied use tended in the 1950's to restrain Chinese military activity in the Far East and perhaps even to forestall serious East German aggression in Berlin.

But today the value of the United States' nuclear capability in preventing or ending a conventional arms conflict has all but vanished, as we are daily reminded by the dispatches from Viet Nam. With Soviet achievement of nuclear capacity to annihilate or incapacitate the United States, we are now like two neighbors each having planted dynamite under the other's house and knowing the probability that throwing the switch on one detonation will close the switch on the other. As China attains a comparable destructive capacity within coming years, it will be seen that even for gigantic powers nuclear weapons are more liability than asset. The value of the bomb will be seen to be *only* the deterrence of a nuclear attack by a hostile power—a value far better preserved by international elimination of all nuclear weapons. Of course, for nations which do not themselves possess nuclear weapons with which to deter or inhibit attack, the existence of nuclear weapons lacks even this minimal deterrent value. It is therefore a fair appraisal that a non-proliferation

THE PROGRESSION FROM HIROSHIMA TO NUCLEAR DISARMAMENT: 1945–2000

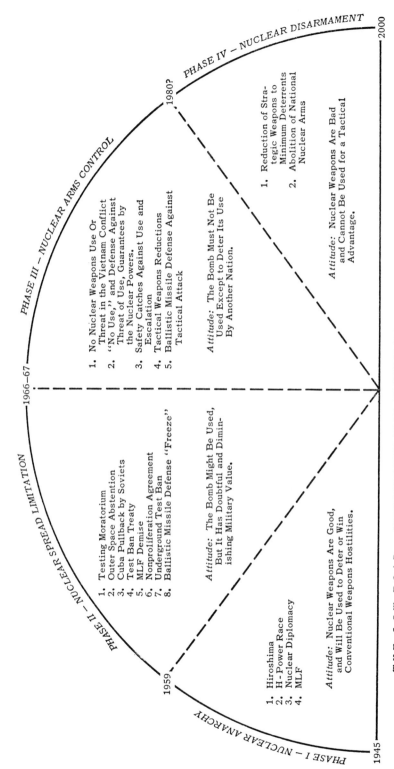

PHASE IV – NUCLEAR DISARMAMENT

1. Reduction of Strategic Weapons to Minimum Deterrents
2. Abolition of National Nuclear Arms

Attitude: Nuclear Weapons Are Bad and Cannot Be Used for a Tactical Advantage.

PHASE III – NUCLEAR ARMS CONTROL

1980?

1. No Nuclear Weapons Use Or Threat in the Vietnam Conflict
2. "No Use," and Defense Against Threat of Use, Guarantees by the Nuclear Powers.
3. Safety Catches Against Use and Escalation
4. Tactical Weapons Reductions
5. Ballistic Missile Defense Against Tactical Attack

Attitude: The Bomb Must Not Be Used Except to Deter Its Use By Another Nation.

1966–67

PHASE II – NUCLEAR SPREAD LIMITATION

1. Testing Moratorium
2. Outer Space Abstention
3. Cuba Pullback by Soviets
4. Test Ban Treaty
5. MLF Demise
6. Nonproliferation Agreement
7. Underground Test Ban
8. Ballistic Missile Defense "Freeze"

Attitude: The Bomb Might Be Used, But It Has Doubtful and Diminishing Military Value.

1959

1. Hiroshima
2. H-Power Race
3. Nuclear Diplomacy
4. MLF

Attitude: Nuclear Weapons Are Good, and Will Be Used to Deter or Win Conventional Weapons Hostilities.

PHASE I – NUCLEAR ANARCHY

1945

THE LOW ROAD: PROLIFERATION, MLFS, TACTICAL WEAPONS THREAT, MISSILE DEFENSE RACE, LIFE UNDERGROUND, NUCLEAR WAR

2000

treaty would become increasingly unstable unless the nuclear powers heeded the legitimate demand by other nations that they themselves begin progress on nuclear disarmament. A beginning on nuclear disarmament is now already being urged by some of these nations; it will in years ahead be increasingly demanded by non-nuclear powers and its achievement would indeed serve the interest of every nation.

When nuclear reductions commence, it is probable that cutbacks will begin with tactical rather than strategic weapons, since these pose the largest threat of kindling an unrestrained annihilative exchange. The nuclear escalation ladder has, after all, a dual logic. Because it has separate ascending rungs, the ladder tends to restrain an ultimate nuclear exchange by virtue of the steps which precede it. But at the same time, there is always the danger that a climb once begun will continue from its own momentum. Accordingly, it is of great importance that the lowest rung of the ladder be as far as possible from the ground. It is for this reason that tactical nuclear weapons pose the greatest threat of kindling an all-out nuclear exchange. Deployed in the field, their use can be too easily rationalized, even short of absolute tactical "necessity," in certain local conflict situations. Perhaps tactical weapons serve the function of maintaining the "credibility" of a strategic

exchange and thus of restraint against conventional arms aggressions. If so, the game is not worth the candle.

Retention of tactical nuclear weapons seems tactically unnecessary in any presently discernible Western military interest. In any event, the risk of retention and thus of potential use—possibly resulting in escalation to a strategic exchange—far outweighs the hypothetical military value. Thus, nuclear disarmament should properly begin with tactical weapons, once it is fully seen that they have become too dangerous to be employed for combat purposes.

But nuclear disarmament is not yet on the agenda. For now the task is to maintain progress in proliferation limitation and nuclear arms control, a task which requires further change in public attitudes concerning nuclear arms. We must more clearly recognize that the existence of nuclear weapons is not an asset but a dangerous liability for every nation, including the United States and the other nuclear powers; and we must emphasize our commitment to ultimate international elimination of all weapons of mass annihilation. If we believe and act upon what we affirm, there is still hope that the "nuclear club" can be held to a maximum of its five present members, and that statesmanship will master these frightful 20th century weapons before they enslave or destroy the civilization which created them.

Vertical Versus Horizontal Proliferation:
An Indian View

By V. C. Trivedi

The international community has been devoting increasing attention of late to the problem of the proliferation of nuclear weapons. During the early 1960's, the emphasis in discussions on disarmament was generally on the principal issue of halting and reversing the nuclear arms race; but during the last two years or so, the particular problem of non-proliferation has been debated as an urgent collateral measure. Earlier, countries like Ireland, Sweden and India had brought it up before the United Nations on several occasions and certain resolutions of a general nature were adopted by that body; but it was only after the explosion of a nuclear weapon device by the Peoples' Republic of China in October, 1964 that people began to speak widely of the danger of proliferation of nuclear weapons and the threat that proliferation posed to international stability and security. The Chinese action was condemned by all peace-loving peoples of the world, particularly as it was accompanied by arrogant bravado and unabashed callousness. There was shock, there was anger and there was anxiety.

Such reactive feelings are, of course, inevitable and natural, but they are not wise counsellors to statesmen or students, to the leaders of men or the peoples of the world. The recalcitrance of the Chinese and their contemptuous disregard of the will and welfare of humanity should not result in frustration, cynical acquiescence or the advocacy of ineffectual remedies on the part of the rest of the world. A sense of urgency should not lead to panic, for measures conceived in an atmosphere of panic are often unwise or unjust. Above all, when one is dealing with fundamental issues affecting the future of humanity, one must avoid resolutely all expedient and spurious remedies, for these do nothing but harm to all concerned.

India has all along maintained that the central and basic problem of international peace and security and of disarmament is that of the nuclear arms race and of the menace posed by ever-increasing and ever more sophisticated nuclear arsenals in the world and that it is not fruitful to deal with the consequences of the arms race unless we

195

also deal with this central problem. India has, therefore, continued to emphasize the imperative need of making progress in halting and reversing the arms race in order to safeguard not only international security but also the survival of civilization. In July 1957, Jawaharlal Nehru said in our Parliament: "We have declared quite clearly that we are not interested in making atom bombs even if we have the capacity to do so and that in no event will we use atomic energy for destructive purposes. I am quite sure that when I say this, I represent every member of this House. I hope that will be the policy of all future Governments. The fact remains that if one has these fissionable materials and if one has the resources, then one can make a bomb, unless the world will be wise enough to come to some decision to stop the production of such bombs."

Whether it was in the context of non-proliferation of nuclear weapons or in the broader framework of disarmament, India tried to make the international community realize that it was essential to come to grips urgently with the nuclear arms menace—particularly the vital problem of halting and reversing the nuclear arms race—for my Government believed that the only efficacious solution was to deal with the cause as well as the consequence of the malaise. India voted for what is called the Irish resolution, but in explaining its vote, it said that the resolution did not go far enough. India supported what is called the Unden Plan and voted for the Swedish resolution in 1961, which specifically called for an inquiry to be made into the conditions under which non-nuclear weapon countries and the nuclear weapon countries might agree to non-proliferation and non-dissemination of nuclear weapons. It is regrettable that

this suggested course of action was not then pursued vigorously.

India's own position in the nuclear field has always been clear. It embarked on a nuclear energy program for peaceful purposes as early as 1954. In fact, India built its own nuclear reactor—designed, erected and commissioned entirely by Indian scientists and engineers —two years before the Peoples' Republic of China was given a reactor by the Soviet Union. During a visit to India, Chou-en-lai told Indian scientists that India was then years ahead of China in nuclear technology. At the same time, India had declared from the very beginning, from the very birth of these dreadful weapons and their early proliferation, that atomic energy must be used only for peaceful purposes. Indian leaders reiterated this position repeatedly in our Parliament as well as in the international forum. In April 1954, for example, when Jawaharlal Nehru sent a message to the Disarmament Commission and the United Nations on suspension of weapon tests, this is what he said: "The general position of this country in this matter has been repeatedly stated and placed beyond all doubt. It is up to us to pursue as best we can the objective we seek. We have maintained that nuclear (including thermonuclear), chemical and biological (bacterial) knowledge and power should not be used to forge these weapons of mass destruction. We have advocated the prohibition of such weapons, by common consent, and immediately by agreement among those concerned, which latter is at present the only effective way to bring about their abandonment."

While, therefore, it was India's policy and national determination to use atomic energy only for peaceful purposes, India was aware that in order to arrive at an international agreement and to obtain an international treaty on non-proliferation of nuclear weapons, it was necessary to stop proliferation of nuclear weapons in all its aspects, that is, the actual proliferation by the nuclear weapon powers themselves, as well as the likely or potential proliferation by the non-nuclear weapon countries. India believed, and continues to believe, that the real problem is in fact that of the existing or vertical or intra-spatial proliferation. Future or horizontal or extra-spatial proliferation is only the consequence and not the cause of the present armaments tension in the world. Once the cause is removed, the consequence is automatically eliminated.

The international community has also been aware of this fundamental verity. Even before the explosion of a nuclear weapon device by the Peoples' Republic of China, the communiqué issued by the Conference of the Non-Aligned Heads of State and Government held in Cairo early in October 1964 requested the Great Powers to abstain from all policies conducive to the dissemination of nuclear weapons and to agree on measures providing for the gradual liquidation of the existing stockpiles. The communiqué then went on to say that as part of these efforts relating to non-dissemination and liquidation of existing stockpiles, the non-aligned countries declared their readiness not to produce, acquire or test any nuclear weapons.

The Disarmament Commission which met in April-June 1965 also adopted a similar approach. The Chinese exploded their second nuclear weapon device while the Commission was in session. In a resolution supported by an overwhelming majority of nations, the Commission deplored these tests. It could do no less. At the same time, the international community was not stampeded into suggesting unjust and ineffective courses of action. As Jawaharlal Nehru said in the statement of April 1954, which I quoted earlier: "Fear and dread do not lead to constructive thought or effective courses of action. Panic is no remedy against disaster of any kind, present or potential." There was thus no support in the Disarmament Commission for the incorrect approach being advocated by some people, namely, that *faits accomplis* be accepted, that the possession and proliferation of nuclear weapons by five countries be sanctified and that only the question of what is called "further proliferation," that is, proliferation of nuclear weapons to new countries, countries other than the U.S.A., the U.S.S.R., the U.K., France and the Peoples' Republic of China, be singled out for international prohibition. The Disarmament Commission, representing the entire membership of the United Nations, did not subscribe to such a discriminatory approach. It refused to use the phrase "further proliferation" and asked the Eighteen Nation Committee on Disarmament to accord special priority to the consideration of the question of a treaty or convention to prevent the proliferation of nuclear weapons, giving close attention to the various suggestions that agreement could be facilitated by adopting a program of certain related measures. An agreement on non-proliferation of nuclear weapons was thus seen as possible in the framework of a program of certain related measures of nuclear disarmament.

When the Eighteen-Nation Disarmament Committee reconvened in Geneva, the eight non-aligned delegations adopted the same approach and submitted a memorandum which declared that a treaty on non-proliferation of nuclear weapons was not an end in itself but only a means to an end. That end was the achievement of General and Complete Disarmament and, more particularly, of nuclear disarmament. The eight delegations also recorded their conviction that measures to prohibit the spread of nuclear weapons should be coupled with, or followed by, tangible steps to halt the nuclear arms race and to limit, reduce and eliminate the stocks of nuclear weapons and the means of their delivery.

As will be seen from this detailed evolution of international thinking on the question of proliferation of nuclear weapons, the world community was defining with progressive precision the basic elements of a genuine and efficacious treaty on non-proliferation of nuclear weapons—elements which would deal with the cause of the malady and not merely some of its symptoms. The latest and the most precise formulation of the views of the international community was expressed in Resolution 2028 adopted on the 19th of November, 1965 by the 20th session of the U.N. General Assembly. This resolution declared, *inter alia,* that an international treaty to prevent the proliferation of nuclear weapons should be based on certain specific principles, one of which was that "the treaty should embody an acceptable balance of mutual responsibilities and obligations of the nuclear and non-nuclear Powers."

It is necessary to pay close attention to this historic resolution. When references are made to views of individual countries on non-proliferation, it is well to remember that there is an international view on this problem. The international community has stipulated quite clearly and in unmistakable terms that a treaty on non-proliferation of nuclear weapons must provide for mutual responsibilities and obligations of nuclear and non-nuclear weapon powers, that

these responsibilities and obligations must be balanced, that this balance must be acceptable to all signatories and that the balance of mutual obligations and responsibilities of the nuclear and non-nuclear weapon powers must be embodied in the treaty. This balance, therefore, must be written into the articles of the treaty itself, and reflected in its application. The international community has clearly rejected the notion that a treaty on non-proliferation of nuclear weapons should embody mainly the obligations and responsibilities of the non-nuclear weapon countries and that as far as the nuclear weapon powers are concerned, they can consider the question of their own obligations and responsibilities separately and under some other agreements which they may hope to debate and negotiate in the future. The international community has categorically rejected the argument advocated by some people that a non-proliferation treaty has to be, by its nature, unbalanced and that it has to cover mainly the obligations and responsibilities of non-nuclear weapon countries. The weakness in that argument is, of course, due to the unwarranted limitation placed on the contours of the problem and due to attempts which have been made to vivisect the single and organic problem of proliferation, severing the actual and existing proliferation by the nuclear weapon powers themselves from the probable and future proliferation to new countries.

The view that India puts forward on non-proliferation is therefore the one that is held generally by the international community. Apart from the nuclear weapon powers, their military allies and others who feel that their security is safeguarded by the existing military alliances, most nations of the world realize what exactly is the danger and what exactly are the means to circumscribe, reduce and eliminate that danger. Broadly speaking, these nations do not think of their national security in isolation either individually or as a group, but in the context of international security as a whole. They are, of course, determined to maintain their freedom and their territorial integrity, their sovereignty and their national unity. At the same time, they believe that their security and independence can be safeguarded not by military alliances, which sustain the Cold War and exacerbate international tensions, but by the rule of law, by observance of the norms of civilized international behaviour, by the outlawry of the use of force to settle disputes and by disarmament. In fact, even among the participants of military alliances three countries went in for national nuclear weapon programs because they were convinced that their security was better maintained by what they called their independent deterrents or national nuclear forces. (The United States, of course, unlike Great Britain and France, acquired nuclear weapons before joining NATO in 1949.)

This historic fact of powerful countries belonging to military alliances going in for national nuclear weapon capabilities provides a clue to the real answer to the problem. Before trying to deal with the question of further proliferation in the future, or proliferation of nuclear weapons to new countries, therefore, it is essential for all serious students of international affairs to examine why further proliferation did in fact take place in the past. This is the only scientific approach to be pursued when one is studying human behaviour at any level up to and including the international.

The countries where further proliferation took place in the past have generally given two reasons for their actions. One is that they wanted to be on "the top table." They wanted their voice to carry weight in international gatherings and they wanted political power. There was, therefore, the consideration of prestige. Secondly, they felt that they could best safeguard their security by possessing an independent nuclear deterrent or an independent striking force. I am referring to responsible powers. An irresponsible and expansionist power like the Peoples' Republic of China may have had a third reason, namely to threaten its neighbors or blackmail those it calls its enemies. Leaving that aside, however, it is the two former considerations of prestige and security which we must bear in mind in our efforts to prevent still further proliferation. One thing is certain. The days have long passed when powerful nations can impose their will on militarily weak but legally sovereign and equal nations. There can be no imposition of a kind of a *Pax Nuclearia* on non-nuclear weapon states. We have, therefore, to look into the real causes of proliferation intrinsically as well as historically and we have to take account of these considerations of prestige and security which have led to further vertical proliferation or proliferation to new countries in the past.

Unfortunately, there is no real attempt being made to deny prestige to the acquisition and possession of nuclear weapons. The United Nations has condemned them and has called them a crime against humanity; and yet many people and their Governments, particularly the Big Powers, continue to act in the context of what they call realities, talk in terms of acceptance of *faits accomplis* and propagate the ideas of exclusive five-power confabulations to solve the problems of the world. There are some who even think of equating possession of these evil weapons with permanent membership of the Security Council of the United Nations, as if the nuclear bomb were a special symbol of the right to enforce the veto. No wonder, therefore, that the world society in general has come to the conclusion that the possession of nuclear weapons does bestow prestige and that consequently the road to sanity lies in taking away these dread instruments from the hands of the five powers rather than placing them in the hands of more countries. India, in particular, with its respectable nuclear know-how and facilities, is a passionate advocate of this thesis. It has eschewed for itself publicly and repeatedly any desire to become a nuclear weapon power: it has urged all other countries to do the same; and yet at the same time, it believes that there is no real answer to this unfortunate problem of prestige unless the existing nuclear weapon powers halt all further production of nuclear weapons and begin a program of reduction and eventual elimination of these weapons and their delivery systems. This is one field where it is nobler as well as safer to lose prestige rather than acquire it.

The question of security is also amenable to the same answer. Military alliances have provided no real or lasting security, as can be seen from the history of three powerful members of alliances who have gone in for independent nuclear weapon programs. What is more, even the two superpowers are continuing to increase their stockpiles, sophisticate their weapons and delivery systems and experiment on producing the ultimate weapon or some kind of technological breakthrough. The so-called balance of terror is, therefore, a misnomer, for one cannot have a real balance without stability. Moreover, this notion of an existing balance of power with five

nuclear weapon powers (apart from its instability) is also fallacious. If there was a balance with only the U.S. and the U.S.S.R. possessing nuclear weapons, on what basis could it be said that the balance remained valid after the addition of the U.K. and France to the nuclear club? If there was a balance till 1964, how can one say that the same balance is maintained or will be maintained in the future, given the decision of China to embark on a nuclear weapon program? At any rate, the fact remains that even according to three members of powerful military defense alliances, the acquisition of their own nuclear weapons was their preferred solution to the problem of their security.

But India and the majority of the international community do not believe that proliferation provides either national security or international stability. India does not wish to go in for nuclear weapons and that is also the desire of other non-nuclear weapon countries and of the international community as a whole. It is the responsibility of the nuclear weapon powers, therefore, to help these countries to maintain their "state of innocence," as a Swiss scholar once put it in a multi-national forum. Countries like India will continue to abide by their national decisions, as repeatedly affirmed by Prime Minister Gandhi and her predecessors, but if there has to be an international treaty, it must be a genuine and non-discriminatory treaty. It cannot be a treaty which gives licence and even encouragement to the existing nuclear weapon powers to proliferate and which imposes controls and prohibitions only on the non-nuclear countries.

In this context, it is imperative to remove the misconception that non-proliferation must be not a means of disarming the armed but merely a measure for ensuring the non-armament of un-armed countries. It is this fallacy which leads to the contradiction between the requirements of security on the one hand and the inadequate notions of pre-vention of further proliferation on the other. International security has not been stabilized by the proliferation which took place in the past and it will not be strengthened by still further prolifera-tion. It can be safeguarded only by put-ting a halt to present or actual prolifera-tion and not by unreal measures calcu-lated to deal with future or probable proliferation.

The international community has laid down in specific terms what should be done to obtain a genuine treaty on non-proliferation of nuclear weapons. The Eighteen Nation Disarmament Commit-tee has been given clear terms of refer-ence by the United Nations in this matter.

The U.N. resolution stipulated five main principles which should form the basis of an international treaty to pre-vent the proliferation of nuclear weap-ons. The non-aligned delegations in the Disarmament Committee have empha-sized in particular that the main prin-ciple is one which specifies that the treaty should embody an acceptable bal-ance of mutual responsibilities and ob-ligations of the nuclear and non-nuclear powers. In fact, this is the only principle out of the five laid down by the United Nations, which stipulates what exactly should be embodied in the treaty.

When we are considering, therefore, what should be the content of an inter-national treaty on non-proliferation and what the relevant articles of the treaty should cover, it is essential that we de-vote detailed attention to the require-ment of mutual balance. The U.S. and the Soviet Union had submitted their draft treaties before the adoption of this U.N. resolution, which placed in proper perspective the two drafts, certain dec-larations of African and non-aligned states, the Italian proposal of a mora-torium and the non-aligned memoran-dum. The two draft treaties will, there-fore, need to be revised so as to embody appropriate provisions in them in ac-cordance with the principle of balance of mutual obligations and responsibili-ties of nuclear and non-nuclear weapon countries.

The U.S. and the Soviet draft treaties on non-proliferation envisage certain obligations and responsibilities on the part of non-nuclear weapon countries. They do not, however, envisage similar mutual or balanced obligations on the part of nuclear weapon countries, ex-cept to a limited extent in regard to the question of dissemination of nuclear weapons and weapon technology. They do not envisage any mutuality or bal-ance in regard to the production of nu-clear weapons nor in regard to the ex-isting stockpiles of these weapons and their carriers. In the U.S. draft treaty, there is also a general reference to International Atomic Energy Agency (I.A.E.A.) or equivalent international safeguards on the peaceful nuclear ac-tivities of non-nuclear weapon countries but not on nuclear weapon activities of nuclear weapon countries. Moreover, a subsequent statement from the U.S. Government indicates that even in re-spect to peaceful nuclear activities, the major nuclear powers would accept in-ternational safeguards only in an in-creasing measure, that is, not entirely in the initial stage while, of course, other countries are required to do so in respect to all nuclear materials and equipment from the beginning.

An appropriate and adequate treaty on non-proliferation of nuclear weapons should, however, deal with the whole problem of proliferation, the single and organic problem of present as well as future proliferation, whether one looks at it from the point of view of disarmament, or of combating the notions of prestige, or of safeguarding international security or the requirements of international law in our modern society of sovereign and equal nations.

The principle of balance in the treaty should apply to the question of weapons as well as that of control. As far as nuclear weapons are concerned, there are three aspects of the problem. Firstly, there is the question of dissemination. The treaty should, therefore, provide that the nuclear weapon powers should not disseminate weapons or material for weapons and weapon technology to any country and that the non-nuclear weapon nations should not receive weapons or material for weapons and weapon technology from any country. This would be a balanced provision and would deal fully with the dissemination aspect of the problem of proliferation.

The second aspect of the weapon problem is that of production. The appropriate provision in an acceptable treaty should prohibit production of nuclear weapons both by the nuclear weapon powers as well as by the non-nuclear weapon powers. This is, in fact, the crux of the problem. One cannot have a balanced or non-discriminatory international treaty if its prohibition is extended only to non-nuclear weapon countries while the nuclear weapon powers are permitted to proliferate, to increase their stockpiles, to conduct experiments and refine their weapons. A provision prohibiting production of nuclear weapons or fissile material for production of weapons by all countries should logically and appropriately be the very first article in a non-proliferation treaty.

The third requirement of balance in a non-proliferation treaty pertains to the issue of the existing stockpiles of these weapons. Unless this question can be resolved, there is no balance and no real solution of the problem of proliferation. The inventories of weapons and missiles which existed even in 1952 or 1960 led to further proliferation in the past. Today, these inventories have increased several-fold and now constitute a multiple over-kill capability. Any appropriate international instrument which purports to deal with the question either of existing proliferation or of future proliferation must, therefore, deal with the problem of the existing stockpiles of nuclear weapons and their means of delivery.

It is realised, of course, that this problem cannot be resolved overnight. Past discussions on the subject have demonstrated that the elimination of the existing stockpiles must be carried out over a period of years. The fact remains, however, that it must be done. As far as a non-proliferation treaty is concerned, the least that the international community will demand is that a beginning should be made in this field and that an agreement be reached on the reduction and eventual elimination of the existing stockpiles of nuclear weapons and the carriers of nuclear destruction. A treaty on non-proliferation should therefore deal first of all with the problem of production of fissile material for manufacture of weapons, secondly with the problem of dissemination and thirdly with the problem of existing stockpiles.

In addition to the questions of dissemination and proliferation of nuclear weapons, there is also the question of control and inspection in a treaty on non-proliferation. There are many views on the subject. For example, there are some who say that control should apply only to measures of disarmament or rather to actual acts of disarmament and that it cannot be extended to armaments. On that principle, even more so, it cannot also extend to measures of non-armament. Then there are others who point out logically and realistically that the real sanction behind the observance by sovereign nations of a treaty of this kind lies in the withdrawal clause. It is in the interest of all signatories to assure others as well as themselves that the treaty is universal and that it is not being violated by any nation. This interest is safeguarded in actual practice by a withdrawal clause of the type incorporated in the Partial Test Ban Treaty. Then there is yet another view held by those who contemplate institution of control either by the I.A.E.A. or by a similar international mechanism in the context of ensuring observance of a non-proliferation treaty. Many of the proponents of control, however, talk primarily of controlling the non-nuclear weapon countries and not the nuclear weapon countries, and of controlling the peaceful nuclear activities of nations and not their nuclear weapon activities.

As far as India is concerned, it believes that if control is to be exercised in the context of a non-proliferation treaty, it cannot be a discriminatory or one-sided control. Such control should be symmetrical and should fully reflect the stipulation laid down by the international community in its resolution 2028 (XX), namely, that the treaty should embody an acceptable balance of mutual responsibilities and obligations of the nuclear and non-nuclear weapon powers. Such a balance is not difficult to achieve; the same mechanism which is to be employed to control the peaceful nuclear activities of nations can with equal facility control the nuclear weapon activities of nations. If there is to be control in a non-proliferation treaty, therefore, it should be instituted for dissemination and production everywhere.

It is obvious that the problem of proliferation cannot be solved by measures of expediency dictated by fear or panic; it can only be solved by a treaty which is based on a correct appreciation of the genesis of the problem and its characteristics and prognosis. Any international edifice that we wish to build to the benefit of world stability and security must be built on firm grounds and on equity and not on the shifting sands of expediency. We should remember that what is at issue is not only a treaty on a collateral measure but a philosophy of international relationships in the second half of the 20th century, the philosophy of the Charter of the United Nations based on the principle of the sovereign equality of all its Members.

Chapter 6

LIMITED WAR
AND INTERNATIONAL PEACEKEEPING

Controlling Local Conflicts

By Lincoln P. Bloomfield

We know a great deal about the theory of superpower wars. Virtually all the literature on the subject of "limited war" has to do with clashes between the U.S. and the Soviet Union in Europe and elsewhere, not using nuclear weapons. There has been quite a lot of experience with individual conflict situations; the postwar history is in many ways one of firefights, brushfires, revolutions, assaults of one kind or another, virtually all outside of Europe and involving the "underdeveloped world." Much has been said about arms control theory, and indeed the most inventive policy literature of our generation has, in my opinion, dealt with the issue of the arms competition and its control. Now we are in the process of trying to educate ourselves about insurgency situations, good and bad, communist or otherwise. Finally, a school of inquiry commonly called "conflict resolution" has been flourishing, often seeming to oscillate between genuine social science and the picket line.

All of these have dealt with parts of the problems of conflict and its control. But there is a dearth of theoretical knowledge tying together these various pieces and yielding up a body of analysis and doctrine on the controllability of less-than-general conflicts outside of Europe. The research I am currently engaged in seeks to bring together the critical masses, so to speak, of our knowledge of local conflict and our growing understanding of arms control, to see what kind of doctrinal detonation they make. At this point I can only throw out a few notions, in a very tentative spirit.

Even the definitions here turn out to be quite inadequate. For among the 52 post-World War II conflicts we are looking at, virtually all are limited not by any natural law but simply because the parties are incapable of making them unlimited. If one recalls that Rome did not need atomic weapons to annihilate Carthage, I think one can get a picture of what some countries and some leaders might do if they had greater capabilities. So "limited" does not necessarily imply deliberate self-denial. In some of the small-bore conflicts we have already witnessed in the postwar years one or another local leader has invoked a threat of bringing on World War III, complete with thermonuclear weapons and the whole apocalyptic package—if he could only do it. A lot of this is of course rhetoric, and we are now consoling ourselves against the further

207

spread of nuclear weapons with the hope that actual possession sobers people up. But I think one wants to be clear that there may not be a qualitative distinction between local wars in Africa, Asia, Latin America, and the Middle East, and what *could* happen if capabilities should increase in various ways.

A related and absolutely crucial point on which we should also be clear is that the physical incapacity of parties to local conflicts to spread the conflicts does not necessarily imply a willingness to reach a settlement. I think this is a very crucial insight, and helps connect up such arms control activity as may be practiced, or contemplated, with respect to India and Pakistan, or between Israel and the United Arab Republic, or in sub-Saharan Africa, with kinds of diplomatic, legal, and other policy activity bearing directly on the resolution of underlying tensions.

As one scans the past, present, and future of our epoch it becomes evident that internal instability is a salient characteristic of the times. This is of course a natural concomitant of the explosive growth of new states often lacking any real attributes of nationhood, with the Congo in 1960 a prime example. And if our topic is local conflict, the most local conflict of all is of course within the boundary of a state. It is precisely these that have turned out to be the hardest of all to control or to stop quickly. We do not often think of these insurrections and rebellions and revolts in the category of "arms control." But there is an excellent reason why great powers, and military staff, and international diplomatic organizations should care at all about these "cats-and-dogs" of the conflict family. The reason is implicit in any discussion of the real-life political security scene in the world. It lies in the ever-present danger of potential involvement. Modern history is replete with civil war situations in which the outside world became enmeshed as a result of the ideological ties between local factions and great external coalitions.

Obvious examples are the Spanish Civil War, the Greek Insurgency, Korea, Cuba, the Congo and now Viet Nam. In our times international security has become indivisible for a great number of reasons, principal among which are the intense ideological warfare being waged, the speed of communications, and the growing mobility of military forces. But in the light of another factor—the excessively destructive nature of nuclear weapons—the effect of making security indivisible is to build in a potential for dangerous escalation in local conflicts virtually anywhere in the world. Of course every local conflict does not escalate, either locally, or in the sense of great power involvement. In fact one highly respected strategic analyst has publicly registered his surprise, looking at Viet Nam, at how hard it is to start a larger war. But again, there is no particular natural law necessarily working itself out here. For all the brickbats thrown at our Department of State and at diplomacy in general, I willingly testify to the continuous, responsible, quiet yet intense processes that have much to do with the fact that many local conflicts do not escalate. In fact, such processes may be as useful, if not more so, than physical controls on weapons, in keeping the peace. Our interest here is to identify, classify, and evaluate *both* as highly relevant to the "controllability" of local conflict. It is evident that the problem is larger than any single category of military or diplomatic or technical activity.

Another interesting issue that arises

early in any broad-gauged analysis of conflict control is a fundamental question of value often buried in unspoken assumptions. There is, I find, no real unanimity as to whether it is a good thing or not to control all conflicts. This is one of the most interesting things to ponder while trying to think through these issues in a general sense. I do not mean the lunatics who are spoiling for bloodshed and seek to apply the military virtues to annihilative weapons. Nor can one linger over the total pacifists except to marvel at their freedom from any sense of responsibility to deal with the situations that arise in real life.

But there are responsible people who seriously believe that the world situation would really have been better if Israel had been permitted to fight it out with the Arabs in 1947-8-9; or if the British, the French and the Israelis had been allowed to overthrow Nasser in 1956; or if India and Pakistan had been allowed to see it through to a conclusion in 1965; or if the Cypriots could have settled their differences once and for all.

In each of these cases I found myself, in some instances officially, totally committed to finding pathways to the earliest possible cessation of hostilities, with or without a political solution in sight. Perhaps when the chips are down I am a pacifist too. Or perhaps I believed that in each case our Government was correct in seeking de-escalation as a top priority because of the dangers of spread —and perhaps also because the United States Government, like me, is also fundamentally pacifist, Viet Nam to the contrary notwithstanding. But I do not think one can just dismiss the advice to fight it out in Palestine or Kashmir as wild-eyed raving. It is based on the recurrent nature and durability of the underlying conflict situation in each of those cases. This in turn is related to the vitally important insight that to stop shooting is not necessarily to supply relief to the claims that are in conflict, particularly legitimate pressures. In some cases—Germany in 1918 is of course the prime example—premature cessation of hostilities leaves one party convinced that it was not beaten, that it could have won if the war had lasted longer, and that nothing had really been settled. Much the same attitude can be found among many Arabs who deny they took a licking in 1948-49. The reverse of course is the sense of humiliation and revenge that occurs if one side *is* decisively beaten.

The main operational matter thus brought up is one that may be the most important of all in the control of international conflict. This is the problem of "peaceful change." Our greatest unfulfilled political requirement is a reliable, acceptable, and orderly procedure for change without war, comparable to what a legislature does domestically in enabling conflicting interests to fight it out relatively peacefully and produce a change in the law that no court could have created. This is a complex and perplexing subject, and here one can only flag its prime relevance to the control of local conflicts and indict it as a very underdeveloped topic.

Related to the question of when to stop a fight, and to the larger question of whether the United States has or should have a more general set of principles to follow regarding local conflicts, is a rather painful but inescapable issue. This is whether the United States does in fact have an interest in fomenting rather than suppressing certain kinds of conflict situations, where the alternative is clearly worse, in certain parts of the world. Arguments on both sides of the issue have to be stared at very carefully case by case, and one approaches the matter of a common policy doctrine very cautiously indeed. Elements of the policy problem can be readily discerned from some of the broad propositions assertable on either side: "Since the Communists foment 'wars of national liberation,' the United States must actively oppose them, even when it means escalating a given conflict"; or "Since Communist domination or takeover is intolerable to us, it may be in our interest to foment rather than suppress certain given conflicts." But: "Since escalation is the greatest danger, it is really never in the U.S. interest to foment conflict"; and, finally, "As a relatively fat, happy, status-quo power with no territorial ambitions it is in our interest on grounds of stability to suppress outbreaks of violence that may come to involve us."

Related to this is a very serious argument that certain kinds of local conflict may have the beneficial result of minimizing a larger conflict. A colleague of mine uses as an example the current Yemen conflict that ties up large Egyptian forces and keeps them from greater mischief-making elsewhere.

All one can conclude at this stage is that it clearly is not a black and white set of arguments. If I had to sum up, I have a general intuition that on balance there is a sort of generalized American interest in the minimization of international conflict and the maximization of international procedures for peaceful change and pacific settlement.

I think also that there is a corollary to this in minimum United States involvement. This may make me a "neo-isolationist," although I don't feel like one. But I think this corollary is arguable, if only on the grounds of C. L. Sulzburger's Fourth Cardinal Rule of

Diplomacy, which is never to get between a dog and a lamppost.

It is evident that others do not share this general intuition that it is a good thing to suppress conflict and a bad thing to foment it. The Chinese Communists with their extravagant dreams when they are in a doctrinaire mood favoring people's revolutionary wars all over the world, or non-Communists with legitimate claims who have little to lose and do not think terribly much of the established order anyway, certainly do not share this conflict-suppression philosophy. But I think the United States probably has it, and that this represents the basic thrust of our policy in this realm.

The ideal form of conflict control is prevention. The UNESCO constitution is correct when it says that wars begin in the minds of men. The trouble is that of course we are lucky indeed if our own diplomats are able to focus on wars after they have started but before they go along too far. I do not think this is cynicism, and I do not propose to worry about ultimate first causes of conflict so much as about the machinery to abort, suppress, terminate, and hopefully, settle them.

To become concrete, policy measures begin with localizing conflict. This is the primordial meaning of local conflict—to limit its geographical scope. And of course this is one of the few measures open to other people to influence the course of events in a local conflict that does not depend entirely on the intentions, capabilities, or goodwill of the people actually doing the fighting. One looks therefore to external aid, specifically to the arms traffic. The Center for International Studies at M.I.T. has made some interesting recommendations on this subject in connection with a study in 1963-64 on Regional Arms Control Arrangements for Developing Countries under a contract with the U.S. Arms Control and Disarmament Agency. It is a first order of business to get under better control the hardware available to countries to expand local conflicts—whether this is done tacitly, unilaterally, or bilaterally; preferably it should be done multilaterally because all those who have the ability must be brought into cooperation.

A second most important measure of conflict control comes under the heading of enforcing the peace. Here one gets into the never-never land of world government. World government just does not seem to me a feasible or perhaps even desirable objective at the present time. And yet a genuine collective security system of enforcement must rest on a consensus and a polity and a decision-making apparatus that add up to an agreed political order. One of the fundamental disputes among students of conflict control comes precisely here. Wholly apart from the possible dangers in a world government, one runs into the belief among some of its proponents that enforcement could be agreed to "if only we could all sit down and talk together," which rests on the further belief that "this thing between us and the Russians is really just a misunderstanding," and so on. I do not happen to believe this, or if I came to believe it about the Russians I would find it very hard to fit the Chinese into such a world order, or even that great mass of newly-independent states who don't think much of the White Western Man's version of the "established order." All things considered, I judge us lucky if we can jack up our efforts that focus on aborting conflicts through good offices, mediation and arbitration, the suppression of conflicts through cease-fires, through observation activities, or through peace forces; and sometimes even to resolution of conflicts, although this is very rare and is becoming increasingly rare. More important than anything else may well be the fidelity with which the Western world and specifically the United States genuinely supports these stages of pacification and practices them in its own actions.

One could argue that international organization machinery, being as imperfect as it is, cannot do very many of these things well. I think it *has* been extraordinarily useful to have cease-fires. But as I suggested earlier, when we have cease-fires the next question is how to keep a conflict from getting worse again, or emerging in a worse form if nuclear weapons spread or if the United States gets rid of its B-47s, or whatever the problem might be. The enforcement-of-peace problem again joins up the stage of cease-fire with the problem of ultimate settlement.

Unfortunately, the Western states have themselves been selective in their various policies about cease-fires. Viet Nam is a case where to focus exclusively on getting the guns to stop would not satisfy the political-strategic purpose of communicating a message to Asian Communists that the United States is prepared to fight to discourage take-over attempts. Cease-fires are often unrelated to the merits of the case, particularly when direct military solutions are being attempted, such as in Goa in 1961, or the recent Indonesian "confrontation" with its neighbor Malaysia. Above all, international organizations are proving unable in this age—as are many national organizations—to cope with the new format of conflict within borders—subversion, terror, insurgency, the whole catalogue of conflict types which so far have baffled the international community. I think there is a serious question whether constitutionally or institutionally the United Nations or any international organization is capable of coping with many problems of internal insurgency. This may be our single most unsolvable problem in the field of conflict control.

In speaking of internal conflict control it seems to be obvious that internal reforms are as important as any single factor in the whole spectrum of civil wars. Their absence creates the role of indigenous Communists, who in the still excellent phrase of Walt Rostow are the "scavengers of the process of modernization." The role of external assistance, however, makes the issue internationally ambiguous. Where the issue is primarily colonial it has not been quite so ambiguous; surely there could have been a great deal more conflict control through a more farsighted colonial policy on the part of certain of our friends. One does not have to be Sophocles to predict the nature of the tragedy that is coming in the southern part of Africa and the Portuguese colonies, where the same kind of history is being repeated with the same kind of predictable results.

Even here rigorous candor compels one to point out that in the short term there may be more conflict control if one retains colonial control. To be intellectually rigorous about this problem *no* flat statement based on an ideal seems to stand up without all kinds of scrutiny. But the argument collapses when one looks at the middle range of time, and short-term suppression of conflict through colonial rule turns out to reflect a consistently unsuccessful policy from 1815 and the Holy Alliance through the Indian, Indochinese, and Algerian experiences in modern times.

There are only hints and clues—perhaps banal and obvious—to a most complex set of issues in the investigation of which all of us are really only at the start. The attempt to find uniformities and regularities that can yield some kind of predictive policy value labors under obvious handicaps. Above all, I think we can be properly cautious of making inferences about the future from the past. Carl Becker once wrote: "In human affairs nothing is predetermined until after it has occurred." But another wise historian of diplomacy also wrote: "I have observed that politicians, unlike diplomats, have no time to learn the lessons of history." This gives us that most valuable thing of all—a place to start.

The Prospects for International Peacekeeping

By William V. O'Brien

Introduction

This assessment of the prospects for international peacekeeping forces proceeds from the assumption that all societies require military or police coercion to maintain law and order. To the extent that arms control and disarmament become a reality, international force will have to replace national force and will inherit all of the material and normative problems faced at present by those who control national force.

Specifically, to the extent that international peacekeeping becomes a serious and frequently recurring phenomenon, the international community will have to clarify two sets of issues:

(1) The legal bases for resort to armed coercion;

(2) The political-military policies and the legal regulations governing resort to armed coercion on behalf of international law and order.

The present paper will not treat those other very important, but perhaps more frequently discussed problems of peacekeeping, namely,

(1) The political bases without which peacekeeping is impossible;

(2) The financing of peacekeeping;

(3) The assurance of sufficient logistical support for peacekeeping and the problem of obtaining it from nations other than the Great Powers;

(4) The issue of *ad hoc* versus stand-by or permanent peacekeeping forces. (In this regard, the reader's attention is referred to the recommendations of the Wiesner Committee.)[1]

The writer is inclined to the view that unless some progress can be made in developing stand-by and permanent peacekeeping forces, the discussion of substantial replacement of national by international force will remain largely academic.

The Legal Bases for International Peacekeeping by the U.N.

Thus far, internationalists have tended to go along with almost any legal argument that justified seemingly necessary peacekeeping activities. Legal "rope tricks" have been welcomed gratefully. However, if the international community is to support more frequent peacekeeping activities in the context of progress in arms control and disarmament and the progressive development

213

of international law, the legal bases for peacekeeping will have to be clarified.

Without a determination of a threat to peace by the Security Council and action under Chapter VII (Articles 39-51) of the U.N. Charter, there exist the following legal bases for peacekeeping:

(1) Military intervention by international peacekeeping forces based, not on Chapter VII, "enforcement orders" of the Security Council, but on allegedly non-enforcement measures of interposition, internal policing and the like, e.g., UNEF (the United Nations Emergency Force) and ONUC (United Nations Organization Command Congo). Such forces have been entrusted to the Secretary General by the Security Council, e.g., under Articles 25, 40 and 49 as in the case of ONUC, and have been received with the consent of the indigenous sovereign.[2]

(2) Voluntary collective action in response to the recommendations of the General Assembly under the Uniting for Peace Resolution of November 3, 1950. However, it would appear that such action would be limited to cases of collective self-defense.

Now there are only two legal justifications for resort to armed coercion (i.e., the threat or use of force in the sense of the Charter and supporting conventional customary international law) today:

(1) Enforcement action authorized by the Security Council;

(2) Individual and collective self-defense (Article 51).

Any action which, in the material sense, results in a level of armed coercion amounting to *war* and which does not fall into one of the two categories would appear *prima facie* to violate the basic law of the international community. At least this would seem to follow from the Charter and authoritative interpretations of it.

Efforts to develop international peacekeeping under present political conditions raise the problem whether the categories of permissible resort to armed coercion should be expanded from two to three. The emerging third category concerns voluntary, non-enforcement actions, invited or acquiesced in by the incumbent government of the nation within which the action is taken, which, because of events in the disturbed area, leads to hostilities between the peacekeeping forces and one or more parties to an internal and/or international conflict. Whether an invited, non-enforcement, peacekeeping force finds itself in a shooting war is a highly fortuitous question which will not necessarily be determined by the intent of *any* of the parties.[3]

From Peacekeeping to Co-belligerency: The U.N. in the Congo

The experience of ONUC in the Congo demonstrates the precarious character of peaceful, non-enforcement military interventions by international organizations. Nicholas describes the ambiguity of ONUC's mandate as follows:

There was from the beginning an ambiguity about the authority and objectives of ONUC which reflected the anomalous position of the Congo itself, a state so newly independent that the *Loi Fondamentale* designed to authorize its constitution had not yet been ratified by the body appointed to do so, the Congolese parliament. In part, ONUC was a routine response to a routine request from a new state for technical assistance; what was novel was that it was for *military* assistance, a category hitherto unknown in United Nations technical aid circles. Simultaneously, however, it was an appeal for United Nations protection against the reintroduction of Belgian troops into the territory of an ex-colony now independent and also, from the United Nations point of view, a necessary safeguard against unilateral assistance pouring in from rival sides in the Cold War. ONUC's role from the outset was consequently a dual one—the provision of both internal and external security. Though the words "international peace and security" do not appear in the Security Council resolution[4] passed at its first meeting concerning the Congo on July 14, 1960, the Secretary-General later stated that his authority to summon the meeting came from Article 99 of the Charter, and any such verbal deficiency was quickly made good in the following resolution of July 22.[5] Thus the force had a role closely analogous to that of UNEF—to facilitate and accelerate the withdrawal of foreign troops and to remove by its presence the justification for any other powers' interference; but it could not assume, as UNEF did, that the host country would look after internal security. Indeed, ONUC's ability to restore internal security was a practical (if not a legal) condition of the successful discharge of its obligations toward international peace and security.[6]

In the case of ONUC, the original rule was that U.N. troops should use force "only in self-defense" and should not exercise "any initiative in the use of armed force." [7] Later, the February 21, 1961, Security Council resolution authorized "the use of force, if necessary, in the last resort to prevent the occurrence of civil war." [8] Oscar Schacter has said that this still did not constitute taking the initiative.

What it did was to authorize the Force, for the first time, to take up positions

for the purpose of preventing civil-war clashes (as in support of cease-fire arrangements and neutralized zones); if the troops were attacked while holding such positions, they could use force in defense, but this did not mean they were entitled to "take the initiative in an armed attack on an organized army group in the Congo." [9]

However, a more realistic interpretation is given by commentators such as King Gordon, who was the Chief Informational Officer for the U.N. in the Congo in 1961-62, who observes:

Adoula's request [for U.N. help in enforcing a Congolese decree of August 24, 1961, calling for the expulsion of all non-Congolese officers and mercenaries serving in the Katangese forces] has been compared with the request of Lumumba for assistance in ending the Katangese secession by force. But there is a basic difference. To have acceded to Lumumba's request would have been to distort the mandate of ONUC by involving it in a domestic constitutional issue and by committing it to military action that was specifically barred. The request of Adoula, in fact, simply placed the sanction of the host government behind a directive that had already been given by the Security Council. The Council had decided that those foreign elements named in the presidential ordinance had no legal status in the country and were known to be acting to prevent the resolution of political differences by the Congolese themselves. For this reason, the Council had called for their withdrawal and requested the Secretary-General to implement its decision.

While the favorable response of ONUC to the request of the Central Government had not in fact altered or enlarged its mandate, it set the United Nations almost inevitably on the road to a head-on clash with Katanga. This clash had been foreshadowed by Tshombe's stand at Tananarive and again at Coquilhatville where he had shown his rage at the Central Government's 17 April agreement with the United Nations. It was easy for Tshombe to interpret the ordinance and Adoula's request for ONUC assistance as an ONUC-Adoula alliance to end the secession.[10]

The prelude to this clash was "Operation Rumpunch" of August 28, 1961, in which 338 prohibited persons were rounded up by U.N. forces in Katanga and the Elisabethville post office and radio station were temporarily occupied by ONUC. This was all done efficiently and bloodlessly.[11] However, Rumpunch was followed by "Operation Morthor" (which Lefever and Joshua refer to as "round one" in the "three round" suppression of the Katangese secession) on September 13, 1961.[12]

Operation Morthor was launched at four o'clock in the morning but, unlike Rumpunch, it was met with alert opposition from Tshombe's forces. Lefever and Joshua tell us:

Within twenty minutes after Morthor got under way, there was an exchange of fire in the vicinity of the post office. It is still not certain whether the Indians or a Katanga sniper fired first. A battle followed . . .

The Indians captured the radio station in hand-to-hand fighting in which twenty gendarmes were killed. Eyewitness reports suggest that the Indians, possibly because of panic, were brutal and shot a number of gendarmes and policemen in cold blood.

By eight o'clock that evening the post office and radio station were in the hands of the UNF. Swedish troops had occupied the Sureté offices. Only one minister, Vice President Jean-Baptiste Kibwe, had been captured. Tshombe, with the aid of the British Consul, had escaped to Northern Rhodesia. The official Central Government party which had flown to Elisabethville in a U.N. plane, was waiting impatiently at the airport under UNF protection.[13]

The purpose of Operation Morthor was clearly revealed when the U.N.'s Conor Cruise O'Brien told reporters at 8:00 p.m., September 13, that "the secession of Katanga is ended." This pronouncement, of course, was patently unjustified, but it shows what the U.N. forces had in mind. Lefever and Joshua summarize the operation as follows:

September 13 was the first and most fateful day of the eight-day clash in which eleven U.N. soldiers, about 50 gendarmes, and a handful of civilians were killed. The UNF captured about 250 prisoners. On September 20 a provisional cease fire was signed between Tshombe and Khiary [who was substituting for Hammarskjold, who was killed in the crash of a U.N. plane on September 17, 1961] in Ndola, Northern Rhodesia. The agreement provided for prisoner exchange; the return of the radio facilities, post office, and other public buildings held by the UNF; a joint commission of four members to supervise the agreement, including the inspection of all military centers in Katanga. Before the cease fire was approved by the Secretariat on September 24, U.N. officials made it clear that it did not imply a recognition of the Elisabethville regime and that its provisions applied only to Tshombe's forces and the UNF in Katanga.[14]

It is believed that Lefever and Joshua are correct in making the following assessment:

In legal, political, and military terms, Round One was a great embarrassment to Hammarskjold, who arrived in Leopoldville in the afternoon of September 13, when O'Brien had hoped the action would be over. Hammarskjold was embarrassed because the UNF had used force, because the effort had failed, and because O'Brien had announced that its purpose was to end secession and that his legal authority to use force was derived from the civil war paragraph of the February 21 resolution. Hammarskjold was also embarrassed because he had not been fully informed and because O'Brien and Khiary apparently had tried to present him with a *fait accompli*. O'Brien frankly stated that the Secretary-General would doubtless have suffered embarrassment "if fighting were actually going on in Katanga while he was in Leopoldville," and recalled Khiary's warning as he left Elisabethville on September 12: "Above all, no half measures." [15]

To meet widespread criticism of Operation Morthor, Secretary General Hammarskjold issued a statement on September 14, the relevant portions of which were summarized in his *Annual Report* as follows:

At dawn of 13 September, the United Nations forces began once again to apprehend and evacuate foreign military and para-military personnel, for this purpose taking security precautions similar to those adopted on 28 August. At that juncture, the United Nations garage was set on fire, and troops proceeding to the garage to extinguish the blaze were fired on from the building in which the Belgian Consulate was located and from houses occupied by non-African residents in which a number of Belgian military personnel were known to be staying. [16]

Conor Cruise O'Brien later disavowed this explanation "as a fabrication designed to appease the critics by obscuring the real purpose of Morthor—ending secession." [17] And Lefever and Joshua get to the heart of the issue we are concerned with when they make the following evaluation of the U.N.'s September, 1961, activities in Elisabethville:

The Secretary-General's public explanation was certainly less-than-honest. Morthor was not simply a continuation of Rumpunch. The use of force was not simply in self-defense. The sending of well-armed troops to capture strategic points in a city and to apprehend cabinet ministers at four o'clock in the morning is hardly a use of force in self-defense. Hammarskjold made no reference to what appears to be well authenticated cases of UNF brutality. He also knew that O'Brien acted to end secession, an objective the United Nations had no authority to pursue by force. In fact, the UNF was not even authorized to use force to arrest mercenaries until the subsequent Security Council resolution of November 24, 1961. [18]

Finally, the November 24, 1961, Security Council Resolution authorized the permissible use of force to apprehend and detain prohibited foreign mercenaries. [19]

This resolution led to the much-quoted response of Tshombe at a large meeting in a stadium on the outskirts of Elisabethville, where he said:

U Thant will launch a war on our territory . . . Tomorrow or the day after tomorrow, there will be a trial of strength. When the time comes, let Katanga fighters arise in every street, on every path, on every highway, in every village. You cannot all have automatic weapons or rifles. But we still have our poisoned arrows, our spears, our axes for cutting down trees, our picks for digging ditches, our hearts to beat with courage. Not a road must remain passable, *not one United Nations mercenary must feel safe in any place whatever*. . . . Katanga, standing between foreign domination through the United Nations and nothing, is ready to choose, with pride, nothing. [20]

The U.N. response was foreshadowed by a communication of Chief U.N. Representative in the Congo Sture Linner to Acting Secretary-General Thant, which stated in part:

Unless the regime alters its course immediately, neither Mr. Tshombe nor his associates may be able to control its direction, and elements of their military forces and of the civil population may initiate further hostilities against the United Nations. Indeed, if this course is pursued, the cease-fire agreement and protocol, which already have been repeatedly violated in nearly every article by the Katanga regime, will cease to exist. In that event the forces of the United Nations will be compelled to employ all legitimate and available measures of force necessary to defend themselves and to bring about conditions under which the mandate of ONUC as laid down in United Nations resolutions can be effectively carried out.[21]

The ensuing U.N.-Katangese clash, "Round Two," is summarized in the authoritative study by Lefever and Joshua, which deserves to be quoted at some length in order to emphasize in some detail the way in which "defensive" military measures can, in practice, become indistinguishable in their form and consequences from deliberately planned offensive measures. Lefever and Joshua say:

In this atmosphere, inflamed by incidents between gendarmes and U.N. personnel, all efforts to discuss differences between Tshombe and the United Nations and between Tshombe and Leopoldville failed. The discipline of the Katangan forces continued to deteriorate. On December 2, Katanga gendarmes fired on UNF troops at the Elisabethville airport and set up two roadblocks in the town to impede U.N.

communications. This was in direct violation of the protocol which prohibited troop movement "to reinforce a garrison or position." The next day, several Swedish medical personnel were abducted by the gendarmerie and a new barricade was set up on the road leading to the airport. Commanded by mercenaries, the gendarmerie had virtually become an instrument of the *ultras.* Tshombe was out of the country. There was some evidence that a coordinated attack against the UNF was about to be launched. Just before Round Two started, U.N. officials claim to have discovered a "battle plan," drawn up by Colonel Faulques, the mercenary leader, to "strangle" the UNF in the Elisabethville area. The Indian officers, who had the largest national contingent in Katanga, were becoming restive under the politically imposed restraints on the Force. The Indian Government was also concerned.

On December 5, the UNF undertook military action to defend its position in Elisabethville. Thant authorized "all counter-action—ground and aerial—deemed necessary" to restore complete freedom of movement in the area. The State Department supported him. After an Indian unit removed the roadblock between the airport and U.N. headquarters, the Katangan forces opened fire with heavy mortars, machine guns, and rifles against UNF positions. This was the beginning of the second clash in which some 206 Katanga troops, 21 U.N. soldiers, and 50 civilians were killed.

On December 9, U.N. headquarters in Leopoldville announced that the restoration of order and the "arrest of foreign mercenaries" were the sole objectives of U.N. military action in Katanga.

When Tshombe was on his way to Kitona to meet Adoula on December 19, 1961, Thant ordered a temporary cease fire. On the same day, U.N. armored columns patrolled the streets of

Elisabethville to reestablish order. . . .

At its peak the December operation involved 6,000 troops, compared with 1,400 in September. Some fifteen jet and other U.N. planes were used. Offensive tactics were employed in the air and on the ground, and U.N. troops were *not* under orders to shoot only in self-defense. Brigadier Raja, UNF commander of the Katanga area, was given greater latitude in exercising military initiative than any former commander. This permitted him to employ offensive tactics and to move his troops into previously unoccupied positions.

All of the fifty civilians killed, including several atrocity cases, were the responsibility of U.N. troops. This was due in part to the fact that the UNF was taking a defended town from which civilians had not been evacuated.

The new U.N. initiative was bound to arouse criticism. . . . Thant said he regretted civilian casualties, but denied other charges, citing "the campaigns of violence, abduction of hostages, assault and battery, murders, the setting up of roadblocks, etc.," carried out by Tshombe's gendarmerie. He insisted that the UNF had shown "great self-restraint," and would have never used military action at all had not the roadblocks prevented "freedom of movement." Thant noted that officials of Union Minière have proudly admitted the manufacture of gendarmerie armored cars and of bombs, and that the mining firm had made it possible for mercenaries to go underground by putting them nominally on its payroll. He denied that the aim of the United Nations was "to force a political solution to the Katanga problem." Thant's assertion was hardly the whole truth, because he was obviously eager to have Tshombe acknowledge the authority of the Central Government. He also believed that the exercise of "freedom of movement" by the UNF in Katanga would contribute to this political objective. Washington shared Thant's views and went even further and openly declared its support for Leopoldville.[22]

Thus, under the rubric of self-defense and insuring freedom of movement, ONUC in fact fought as a co-belligerent on the side of the Congolese government in its civil war with Katanga. Round Two was followed by Round Three, "Operation Grandslam." Lefever and Joshua give this account of the operation:

Considerable evidence suggests that the U.N. command was prepared to initiate the use of military force to end Tshombe's secession, doubtless citing as its legal justification its authority to apprehend mercenaries or to exercise freedom of movement. But as matters developed, Round Three was actually ignited by the one-sided harassment of Katanga gendarmes. After four days of intermittent firing, which Tshombe seemed powerless to control, the UNF on December 28 started to move against the gendarmerie strong points in Elisabethville. They were literally moving in self-defense.

What fortuitously started as a defense of existing positions in Elisabethville soon became Operation Grandslam, the code word given by the Indian officers to the plan to establish freedom of movement throughout Katanga. All three phases of the operation were finally completed on January 21, 1963, when the UNF entered Kolwezi without resistance and were received by Tshombe personally. This marked the end of the military phase of bringing Katanga under the control of the United Nations and the Central Government.

Round Three, in contrast to the two previous clashes, was conducted with discipline and restraint. Major General Prem Chand was a competent and respected commander. Throughout the operation the UNF encountered little resistance. The mercenaries, now largely

French and South African, were considerably more disorganized than in the earlier rounds. During or shortly after Round Three, most of the remaining mercenaries left Katanga by the way of Angola. Tshombe's appeals for a "scorched earth" policy went largely ignored. For these reasons casualties on both sides were light. Noting this fact, Thant said: "For a peace force, even a little fighting is too much, and only a few casualties are too many.[23]

In summary, then, Lefever tells us:

In considering the problem of atrocities or other illegal acts committed by men serving in the UNF, it is important to note that in military terms the three rounds in Katanga were modest police actions in which probably fewer than 300 Katanga gendarmes and 50 civilians, including a dozen Europeans, were killed by U.N. troops. On the U.N. side, 42 soldiers and officers were killed and approximately 200 wounded.

Though small in scale, the U.N. forces in Katanga were engaged in hostilities of a war-like character, whatever their legal status may have been. Prisoners were taken and exchanged. Innocent civilians were killed. Atrocities were committed by and against U.N. troops. The Secretary-General has been rightfully criticized for his reluctance to acknowledge in more explicit terms than he has the atrocities committed by members of the UNF.[24]

In retrospect, we must admit that we were very lucky in the Congo. ONUC was, in effect, a co-belligerent on the side of the central government in a civil war. Had the civil war reached a more intensive level, ONUC would have been involved in that kind of military coercion which at present can only be justified as self-defense or as enforcement, and all parties concerned agree that ONUC was *not* an enforcement force.

The Perils of Peacekeeping: The U.N. in Cyprus

A Security Council resolution of March 4, 1964, empowered the Secretary-General to establish a peacekeeping force in Cyprus with the consent of the Cypriot Government and in consultation with the governments of the United Kingdom, Greece, and Turkey.[25] The force was deemed necessary because of civil strife between Greek Cypriots and Turkish Cypriots in which both Greece and Turkey were intervening. Indeed, direct hostilities between Greece and Turkey appeared imminent. Potentially this was a much more difficult peacekeeping mission than that of ONUC in the Congo. Well-established civil war adversaries were being openly backed by outside powers with close historic and ethnic ties to Cyprus. Moreover, whereas the adversaries in the Congolese-Katangese confrontations were, with the exception of the mercenaries, rather more inclined to release their energies in random lawless behavior and atrocities, the Greek and Turkish Cypriots were fanatical and skillful soldiers willing to fight for their respective causes and, in the case of the Turkish Cypriots, for their very existence.

Operating under what Wainhouse describes as "vast executive powers in addition to the administrative powers he already possessed under the Charter," [26] Secretary-General U Thant organized a force, UNFICYP, consisting of British troops already in Cyprus by treaty rights, and of contingents from Canada, Finland, Ireland, Sweden, and Austria. They were commanded by Lt. General P. S. Gyani of India.[27] Their mission, as outlined in the resolution, was as follows:

. . . the function of the force would be, in the interest of preserving international peace and secrurity, to use its best efforts to prevent a recurrence of fighting and, as necessary, to contribute to the maintenance and restoration of law and order and a return to normal conditions; . . .[28]

Wainhouse observes that, "This language implies that the U.N. force may use force not only in self-defense but to take appropriate steps to maintain and restore law and order." [29]

Despite denials that ONUC had intervened on the side of the Congolese Government in a civil war with Katanga in 1962 and 1963, the states who were asked to furnish troops to UNFCYP were very concerned not only about the possibility that their peacekeeping troops would end up in a shooting war but that they would in fact be obliged to take sides in a civil war.[30] Fortunately, direct engagement in hostilities was comparatively rare and usually both short-lived and minor in character. Once again, international peacekeeping forces turned out to be lucky. The issue of taking sides plagued the force and many issues remain unresolved to this day. The Turkish Cypriots complain that, on the whole, UNFICYP favored the Greek Cypriots and the Greek-dominated government over the "rebels." [31] The Turkish Cypriots and their supporters in Turkey also complained that the U.N. force did not restore the constitutional arrangements balancing Greek and Turkish Cypriot participation in the government by force.[32]

Although UNFICYP operations fortunately did not require major combat engagements, their brushes with danger were numerous and the possibility for major involvement in hostilities was often present. For example, British troops were deliberately fired upon, disarmed and taken hostage by Greek Cypriots.[33] In April, 1964, Canadian troops were obliged to fire at Turkish Cypriots. By late April 1964, there were increasing demands that UNFICYP be permitted to use at least enough force to avoid outright humiliation.[34] The most humanitarian concerns at times resulted in acts that could lead to fighting. Thus when Swedish troops were unsuccessful in their attempts to arrange a truce at Kohhina to remove women and children, the U.N. forces entered the village in armored cars and evacuated refugees.[35] Subsequently, U.N. posts manned by Swedish troops were set up between the lines of the Turkish Cypriot defenders of Kohhina and the besieging Greek Cypriot forces.[36] With a bit of ill chance this kind of interposition could obviously lead to serious U.N. involvement in the conflict.

The hazardous character of the UNFICYP operation was well recognized by U Thant, who stated that at the time of its deployment, the force

. . . is in the most delicate position that any United Nations Mission has ever experienced, for it is not only in the midst of a bitter civil war, but it is dangerously interposed between the two sides of that war.[37]

Wainhouse summarizes UNFICYP's first and most critical year as follows:

In December 1964, the Council again reviewed the Cyprus situation in the light of the Secretary-General's report. From March to August, the major effort of the U.N. force was focussed on stopping the shooting and arranging separation of the combatants. After the August session of the Council calling for a cease-fire, the active fighting had virtually ceased, and "owing to UNFICYP's steady efforts and the restraint of the parties," the military situation in general remained quiet. These developments enabled the U.N. forces "to concentrate its activities on promoting a return to normal conditions" as called for in the Council's March 4 resolution. An agreement was reached with the Governments of Cyprus and Turkey for the rotation of the Turkish national contingent, and for the reopening of the Kyrenia road under UNFICYP control. The easing of economic restrictions against the Turkish population, together with an easing of restrictions on freedom of movement, led to a general relaxation of tension in most parts of the island.[38]

Yet all concerned agree that the underlying sources of conflict are substantially unaffected and that serious civil and international conflict could break out again.[39] If it does and if the U.N. engages once more in peacekeeping in Cyprus, the possibility of large-scale U.N. involvement in warfare remains, limited principally by the probability that the traditional sources of peacekeeping troops may not be as readily tapped after the collisions and near-misses of ONUC and UNFICYP operations.

Peacekeeping by Regional Organizations: The Intervention in the Dominican Republic.

Given the many difficulties of organizing and justifying legally U.N. peacekeeping forces, the United States has increasingly been interested in peacekeeping by regional organizations. The basic legal problem is this: Given the two-fold bases for permissible resort to military coercion, regional peacekeeping must be based either on

(1) a Security Council decision to "utilize" a regional organization for "enforcement action" under Article 53,[40] or,

(2) collective self-defense (Article 51).

At present, there is no legal possibility of a regional organization operating under the Charter (as do all those to which the United States belongs) assuming the right to initiate "enforcement action."

The official U.S. position, however, apparently denies this. In both the Cuban Missile Crisis and the Dominican Intervention, the U.S. has taken the position that the OAS can initiate enforcement action or intervention in civil strife in the form of overt armed coercion (quarantine) or in the form of a massive military intervention which could and did lead to hostilities.

In the Cuban Missile Crisis the United States justified the quarantine under Articles 6 and 8 of the Rio Pact of 1947 and Article 53 of the Charter. But the Security Council never initiated enforcement action nor decided to "utilize" the OAS. The United States was later to claim that silence on *the part* of the Security Council constituted tacit, retroactive acquiescence in the unsolicited "enforcement action." Self-defense was not claimed.[41]

In the Dominican Intervention, the United States initially acted unilaterally, first of all to save American and other lives—a justification that, at best, could not be used indefinitely, as Mr. Art Buchwald observed at the time—in response to an invitation from the *junta*.[42] Secondly, the intervention was justified in terms of preventing a take-over by communists within the "rebel" forces.[43] Then, the United States collectivized the intervention by bringing in various units of soldiers and police from other American States.[44]

We know that the U.S.-OAS force *fought* in the Dominican Republic. We watched them on television. This was akin to ONUC's "prevention of civil war" except that it was more clearly "repression" of civil war.

One may find either or both of these cases of resort to armed coercion justified in terms of strategic necessity or the higher values at stake. One might discount the frequent official U.S. avowals of dedication to international law as rhetoric, propaganda, absent-minded utopianism or whatever. One might say quite honestly, as some overly frank German statesmen did half a century ago, that necessity knows no law.

But it is more harmful, in my opinion, to the progressive development of international law to attempt to justify all measures deemed necessary as also legal by perverting the law we ourselves helped to create. Moreover, it is questionable whether it is good policy to encourage such justifications. One can imagine other regional organizations ordering themselves to carry out "enforcement actions" which might produce evil results both for international law and for U.S. foreign policy —e.g., the Arab League suppressing Israel, or the Organization of African Unity undertaking "police actions" in Mozambique, Rhodesia, or South Africa.

This problem of finding suitable legal justifications for U.N. or regional peace-keeping should be recognized, not swept under the rug. If the present law is unrealistic, we should think about changing it, i.e., change regional organization charters to authorize enforcement actions and recognize that this is at vari-ance with the U.N. Charter. We should not pretend that the present distribution of authority is adequate for a world in which international peacekeeping will be a prominent phenomenon.

The Regulation of International Peacekeeping Forces

U.N. and OAS peacekeeping forces have:

(1) fought with conventional weapons;

(2) destroyed the lives and property of non-combatants;

(3) taken prisoners and exchanged prisoners;

(4) undertaken the equivalent of occupation duties; and

(5) negotiated truces and surrenders.[45]

Clearly, there is a need for study of the applicability of the international law of war to such forces. Moreover, there is an urgent need for political, military, legal and moral analysis of the policies that international peacekeeping forces should follow in the use of controversial means of warfare.

Depending on the degree of progress achieved, arms control and disarmament measures could produce a requirement for international forces to cope with the full range of deterrence and conflict from sub-conventional to conventional to CBR. Leaving aside for the moment the ultimate questions of nuclear deterrence by an international authority, what about the following?

(1) The issue of non-lethal gas.

(2) The limits of counter-insurgency.

With regard to the former, Lincoln

Bloomfield says in *International Military Forces*:

Nerve gases, tranquillizer dart guns, psychochemicals, and other temporarily disabling or paralyzing organic agents all may be high in the armorarium of an international police. For, at least arguably, such agents of persuasion and coercion would be likely to do the job in more appropriate and humane ways than more conventional military weapons whose efficient use depends upon the existence of the very kind of military targets that disarmament planners assure us will be outlawed.[46]

Dr. Bloomfield is projecting ahead some distance. But what about the use of non-lethal gas in contemporary counter-insurgency operations in which international peacekeeping forces become involved? Ironically, it may make a difference whether the situation is viewed as only a *civil disturbance* in which the international forces should have the right to use those riot-control gases used normally by governments against their own people or a *civil war* amounting to a conflict covered by international law. In the latter case, the use of any kind of gas, even of the non-lethal kinds presently in use in Vietnam, is probably not legally permissible.

With regard to the limits of counter-insurgency, it is hard to find a counter-insurgency effort that does not involve unpleasant repression of innocent populations, reprisals, indiscriminate attacks on "guerrilla territory" and torture. Will world opinion be less sensitive to living color photographs of interrogation by torture in *Life* if the torturers are wearing blue and white helmets?

In the light of the Congo experience, what degree of control will international authorities have over national units in international forces committed to ugly counter-insurgency operations?

All in all, it is clear we need to think about these hard questions and to encourage research and planning on them by international, national, governmental, and private institutions and organizations. In these and other important problem areas, the prospects for international peacekeeping depend in large measure on recognition of the fact that peacekeeping is not necessarily or perhaps even normally a peaceful activity.

Notes

[1] The Committee on Arms Control and Disarmament of the National Citizens' Commission, *Report Prepared for the White House Conference on International Cooperation* (New York: United Nations Association of the United States of America, 1966), pp. 28-29.

[2] Ernest W. Lefever and Wynfred Joshua, *United Nations Peacekeeping in the Congo: 1960-1964—An Analysis of Political, Executive, and Military Control.* Draft Report prepared for the United States Arms Control and Disarmament Agency under Contract Number ACDA/RS-63. Dated November 15, 1965. Foreign Policy Studies Division, The Brookings Institution, Washington, D.C. [hereinafter cited Lefever and Joshua, *U.N. Peacekeeping in the Congo*], p. 46. Permission to quote from the draft of this definitive study was generously granted by Dr. Lefever.

Article 40 provides: "In order to prevent an aggravation of the situation, the Security Council may, before making the recommendations or deciding upon the measures provided for in Article 39, call upon the parties concerned to comply with such provisional measures as it deems necessary or desirable. Such provisional measures shall be without prejudice to the rights, claims or position of the parties concerned. The Security Council shall duly take account of failure to comply with such provisional measures."

Implementation of actions authorized under Article 40 does not rest upon the kind of legally mandatory orders envisaged in Article 42, which states: "Should the Security Council consider that measures provided for in Article 41 would be inadequate or have proved to be inadequate, it may take such action by air, sea, or land forces as may be necessary to maintain or restore international peace and security. Such action may include demonstrations, blockade, and other operations by air, sea, or land forces of Members of the United Nations."

Rather, Security Council recommendations made in virtue of Article 40 are implemented in accordance with Articles 25 and 49 which provided: "Article 25. The Members of the United Nations agree to accept and carry out the decisions of the Security Council in accordance with the present Charter." "Article 49. The Members of the United Nations shall join in affording mutual assistance in carrying out the measures decided upon by the Security Council."

Lefever comments: "An analysis of the first three Council resolutions, July 14 and 22 and August 9, 1960 (the significant ones as far as the establishing of the U.N. Force was concerned), and the debate preceding these resolutions, leads to the conclusion that member states had a moral obligation to support, at least passively, the U.N. peacekeeping operation." (Lefever, *U.N. Peacekeeping in the Congo*, p. 47.) He cites as supporting authorities: Oscar Schachter, director of the U.N. General Legal Division, and D. W. Bowett of Cambridge University. See E. M. Miller [Oscar Schachter], "Legal Aspects of the United Nations Action in the Congo," *American Journal of International Law*, Vol. 55, No. 1 (January 1961), pp. 1-28. For a slightly different line of argument, see D. W.

Bowett, *United Nations Forces: A Legal Study* (New York: Frederick A. Praeger, 1964), pp. 174-182.

[3] Herbert Nicholas, "An Appraisal," *International Military Forces*, Lincoln Bloomfield, editor (Boston: Little, Brown and Company, 1964), pp. 105-125.

[4] S/4387, 14 July 1960. *The Security Council,*

Considering the report of the Secretary-General on a request for United Nations action in relation to the Republic of the Congo,

Considering the request for military assistance addressed to the Secretary-General by the President and the Prime Minister of the Republic of the Congo (document S/4382),

1. *Calls upon* the Government of Belgium to withdraw their troops from the territory of the Republic of the Congo;

2. *Decides* to authorize the Secretary-General to take the necessary steps, in consultation with the Government of the Republic of the Congo, to provide the Government with such military assistance as may be necessary, until, through the efforts of the Congolese Government with the technical assistance of the United Nations, the national security forces may be able, in the opinion of the Government, to meet fully their tasks;

3. *Requests* the Secretary-General to report to the Security Council as appropriate. [This resolution was adopted by eight votes—Argentina, Ceylon, Ecuador, Italy, Poland, Tunisia, the U.S.S.R., and the United States—to zero, with three abstentions—China, France, and the United Kingdom.] See Arthur Lee Burns and Nina Heathcote, *Peace-Keeping By U.N. Forces* (New York: Frederick A. Praeger, 1963), pp. 249-250.

[5] S/4405, 22 July 1960. *The Security Council,*

Having considered the first report by the Secretary-General on the implementation of Security Council resolution S/4387 of 14 July 1960 (document S/4389),

Appreciating the work of the Secretary-General and the support so readily and so speedily given to him by all Member States invited by him to give assistance,

Noting that as stated by the Secretary-General the arrival of the troops of the United Nations force in Leopoldville has already had a salutary effect,

Recognizing that an urgent need still exists to continue and to increase such efforts,

Considering that the complete restoration of law and order in the Republic of the Congo would effectively contribute to the maintenance of international peace and security,

Recognizing that the Security Council recommended the admission of the Republic of the Congo to membership in the United Nations as a unit,

1. *Calls upon* the Government of Belgium to implement speedily the Security Council resolution of 14 July 1960, on the withdrawal of their troops, and *authorizes* the Secretary-General to take all necessary action to this effect;

2. *Requests* all States to refrain from any action which might tend to impede the restoration of law and order and the exercise by the Government of the Congo of its authority and also to refrain from any action which might undermine the territorial integrity and the political independence of the Republic of the Congo;

3. *Commends* the Secretary-General for the prompt action he has taken to carry out resolution S/4387 of the Security Council and his first report;

4. *Invites* the specialized agencies of the United Nations to render to the Secretary-General such assistance as he may require;

5. *Requests* the Secretary-General to report further to the Security Council as appropriate. [This resolution was adopted unanimously.] See Burns and Heathcote, *op. cit.,* p. 150.

[6] Nicholas, *op. cit.,* pp. 114-115.

[7] United Nations, *Security Council Official Records* [hereinafter cited U.N., *SCOR*], Supplement for July, August, September, 1960, Document S/4389 (July 18, 1960), pp. 16-24. Lefever and Joshua, *U.N. Peacekeeping in the Congo,* p. 69.

[8] S/4741, 21 February 1961. *The Security Council,*

Having considered the situation in the Congo,

Having learned with deep regret the announcement of the killing of the Congolese leaders, Mr. Patrice Lumumba, Mr. Maurice Mpolo and Mr. Joseph Okito,

Deeply concerned at the grave repercussions of these crimes and the danger of wide-spread civil war and bloodshed in the Congo and the threat to international peace and security,

Noting the report of the Secretary-General's Special Representative (S/4691) dated 12 February 1961 bringing to light the development of a serious civil war situation and preparations therefore,

1. *Urges* that the United Nations take immediately all appropriate measures to prevent the occurrence of civil war in the Congo, including arrangements for cease-fires, the halting of all military operations, the prevention of clashes, and the use of force, if necessary, in the last resort;

2. *Urges* that measures be taken for the immediate withdrawal and evacuation from the Congo of all Belgian and other foreign military and para-military personnel and political advisers not under the United Nations Command, and mercenaries;

3. *Calls* upon all States to take immediate and energetic measures to prevent the departure of such personnel for the Congo from their territories, and

for the denial of transit and other facilities to them;

4. *Decides* that an immediate and impartial investigation be held in order to ascertain the circumstances of the death of Mr. Lumumba and his colleagues and that the perpetrators of these crimes be punished;

5. *Reaffirms* the Security Council resolution of 14 July, 22 July, and 9 August 1960 and the General Assembly resolution 1474 (ES-IV) of 20 September 1960 and reminds all States of their obligation under these resolutions. See Burns and Heathcote, *op. cit.*, p. 253.

[9] Oscar Schachter, "Preventing the Internationalization of Internal Conflict: A Legal Analysis of the U.N. Congo Experience," *Proceedings of the American Society of International Law,* 1963, p. 218.

[10] King Gordon, *The United Nations in the Congo, A Quest for Peace* (New York: Carnegie Endowment for International Peace, 1962) [hereinafter cited Gordon, *U.N. in the Congo*], pp. 122-123.

[11] Lefever and Joshua, *U.N. Peacekeeping in the Congo,* pp. 112-113.

[12] *Ibid.,* p. 115.

[13] *Ibid.,* pp. 118-119.

[14] *Ibid.,* pp. 119-120.

[15] *Ibid.,* p. 120.

[16] *Annual Report of the Secretary-General on the Work of the Organization,* 16 June, 1961, to 15 June, 1962, U.N. Document A/5201, p. 4. (The full statement is found in U.N. Document S/4940 (September 14, 1961), p. 103.) Lefever and Joshua, *U.N. Peacekeeping in the Congo,* p. 121.

[17] *Ibid.,* p. 122.

[18] *Ibid.*

[19] S/5002, 24 November 1961. *The Security Council,*

Recalling its resolutions S/4387, S/4405, S/4426 and S/4741,

Recalling further General Assembly resolutions 1474 (ES-IV), 1592 (XV), 1599 (XV), 1600 (XV) and 1601 (XV),

Reaffirming the policies and purposes of the United Nations with respect to the Congo (Leopoldville) as set out in the aforesaid resolutions, namely:

(a) To maintain the territorial integrity and the political independence of the Republic of the Congo;

(b) To assist the Central Government of the Congo in the restoration and maintenance of law and order;

(c) To prevent the occurrence of civil war in the Congo;

(d) To secure the immediate withdrawal and evacuation from the Congo of all foreign military, para-military and advisory personnel not under the United Nations Command, and all mercenaries; and

(e) To render technical assistance,

Welcoming the restoration of the national Parliament of the Congo in accordance with the *Loi fondamentale* and the consequent formation of a Central Government on 2 August 1961,

Deploring all armed action in opposition to the authority of the Government of the Republic of the Congo, specifically secessionist activities and armed action now being carried on by the Provincial Administration of Katanga with the aid of external resources and foreign mercenaries, and *completely rejecting* the claim that Katanga is a "sovereign independent nation,"

Noting with deep regret the recent and past actions of violence against United Nations personnel,

Recognizing the Government of the Republic of the Congo as exclusively responsible for the conduct of the external affairs of the Congo,

Bearing in mind the imperative necessity of speedy and effective action to implement fully the policies and purposes of the United Nations in the Congo to end the unfortunate plight of the Congolese people, necessary both in the interests of world peace and international cooperation, and stability of Africa as a whole,

1. *Strongly deprecates* the secessionist activities illegally carried out by the provincial administration of Katanga, with the aid of external resources and manned by foreign mercenaries;

2. *Further deprecates* the armed action against United Nations forces and personnel in the pursuit of such activities;

3. *Insists* that such activities shall cease forthwith, and *calls upon* all concerned to desist therefrom;

4. *Authorizes* the Secretary-General to take vigorous action, including the use of requisite measure of force, if necessary, for the immediate apprehension, detention pending legal action and/or deportation of all foreign military and para-military personnel and political advisers not under the United Nations Command, and mercenaries as laid down in paragraph A-2 of the Security Council resolution of 21 February 1961;

5. *Further requests* the Secretary-General to take all necessary measures to prevent the entry or return of such elements under whatever guise and also of arms, equipment or other material in support of such activities;

6. *Requests* all States to refrain from the supply of arms, equipment or other material which could be used for warlike purposes, and to take the necessary measures to prevent their nationals from doing the same, and also to deny transportation and transit facilities for such supplies across their territories, except in accordance with the decisions, policies and purposes of the United Nations;

7. *Calls upon* all Member States to refrain from promoting, condoning, or giving support by acts of omission or commission, directly or indirectly, to activities against the United Nations often resulting in armed hostilities against the United Nations forces and personnel;

8. *Declares* that all secessionist activities against the Republic of the Congo are contrary to the *Loi fondamentale* and Security Council decisions and specifically *demands* that such activities which are now taking place in Katanga shall cease forthwith;

9. *Declares* full and firm support for the Central Government of the Congo, and the determination to assist that Government in accordance with the decision of the United Nations to maintain law and order and national integrity, to provide technical assistance and to implement those decisions;

10. *Urges* all Member States to lend their support, according to their national procedures, to the Central Government of the Republic of the Congo, in conformity with the Charter and the decisions of the United Nations;

11. *Requests* all Member States to refrain from any action which may directly or indirectly impede the policies and purposes of the United Nations in the Congo and is contrary to its decisions and the general purpose of the Charter. [This resolution was adopted by nine votes to zero, with two abstentions—France, the United Kingdom.] See Burns and Heathcote, *op. cit.,* pp. 254-256.

[20] Gordon, *U.N. in the Congo,* pp. 139-40.

[21] *Ibid.,* pp. 140-141, citing United Nations Doc. S/4940/Add.15, 30 November 1961, pp. 6-7.

[22] Lefever and Joshua, *U.N. Peacekeeping in the Congo,* pp. 125, 126, 127, 128.

[23] *Ibid.,* pp. 133-134.

[24] *Ibid.,* p. 72.

[25] David W. Wainhouse and others, *International Peace Observation: A History and Forecast* (Baltimore: The Johns Hopkins Press, 1966), pp. 444-447.

[26] *Ibid.,* p. 447.

[27] *Ibid.,* p. 449.

[28] U.N. Security Council S/PV.1102, March 4, 1964, p. 22. See Wainhouse, *op. cit.,* p. 445.

[29] *Ibid.,* p. 447.

[30] *Ibid.,* p. 449. See also *The Economist* [London] CCX (March 21, 1964), p. 1093.

[31] *Ibid.;* Wainhouse, *op. cit.,* p. 451.

[32] *Ibid.*

[33] See *The Economist* [London] CCXI (April 11, 1964), 118.

[34] *The Economist* [London] CCXI (April 25, 1964), 368.

[35] Time (August 14, 1964), 20-21.

[36] *Time* (August 28, 1964), 28.

[37] Wainhouse, *op. cit.,* p. 452.

[38] *Ibid.,* pp. 452-453.

[39] See U.N. Security Council, S/6102, December 12, 1964. Wainhouse, *op. cit.,* p. 453.

[40] Article 53 states: "The Security Council shall, where appropriate, utilize such regional arrangements or agencies for enforcement action under its authority. But no enforcement action shall be taken under regional arrangements or by regional agencies without the authorization of the Security Council, with the exception of measures against any enemy state, as defined in paragraph 2 of this Article, provided for pursuant to Article 107 or in regional arrangements directed against renewal of aggressive policy on the part of any such state, until such time as the Organization may, on request of the Governments concerned, be charged with the responsibility for preventing further aggression by such a state.

"2. The term 'enemy state' as used in paragraph 1 of this Article applies to any state which during the Second World War has been an enemy of any signatory of the present Charter."

[41] See Leonard C. Meeker, "Defensive Quarantine and the Law," 57 *American Journal of International Law* (July, 1963), 515, 517-518; Carol Q. Christol and Commander Charles R. Davis, "Maritime Quarantine; The Naval Interdiction of Offensive Weapons and Associated Matériel to Cuba, 1962," 57 *American Journal of International Law* (July, 1963), 525, 526; Lyman M. Tondel, ed., *The Inter-American Security System and the Cuban Crisis* (Dobbs Ferry, New York: Oceana, 1964), p. 27; Abram Chayes, "The Legal Case for U.S. Action on Cuba," 47 *U.S. Department of State Bulletin* (1962), 763-765; "Law and the Quarantine of Cuba," 41 *Foreign Affairs* (1963), 522; "Remarks," *Proceedings, 57th Annual Meeting, American Society of International Law* (1963), 10-21.

[42] In a request of April 28, 1965, the *junta* wrote:

> DEAR MR. AMBASSADOR: Regarding my earlier request I wish to add that American lives are in danger and conditions of public disorder make it impossible to provide adequate protection. I therefore ask you for temporary intervention and assistance in restoring order in this country.
> Truly yours,
> PEDRO BARTOLOME BENOIT
> Colonel, Presidente de la Junta Militar del Gobierno de la República Dominicana

U.S. Congress, Senate, Subcommittee To Investigate the Administration of the Internal Security Act . . . of the Committee of the Judiciary, *Organization of American States Combined Reports on Communist Subversion,* 89th Cong., 1st Sess. (Washington: Government Printing Office, 1965), p. 114.

On the same day President Johnson told the American people:

"The United States Government has been informed by military authorities in the Dominican Republic that American lives are in danger. These authorities are no longer able to guarantee their safety, and they have reported that the assistance of military personnel is now needed for that purpose.

"I have ordered the Secretary of Defense to put the necessary American troops ashore in order to give protection to hundreds of Americans who are still in the Dominican Republic and to escort them safely back to this country. This same assistance will be available to the nationals of other countries, some of whom have already asked for our help." U.S. Department of State *Bulletin* (May 17, 1965), 738.

[43] On May 2, 1965, President Johnson stated in a major address to the nation:

"The Revolutionary movement took a tragic turn. Communist leaders, many of them trained in Cuba, seeing a chance to increase disorder, to gain a foothold, joined the revolution. They took increasing control. And what began as a popular democratic revolution . . . , very shortly moved and was taken over and really seized and placed into the hands of a band of Communist conspirators.

"Many of the original leaders of the rebellion, the followers of President Bosch, took refuge in foreign embassies because they had been superseded by other, evil forces . . . The revolution was now in other and dangerous hands." *The New York Times,* May 3, 1965.

[44] The Resolution of May 6, 1965 creating the OAS force was passed 14-5 with one abstention. In order to obtain the necessary two-thirds majority, the controversial inclusion vote of the Do-

minican representative was required. See Pan American Union, *Resolutions Approved by the Tenth Meeting of Consultation of Ministers of Foreign Affairs as of June 2, 1965* (Washington: Pan American Union, 7 June 1965).

As of July 3, 1965, the OAS force was composed as follows: Brazil—1,115 soldiers, marines, and officers; Costa Rica—20 policemen; El Salvador—3 officers; Honduras—250 army troops; Nicaragua—164 army troops; Paraguay —183 army troops; and the United States—10,900 troops (the peak U.S. force was around 22,000). 1 *The OAS Chronicle* (August, 1965), 5.

[45] For example, Burns and Heathcote tell us: "Further, we argued that the U.N. would have difficulty in terminating operations conducted for political ends. In fact, it has now successfully terminated such action. It did however encounter certain difficulties, notably in the Jadotville confusion. There the local U.N. commander accepted the town's surrender as though he had been the officer of a national military force operating under the laws of war. But the U.N. seems to have made no prior arrangements anywhere in Katanga, despite its phased plan for the occupation of towns, either for the legal surrender of towns or for the taking of prisoners, except in the case of mercenaries. In the earlier diplomatic phase of the Thant plan, however, the absence of a termination procedure for UNOC as a whole enabled Tshombe to temporize." Burns and Heathcote, *op. cit.,* pp. 220-221.

[46] Bloomfield, *op. cit.,* p. 23.

Armaments and Order in Civilized Society

By Charles C. Price

The age in which we live may well be one of the most interesting periods in all of history. In the broader view, the twentieth century has certainly been one of the most revolutionary of all time for its impact on the way of life of mankind. In a narrower view, there are signs that perhaps we are coming to the end of that era in which the policies of the United States have been based on the containment of Communism. We find ourselves at the end of that era not because the policy was a failure, but because it has been a success; and if it has indeed been successful, then we need to address ourselves now to what should be the basis of our policy for the decades ahead.

Let me begin by expressing my strong belief that there is an urgent need for a more cooperative, orderly and civilized world society, even though this may still be only a fond hope. Many people have reached a similar conclusion concerning the need for world order for a variety of reasons. Perhaps it is worth noting that part of the rationale for my own relatively optimistic position can be traced all the way back to the beginning—to the understanding of the remarkable physical and biological evolution which has made man's life possible here on this planet. It would be fitting, therefore, to start with a brief bit of background into what seems to me as a scientist to be an important new conception of man's role on earth—a conception which has actually become possible only in recent decades. We have in the lifetime of our generation witnessed revolutions in understanding and control of our physical world which have brought man to the threshold of a civilized world society. However, the incredible explosion in scientific knowledge has not merely given us the power to travel at speeds fast enough to leave the planet, to communicate virtually instantaneously around the globe, to conquer disease, hunger and poverty everywhere, but it has also brought us to amazing new insights into the universe, the origin of matter, and even of life itself, which puts new perspective on the meaning and purpose of human existence.

We know, for example, that the elementary particles of matter, electrons and protons, when attracted by gravity into a huge mass the size of our sun or larger can be forced to combine against strong natural repulsion, liberating vast amounts of energy and giving much more complex, highly organized structures, the nuclei of the hundred chemical elements. Under other conditions, such as those which exist here on earth, these elements can combine in orderly arrangements known as molecules, eventually elaborating the varied large and complicated molecules necessary for living systems, and thus leading to the highly organized chemical society of a living cell. We now understand a great deal about how a simple living cell, guided by the information stored in its nucleic acid, could gradually undergo mutation and adaptation to form the wondrous variety of complex living beings culminating in man and his remarkable intellect.

The key direction of this physical and biological evolution has been towards order by means of cooperative phenomena. Man has now used his reason and imagination to create institutions to guide his progress up the path toward what we may hope will be a more orderly, more cooperative, more civilized society. In this century this struggle has been culminated by efforts to create world-wide institutions to bring some degree of order among the nations of the world. The entire vista of physical, biological and social evolution thus points to order as the key to greater purpose and power, the key to a higher level of life and accomplishment.

Our efforts today, it seems to me, must have this as a prime purpose. We must do our utmost to understand— and it is not easy to grasp the full import of this—that in this more complex, more civilized society we are building, the prime value of order must be recognized over that of unbridled and uncontrolled freedom. In this twentieth century we may well be at the culmination of man's struggle up from a barbaric and violent past to a new golden era of peace and plenty. At least this is one of the alternative prospects confronting us, one that we can realize if we work at it with enough imagination, determination and a bit of good luck!

Looking at man's history in this larger framework, it seems that the foreign policy of the United States should now put prime emphasis on two major objectives. The first is building the United Nations as an institution of international order. Such a task will require that power over major armaments must be transferred by all nations to an international organization appropriately altered in structure, power and function to accept such responsibility. Secondly, we must channel much of the resources now being allocated for armaments into the massive efforts necessary to close the growing gap between the industrialized and the developing nations. These, it seems to me, ought now to be the two fundamental interrelated objectives of American policy.

Now that the containment policy has been sufficiently successful to enable us to go beyond it, the key to success in the coming decades will be a new policy, based on establishing more friendly, more normal relations with the U.S.S.R. and China, of seeking ways to cooperate for our mutual benefit. A policy aimed at cooperation is, of course, seriously undermined by a situation in which the parties manifestly pose major threats of mutual annihilation. Clearly, therefore, one of the rational ways for the major powers to achieve security for their peoples and for world order necessary to build a more civilized and productive world community is to place the control of armaments under a United Nations invested with the resources and authority commensurate with its great new global responsibility.

Just as one might say that the six-shooter became both the great equalizer and the harbinger of civilization to the American Far West a hundred years ago, so the atom bomb may become the great equalizer and the harbinger of a civilized order to the world in this century.

Before men can make this come to pass, they must find ways to overcome both militant anti-Communism and militant anti-Capitalism in order to be ready to take this next significant great step in their social evolution. These militant extremist views feed on the tension and fear bred by the arms race and the balance of terror in which we are now so deeply involved. At any time they could conceivably get beyond the control of reasonable elements in all the countries now parties to ideological, national and other conflicts.

No doubt these fears, expressed by Presidents Eisenhower and Kennedy and others, have led to efforts to curb the arms race. Many well-conceived proposals for general and complete disarmament have been put forth during this decade. There have been well-advertised proposals for general and complete disarmament in the form of draft treaties presented by both the United States and the U.S.S.R., and the United States, reflecting many of the creative ideas suggested by Philip Noel-Baker[1] and by Grenville Clark and Louis Sohn.[2]

Both the U.S. and Soviet plans call for the nations to abandon all major armaments with final verification by complete international inspection, but there have been acrimonious debates between the Americans, who accuse the Soviets of seeking disarmament without control, and the Soviets, who charge that the Americans want control without disarmament. Louis Sohn, in an effort to bridge the gap between the two positions, has proposed the interesting idea that each nation divide its territory into, say, six regions, one of which would then each year be chosen by the U.N. (not by the nation) to be completely disarmed with full U.N. inspection to verify the process in that particular region.[3]

Some such plans could perhaps break the impasse over the relative degree of inspection and disarmament at each stage of present plans which has blocked any serious consideration to date. But if we are to make civilized order realistic in a nationally disarmed world, if that really is an objective of our policy and that of the Soviet Union, then the U.N. itself must become the deterrent to aggression. We do indeed need a deterrent to aggression, but it is extremely dangerous for each nation to attempt to set itself up as judge and executioner, supplying its own deterrent for all forms of aggression. Therefore, we need to find a way in which the U.N. may become the central deterrent to all major aggression by retaining in being and in readiness a sufficient amount of the military power transferred to it from the nations during the process of general and complete disarmament.

If this is to happen, there must be acceptable procedures for mediation and adjudication of major international conflicts. In addition, the U.N. must then have a direct and reliable source

[1] Philip Noel-Baker, *The Arms Race: A Programme for World Disarmament,* New York: Oceana Publications, 1960.

[2] Grenville Clark and Louis Sohn, *World Peace Through World Law,* Cambridge: Harvard University Press, 1958.

[3] Cf. Louis B. Sohn, "Zonal Disarmament and Inspection: Variations on a Theme," *Bulletin of the Atomic Scientists,* Vol. XVIII, September 1962.

of revenue and not be dependent on voluntary contributions from national governments. The U.N. envisaged here, of course, is not the U.N. as it exists at the moment.

If such a U.N. is to be responsive to the needs and purposes of mankind, it should be endowed with some direct relations to the world's citizenry, as, for example, by having a second major parliamentary body parallel to the General Assembly but representative of and preferably directly elected by the people. This revised U.N. would require the right to deal directly with people in matters of international law, and not be limited to dealing just with governments as is now the case.

One of the requirements, then, must be a much more direct relationship of the U.N. with citizens of the world; and in order for this to be acceptable to us there must also be a clear bill of rights to protect the basic human rights of all the world's citizens against infringement by this stronger, more powerful United Nations.

It is, of course, exceedingly easy to point out how difficult it will be to endow the U.N. with the necessary structure, procedures, authority and resources to become an effective supranational instrument for resolving international disputes in an orderly way. Anybody with any intelligence can easily see the immense problems, barriers and obstacles in the direction of what is suggested here.

But the entire journey up from the cave has been difficult. Today nothing less than assigning the U.N. the sole responsibility for major weapons of aggression can bring us up the next step of the ladder of progress toward a civilized world society, and a step further away from the ever-present alternative to progress: extinction. When the stakes are so high, man must contemplate running the risks which his bold, creative intelligence deems necessary.

Chapter 7

COMMENTS ON
THE PRECEDING PAPERS

Arms Limitation and Integrative Activity as Elements in the Establishment of Stable Peace

By *Kenneth E. Boulding*

An alternative title of this paper might be "The Claws of the Dove." I am very anxious to preserve the dialogue between the doves and the hawks, but I feel it has become so hopelessly one-sided that there is a strong danger of the doves simply withdrawing from it, and as a dove, I regret this. The dialogue, however, must go on, even if the voice of the dove is reduced to a whisper. Furthermore, it is spring, and in the spring, as Tennyson remarks, "a livelier iris changes on the burnish'd dove." Fully burnished then, and with claws slightly extended, let me plunge into this intellectual combat.

Virtually all systems exhibit phases, and the theory of phases is a very important general system. A phase may be defined as an identifiable state of a system, identified by a number of related characteristics, which is stable only within certain limits or limiting values of the parameters which define the system. Thus water can exist either as ice, liquid water, or steam; and indeed there are at least seven varieties of ice. A diagram like Figure 1 shows what particular phases are stable at different combinations of temperature and pressure.

Phases are divided by a phase boundary, which is almost universally characterized by the absorption or release of large quantities of energy, depending on which way we are going. Thus melting ice into water requires the input of a lot of energy; as water crystallizes into ice, heat is released. The phase boundary is also apt to be characterized by a peculiar phenomena involving, for instance, nucleation.

An international system exhibits phases like any other. It has a great many more parameters than a simple system like the phases of water, but nevertheless there are surprising parallels. These phases are illustrated in Figure 2. Oddly enough, the two major parameters which determine the phases of water have striking parallels in the international system. Corresponding to temperature there is something which I have called "warmth," which is a property of the integrative system. This could be measured by content analysis of international communications; as we move from left to right in the figure, hostility diminishes, a sense of friendship and community increases, communications themselves increase, the sense

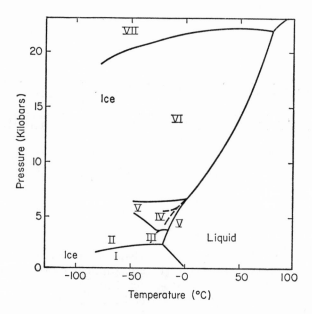

Figure 1

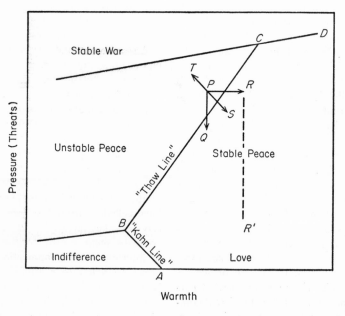

Figure 2

of common interest increases, and the integrative structure is strengthened. The vertical dimension I have called, again by analogy with the water-ice system, "pressure." It could be measured by the magnitude of the war industry of the system or subsystem, modified, perhaps, by some index representing the specificity of threats, as we move vertically in the diagram; that is, the threat system becomes larger as we move up, smaller as we move down.

I have distinguished only four phases of the international system, for the sake of simplicity. Many more could probably be distinguished. These are: stable peace, which corresponds to the liquid water of Figure 1; stable war, unstable peace, and indifference, which corresponds to ice. History provides examples of all these phases. We have stable peace over certain subsets of the international system, for instance, in North America, between the United States and the British complex, among the Scandinavian countries, and probably among the countries of the socialist camp. This is the state of the international system in which the probability of war is so small as to be below what might be called the just noticeable difference in political behavior. It is characterized by disarmed boundaries, the absence of a specific threat system, and strong integrative links. That is, stable peace will be found in that area of the diagram where warmth is high and threats are low.

Stable war has also characterized many systems. Europe in the early medieval period before the "Truce of God," the relationships between Christendom and Islam at certain times, many centuries of Indian history, and many, though not all, primitive societies exhibit this phase. The boundary between stable war and unstable peace is not a clear one, though it may be useful to make the distinction. The instability of peace may be measured, perhaps, by the proportion of time spent in war, which will be higher towards the top of the diagram and lower towards the bottom. It seems not unfair, however, to describe the state of the international system which prevails over much of the world today as unstable peace, as the proportion of the time actually spent in war is small enough so that the society visualizes peace as normal and war as abnormal. This perhaps is the major basis for the distinction. In unstable peace, however, the probability of war is great enough so that it is a major determinant of national policy. At very low levels of pressure and warmth, I have distinguished a phase which I have called indifference, which would characterize, for instance, the international relations of states such as Nepal and Peru, which are really too far apart to interact. Social distance might produce this as much as geographical distance.

As I have drawn the diagram, I have preserved the peculiar kink in the stable-peace boundary, which might be called the "Thaw Line," at point B. In the water-ice diagram, the kink accounts for the fact that ordinary ice floats, which is fortunate for us, as otherwise the world would probably be uninhabitable. In Figure 2 I have made the thaw line from A to B backward-sloping in order to take care of Mr. Kahn, who has argued that sometimes an increase in the threat system can produce stable peace. Line AB, therefore I call the "Kahn Line." It will be noticed, however, that it only separates the region of indifference from the region of stable peace, and it simply represents the fact that people are apt to notice each other a little more under the impact of an increase in the threat system. In practice, I suspect that we are far above this point, and this phenomenon is only significant if the levels of the threat system are very far below what they are today. While I am prepared to admit the point in theory, therefore, it seems to me of no practical importance.

I have assumed that the thaw line from B to C is positively sloped. This means that if we are in a region of unstable peace, we can reach stable peace across the thaw line either by a reduction of pressure or by an increase of temperature. Thus from a point P in the region of unstable peace, we could move to stable peace either by moving from P to R, that is, increasing the warmth of the system, or by moving from P to Q, that is, diminishing the threats through arms control and disarmament. Beyond point C, I suppose that the boundary of stable peace becomes almost horizontal, indicating that there is some level of the threat system above which stable peace is virtually impossible and stable war virtually inevitable. Above point C, therefore, an increase in the warmth of the system is ineffective in producing stable peace as well as very difficult, and the only method is by disarmament.

A very crucial question which is not easy to resolve is what is the slope of the line BC. If this is steep, then from any point in the region of unstable peace to the right of point B, there will have to be a relatively large decrease in the threat system in order to reach the thaw line, whereas a relatively small increase in the warmth of the system will enable us to reach it. If on the other hand the thaw line is rather flat, the reduction in the threat system will be highly effective, the increase in warmth rather ineffective. The epistemological problem here, unfortunately, is very difficult. It is always hard to know where any boundary is until we have crossed it. Hence the perception of the boundary is more apt to be a function of the value system of the perceiver rather than the realities of the case. Those who are personally incapable of warmth because of traumatic experiences in childhood or adolescence when they have been rejected by those to whom they offered warmth are apt to be "hawks," who perceive the thaw line as steep and warmth as ineffective. Those whose personal experience has been happier are likely to be "doves" who perceive warmth as effective and threats as ineffective.

It is the dynamics of this system which is its most important and at the same time its most difficult aspect, mainly because of the great importance of random elements in it. The dynamics of the system are complicated also by the fact that the parameters are strongly related, that for instance an increase in pressure is likely to result in a decrease in warmth and vice versa. Hence we rarely get pure horizontal-vertical movements, but from the point P, for instance, we are likely either to go "southeast" towards S, with warmth increasing and threats diminishing, or "northwest" towards T, with threats increasing and warmth diminishing. About the best we can do is to outline some rather general considerations which lead to movement in one direction rather than in the other.

In the first place, the threat system taken by itself has a certain tendency to escalate. That is, the threat system introduces a constant pressure to move upward in the figure. There are many reasons for this. One of the principal reasons is that there is a marked asymmetry in the perception of threat as between the threatener and the threatened. The threatener frequently perceives his own threat system as essentially defensive and a counter-threat; the threatened perceives the threat to him as being much greater than the threatener perceives it, and produces another counter-threat, which in turn is perceived by the first party as a greater threat to him than the second party perceives it. It is not surprising, therefore, that we get arms races and escalation, and that in the absence of a sufficient degree of warmth in the system we are all caught in the dynamics of the Prisoner's Dilemma which makes us all worse off and eventually drives us to disaster.

Another reason for the dynamic instability of the threat system is that in a condition of unstable peace there is always a positive probability of war occurring. Over a sufficient length of time, therefore, war will occur, and this frequently intensifies the threats and the fears of the system. This is why "stable deterrence" is a pure myth of the military intelligentsia's imagination. Deterrence, that is, a system of threat and counter-threat, may be stable in the short run, but if it is to be effective at all, there must be a positive probability of it failing, that is, of its degeneration into war. Deterrence will not deter unless it is credible; it will not be credible unless there is a positive probability of its failing; over the long run, therefore, it must fail. This logic seems to me irrefutable, and as Mr. Kahn himself has suggested, all that deterrence does is give us time to change the system, and we are not doing very much with the time that it gives us.

There are other complex historical forces making for the increase of threats, which involve for instance the alliance of the threat system with what I have sometimes called the "masculine mystique" of potency, as satirized so eloquently in the movie "Dr. Strange-love." Unfortunately we do not know much about the dynamics of the distribution of sexual disorders, and the extent to which child-rearing and educational practices produce "masculinismo" and the covert sadism and masochism which feeds the threat system. That there is a malevolent dynamic at work here, however, can hardly be doubted, and while I would not wish to accuse the hawks of sexual impotence, the idea that love and war are substitutes for each other has at least a germ of truth in it.

Even apart from psychoanalytic considerations, one can identify perverse political learning processes which produce what might be called political superstition. Superstition, as B. F. Skinner produces it in pigeons, is a derivation of a nonrandom system or image of the world from what are essentially random events. There is also a problem which arises in political learning, as in other forms of learning, because we have learned from salient, rather than from important, experiences. Experiences furthermore have a much greater degree of salience in adolescence and young manhood than they do in later life. Hence the decision makers of one generation, who are apt to be in middle age, tend to be traumatized by the salient experiences of their youth, and so develop political superstitions. In the present generation of decision makers, for instance, the "Munich trauma" is so enormous that it has produced a vast amount of political superstition and unreal images of the present world. We will probably have to wait until the present generation passes away before more realistic images of the international system in the minds of the decision makers can be developed. By that time, of course, another set of traumas may cause trouble. Here, however, there is a ray of hope. If with a bit of luck we can get through two generations without serious trauma, more realistic learning processes are apt to assert themselves.

The upward instability of the threat system is unfortunately reinforced by its effects on the integrative system, for the lower the level of warmth of the system, the more unstable the threat system, the greater the upward pressure. An increase in the threat system, on the other hand, tends to lower the warmth of the system, so that what we seem to have is a very disagreeable system indeed, in which an initial instability of the threat system results in an increase in pressure. This lowers the temperature, which leads to a further acceleration in the increase of the pressure, and under these circumstances it would hardly be surprising if all systems ended up in stable war. It is certainly not surprising that stable war has been such a common system in human history. Nevertheless, neither is it a universal system, and it has tended to decrease. Historically the movement has been from stable war into unstable peace into stable peace, in the course of what we might call political development in those subsections of the system which have had successful development.

There must, therefore, be strong forces operating in the opposite direction to the threat system towards increasing the warmth of the system and the strength of the integrative system, and some of these forces can certainly be identified. The first and perhaps the most important is simply that stable peace has very large payoffs in terms of human wealth and welfare. Economic development is almost impossible under stable war; the chance of it increases as we move in Figure 2 downward and to the right. It is only possible where stable peace prevails over considerable areas, as it does within nation-states; and though it is possible under unstable peace in the international system, there is a great deal of historical evidence that suggests that the less the probability of war, the greater the possibility of economic development, even though there have been occasions when a relatively small threat, as in the case of Japan, stimulated a system change into economic development. Where the payoffs for something are very large, therefore, no matter how difficult the dynamic process, work will be put into it.

Another hopeful sign is that the integrative system has a certain dynamic of its own. Even Lewis Richardson pointed out that falling in love was a pattern of behavior quite similar to the arms race. I recall, indeed, a popular song some years ago which ran, "Lay down your arms and surrender to mine." If the masculine mystique supports the threat system in the arms race and gets its sexual satisfaction out of death and pain, perhaps the feminine mystique creates the love race, warms up the system, and relates sexual satisfaction to birth and life. It is easy to push this analogy over the edge of absurdity, but until it falls over that edge it is not absurd. One would certainly like to know more about the extent of frigidity among belligerent and nationalistic women, who are often much more belligerent than men.

Here again the payoffs to love and benevolence are very large. The more we are together, the merrier we shall be. If my welfare pleases you and your welfare pleases me, cooperation is easy and we all plunge into the pleasant positive-sum games of getting rich together, as over against the essentially negative-sum game of the threat system. It seems to me clear therefore that the long run dynamic and long run legitimacy is on the side of warmth and will carry us eventually into stable peace. I am not ashamed, therefore, of being a long-run optimist, however bleak the next century may look.

Another element which we cannot neglect in the dynamics of the international system is luck. The road to stable peace is something like a hurdles race. If we clear four hurdles, we are in; if we only clear three of them, we will fall back. Hence the achievement of stable peace in the various subsystems where it occurs in the past has often been the result of a succession of lucky accidents. The relations of Canada and the British Empire to the United States in the 19th and 20th centuries are a very interesting case in point. A wise man looking at the world in 1815 might have predicted with a good deal of confidence that some time within the next hundred years there had to be a great war between Britain and the United States, and it would probably be fought in Oregon. That this did not happen was, I suspect, the result of good luck rather than good management. We got the Rush-Bagot agreement in 1817, which gave us a partial and incomplete disarmament of the Great Lakes; we did not get 54-40 and we didn't fight; and the 49th parallel ran peacefully and slightly absurdly to the Pacific. There may have been four or five occasions when we came to a hurdle, and with a little bit of luck we cleared it. The doves won out, the hawks were beaten down. As a result, today we have quite astonishingly stable peace, even though Mr. Kahn might produce a scenario in which the United States Marines march on Ottawa, especially if the Canadian society would rather not be a nuclear battleground. The mere suggestion, however, raises smiles in an American audience, and if one suggested Ontario as a pistol pointed at the industrial heart of America, which is what it looks like on the map, the suggestion is received with laughter.

I am not enough of a historian to know how the Scandinavian countries arrived at stable peace among themselves, and why the last battleground of the Swedes and the Danes has become the Tivoli in Copenhagen, the most delightful Disneyland in the world; but I am sure it was likewise a process of lucky accidents, combined with what one might call a long-term warming drag, simply because of the payoffs of stable peace, which to a practical-minded people become apparent. An interesting example of this was the separation of Norway from Sweden in 1904. Here again there were some hawks who wanted to have a civil war in order to preserve the union, but wiser counsels prevailed and no one is any the worse off for this. It is hard not to conclude that if the doves had won before the American Civil War and the South had been allowed to secede peacefully, this would have been a much happier society and that slavery would soon have been abolished in the South without the enormous trauma which its forcible abolition created.

What, then, in these dynamic processes, is the role of activity directed towards arms control and disarmament? Theoretically we could move from unstable peace to stable peace, as from P to R in Figure 2, without disarmament, simply by an increase in the strength of the integrative system. Once we got to R, as a matter of fact, disarmament would become very easy, and the payoffs for this would almost certainly take us down, shall we say, to R'. If we are in the unstable peace phase, disarmament is extremely difficult, because the dynamics of the system are all against it. In the stable peace phase it becomes fairly easy. We could argue, therefore, that those of us who are interested in crossing the thaw line should concentrate all our attention on the integrative system, on things like cultural exchange, friendship societies, travel, penpals, and the like, which build up the integrative system, and should not worry about disarmament. There are, however, strong arguments against this point of view. In the first place, the level of armaments is now so great that it threatens the whole integrative system. We are dangerously close to the stable war boundary, even if we are now in unstable peace; and a measure of disarmament may be a necessary prerequisite to any successful operation on the integrative system. We see in Vietnam how one cannot come bearing napalm in one hand and economic assistance in the other. Activity directed towards arms control and disarmament, therefore, strongly increases our chances of developing a stronger integrative system, simply because almost any common activity creates integration. Even if we quarrel at disarmament conferences, the fact that we are sitting down together is important, and the fact that we have a common objective, however difficult the negotiating path towards it, is important. I am strongly of the opinion, therefore, that we should not give up on disarmament but should continue to press for it, in spite of the difficult dynamics of the system. In a very real sense, moving "down" in Figure 2, say from P to Q, is walking uphill. It requires work, and intellectual and emotional work of a high order. Nevertheless, it is work that can be done, and there is no law which says it cannot be done, in spite of the forces arrayed against it. Given the right parameters of the system, even disarmament races are possible, and we need to study these, as they have happened in history, both between nations and in regard to personal disarmament.

Even arms control, which Schelling has defined as military cooperation with potential enemies, is capable of expanding the integrative system. Once one begins to cooperate with enemies on any score, the enmity tends to diminish. One begins to see even the enemy as a real person with real needs and problems, and a thin thread of community is established between us. Even though, therefore, it is easy to regard arms control as essentially a piece of militaristic hypocrisy designed to take pressure off the process of de-legitimizing the military, this interpretation, while it may have some subjective truth, is objectively mistaken. The pressures toward stable peace, like God, move in mysterious ways their wonders to perform, and can turn even hypocrisy to their own ends. Arms control, therefore, even if it only represents a diminution of the upward pressures in the threat system, creates as it were a system which hovers at the point P rather than going off to T, and by this very means improves the chance of strengthening the integrative system.

One of the most important and I think hopeful things which is happening at the present time is the development of self-consciousness about the integrative system. It is only in the last hundred years that the international system has exhibited any consciousness of the integrative system at all, and has developed what might be called integrative foreign policies such as cultural exchange, cultural propaganda, and the support of international organizations. In terms of actual resources we put very little into the integrative system, and what we have put into it I think has paid off handsomely. If, for instance, there is a relaxation of tensions between the United States and the Soviet Union today, a great deal of the credit must be given to the Pugwash movement and to the good luck of having two rather warm individuals, Eisenhower and Khrushchev, in positions of power at a crucial moment of history. When one looks at the world war industry, however, which is now probably close to $140 billion a year, and compares this with the minuscule resources which we put into all the international agencies, which is not much more than a third of a billion, the fantastic disproportion of the threat system and the minuscule effort devoted to the integrative system is all too apparent. Nevertheless, the United States national image is enormously weighted on the side of the threat system. In President Kennedy's last year I was shocked to find plastered all over the walls of the White House offices a cartoon of the American eagle bearing the familiar olive branch in one claw and the arrows in the other, with the slogan under it, "Don't Forget the Arrows!"—this at a time when we were devoting almost ten per cent of the gross national product to the arrows and about one thousandth of this to the olive branch. My own image, I am afraid, is that of a totally grounded eagle, clutching a vast sheaf of missiles in one claw, a pitifully withered olive leaf in the other, and completely unable to get off the ground as a result. When one reflects, for instance, that the ordinary budget of the United Nations is only about half that of my own University, one realizes what a fantastically small amount of resources we put into peace. As a corollary of what my computer friends call the GIGO principle, that is, garbage in, garbage out, I have

offered the NINO principle, that is, nothing in, nothing out; and this seems pretty close to describing the integrative system. Considering indeed how little we put into it, we get a fantastic amount out, and such a high marginal productivity would suggest that expansion would be profitable.

Let me suggest in conclusion that the real problem before us is not that of fine rational argument but of rhetoric. The real question is how can we desacralize the national state. It has become a Moloch, demanding ever-increasing blood sacrifices and sanctifying itself by the blood shed. What rhetoric will reduce its emotional affect, will make it a useful workhorse like the corporation, a public convenience for the betterment of mankind, not an object of obsessive love, loyalty, and self-sacrifice? As a naturalized American, I have had a long stormy love affair with this country. For the native-born, this country is more like a mother, but for the naturalized, more like a wife, with all the attendant emotional complications that that implies. When I became a citizen, I "married" the United States, for better or worse, in sickness or in health. I am horrified, however, by its moral degeneration in the last twenty-five years, a degeneration to the point where we now boast of our own atrocities. I am comforted, however, by the story of the One-Hoss Shay. The dynamics of legitimacy often operates in this way. An institution seems unshakeable in its pride, its majesty, and its might; and one fine morning, it is a pile of dust in the road. In our pursuit of power or even our fear of impotence, we are following a course so monstrous that it can only lead to the loss of that legitimacy which is the only breath of life for organizations. Many American strategists seem to me to belong to a new religion, NonChristian UnScience, with the doctrine that only evil is real. Our world has become so one-dimensional along the lines of the threat system that we have altogether lost sight of the integrative system which ultimately dominates it.

Nevertheless, to go back to the analogy of ice again, there can be a thaw. The Catholic Church has had a thaw; even the Soviet Union has had a thaw, though a thaw is apt to make so much mess there are apt to be attempts at refreezing. The United States seems to me to be still frozen solid in the ice of its own fear and pride. Even the United States, however, can have a thaw. I attribute many of our present disorders to a process of overlearning. The lead-ing decision makers of the present day were deeply traumatized by the 1930s, which was a very unusual decade. They have made many false generalizations from this, such as the Munich trauma, or even what I call the "mantle of Elijah" complex, which sees us as inheriting the bloody mantle of the British Empire, which is much better put in the ash can. In the '30s we decided that naive idealism did not pay off; hence we threw away the idealism. We became almost as hard and evil as our teacher, Adolf Hitler. It is still not too late to throw away the naiveté and recover the idealism. This goal, ideally, should characterize the new direction of arms control inquiry.

Commentary

By Betty Goetz Lall

My task is to give a commentary on what has been said in the preceding sections of this book in terms of direction for U.S. policy. This is difficult because I have been greatly stimulated by the many new ideas. There is much one would like to say and only a limited space in which to say it.

In this paper my approach will be to evaluate many of the proposals discussed and analyses propounded in terms of what I consider to be perhaps the three most serious problems on the international scene today. With these in mind I shall mention directions in which we might prudently move.

The first problem is the future of the Atlantic Alliance and the U.S. relation to it. The second is the growing gap in living standards and economies between the developed and developing countries. The third is the question of handling conflicts in those parts of the world where nationalism is a very important factor affecting polities and attitudes and which we have not yet properly understood; in these areas there are special problems of instability and revolution and there are predominantly authoritarian governments existing amidst severe poverty.

These three problems are perhaps the most crucial facing us today. Therefore, such problems as preventing the proliferation of nuclear weapons and preserving a stalemate of the strategic balance between the U.S. and the U.S.S.R. belong to a second priority of problems at this particular time. I don't mean to say that these matters aren't important or that they shouldn't be dealt with, but for the moment, I rate the other three as more crucial; we need to devote our attention to them.

U.S. Policy Toward Europe

First, the future of the Atlantic Alliance, of Europe, and of U.S. relations with Europe. Europe should not be considered the number one priority in the total context of U.S. foreign policy in the sense that all other problems must be dealt with in light of their effects on our policy toward Europe. This has tended to be our approach for the past twenty years.

The United States, which is still the greatest military and economic power in the world today, must consider the entire world situation and should not put its emphasis on one region irrespective of the total galaxy of international issues. There are many people in Europe who also believe that these crucial problems in the world reside primarily outside of Europe, and who would not be unhappy if the United States adopted a broader perspective. This is not to say, however, that we don't have a great affinity with European countries, because of history, culture and similar political systems of government. I think we do.

One might ask, how has a disproportionate emphasis on Europe adversely affected U.S. interests? For one thing, we have tended to view the Soviet threat to Europe as unchanging, and have tried to convince European governments that the level of defense efforts and expenditures should be maintained at levels determined at a time when the military threat was more imminent. With this preoccupation about NATO defense strategy and organization, we have not been able to pursue some arms control steps that would have contributed to the reduction of tensions and to an increase in stability in the world. Furthermore, we have dealt with certain economic questions, such as how to achieve a better balance in our international payments, principally in terms of how the balance looked vis-à-vis Europe.

Finally, we have thought that NATO countries and the U.S. ought to have a common policy on all issues arising outside of Europe. In many respects this has been a frustrating experience for all the countries involved because often the individual national interests could not be submerged effectively into a common bond, e.g., the Portuguese position on Angola, the French in Algeria, the U.S. in Vietnam, and the British recognition of China. If we had not been so desirous of attaching ourselves to Europe more than to other parts of the globe, these frustrations would not have been so great and each nation could have been more relaxed about diverging occasionally from the policy of the majority without so much strain placed on the alliance as a whole.

Our policy toward Europe itself appears to be largely determined by our preoccupation with preserving the present form of NATO military organization and especially to lock the Federal Republic of Germany tightly into a form of military integration with the other NATO powers. Our rationale for the policy hardly seems to be based on fear of the Soviet Union; rather, it is based on two other fears. One is that unless we wed ourselves irrevocably to NATO, isolationist pressures within the United States may force the U.S. to abandon its international involvement in Europe and elsewhere. The second fear is that unless Germany is permanently committed to be part of the collective security of the West, pressures within Germany may force that country to seek military adventures on her own, thus embroiling the world once again in war. I think both of these possibilities are exaggerated, but if we continue to base our policy on the probability of their existence, we may unwittingly promote the very things we wish to avoid.

The major emphasis of our policy toward Europe and Germany ought not to be the question of the military integration of NATO and the military integration of West Germany into NATO. Instead, it ought to be the question of the total unity of Europe—not all the way to the Urals, that is an anachronism—we should stop at the Western borders of the Soviet Union. United States policy also ought to be directed to seeking the full participation of Germany in the international community and the strengthening of its democracy. This means eventual reunification.

For those who are concerned with non-proliferation, particularly with respect to West Germany, there is a better chance of realizing effective non-proliferation in this context than in the continued emphasis, almost forced continued emphasis, of a certain form of military integration.

An examination of the two types of fears I mentioned should be undertaken more candidly. Looking at the American aspect for a moment we seem to think that the United States will become isolated if we begin to withdraw militarily from Europe. In the past twenty years we have come to equate internationalism with military power projected abroad and we have also come to equate military withdrawal with isolationism. These are false equations and this is one of the psychological factors at the root of the fear about the U.S. relationship to NATO and NATO military integration.

With respect to our fear about Germany, it ought to be obvious that Germany today is not in a position to threaten other countries militarily and would not even be in such a position if reunification were achieved. The military power of the United States and the Soviet Union, combined or separate, is sufficient to stop quickly any German military aggression in the unlikely event such a venture could be started. But what is troublesome is that potential German demagogues could generate substantial support by claiming that Europe, the Soviets, and the United States were deliberately keeping Germany in a subjugated state by maintaining their troops on its soil for too long a time and not allowing unification to take place. Demagogues coming to power would still have difficulty in building a German military machine, without outside help, to a point where it could effectively

match U.S. and Soviet power and threaten the peace, but such a development could destroy the democracy that has been so laboriously nourished in the West German Republic these past twenty years.

The United States should encourage the element in Germany—and it is strong and growing—that wants to make small overtures to the East. We have seen some small steps of this type taken since the recent German election. The United States should not give the impression to the Germans it is opposed to taking these steps.

Furthermore, we could be more relaxed about the nature of the military form of the organization of the alliance in peacetime. We seem to be over-reacting to some of the things President de Gaulle is trying to accomplish. In the arms control context, we should look for possible steps to reduce—and I emphasize the word reduce and not totally withdraw—our troops from Germany and the Soviet troops from Eastern Germany and other parts of Eastern Europe. This is an arms control proposal that may be ripe for solution, particularly if troop reduction in Germany could be achieved in the context of the type of proposal the Soviets sought on the prevention of surprise attack in Europe. This, incidentally, is the only limited arms control proposal, other than the test ban, where the Soviet Union indicated a willingness to accept some inspection on its soil.

In concluding the section on Europe I want to stress another arms control area that could be stressed. We could spend more time trying to reduce the Soviet intermediate range ballistic missiles aimed at Western Europe. This would certainly ease the problem of the sharing of the nuclear weapons. If the United States earnestly wants to have a working partnership with Europe, we should consider offering to trade off some of our ICBM's for Soviet IRBM's.

U.S. Policy
Toward the Developing Areas

The second problem area I have chosen is bridging the economic gap between the developing and the developed nations. We have all heard much about this question, but not long ago I was startled to read some figures which showed, given present trends, what will be the percentage of the total world's resources in certain fields to be used by the United States in the period 1975-1980—something like 60 per cent of the world's fuel and a high percentage of the total supply of many other resources. If this trend keeps on, and becomes dramatized, people and governments of the developing countries eventually are going to start to gang up against the United States. This may be far in the future, but we should start worrying about it now in terms of devising policies to prevent a bad reaction to the United States from occurring. I will go so far as to say that for the richest and the most powerful nation in the world today to have to hoard its gold and adopt policies to preclude an uninterrupted flow of capital to developing nations is morally wrong. We have to try to rectify that kind of situation. One of the ways we can rectify it is to look more critically at what we spend in the military field.

Unnecessary military spending should be channeled into international development projects, primarily administered through international institutions. It can be argued that politically neither the Congress nor the American public is willing to allow a transfer of resources of this type to take place. I doubt this.

The American Congress has a more open and flexible outlook than many intellectuals and government bureaucrats are prepared to concede. If intellectuals, academic and other experts, business leaders, and government officials made an effective case for channeling more funds from military to international economic projects, there is little doubt that this would be received sympathetically by the public and its representatives in the Congress.

Making an effective case for the transfer of some military spending to international economic development projects requires acknowledgment that the military threat from the U.S.S.R. has diminished, that the Chinese for some years will not be an effective threat to U.S. security, and that what can become a substantial challenge to U.S. well-being is allowing the gap between rich and poor nations to continue, or worse, allowing it to grow. Finally, the marshalling of these facts alone will not be totally convincing to the American public unless it also sees these conditions in terms of the values it holds when it makes decisions about the allocation of the resources of the nation. A country need not forever have a value system based on spending up to $22 billion a year for the kind of war the United States is fighting in Vietnam, while appropriating only a few million dollars a year for the special United Nations fund for economic development.

I believe that the question of whether to produce and deploy an anti-ballistic missile system should be evaluated in terms of the priority of the allocation of resources. Given the nature of the strategic military balance between the United States and the U.S.S.R., given the relative ineffectiveness of present ABM systems, given the cost of the systems compared to their effectiveness, and given the need to use our resources in dealing with the more crucial issues affecting our security, we should postpone full production and deployment of an ABM on the ground that the Soviets are installing a system, because the Chinese several years hence may have ICBM's that need to be counteracted, or because this is a way to keep industrial plants and scientific manpower occupied. Deploying the system would be a luxury that the nation can ill afford.

Another reason for raising the question of the development gap is in relation to the growth of democracy and freedom. When one looks around the world one sees how very slow this growth has been. I made a computation about the rate of countries going Communist, and the rate of countries going democratic since World War II. In both cases within the last fifteen years the rate is downward. For example, since 1950 only two states have turned Communist; only four new ones have been able to follow consistently a democratic form of government. The rest of the world has adopted in varying degrees non-Communist authoritarian systems, with about five leaning toward communism and about twelve leaning toward democracy. If one accepts the principle that freedom and democracy flourish best in an atmosphere of economic well-being, then this is another compelling reason why one of the main directions in U.S. foreign policy should be to devise ways to bridge the development gap.

Some may argue that it will take a long time before the poorer nations can hurt the United States. This, however, is a short-sighted view. In the beginning we may only witness a reaction at the United Nations in the form of the voting on resolutions; we may experience a shift in voting so that instead of being on the majority side most of the time the United States will increasingly find itself in a minority at the United Nations. The disaffection of countries toward the United States is likely to be demonstrated eventually in other ways outside the United Nations. It is essential for the United States to avoid being isolated politically, economically, and emotionally from the emerging nations. Such isolation, if it came about, would give the Soviets, the Chinese, and the whole Communist world a very great inroad, because in a sense they are still looked upon as underdeveloped by most of the developing nations. This would be an important disadvantage to the national interests of the United States.

Having developed the thesis that bridging the economic gap between the developed and developing nations is one of the crucial current problems facing the United States, I ought to prescribe some possible solutions. This is not the place for a complete prescription, but I shall, however, indicate some directions in which to proceed.

One possible type of solution is to have the United States work more closely with international institutions in conceiving and implementing regional development projects that affect more than one nation and cross industry lines. International commissions for the regional comprehensive development of large river basins is one example. Another direction is to find a more effective system for balancing international payments so that the flow of capital is not as restricted as it is today. A third direction is a better working relationship between U.S. business and government so that U.S. business can provide technology to developing countries for a fee but without necessarily requiring a capital input that must be paid back with interest. And where U.S. business does provide capital there should be greater willingness to permit control to be exercised by the host government or private company. Finally, the United States needs to be ever conscious of adjusting its foreign trade, tariff, custom, and shipping laws so as to give preference where necessary to developing countries.

If the United States does in fact become more critical in evaluating the level and purpose of its military expenditures with the consequence that some projects can be postponed, cut back, or abandoned, we shall then be faced with the need to know more precisely our military turn-around capability. In the U.S. Arms Control and Disarmament Agency we discussed this matter often. If weapons are reduced and destroyed and the world situation changes, how does the government revise its policy and begin to take immediate steps to produce weapons if this becomes necessary? This is an important factor in managing our national security. If we destroy, for example, some of our nuclear weapons, we know we have the capability and the resources to produce new weapons; this cannot be destroyed in any disarmament plan. The question is: how fast, in relation to the opponent, can the turn-around capability be put into effect? This is an area for continued research.

Handling Local Conflicts Between Nations

The third area on which I have chosen to comment is the handling of conflict between nations where nationalism is a potent force. My first point is that the concept of nuclear guarantees is not a realistic concept because it flies in the face of nationalism. Some at this conference have talked as though countries which have just gained their independence want to turn around and say, "we will mortgage our defenses and let the previous colonial or other powers be responsible for our security by guaranteeing our defense in the event of a nuclear attack on us." If we want to avoid the proliferation of nuclear weapons to these countries, means other than these nuclear guarantees must be found.

One proposal which, while not sufficient in and of itself to meet the problem of proliferation, may provide some answer is an international no-first-use agreement in areas where nuclear weapons do not exist. There is a relatively new Soviet proposal on this subject which might constitute the basis for serious negotiation with the United States. It would require that nuclear weapons powers agree not to be the first to use nuclear weapons against countries that do not possess nuclear weapons or allow them to be stored on their territory. A no-first-use agreement of this type would put an interesting challenge to China in that it would be asked to agree not to use its nuclear power against non-nuclear powers. A no-first-use position applying to non-nuclear weapon states would not appear to endanger U.S. security, or the security of any alliance we have joined, and it would be one way, short of nuclear disarmament, to begin to deal with the coming nuclear power of China.

The second point I wish to make under this third topic is to suggest that new ways must be found to handle the type of conflict represented by the current war in Vietnam. The use of the armed forces of a single nation as a result of an appeal by a country, which charges it is the victim of aggression, must be avoided. But if this is to be avoided there must also be ways of dealing more effectively with genuine cases of subversion and infiltration. Unilateral acts of intervention with armed force need to be avoided because they raise the possibility of intervention by other countries, thus enlarging the conflict. Furthermore, the force of nationalism in many countries increasingly will result in requests for the withdrawal of foreign military power from their territory. To fill any vacuum caused by a withdrawal of U.S. military power new approaches must be tried.

An approach I would advocate is the negotiation of a world-wide non-intervention treaty with effective enforcement machinery. Such a treaty ought to provide for automatic U.N. involvement if a country suspects it is being the victim of armed infiltration and intervention. The United Nations should have authority to send an investigating team to report on suspected infiltration. In the past such investigating teams, such as those in Vietnam, have not been effective because members of the team lacked either the capability or motivation to identify infiltrators. This problem might be corrected by having host country nationals accompany or serve on the investigating team. Of course to make such a non-intervention treaty work in all areas all important powers would have to be in the United Nations and the treaty would need to be acceptable to the Soviet Union and China as well as to the United States and other countries with military power.

Another point I wish to touch on in the handling of conflict between nations is the extent to which there may be other areas in the peacekeeping field in which progress might be realized if further attention were devoted to them

particularly by the United States and the Soviet Union. I shall mention a few possibilities which need further development. One promising area is Article 43 of the U.N. Charter; this specifies that countries should make agreements with the Security Council on the use of their armed forces when the Security Council so requests. We in the United States have considered this clause something of a dead article because of the Cold War, but it might be revived in some interesting and innovative ways to advance the application of peacekeeping machinery.

A second area where I would look for progress is the possibility of combining the financing formula in peacekeeping operations with Security Council resolutions on specific cases of peacekeeping. I agree with Herman Kahn when he states that when the Security Council works this can run the world. On those occasions when it does work should not the financing formula be placed as an integral part of the Security Council resolution? We could thereby avoid the type of financing problem that we are now facing in the Cyprus case where there is unanimity in the Security Council but no funds, other than those provided by voluntary contribution, to pay the forces sent to maintain peace in Cyprus.

Third, we need to reach better understanding with the Soviets on peacekeeping research. This may sound like a small matter, but progress in many areas is held up because our concepts about procedures to use to maintain international order are still very different from those of the Soviet Union. One of the ways to begin to resolve our differences is having some joint research or at least negotiating with the Soviet Union to permit the United Nations or some other international institutions to carry on some research.

My comments have been in the form of suggestions for direction of U.S. policy. They necessarily have not been developed here fully. They are obviously minority opinions. They are not policy and most of them have not yet begun to form part of the consensus leading to policy, but they are directions that could profitably absorb our attention.

Commentary

By *Klaus Knorr*

Before responding to the issues explored in this book, I feel called upon to disclose my philosophic credentials. To put it succinctly, given modern arms technology, the traditional system of sovereign nation-states as the custodians of military power cannot—according to my belief—afford a satisfactory degree of security to any nation, including the United States. To put it differently, if mankind is to have a reasonable degree of military security, we need a radical change in the way military power is organized in the world. We require a drastic system change. This makes me, I believe, a realist, not an idealist.

One of those contributing to the volume remarked that the arms control and disarmament movement has its ups and downs, and that it is at present in a down-movement. I agree. Richard J. Barnet offers an explanation of this fact by pointing to the deep preoccupation of governments, publics, and disarmament proponents with the conflict raging in South Vietnam. Perhaps there is also a more profound reason. According to my observations, the proponents of drastic arms control and disarmament manifest a certain fatigue; the words and emotions they have been using are somewhat exhausted; there is a noticeable disheartenment. The early hopes for quick solutions have been dashed.

The plain fact is that nothing of importance has happened, or is in the offing, in terms of radical negotiated measures of arms control. And current expectations are low. If the arms control and disarmament movement has its ups and downs, they are ups and downs around a very low level. The immediate reason for such inaction is obvious. Practically all governments and publics, if they have a genuine interest in drastic measures at all, regard them as a very long-run issue; and to regard something as a long-run issue means that it gets little action, no central attention, and that its requirements do not affect current policy. It is the habit of governments anywhere to be preoccupied with short-run problems. Now, why drastic arms control and disarmament—involving a drastic system change—is regarded universally as a long-term, if not utopian, issue is a more difficult question. It is a question that has received little serious speculation and attracted virtually no research. Yet it is a subject for research worth commending.

It should be clear from these remarks that I am profoundly pessimistic about the chances of anything drastic happening in arms control and disarmament, although I am not denying that the governments of nuclear nations have adapted themselves with considerable prudence to the fact that unprecedented weapons of mass destruction are at their command in an existential situation of international anarchy. Mr. Silard's chart guide (p. 193) to general and complete disarmament by the year 2000 has, in my opinion, not the slightest utility. We may achieve full disarmament by the year 2000. But if we do, it is more likely to have happened because we traveled on the low road, along the lower and neglected circle of his chart, marked by bouts of destruction, which means that things are likely to get a great deal worse before they can get better. There is, in fact, historical backup for this observation. Over the past, nations and governments have been ready to consider and attempt basic system changes only in the wake of highly destructive warfare. This happened after the Napoleonic wars, when the Holy Alliance was organized; after World War I, when the League of Nations was established; and after World War II, when the United Nations organization came into being. In each case, at least an attempt at drastic system change was made although, before long, the old rigidities and reflexes took over, and not only precluded further development of the experiment, but reduced the effectiveness of the new institutions. Still, if so far only visitations of disastrous war have generated the flexibility required for drastic change, this is, in the nuclear age, hardly a happy conclusion.

In the meantime, we must, of course, do whatever little things can be done to make the received traditional system operate a bit better, to minimize the risk of major war, indeed of any war, even though—and this is a dilemma—we

will thereby make a fundamentally unsatisfactory condition for security look a little more tolerable, and thus deflate whatever feeble pressure there is toward basic change. Nevertheless, it is only sensible to apply some discount to the future and to alleviate, as best one can, the problems of the moment, even in the most marginal ways.

Herman Kahn proposes a somewhat bolder posture. According to his message, the little things in arms control that can be done readily will not do much good, while the big things are not feasible; hence we should concentrate on medium-size remedies. Yet no such proposals are advanced in this book.

Following these preliminary remarks, I will react to some of the points made in the preceding papers, though I can do this only very selectively in the space available. As far as I can see, the new or fresh things that were said mostly concerned the problems of nuclear proliferation and ballistic-missile defenses.

I do not know whether the modest anti-proliferation treaty now at issue at Geneva has much chance of being adopted. I am for the treaty, but I do not think it very important. I go a long way with James Schlesinger in believing that a further spread of national nuclear forces is not going to be quite so catastrophic as some people believe; and, as Hedley Bull remarks, there are some ways in which we can manage to minimize the risks of living in a world of many nuclear powers. It is nevertheless indisputable that further nuclear proliferation will increase world insecurity. It is hence worthwhile to impede, if not arrest, nuclear spread. The kind of anti-proliferation treaty now under negotiation will hardly stop such spread; but it should impede it somewhat. If a government, having signed a treaty, must invoke the escape clause and withdraw before going nuclear, this means overcoming one additional obstacle, and this may make a difference in states in which there is considerable opposition to exercising the nuclear option.

But—and here I again cite James Schlesinger—if one does not think this kind of anti-proliferation treaty very important, one is logically unwilling to pay a high price for it. The price on which this book focuses—which is also the focus at Geneva—is the abandonment of nuclear sharing within NATO. This is a price demanded by the U.S.S.R., and one which, it was said, would, if paid, cause a serious decline in NATO cohesion. I am not quite as worried about a Europe without NATO as Robert Strausz-Hupé appears to be in his eloquent paper. I do share the view that the Soviet threat to Europe has declined, at least for the time being, and I believe therefore that NATO does not require as much cohesion as it had in the past, especially in the rather distant past. On the other hand, in the absence of drastic arms control and disarmament, I believe that some sort of NATO should continue to play a constructive part in keeping Europe a militarily stable area. And the fact is that NATO has already lost considerably in cohesion over recent years, so that a unit of NATO cohesiveness has tended to rise in value. It is not therefore clear to me that a mildly useful anti-proliferation treaty is worth the price of a further, and perhaps sharper, diminution of NATO cohesion.

Ambassador Trivedi reports that the non-aligned, non-nuclear countries in the U.N. are inclined to ask a rather stiff price from the nuclear powers in exchange for giving up their right to proliferate. That is really like attaching to a mild arms control measure a rider requiring a firm commitment and plan for general and complete disarmament. But the problem is not that simple. I appreciate the moral right of the non-aligned and non-nuclear nations to demand that the nuclear powers disarm. Yet I do not think that this is practical politics.

Much is said in this book about improving the prospects of non-proliferation by means of guarantees on the part of the nuclear states against nuclear threats to the non-nuclear states. For three reasons I am rather skeptical about such "nuclear guarantees." First, they require the nuclear powers to assume world-wide carte-blanche responsibilities—an extension of responsibilities which is not without risks in terms of dangerous confrontations between the nuclear countries themselves. Second, the non-nuclear countries may well nurse doubts about the credibility of such guarantees; and the historical record of collective security arrangements is not calculated to dissipate such doubts. Third, prospective candidates for the nuclear club may desire nuclear capabilities for other reasons than security from nuclear attack. This last point especially is made by several contributors to this volume. And the fact is that both France and China enjoyed nuclear guarantees from an ally at the time they decided to opt for an independent nuclear posture.

Herman Kahn makes an interesting proposal. Some people have advocated a collective nuclear force in Europe (such as the MLF) as an anti-proliferation device. The rationale is that deterrent protection available through participation in a collective force diminishes any incentive toward acquiring an independent national force. Kahn proposes two such capabilities, which he calls "international forces"—one for Europe and another for Asia. He gives the MLF a new twist by proposing that the function of these forces should not be that of threatening massive nuclear reprisal—on which the participants could probably never agree in an emergency—but that of exercising tit-for-tat limited threats and reprisals. A restriction to very limited nuclear threats and strikes would solve the trigger problem in a collective system.

I rather doubt that this is a very promising idea. Aside from larger political obstacles to the establishment of such forces, it seems to me that a tit-for-tat strategy involving nuclear weapons would require superb control, superb flexibility in rapid decision-making, and continuous political inputs. It seems to me unlikely that these requirements could be met by a collective system involving a number of sovereign states. Moreover, a nuclear tit-for-tat capability must necessarily include the ability to deter escalation by a tit-for-tat opponent. Unless this capability were provided from outside the system, it must also be provided by the collective force; and this would seem to raise the X-finger-on-the-safety-catch problem that bedeviled the MLF proposal.

Turning to the ABM problem, the several papers presented here are sharply divided on whether or not the United States should develop, produce, and deploy ABM defenses.

I begin with two observations. If either the Soviet Union or the United States invents ABM systems that are technologically efficient, that is, exact a decisive attrition on attacking missiles, and that are economically feasible, then either country is, in my opinion, very likely to deploy such defenses, even if the other one did not. I say this because, on the assumption made, the one-sided introduction of such defenses would greatly improve the military position of the deploying power vis-à-vis the other power. Furthermore, as John Herz has reminded us, to give military protection to civilian society, to surround this soft society with a hard military shell, is the very raison d'être of the sovereign nation-state. The vast offensive superiority of nuclear missiles over military defenses deprived the nation-state of the capability of fulfilling this raison d'être; and the development of very efficient ABM defenses would permit the sovereign nation-state to recover a good deal of its protective function. Hence, if efficient ABM defenses became available, the case for deploying them seems to me politically irresistible. After all, the idea of making cities and civilians hostages to the good behavior of their governments is a rather sophisticated idea, and surely one which most prospective hostages would reject if they had a choice.

What I have just said is conjecture about what is likely to happen in a specific contingency. I must now add that I see a net advantage in ABM deployment, both in the Soviet Union and in the United States, as long as rapid progress in the direction of General and Complete Disarmament is unfeasible, and provided ABM defenses are highly efficient.

I come to this conclusion, despite the cogent arguments advanced by Joseph Coffey, Jeremy Stone, and Hedley Bull, chiefly because I do not believe the balance of terror to be all that stable and dependable, in the short run or in the long run, and hence I see virtue in the protection of civilians in the event deterrence fails. I realize that the opponents of ABM defenses do not wish to jeopardize the emergent balance of terror. But I hold this balance to be precarious, and this especially in view of the probability that additional nuclear proliferation will take place. Good ABMs look rather attractive in a world of many nuclear powers; and it is a mistake to think of the deterrence problem only as a problem limited to the United States and the Soviet Union. Besides, even at best, ABMs will not be good enough to remove civilian populations entirely from the threat of a nuclear superpower. Enough civilians will remain hostages to sustain a high degree of deterrence, or self-deterrence. At the same time, as Dr. Teller points out, effective ABM defenses diminish further any incentives to mount a preemptive strike, and also lessen the risk of nuclear war by inadvertence.

Concerning the effects of ABM deployment on the prospects of arms control and disarmament, Joseph Coffey and Jeremy Stone argue keenly and forcefully that these effects would be deleterious. Coffey avers that ABMs "promised so little and risked so much." But again, the critical issue is the efficiency of such defenses. They certainly promise little if their efficiency is low. But, as I have stated, they promise a great deal if their efficiency is high (though not necessarily perfect). The efficiency question is one which only Research & Development can settle. But should their efficiency turn out to be high, would ABMs really risk so much in terms of what Coffey calls "the already slim chance for arms control and disarmament"?

As Stone points out, their introduction would indeed mean a significant new phase in the arms race. However, as long as we cannot get away from reliance on national armaments at all, I find an arms race in strictly defensive weapons rather tolerable, and even supportable. Nor does ABM deployment preclude substantial steps toward arms control and disarmament. Indeed, here I find myself in agreement with Donald Brennan's argument.* He proposes that ABMs "might make real arms control and disarmament possible unless ABMs are offset by large additions to offensive forces on the other side." This means precisely that the efficiency of ABMs is the crucial issue. If they are inefficient, they can and will be negated by additional offensive systems, including penetration aids. In that case, little is gained for either defense or for arms control. If ABMs are efficient, however, they might facilitate substantial controls over, and reductions of, offensive weapons. They would do so by vastly reducing the problem of cheating and the associated demands for inspection which have been a stumbling block in disarmament negotiations. If ABM defenses were efficient and deployed, it should be easier to negotiate a freeze, and even sizable reductions, of offensive forces; and this would be a truly big step in the direction of disarmament. If it ever came to drastic disarmament, good ABM defenses would logically be the last strategic weapons to go.

* [Editors' note: Although Dr. Brennan addressed the Symposium, his paper was not submitted for publication.]

INDEX

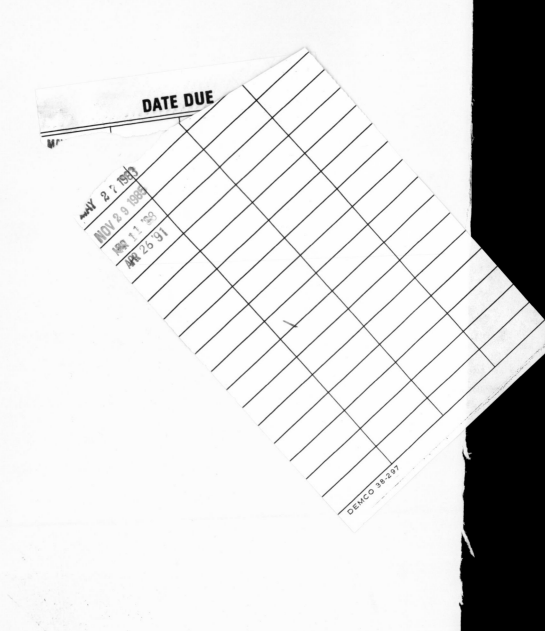